Freedom's Debt

THIS BOOK WAS
THE WINNER OF THE
JAMESTOWN PRIZE
FOR 2009

WILLIAM A. PETTIGREW

Freedom's Debt

*The Royal African Company and the
Politics of the Atlantic Slave Trade, 1672–1752*

Published for the Omohundro Institute of Early American
History and Culture, Williamsburg, Virginia, by the
University of North Carolina Press, Chapel Hill

The Omohundro Institute of Early American History and Culture is sponsored jointly by the College of William and Mary and the Colonial Williamsburg Foundation. On November 15, 1996, the Institute adopted the present name in honor of a bequest from Malvern H. Omohundro, Jr.

© 2013 The University of North Carolina Press
All rights reserved

Set in Bembo
by Tseng Information Systems, Inc.

Library of Congress Cataloging-in-Publication Data
Pettigrew, William A. (William Andrew), 1978–
Freedom's debt : the Royal African Company and the politics of the Atlantic slave trade, 1672–1752 / William A. Pettigrew.
pages cm
"Published for the Omohundro Institute of Early American History and Culture, Williamsburg, Virginia."
Includes bibliographical references and index.
ISBN 978-1-4696-1181-5 (cloth : alkaline paper)
ISBN 978-1-4696-2985-8 (pbk. : alkaline paper)
ISBN 978-1-4696-1182-2 (ebook)
1. Slave-trade—Political aspects—Great Britain—History—17th century. 2. Slave-trade—Political aspects—Great Britain—History—18th century. 3. Royal African Company—History. 4. Slave-trade—Africa—History. 5. Slave-trade—West Indies, British—History. 6. Slavery—Law and legislation—Great Britain—History. I. Omohundro Institute of Early American History & Culture. II. Title.
HT1162.P48 2013
306.3'6209—dc23

2013037641

The paper in this book meets the guidelines for permanence and durability of the Committee on Production Guidelines for Book Longevity of the Council on Library Resources.

The University of North Carolina Press has been a member of the Green Press Initiative since 2003.

For Gem

Contents

List of Illustrations and Tables ix

PROLOGUE
"This *African* Monster" 1

Part One. Deregulation, 1672–1712

ONE
The Politics of Slave-Trade Escalation, 1672–1712 11

TWO
The Interests: "A Well-Governed Army of Veteran Troops" versus "an Undefinable Heteroclite Body" of "Pirates" and "Buccaneers" 45

THREE
The Ideas: Challenging the "Tales of . . . Mandevil" 83

FOUR
The Strategies: *"As Witches Do the Devil"* 115

Part Two. Re-regulation, 1712–1752

FIVE
The Outcomes: Tropical Burlesques 153

SIX
The Legacies: Free to Enslave 179

EPILOGUE
Confused Commemorations 211

APPENDIX 1
Data Supplements for Annual Slave-Trading
Voyages, 1672–1752 *219*

APPENDIX 2
A Directory of Independent Slave
Traders, 1672–1712 *227*

APPENDIX 3
A Directory of Lobbying Independent
Traders, 1678–1713 *235*

APPENDIX 4
A Directory of Royal African Company
Directors, 1672–1750 *237*

APPENDIX 5
Africa Trade Petitions to Parliament on the Royal
African Company's Monopoly, 1690–1752 *240*

Acknowledgments *247*

Index *249*

List of Illustrations and Tables

Plates

1. *Sir Gilbert Heathcote* 54

2. *Humphrey Morice* 63

3. "Advertisement by Order of the Royal African-Company of England" *140*

4. *William Ansah Sessarakoo* [The Royal African] *202*

Figures

1. Slave-Trading Voyages, Great Britain, France, Portugal / Brazil, and the Netherlands, 1672–1752 12

2. Slave-Trading Voyages, Royal African Company (RAC), Separate Traders (ST), and South Sea Company (SSC), 1672–1752 13

3. Slave-Trading Voyages, London, Liverpool, and Bristol, 1672–1752 14

4. Petitions for and against the Royal African Company's Monopoly by Location during the Africa Trade Debates, 1690–1752 122

Tables

1. Elite Separate Traders, 1690–1712 78

2. Origins and Incidence of Petitions during the Africa Trade Debates, 1707–1713 120

PROLOGUE

"This *African* Monster"

Cape Coast Castle, West African Coast, February 1685

When a wave broke directly onto the outer wall of the castle prison, its force conducted along the arches of the ceiling, drowning out the noise as much as the darkness obscured the captives' sight of one another. The vibration and the wind that followed it nonetheless provided some comfort to those contained within. They were a small group of captives, perhaps a dozen. Seized near the Gambia River on pretense of theft, they awaited the unknown, their goods taken from them. Starved and "harassed with the hardships of Imprisonment . . . [and] Sickness," the men were further taunted by the "violent Heats . . . [and] Pestilent Air" of the castle's dungeon. Their confinement presented "a continual Scene of Miseries of all sorts."[1]

Nearly a hundred Royal African Company soldiers paraded around the stone platforms and parapets above the prison. Henry Nurse, the company's chief agent at Cape Coast Castle, presided over the garrison and the prisoners. Captain John Castell, commander of the frigate *Orange Tree,* patrolled the length of the coast looking for more to stock the castle's human stores. For those already detained, the likelihood of death equaled the chances of a return home "by reason of the barbarous usage." The "extream hardships" of their situation led one of their number into a state of desperate depression. "The companion of his sorrows; not being able to endure the hardships imposed by Captain John Castell," he took his own life. Suicide evidently provided the best prospect of a homeward voyage.[2]

These captives at Cape Coast Castle were not African slaves, however, but English slave traders. They were detained, not because of the immorality of their trading activity, but because of its dubious legality. Since 1672, the Royal

---

1. This captive narrative is from William Wilkinson, *Systema Africanum* . . . (London, 1690), 3, 18, 19; and Wilkinson, *The Case of William Wilkinson, Late Commander of the Ship Henry and William of London, 1684–1685* . . . ([London, 1690?]), 1.
2. Wilkinson, *Systema Africanum,* 3; Wilkinson, *Case of William Wilkinson,* 1. For an account of the soldiers employed at Cape Coast Castle in the late seventeenth century, see William St Clair, *The Grand Slave Emporium: Cape Coast Castle and the British Slave Trade* (London, 2006), 13.

African Company had enjoyed a monopoly of all English trade with the west coast of Africa and of the slave trade to the American colonies as well as a predominant position in the trade that imported Caribbean sugar into England. Those who sought to infringe upon the company's monopoly (like the suicidal Henry Wilkinson) were subject to interception by Royal Navy frigates (like the *Orange Tree*), the seizure of their vessels and cargoes (in the above case, valued at three thousand pounds), a trial without jury in an Admiralty court, and indefinite imprisonment. Company officials, like Captain Castell, swore to "shew more mercy to a TURK than to an INTERLOPER." The above account, by freed captive and brother of Henry, William Wilkinson, went one step further by depicting the victims of the African Company's monopoly as chattel slaves—captured, imprisoned, starved, and reduced to suicide.[3]

Henry Wilkinson's suicide led William to seek vengeance against the Royal African Company. He did not seek redress in combat or in the law courts. He chose to mount a propaganda campaign in print against what he called "this *African* Monster." Wilkinson believed that William III and Mary II "together with the present Parliament now Assembled" ought to be appealed to "for a Redress of these Abuses." His strategy worked. Other merchants came forward with petitions to Parliament detailing that the Royal African Company had "beaten, abused, and imprisoned" them and that their attempts to sue the African Company to recover the property the company had seized from them had led to their imprisonment in England.[4]

This political dispute between the Royal African Company and its independent slave-trading opponents would politicize the transatlantic slave trade. It would place discussion of the regulation of that trade into a shifting and uncertain political context in which both sides in the dispute would use contrasting political strategies and polarized ideologies to advance their interests. By 1712, opponents of the African Company's monopoly had succeeded in their aim. They had deregulated Britain's transatlantic slave trade. They did so by mounting a lobbying campaign that championed the right to trade in African slaves as a deeply cherished English liberty. Freedom became

---

3. Wilkinson, *Systema Africanum*, 3. The value of this cargo is detailed in "A Petition of Thomas Byfeild, and Others, Owners of the Ship *Henry and William*," Apr. 29, 1690; see *Journals of the House of Commons*, I–LI (London, 1803), X, 392 (hereafter cited as *Commons Journals*).

4. Wilkinson, *Systema Africanum*, 6, 26; *The Case of E. H., W. Dockwra, J. Thrale, and T. Jones, Merchants, and Their Partners* ([London], 1695), 1. For further petitions detailing African Company seizures and abuses, see "Petition of John Thrale, and John Tutt, and Others, Owners and Freighters of the Ship *Delight*, of London," Apr. 21, 1690, "Petition of Benj[amin] Rawlins," Apr. 30, 1690, both in *Commons Journals*, X, 382, 394.

the rallying cry for those who wished to participate in the largest intercontinental forced migration in history.

THE MODERN WORLD cannot ignore the legacies of the transatlantic trade in enslaved Africans, a system that destroyed the lives of more than twelve million women, men, and children and many millions of their descendants between the fifteenth and the nineteenth centuries. Although these legacies have been richly explored, explanations for the trade are still less well rehearsed. To reconcile the parts played by the slave trade in Britain's history with modern, liberal politics, examinations of the trade's culture and politics have often focused attention on the ending of slavery and have remained quiet about its beginnings. In Britain, the abolition of the slave trade and of slavery remains a source of national pride—a profound achievement in which politicians and institutions continue to bask. Despite Britain's perfecting the slave trade and shipping across the Atlantic more enslaved Africans than any other European nation (before abolition), it is the story of abolition that defines Britain's relationship to slavery. The explanation for this focus on response rather than cause is clear. Perpetrations of inhumanity on this scale make unlikely resources for triumphant, liberal, national narratives. The campaign to abolish the slave trade and slavery, on the other hand, redeemed and reinvigorated Britain's political system, its political institutions, and its empire. It proved that Britain's politics could rise above greed and avarice to lead the world in a bold crusade against inhumanity.

Historians of abolition have largely perpetuated this view. The literature on British antislavery describes a triumphant legislative movement with a broadly based constituency and coherent strategy led by heroic protagonists against a formidable opposition. The early pioneers of English slave trading are viewed, for the most part, as primeval economic men, devoid of reflection and intention and hypnotized by the prospect of material gain or predisposed to commit racial violence. This "Whig" view comforts present sensibilities because it makes the end of slavery contingent on intentional political intervention and modern political institutions and dissolves any responsibility for the development of the slave trade into the circular interaction of demand and supply and man's primordial avaricious instincts. The story of the abolition of the slave trade and of slavery remains the ultimate promoter for modern, liberal, Anglo-Saxon politics. Despite the celebrated political features of the abolitionist movement, we have no political account of the development of the transatlantic slave trade or of American slavery. Unlike the story of abolition, there is no corresponding "intentionalist" school describing the slave-trade protagonists, analyzing the ideas, the disputes, the compromises—in short, the politics—that established England's involvement in and later dominance of the transatlantic slave trade.[5]

This book offers such an account. It focuses on the story of the Royal African Company, a corporation provided in 1672 by Charles II with a chartered monopoly over all English trade with Africa for a thousand years. It locates the story of the Royal African Company and of the transatlantic slave trade within the political history of trade regulation. Seventeenth-century English history has often been defined by the polarized political disputes about the English constitution. Ought the legitimacy of the English state to derive from the crown or from the subjects of the crown? As a derivative of the royal prerogative, the African Company's charter placed it unequivocally on one pole of that debate. It proposed a method of state regulation of the economy based upon the constitutional validity and power of the royal prerogative. Because state regulation was (and is) a political concern, the African Company's charter politicized England's transatlantic slave trade, setting in motion a political debate about the management of the slave trade that would last until the middle of the eighteenth century. This debate would produce an expanded supply of slaves for the English plantations in the Caribbean under the terms of the African Company's monopoly and would then see a massive expansion of slave trading as the company's independent slave-trading opponents used political means to deregulate the trade. This deregulation provided a reliable supply of slaves to the mainland American colonies for the first time. It is therefore central to our understanding of the causes of American slavery. For political reasons examined here, the African Company endured this deregulation to persist, and, with another changed political environment in the second quarter of the eighteenth century, its early arguments in favor of slave-trade regulation came to inform the politics of antislavery in the second half of that century.[6]

The politicization of the slave trade is at the center of this study, that is, the ways in which, in seventeenth-century England and its overseas domains, constitutional changes altered the relationships (expressed ideologically and

---

5. Roger Anstey supplied the classic political narrative of British abolitionism; see *The Atlantic Slave Trade and British Abolition, 1760–1810* (Atlantic Highlands, N.J., 1975), 406. The first historian of abolition, Thomas Clarkson, developed this Whiggish tendency; see Clarkson, *The History of the Rise, Progress, and Accomplishment of the Abolition of the African Slave-Trade by the British Parliament* (New York, 1836), 45.

6. The slave trade was deregulated, that is, within the context of the Navigation Acts, which stipulated that English trade in the Atlantic be restricted to English-made ships and English personnel.

institutionally) between phenomena traditionally reified as either economic or political. These changes are examined through an analysis of the dialectical interactions between economic interests, political ideologies, and public strategies for both the Royal African Company and its independent slave-trading disputants. The study compares these interactions to the regulatory outcomes for both the Royal African Company and its political opponents and links these outcomes to the rapid development of the transatlantic slave trade and some of the earlier political opposition to the slave trade that developed in this period.

The African Company's monopoly was politically constituted. Its interests included its employees, shareholders, creditors, and the king. In the 1670s and 1680s, the political and constitutional context supported these interests by protecting the company's charter. Once involved in the need to publicly justify its monopoly, the company sought to ensure the loyalty of these interests and gather further support by associating its interests with broader, ideological concerns, such as the way in which a monopoly company could satisfy the national good better than self-interested independent merchants. It marshaled ideas that reflected its interests, but, from the 1690s, it failed to develop a political strategy that reflected how the political context had changed. The royal prerogative could no longer be celebrated as the primary source of regulatory initiative and control in the national economy. Without a successful political strategy that matched the company's ideological posturing to the political context, the company could not look after its interests.[7]

The company's opponents formed a lobby that represented a large population of independent merchants active primarily in the Atlantic economy. Before the Glorious Revolution, they did not enjoy a political context propitious to asserting their own interests. But, by the 1690s, Parliament was in charge of regulation, and it emphasized the importance of broad public support for regulation and political tactics that complemented the political and legislative processes. The independent traders could thus uphold their interests and engineer a vastly expanded slave trade.

The politicization of the slave trade therefore allowed the African Company to develop the slave trade in the 1670s and 1680s. It polarized debate about regulation, which helped opposing interests to form, cohere, and endure. This polarization had much to do with the formation of the two main political parties in this period, the Whigs and the Tories. Throughout the debate between the company and independent traders, the complex shifting

---

7. Robert Brenner, *Merchants and Revolution: Commercial Change, Political Conflict, and London's Overseas Traders, 1550-1653* (Princeton, N.J., 1993), 669–670.

ideological distinctions between the two parties shone through the ideological assertions of the company and the traders. But the political disputes between the two factions are not reducible to the disputes between the parties. The parties had a negligible influence on the primary focus of this study: the connection between the outcomes of the political disputes between the African Company and the independent traders and the changes in the capacity, geography, legitimacy, and morality of the trade in enslaved Africans. My depiction of the debate between the company and the separate traders offers a more nuanced interpretation of the reciprocal connections between interests, ideas, strategies, and outcomes than one in which the political parties are monolithic arbiters and authors of government, ideology, and empire.[8]

The constitutional changes of the 1690s intensified the politicization of the slave trade by broadening participation and enriching the ideological disputes as the dialogue between the company and its opponents forged new ideas, new strategies, and, in turn, new contexts—all celebrated as conducive to "freedom," but all instrumentally involved in the entrenchment of slavery.

Persuading Parliament to support a totally unregulated slave trade—one without any statutory management—was a key lobbying strategy of the independent slave traders. Because of Parliament's supremacy over national regulation, the independent slave traders' defeat of the African Company's attempts to achieve statutory support for their monopoly ensured that the slave trade would default to an unregulated state. The independent traders veneered this lobbying tactic by celebrating the right to trade in enslaved Africans, without state interference, as a natural right. The British decision to foster the slave trade through the free market was, therefore, a political one, founded on a distinctively British conception of freedom. This freedom became a rallying cry for the maintenance and protection of the English and then the British Empire. The debates about the regulation of the slave trade suggest that this empire needed broader political support than crown-sponsored monopoly companies, like the Royal African Company, could provide.

The independent slave traders' parliamentary victory did not end the politicization of the slave trade. The British state responded to this deregulated trading model, however, throughout the eighteenth century by instituting tighter regulation of the transatlantic economy with the help of statutory initiatives to occupy the legislative vacuum that the independent slave traders engineered from 1712. By the 1770s, the British Parliament's regulatory fervor

---

8. For the principal case made that the Africa trade issue exhibited a party aspect, see Tim Keirn, "Monopoly, Economic Thought, and the Royal African Company," in John Brewer and Susan Staves, eds., *Early Modern Conceptions of Property* (London, 1995), 430. See also Steve Pincus, *1688: The First Modern Revolution* (New Haven, Conn., 2009), 375.

had alienated the American colonists. In the early decades of the nineteenth century, it ended the slave trade and slavery in the British Empire.

Public deliberations about the slave trade broadened discussion of narrow economic interests into all their noneconomic connotations. This broadening gave the dispute between the African Company and the independent traders a pronounced ideological dimension. Once the independent traders had persuaded Parliament to countenance their expanded version of the slave trade, the dialogic impetus between the African Company and the independent traders did not die down. In the 1740s and 1750s, in response to an impressive resurgence of competition from the French, the company began to fashion ideological justifications for itself (and rework older ones) that celebrated the importance of state regulation of trade. These rationales would play a part as important in informing the rhetoric of early discussions of the abolition of the slave trade as the independent slave traders' fixation with natural rights and with freedom. The politicization of the transatlantic slave trade between 1660 and 1752 would underpin the initial political dialogues about the abolition of the slave trade.

Examining this process of politicization and its influence on the regulation, deregulation, and re-regulation of the slave trade provides a means to bridge explanations of the "origins" of the slave trade and slavery with explanations of their abolition. The focus on politics helps to provide a richer account of the publicly articulated intentions that willed the slave trade and slavery into existence to set alongside the political accounts of the trade's abolition. The African Company had to justify and explain its monopoly. The movement to enlarge Britain's slave trade used new political means to achieve its economic ends. It took advantage of changed political and constitutional structures; it developed and articulated a political creed; and it implemented an ingenious political strategy to achieve success. All of these features of the politicization of the slave trade allow historians to learn about the intentions of the architects of the transatlantic slave trade and of American slavery.[9]

Concentrating on politicization also allows a broader, transatlantic analysis of the institutional contours of the slave-trading regimes that enables a balanced depiction of the trade's demand and supply sides. Both factions in what became known as the Africa trade debates sought to influence Britain's im-

---

9. The escalation of the slave trade allowed for a responsive supply of enslaved Africans for the mainland American plantations for the first time. It therefore offers a political embellishment for those accounts of the development of slavery that fixate either on the history of racial prejudice or on the changing prices of enslaved Africans. For a recent intervention that pieces together the development of racial prejudices among a similar population at the same time, see Catherine Molineux, *Faces of Perfect Ebony: Encountering Atlantic Slavery in Imperial Britain* (Cambridge, Mass., 2012).

perial policy. Focusing on both the African Company and its lobbying opponents also helps to show the implications of the political union of Britain and the American colonies during slavery's development.[10]

Most important, the politicization of slavery forces us to interrogate modern, liberal conceptions of freedom and liberty and their instrumental connections with the kidnapping, enslavement, transportation, torture, and murder of hundreds of thousands of African women, men, and children. The African Company's independent slave-trading opponents mounted a campaign to escalate the slave trade with reference to their freedom to trade and made use of modern, liberal political institutions like Parliament and the free press. Slavery and the slave trade were not the relics of a traditional, precapitalist society; they were the distillate expressions of modern society's dynamic founding moments. Focusing on the politicization of slavery shows us that freedom's interaction with slavery was not only ironic. Freedom, in multiple ways, caused slavery. As such, it has a debt to pay.

10. The desire to emphasize the connectedness of the colonies and the mother country and therefore to add contingency to American independence represents one of the goals of "Atlantic history." For the multifarious aims and definitions of this historiographical tradition, see, especially, the forum "The New British History in Atlantic Perspective," *American Historical Review*, CIV (1999), 426–500; David Armitage and Michael J. Braddick, eds., *The British Atlantic World, 1500-1800* (Bakinstoke, 2002). See also Elizabeth Mancke and Carole Shammas, eds., *The Creation of the British Atlantic World* (Baltimore, 2005). This view contests the persistence of a perspective on empire content to deploy the abstractions of center and periphery; see, especially, Alison Games, *The Web of Empire: English Cosmopolitans in an Age of Expansion, 1560-1660* (New York, 2008), 10–11; and J. H. Elliott, *Empires of the Atlantic World: Britain and Spain in America, 1492-1830* (New Haven, Conn., 2006), xiv–xvii. Christopher Tomlins, in *Freedom Bound: Law, Labor, and Civic Identity in Colonizing English America, 1580-1865* (Cambridge, 2010), 417, 418, mentions the importance of documenting the intention to develop slave regimes. Any attempt to isolate primary causes, and, indeed, evidence of intention, within a purely economic understanding of the British Atlantic empire in which artificial political distinctions separate center from periphery along with their economic impersonations, supply and demand, is unlikely to succeed. The absence of coordination between the center and the periphery has been an important theme within the literature explaining slavery's creation story. Slave-trade historians have often relied on oscillating colonial commodity prices, the changing availability of white indentured labor, and productivity improvements in slave trading to explain the rise and fall of slave-trade volumes. As with accounts of the development of slavery that concentrate on the periphery of power rather than the imperial center, economic accounts of the development of slavery suffer by an inclination to minimize the role public bodies played in Africanizing the American plantation labor force. For a (nonetheless) brilliant overemphasis on the demand side, see Edmund Morgan, *American Slavery, American Freedom: The Ordeal of Colonial Virginia* (New York, 1975), 295–315. For an assertion that the shift from indentured servitude to slavery proceeded without transatlantic coordination, see Russell Menard, "From Servants to Slaves: The Transformation of the Chesapeake Labor System," *Southern Studies*, XVI (1977), 363, 389. For the belief that the rise and fall of slave-trade volumes were determined primarily by economic factors, see Richard Nelson Bean, *The British Trans-Atlantic Slave Trade, 1650-1775* (New York, 1975), 73. Africa trade refers to all aspects of England's trade with Africa, including the sizable imports of ivory, redwood, and gold.

Part One
Deregulation, 1672–1712

ONE

The Politics of Slave-Trade Escalation, 1672–1712

The Royal African Company of England shipped more enslaved African women, men, and children to the Americas than any other single institution during the entire period of the transatlantic slave trade. From its foundation in 1672 to the early 1720s, the African Company transported close to 150,000 enslaved Africans, mostly to the British Caribbean. It played a central role in establishing England's transatlantic slave trade, stealing market share from the Dutch and French slave trades, and in Africanizing the populations of England's Caribbean plantations. In 1673, soon after the company's foundation, the English had a 33 percent share in the transatlantic slave trade. By 1683, that share had increased to 74 percent.[1]

Nevertheless, from the mid-1670s forward the company's monopolistic restrictions precipitated complaints from many American colonists and transatlantic English merchants. Independent slave traders, known from 1698 as the "separate traders to Africa," mounted a campaign to satisfy the demand for slaves. In the aftermath of the Glorious Revolution, they were able to carry on a political movement that transformed the contours and capacity of Britain's slave trade. The annual average peacetime capacity of the trade when the African Company's monopoly came closest to being enforceable, from 1673 to 1688, was twenty-three voyages. An equivalent period of peace after deregulation, from 1714 to 1729, saw free trade produce an average of seventy-seven voyages annually. Between 1687 and 1720, the company's market share reduced from 97 percent to 4 percent. Despite the remarkable scale of human trafficking conducted by the company, its maximum capacity could not match that of the deregulated trade. Even if the African Company had endured the changing political climate of the 1690s, England's contribution to

---

1. See *The Trans-Atlantic Slave Trade Database (Voyages Data Set)*, "Estimates" spreadsheet (2010), http://www.slavevoyages.org/tast/database/download.faces#extended. All statistics relating to slave-trade numbers are drawn from this invaluable source, unless otherwise stated. For the data on which Figures 1–3 are based, see Appendix 1, below.

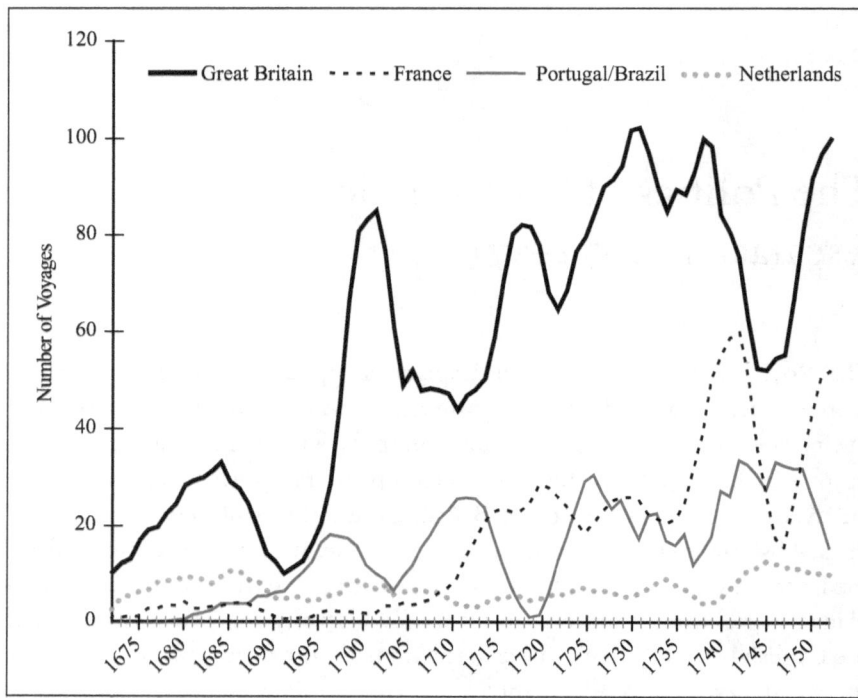

FIGURE 1. Slave-Trading Voyages, Great Britain, France, Portugal / Brazil, and the Netherlands, 1672–1752. Data represents five-year running averages. *The Trans-Atlantic Slave Trade Database (Voyages Data Set)*, "Estimates" spreadsheet (2010), http://www.slavevoyages.org/tast/database/download.faces#extended.

the transatlantic slave trade would have been far smaller and, in all likelihood, would have lagged behind those of its European competitors. If we assume an average of 350 slaves per voyage, this 230 percent increase accounted for an additional 1,474,200 slaves between 1729 and 1807.[2]

The separate traders' victory affected the geography of the British slave trade in ways that became formative for the trade's zenith in the second half of the eighteenth century. The separate traders were a broadly based interest group that sought to wrest control of the slave trade from the African Company in London and extend the opportunity of slave trading to provincial "outports," such as Bristol and Liverpool. The average number of slave voyages that departed from an English port outside London between 1672 and 1711 was five per year. From 1712 to 1751, that annual average improved

2. This dramatic increase of 230 percent in the trade's capacity is all the more remarkable because it took place when sugar and tobacco prices were declining.

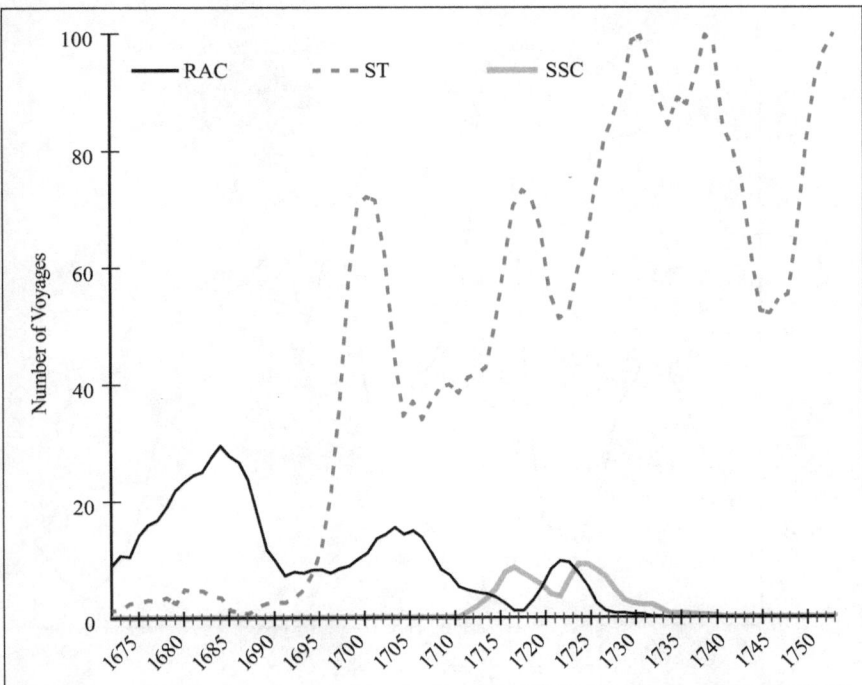

FIGURE 2. Slave-Trading Voyages, Royal African Company (RAC), Separate Traders (ST), and South Sea Company (SSC), 1672–1752. Data represents five-year running averages. *The Trans-Atlantic Slave Trade Database (Voyages Data Set)*, "Estimates" spreadsheet (2010), http://www.slavevoyages.org/tast/database/download.faces#extended.

to forty-six (in the same periods, the averages for London decreased slightly from twenty-four to twenty-three). The great cloth-producing areas for the company, such as Kidderminster, declined as the West Country suppliers for the separate traders grew.

The statutory deregulation of the trade that occurred in 1698 with An Act to Settle the Trade to Africa produced a craze for independent slave trading in the capital. A large proportion of the voyages that occurred during the "spike" year of 1701 came from London, 65 percent. War with France did encourage Atlantic-facing ports such as Bristol to develop their transatlantic trades at the expense of London in this period. But London's vitality as a commercial center and its proximity to the public debates about the slave trade in Westminster continued to ensure that the most successful separate traders of this period were London-based.

The politics of slave-trade escalation also influenced which colonies received an increased supply of enslaved Africans. Those colonies and boroughs

14 · DEREGULATION, 1672–1712

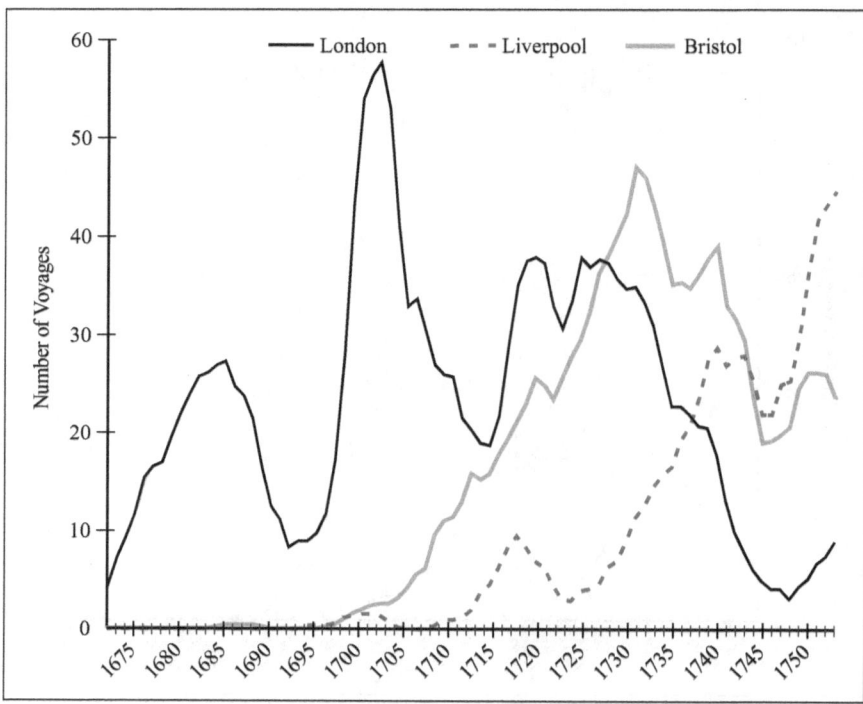

FIGURE 3. Slave-Trading Voyages, London, Liverpool, and Bristol, 1672–1752. Data represents five-year running averages. *The Trans-Atlantic Slave Trade Database (Voyages Data Set),* "Estimates" spreadsheet (2010), http://www.slavevoyages.org/tast/database/download.faces#extended.

with burgeoning slave trades and well-established means of lobbying Parliament benefited from the separate traders' political campaign. Jamaica and the Chesapeake colonies (who ironically had, as crown colonies, the same constitutional support as the company) received more slaves after the African Company's demise because their merchants had been persistent and energetic political opponents of the company. Jamaica took in thirteen slave cargoes in 1687. By 1729, that figure had increased to forty-nine. The mainland American colonies, in particular, benefited from the African Company's collapse; in particular, the greater availability of slaves catalyzed the shift from white indentured labor to African slave labor in the tobacco colonies. The average number of slave voyages that departed to the American mainland between 1672 and 1711 was four per year. From 1712 to 1751, that annual average improved to fourteen. In the fifteen years before the 1698 act, slavers transported close to fifty-five hundred slaves to North America. In the fifteen years after, that figure increased by nearly 300 percent to more than fifteen thousand. One separate-trader pamphlet argued that the deregulation of the slave trade had saved Maryland, in particular, from ruin: "Before opening the Trade to *Africa*, the Planters there, Owners of many 1000 Acres of good Land, were obliged to work barefoot and bareleg'd in cultivating their own Grounds themselves, and were resolv'd to have deserted that Province, had they not been supplied with Negro Servants." The separate traders achieved a much larger direct supply of enslaved Africans from Africa to the mainland American colonies than the African Company was able to provide. The Africa trade debates therefore played a critical part in entrenching African slavery as the preferred solution to the American problem of labor supply.[3]

The shift from a monopolistically organized trade to a free trade in slaves also altered the purchasing points and, therefore, the ethnic mixtures of the enslaved population in America. It decreased the proportion of slaves imported to America from the area around the Bight of Benin and southeast Africa and increased the number whose enforced embarkation began in west central Africa and Senegambia, trading arenas opened up to the English by the separate traders.[4]

The outcomes of the Africa trade debates determined the distinctive mechanics of the eighteenth-century transatlantic slave trade. The separate traders pursued a lobbying strategy that ensured that the slave trade became an early example (by 1712) of an almost entirely unregulated overseas trade. Participants on the Atlantic periphery, rather than the British state, regulated the trade. African vendors had always required bribes (or "dashees") and gifts to encourage their business. Colonial governments repeatedly attempted to benefit from the expansion in the slave trade by levying duties on slave imports. Colonial officials claimed that these taxes sought to limit slave imports to prevent planters from becoming overly indebted to British merchants. The levies, however, proved invaluable money-raising strategies because, by the second decade of the eighteenth century, plantation owners became less sen-

---

3. *A Letter to a Member of Parliament concerning the African Trade* ([London, 1709]), 1. For the importance of the changing availability of white indentured labor, see Russell Menard, "From Servants to Slaves: The Transformation of the Chesapeake Labor System," *Southern Studies*, XVI (1977), 363; and David W. Galenson, *White Servitude in Colonial America: An Economic Analysis* (Cambridge, 1981), 152. Although the African Company increased its interest in the mainland colonies after 1698, this increase cannot explain the dramatic improvement in the supply of slaves to the Chesapeake.

4. The percentage changes across the periods 1672–1711 and 1712–1751 are as follows: Bight of Benin (reduction from 20 percent to 10 percent), southeast Africa and the Indian Ocean (reduction from 5 percent to 1 percent), west central Africa (increase from 11 percent to 16 percent), and Senegambia (increase from 11 to 14 percent).

sitive to the price of slaves. In Virginia, for example, the duty on slave imports helped pay for the new Capitol building in Williamsburg.[5]

The expansion of the slave trade that resulted from the demise of the Royal African Company led to an enlargement of the sugar and tobacco industries, which the British government taxed. One contemporary disputant in the Africa trade debate believed that each slave contributed an extra thirty to forty shillings per annum to the fisc. If the failure of the African Company increased the volume of the slave trade by 59 percent (a conservative estimate), this increase represented more than thirty thousand pounds of additional customs revenue for the state per year and almost four million pounds between 1712 and 1807. What explains the separate traders' victory? This chapter views the separate traders' triumphant deregulation of the English slave trade through the lens of politics. It offers an introduction to the politics of slave-trade escalation.[6]

THOSE WHO HAVE formulated an explanation for the demise of the African Company have focused on the perceived failures of the company rather than the successes of the separate traders. In 1709, at the height of the Africa trade dispute, Nicholas Morice made his assessment of the causes of the African Company's downfall in a letter to his nephew, Humphrey Morice, a leader of the separate traders' parliamentary campaign: "the frauds and cheats of their [the Royal African Company's] factors . . . [and] that the planters in the several lands of America were men without justice and common honesty, and never willingly paid a just debt, so that the companie came to great losses by their means." Most historians have shared Morice's view about the causes of the Royal African Company's downfall. Scholars who believed that the company's monopoly could not be enforced explained its demise with reference to what they viewed as the natural structural inefficiencies of monopolies, which, as Nicholas Morice said, offered insufficient incentives to employees. Some historians cited the difficulty that the company faced in retrieving colonial debts, as Morice also mentioned. Others saw evidence of the African Company's inefficiency as proof of the absence of monopoly power and argued that the costs of maintaining the company's forts on the African coast prevented the company from competing with its "free riding" interloper competitors. The company's principal historian, K. G. Davies, attributed the

5. See Spotswood to the Board of Trade, Mar. 6, 1710, Journal of Alexander Spostswood, 45, Virginia Historical Society, Richmond.
6. See *Some Considerations: Humbly Offered to Demonstrate How Prejudicial It Would Be to the English Plantations, Revenues of the Crown, the Navigation and General Good of This Kingdom, That the Sole Trade for Negroes Should Be Granted to a Company with a Joynt-Stock Exclusive to All Others* [London 1698?], 2.

Royal African Company's fall to the disruptive impact of the wars on either side of the turn of the eighteenth century and the directorate's erroneous and often dishonest financial policy (with the political changes associated with the fall of James II as a hastening factor). Davies also noted a dissonance between the design of the African Company and the interests of its stockholders. He compared the company's operation to that of a public utility and saw its financial failure in terms of the unwillingness of the company's shareholders to subsidize imperial policy.[7]

Explanations for the African Company's foundation might have recognized its political position, but accounts of the company's downfall have largely concentrated on economics, favoring the company's natural inefficiency as a monopoly or its inability to compete with the separate traders. It is tempting to explain the separate traders' success in terms of their trading achievements. These independent traders benefited from undoubted economic advantages over the African Company. They made slave trafficking more efficient and profitable. In 1707, Royal African Company officials complained to one of their representatives on the African coast that separate traders could complete two journeys in the time it took for the company to dispatch a single ship. Rather than using (and having to fully finance) the company's African forts, like those at Cape Coast, the separate traders cut costs by dealing with vendors from their ships. They also prided themselves on having lower mortality rates among their slave cargoes. One African Company sympathizer, John

---

7. Nicholas Morice to Humphrey Morice, Mar. 25, 1709, Letterbook of Humphrey Morice, Humphrey Morice Papers, Bank of England Archive, London. For classical economic accounts of the Royal African Company's downfall, see S. R. H. Jones and Simon P. Ville, "Theory and Evidence: Understanding Chartered Trading Companies," *Journal of Economic History,* LVI (1996), 925–926. See also William Robert Scott, *The Constitution and Finance of English, Scottish, and Irish Joint-Stock Companies to 1720,* vol. II of *Companies for Foreign Trade, Colonization, Fishing, and Mining* (Cambridge, 1910), 21–32; David W. Galenson, *Traders, Planters, and Slaves: Market Behavior in Early English America* (Cambridge, 1986), 146–150; Ann M. Carlos and Stephen Nicholas, "Theory and History: Seventeenth-Century Joint-Stock Chartered Trading Companies," *JEH,* LVI (1996), 916–924; and K. G. Davies, *The Royal African Company* (London, 1957), 120–152, 346–349. Davies, although sensitive to both economic and political factors (but characterizing their interaction as accidental, 346) and to the role played by the colonies in opposing the company, emphasizes the importance of the African Company's structural faults and the interlopers' commercial advantages when explaining the company's demise. He did not sufficiently consider the separate traders' political acumen and the political conditions that favored their rise (see 120–152). Davies also underestimated the significance of the expiration of the 1698 act in 1712 for the future development of the slave trade. He described the debates before the expiration as "utterly barren of consequence." Limiting the impact of the expiration to the emergence of provincial slave trading, he remained dismissive about the political and ideological aspects of debate between 1708 and 1712 (130, 152). See also Adam Smith, *An Inquiry into the Nature and Causes of the Wealth of Nations,* ed. R. H. Campbell (Oxford, 1976), 741.

Atkins, described the separate traders' selling their goods to African vendors more cheaply and then beating the African Company ships across the Atlantic to corner the slave markets of America: "Separate Traders are not under the delays they [the African Company] are subject to: They take the whole Coast in their way, while the other is consigned to the Governour, and can afford to undersel their Goods (necessary Requisites for Dispatch and Success) because they stand exempt from all Coast-Charges." The separate traders worked faster in better managed, bigger ships. They therefore received higher prices for their larger human cargoes.[8]

The Royal African Company's economic and financial failings are also well rehearsed. It used dishonest financial methods to raise money in England, and its employees on the African coast and in the colonies, as Nicholas Morice mentioned, could not be relied upon to act in its interest. The separate traders preferred to stress the inevitability of the African Company's demise to make their case for opposition to the company's monopoly undeniable: "They were ruined before ever the Parliament broke in upon their charter," explained a supporter of deregulation some years later. But an economic interpretation of the separate traders' victory reduces a complex political story to the rhetoric of the victors.[9]

Explanations for all of the African Company's economic failures ought to acknowledge the importance of political phenomena. To explain the Royal African Company's collapse solely with reference to the company's economic failings is insufficient. Although the prospect of economic success made the company (and monopoly companies in general) more attractive to the state as

---

8. Royal African Company to Sir Dalby Thomas, Dec. 30, 1707, Treasury (T), 70/52, 210, National Archives, Kew; "Voyage of John Atkins to Guinea," in Elizabeth Donnan, ed., *Documents Illustrative of the History of the Slave Trade to America*, 4 vols. (Washington D.C., 1930–1935), II, 273. Company officials observed the separate traders' superior victualing; see Thomas Stewart and Raynes Bate to Royal African Company, Sept. 19, 1711, T 70/8, 114–115. See also Stewart and Bate to Royal African Company, [September 1711], T 70/26, n.p. For the separate traders' use of more experienced captains, see Sir Dalby Thomas to Royal African Company, Mar. 26, 1706, T 70/26, n.p. For the larger ships used by the separate traders, see *Some Remarks on a Pamphlet, Call'd, Reflections, on the Constitution and Management of the Trade to Africa* . . . ([London], 1709), 12. For the separate traders' claim to have lower mortality rates on their ships, see *The Improvement of the African Trade Farther Demonstrated by Separate Traders, in Answer to a Scurrilous Paper, Called, The Falsities of Private Traders Discovered* . . . ([London], 1708), 1. For the separate traders' superior speed at crossing the Atlantic and their being the first to supply planters each year, see John Hussam to Royal African Company, Aug. 27, 1711, T 70/8, 114. Edmund Jenings recorded Virginia planters' greater willingness to pay more for slaves from the separate traders in his response to the Board of Trade's 1708 inquiry about the management of the slave trade; see "Report of the Board of Trade to the House of Commons," Dec. 19, 1709, in Donnan, ed., *Documents*, II, 106.

9. *A Short View of the Dispute between the Merchants of London, Bristol, and Leverpool* . . . (London, 1750), 12.

a potential source of government finance as well as to potential shareholders, in the context of imperfect competition political support alone could ensure that economic success. London's capital market acknowledged this truth as the Royal African Company's stock price responded to political developments as much as to short-term cash flow. The African Company's political position might have been sustained, but this contingency would have limited the scale of England's contribution to the transatlantic slave trade. The expansion of the slave trade resulted, not from the separate traders' economic success, but from the separate traders' innovative political strategy, which better exploited changing political circumstances than the African Company's.[10]

The company's ability to enforce its monopoly and collect its colonial debts depended upon its political position in the colonies. Employees' dishonesty indicates their belief that the company's preferred position might excuse such behavior; and the belief that the company might enjoy good will as a public utility rather than as a profit-making enterprise suggests a public-spiritedness on behalf of its investors that derived from a political viewpoint now deemed obsolete. Similarly, the economic successes of the company's challengers would not have become significant until they had won a political campaign to legalize independent slave trading. Despite assertions by economists and the separate traders, nothing was inevitable about the Royal African Company's demise. As one contemporary pamphlet concurred:

> IT's most certain, that no Establish'd Company in that trade, ever Fail'd or became Bankrupt, upon Account (or by reason) of their being a Company; . . . And it always was the Interlopers breaking into the Company's Charters, and the Obstructions given to the Trade thereby, . . . which Reduced every Establish'd Company, to all the Misfortunes that can be Charged.[11]

The African Company's monopoly produced a slave trade with a lower capacity than that produced by deregulation under the separate traders' management. This observation does not explain the victory of the separate traders; rather, the insight derives from a timeless assessment of an economic form. It was not enough for the separate traders to argue that a deregulated slave trade would enlarge or had expanded the trade. The economic connotations of these differing arrangements—free trade versus monopoly—depended

---

10. Conversely, the Royal African Company repeatedly encouraged investment in its stock by MPs on the grounds that parliamentary confirmation of its charter would have improved its stock value; see Royal African Company to Richard King, Nov. 30, 1708, T 70/44, n.p.

11. *Reasons for Settlement of the Trade to Africa, in a Joynt-Stock, with the Arguments of the Separate-Traders against It, Answer'd* ([London, 1711?]), 1.

upon political turning points. In this period, such turning points hinged on more than economic success. Protagonists understood that, before 1688 (and to a lesser extent afterward), political position could sustain economic opportunities for companies without evidence of those companies' economic superiority. Political factors (ideologies, institutions, and strategies) mediated economic interests. This mediation could refract the economic outcome, as in this case. For the African Company and the separate traders, these elements enabled the realization of economic efficiency—a vastly expanded transatlantic slave trade.

Politics becomes even more important when attempting to explain the "breaking in" of the separate traders. The African Company's opponents used political as well as economic methods to defeat the company. Just as the creation, enforceability, and maintenance of the Royal African Company's charter depended upon political support, the separate traders' capture of the slave-trading market required the political center of gravity to shift away from interests sympathetic to the African Company and toward those who favored unregulated trade.

Disputes about various monopolies during the period 1672–1712 indicate the importance of political lobbies to the prospects of company charters. Several joint-stock monopoly companies victimized by interest groups included the Russia Company, the East India Company, and the Hudson's Bay Company. In all cases, whether opponents incorporated themselves within the company as in the East Indian case, failed as in the Hudson's Bay case, or eclipsed the company as in the Russian and African cases, company reform depended on the emergence of an external political opposition. The Royal African Company was uniquely vulnerable because its American customer base (unlike the nondomestic customers of the East India and Hudson's Bay Companies) was able to assert its opposition within the British Parliament by 1690.[12]

Comparing the fortunes of the Royal African Company with its continental European counterparts further buttresses the view that political phenomena were central to the former's failure. The French trading companies' monopolies endured longer. When deregulation occurred in France, it was subject to strict limits. Although independent slave traders from Nantes per-

---

12. The differing outcomes of the disputes between the East Indian Company and the Royal African Company and their respective interlopers reflect the power of the Atlantic interests antithetical to the African Company. For an assessment of the interests that attacked the East India Company's monopoly, see D. W. Jones, "London Overseas-Merchant Groups at the End of the Seventeenth Century and the Moves against the East India Company" (D.Phil. thesis, University of Oxford, 1970), 264–373.

suaded the French authorities to dismantle the French Guinea Company in 1713, this legislation limited the traders' activities to twelve sailings per year. Liberalizing legislation in 1716 allowed only four cities to dispatch African cargoes, and, unlike the British trade, the French government levied taxes on their activities to support French forts on the coast of Africa. The French state did not open the slave trade to the Gold and Slave Coasts of Africa to all French subjects until 1741, and the French Senegal Company maintained its monopoly farther north throughout the eighteenth century. Legislation opened the Dutch slave trade between 1730 and 1734, but, again, charges limited the independent Dutch slave traders' profits. The Dutch arrangement is not comparable to the British situation of 1698 until 1738, when the Dutch West India Company lost its monopolistic privileges.[13]

The Dutch West India Company incorporated within its management structure many of the provincial and colonial interests that would emerge to oppose the Royal African Company. This strategy preempted political opposition for a while but limited the size of the Dutch transatlantic slave trade during the first few decades of the eighteenth century. The Dutch did not achieve more than ten voyages a year from 1701 until the 1730s, when the deregulated English trade exceeded a hundred voyages a year. In France, the absence of open, deliberative political institutions, like the post-1688 English Parliament, deprived independent French slave traders of a political platform to mount a viable deregulation movement. British merchants had sufficient political power to successfully intervene within a more inclusive system. They enlarged their economic opportunities by completely deregulating the British African trade decades in advance of their French rivals, and, unlike their Dutch rivals, the British traders confronted a monopoly that made concerted efforts to exclude them.[14]

Those historians who admit some role for politics in the demise of the Royal African Company's monopoly confine it to the developments of 1688, which, because of the flight of the company's governor, James II, left the company cut adrift from the nurturing and protecting influence of the monarchy. Others have misconstrued the statutory regulation of the company's monopoly by Parliament in 1698 as a blow to the company's fortunes that re-

---

13. See Robert Louis Stein, *The French Slave Trade in the Eighteenth Century: An Old Regime Business* (Madison, Wisc., 1979), 6–17; and Johannes Menne Postma, *The Dutch in the Atlantic Slave Trade, 1600–1815* (Cambridge, 1990), 126–148, 201–202.

14. See Postma, *The Dutch in the Atlantic Slave Trade*, 127; and Stein, *The French Slave Trade*, 6. A comparison with European slave trading suggests that there was nothing natural about the demise of monopoly companies in this period. See Robin Blackburn, *The Making of New World Slavery: From the Baroque to the Modern, 1492–1800* (London, 1997), 389.

sulted from a broad Whig movement to reform monopolies associated with the discredited royal prerogative. The years 1688, 1689, and 1698 saw severe setbacks to the African Company's fortunes, but the company was not dead in the water as a slave-trading operation until 1712, after the separate traders had deployed all of their lobbying resources and skills. Institutional and ideological change within the British American political sphere proved more influential for England's eighteenth-century transatlantic slave trade than the surface changes in political personnel.[15]

The explanation for Britain's supreme contribution to the eighteenth-century transatlantic trade in enslaved Africans thus lies in a careful examination of the politics of the African Company and its independent trading opponents. The company derived its economic position from the political support it received from the monarchy. Any objections to the company's monopoly power would therefore need to be expressed politically (and often constitutionally). Changes to politics in England and in the colonies after 1689 exposed the company to the independent traders' lobbying campaign. This campaign undermined the company's commercial legitimacy and promoted a deregulated expanded trade that the traders deemed to be conducive to national happiness and strength—an enterprise consented to by the public and supportive of the natural rights of Englishmen throughout the British Atlantic world.

THE ENGLISH MONARCHY'S desire to expand and control the shipments of enslaved Africans to its colonies in the Caribbean was founded on political concerns and methods as much as economic ones. From the Restoration of the monarchy in 1660, Charles II wished to use a monopoly company to supplant the Dutch competition in the Atlantic trades, develop trade with the cash-rich Spanish Americas, and secure and expand English interests in Africa by establishing plantations there, thus supplying gold for the mother country as well as enslaved Africans for England's Caribbean plantations. The king, so it was hoped, could use the revenues from such a company to augment the glory of his restored monarchy.

In 1660, Charles founded the Company of Royal Adventurers Trading to Africa. This company was itself the latest in a long line of slave-trading initiatives supported by the English monarchy that began with Elizabeth I's endorsement of the slave-trading voyage of John Hawkins in 1562. The crown

---

15. See Davies, *Royal African Company*, 130, 152. See also Ann M. Carlos and Jamie Brown Kruse, "The Decline of the Royal African Company: Fringe Firms and the Role of the Charter," *Economic History Review*, 2d Ser., XLIX (1996), 291–313; and George L. Cherry, "The Development of the English Free-Trade Movement in Parliament, 1689–1702," *Journal of Modern History*, XV (1953), 107–119.

first experimented with a monopoly company to Africa with the Senegal Adventurers in 1588, which traded between Gambia and Senegal for ten years. The first incorporated monopoly company to manage English interests on the coast of Africa was the Governor and Company of Adventurers of London Trading to Gynney and Bynney in 1618. Competition from slave traders from other nations and interloping slave traders from England limited this company's success, though it built England's first fort on the African coast at Kormantine. From the 1630s to the 1650s, the Crispe family appears to have managed England's African trade. The scale of England's slave trade in the first half of the seventeenth century was, however, small. The political backing of the restored Stuart monarchy would be required to develop the trade's capacity.[16]

The Company of Royal Adventurers Trading to Africa brought fresh initiative and organization to the African trade. The king's brother, James, duke of York, managed this company along with his cousin Prince Rupert and a group of aristocratic supporters. After a series of false starts, Charles reorganized the enterprise as the Company of Royal Adventurers in 1663. The company advanced the same aims as its predecessor. It made an impressive contribution to the slave trade, but the Dutch, whose interests dominated the west coast of Africa, resented England's burgeoning interest there. The area became a central battleground in the second Anglo-Dutch War (1665–1667), with the African Company's serving there as part of the Stuart's military operation. This conflict greatly disrupted trade. England's growing cohort of independent slave traders filled the breach and helped to sustain an adequate supply of slaves to England's Caribbean plantations from 1665 to 1672. The Company of Royal Adventurers nevertheless played a critical role in the establishment of the English slave trade, shipping more slaves in the 1660s than separate traders had in the 1650s. But losses in the first Anglo-Dutch War led Charles II to again reconstitute the court-sponsored company as the Royal African Company in 1672.[17]

The Royal African Company expressed the regulatory potency of the royal prerogative. As the Company of Royal Adventurers' charter stated, its license was "a Prerogative of the Crown, . . . and therefore is free to be placed where his Majestie shall please, without giving any just cause of complaint of any others, that share not in it." These monopolistic charters and the trade they managed represented properties that derived from the constitutional position

16. Hugh Thomas, *The Slave Trade: The Story of the Atlantic Slave Trade: 1440–1870* (London, 1997), 174–181.

17. These aristocratic supporters of the Company of Royal Adventurers Trading to Africa included George Monck, duke of Albermarle, George Villiers, duke of Buckingham, Edward Montagu, earl of Sandwich, and John Grenville, earl of Bath.

of the monarchy in the 1660s and 1670s. Monopoly companies' control over markets reflected their royal benefactors' absolutist pretensions. The Stuart kings viewed their subjects' economic opportunity as a personal fiefdom and parceled it out to favorites in the form of monopolies, and these monopolies governed England's overseas and domestic markets. The monarchs also aimed to generate a revenue stream that would prevent their financial reliance on Parliament.[18]

In the 1660s and 1670s, the powers of the English monarchy projected aggressively into the world of the English Atlantic. The Restoration of the monarchy in 1660 encouraged a version of overseas empire based upon formal imperial institutions such as monopoly trading companies that expressed both the desire to extend state power overseas and the widespread belief in the importance of regulated overseas markets. Although statutory mechanisms— the Navigation Acts—had been created to channel the benefits of Atlantic trade through the coffers of the English state, the period saw a striking tendency for the state to deploy the law of the royal prerogative and for civil law courts, like the Admiralty courts, to manage the English Empire. This Restoration system proposed to move power into London, to engross profit within the executive branch of the constitution, and to govern through formal structures like the Lords of Trade and Plantations. The Lords of Trade was designed to assist in enforcing the Navigation Acts and impose royal government on the proprietary and charter governments in the colonies. As a committee of the Privy Council, the Lords of Trade could "command the respect, attendance, or opinion" of the Admiralty and Treasury. It acted as an executive body, ruling, without consultation, on all issues to do with England's growing overseas empire. From the 1670s, Charles II and, later, his brother, James, duke of York, attempted to tax the Atlantic economy more heavily.[19]

The Royal African Company was designed to be central to this system. The company's charter provided it with every conceivable means to attempt to enforce its monopoly, including the capability to erect Admiralty courts

---

18. Company of Royal Adventurers to King Charles II, Feb. 26, 1663, Colonial Office (CO), 1/17, no. 4, National Archives, Kew.

19. See I. K. Steele, *Politics of Colonial Policy: The Board of Trade in Colonial Administration, 1696-1720* (Oxford, 1968), 9 (quotation), 125. See also R. M. Lees, "Parliament and the Proposal for a Council of Trade, 1695-6," *English Historical Review*, LIV (1939), 38-66. For the use of Admiralty courts, see George F. Steckley, "Merchants and the Admiralty Court during the English Revolution," *American Journal of Legal History*, XXII (1978), 137-175. For the relevance of the distinction between formal and informal imperial institutions, see Bernard Bailyn, *Atlantic History: Concept and Contours* (Cambridge, Mass., 2005), 60. As Agnes M. Whitson noted, the Lords of Trade sought to improve the enforceability of the crown's will in the colonies; see Whitson, *The Constitutional Development of Jamaica, 1660 to 1729* (Manchester, 1929), 70.

on the African coast and in the colonies to prosecute those interlopers who infringed its charter. These courts were a significant innovation and added to the powers the Royal African Company's predecessors had enjoyed. The company's charter stipulated that these courts would have the "cognizance and power to hear and determine all cases of forfeiture and seizures of any ship or ships goods and merchandises trading and coming upon any the said coasts." The legal powers conferred on these courts were extraordinary for prerogative-sponsored trading companies (the East India Company did not receive this power until 1683). The formation of the African Company's own "vice-admiralty" jurisdiction would remain hugely controversial into the late 1680s, before that power was undermined completely. Charles II instructed colonial officials to enforce the terms of the company's monopoly by prosecuting "interloping" slavers and encouraging colonists to pay their debts to the company as it began to supply them with slaves.[20]

Powerful people supported the Royal African Company. Of all the monopoly companies, it enjoyed perhaps the closest relations with the sovereign power of the ruling monarch between 1672 and 1688. The duke of York had been the African Company's governor since its creation and was its largest shareholder. The African Company's charter and its intimacy with the royal family proved attractive for investors. Conspicuous among early subscribers were those at the heart of Charles II's circle (including four of five of the Cabal, the king's select group of advisers): Sir Edmund Andros, Henry Bennet, earl of Arlington, George Villiers, Lord Buckingham, Sir George Carteret, Sir Thomas Clifford, Sir Peter Colleton, Sir William Coventry, William Craven, earl of Craven, Lawrence Du Puy, Ferdinando Gorges, Lord Francis Hawley, John Locke, Thomas Povey, Prince Rupert, Sir Joseph Williamson, and Matthew Wren. Many of these men had experience of the Atlantic economy. Sir Peter Colleton owned vast plantations in Barbados. Sir Edmund Andros had been governor of New York and would become James II's governor of his Atlantic supercolony, the Dominion of New England. Ferdinando Gorges had estates in New England, and Sir George Carteret was a lord proprietor of the Carolinas. John Locke's expertise in transatlantic issues is also well known. As a result, the Royal African Company made an impressive contribution to the English slave trade throughout the 1670s and 1680s.[21]

The Royal African Company's monopoly, however, was both deeply un-

20. Instructions to Sir Jonathan Atkins, governor of Barbados, Dec. 19, 1673, CO 1/30, no. 93; Cecil T. Carr, ed., *Select Charters of Trading Companies, A.D. 1530–1707* (London, 1913), 192. See also Philip J. Stern, *The Company-State: Corporate Sovereignty and the Early Modern Foundations of the British Empire in India* (New York, 2011), 59.

21. See Davies, *Royal African Company*, 25.

popular and difficult to enforce. It was particularly divisive in the colonies, where it had been a source of frustration to colonists from its inception, and there are ample references to interloping voyages. In 1675 in Barbados, the extent of ill feeling among the islanders led the governor there, Sir Jonathan Atkins, to appeal to the Lords of Trade to liberate the slave trade from the African Company's grip. The Lords of Trade in London, however, censured Atkins for his recalcitrance in challenging the king's right to monopolize trade. The company argued that embarking on independent slave-trading voyages represented a form of piracy and should be treated as such under Admiralty law. Anticompany colonists made it difficult to prosecute interlopers, though, despite the company's charter right to assemble Admiralty courts to try them.[22]

In 1676, a difficult year for the administration of the colonies, company interests, with the help of Governor John Lord Vaughan of Jamaica, seized the interloping ship the *Saint George*. Colonial elites rejected the company's suit for condemnation, using the rationale that an act of the Jamaican legislature made the water where the seizure took place a part of the local Jamaican parish of Saint Dorothy and, as a result, it was not under Admiralty jurisdiction. Prevented from upholding the seizure of the *Saint George*, the company began to seek means of supporting its prerogative in the colonies. The attorney general ordered Vaughan to "take care to preserve the jurisdiction of the Admiralty, and that the King's prerogative be not called in question concerning forfeitures." The island's council pressed on with their opposition to the company by passing the Act for Free Importation of Negroes, which the Lords of Trade rejected. Opposition to the company often expressed the constitutional position of the assembly, as the Jamaican council in this instance had asserted the rights of its legislature as equivalent, not subordinate, to the English Parliament. Convicted interlopers used common law courts in the colonies to obtain redress. In 1682, for example, a Jamaican court awarded damages of £1,627 to an interloper after seizure by the African Company in Jamaica. The company therefore became more timid in enforcing its monopoly in the colonies, especially in Jamaica. Colonial interlopers, as a result, eroded the company's share of the transatlantic market in enslaved Africans throughout the 1670s.[23]

---

22. Petition of the Barbados Council and Assembly to Charles II, 1675, CO 1/66, no. 931; Minutes of the Lords of Trade, Nov. 24, 1676, CO 391/1, 256; Mark Gillies Hanna, "The Pirate Nest: The Impact of Piracy on Newport, Rhode Island, and Charles Town, South Carolina, 1670–1730" (Ph.D. diss., Harvard University, 2006), 25.

23. Journal of the Lords of Trade and Plantations, July 13, 1676, in W. Noel Sainsbury et al., eds., *Calendar of State Papers, Colonial Series, America and West Indies* . . . , 44 vols. (London, 1860–1969) (hereafter cited as *CSPC*), IX, no. 988, 430–431, and Governor John Vaughan to Sir Robert South-

Clearly concerned about the legality of its vice-admiralty courts, the African Company in late 1677 sought the advice of three respected lawyers, Thomas Corbett, Sir John Maynard, and Thomas Turnor. These lawyers worked to deny the accusation, presumably made by independent slave traders, that the African Company's vice-admiralty courts were illegal and, by implication, that a common law right to free trade ought to extend to the west coast of Africa, as colonists had argued successfully that it did in Jamaica. Their opinion served to broaden the prerogative justification of the company's monopoly and its vice-admiralty courts in particular. Corbett's opinion supported the company's right to enjoy "Navall and Military Power," which allowed them to prosecute interloping merchants as "Rebeles to the King's Authority," quoting John Selden's 1635 tract *Mare Clausum* as a supportive authority. Corbett added that the 1628 Statute of Monopolies had made special exception for overseas trading monopolies and that its vice-admiralty courts were legal because they would be located outside England, where "the King about may give to any Countreys conquered by him, what Lawes he pleaseth whc are not contrary to the Lawes of Nature, or to natural reason and also may prescribe a way, manner, or course of Proceeding and Tryalls, different from the course of our common Lawes of this Land, bt canot doe soe in England." Corbett noted that Sir John Maynard, the king's sergeant and chief prosecutor and one of the kingdom's most important lawyers, confirmed the legality of Corbett's opinion. Thomas Turnor added that the common law could not operate in Africa "because the Comon Law cannot run where Writs cannot be executed, and Writs cannot be executed in this Territory for want of Sherriffs, and other Officers, And none but the King can constitute a Sheriff." Turnor went on to suggest "the superinduction of the Common Law into conquerd Countries is a Ray or Emanation of the King's own free and spontaneous Grace and Favour vouchsaf'd . . . to his own very English Subjects." The three respected lawyers thus provided legal authority to the company's forfeiture power.[24]

Added legal authority encouraged interlopers to seek to erode the company's trade using public political, rather than legal, means. They expressed their opposition to the company and sustained it with the help of constitutional arguments. In the 1670s and 1680s, though, when the company en-

---

well, Oct. 30, 1676, IX, no. 1094, 478; Hanna, "The Pirate Nest," 27; "Letter from Lord Vaughan about an Interloping Ship," Apr. 4, 1676, CO 138/3, 52–54; Dr. Lloyd's Report on the Case, CO 138/3, 56–59; Joseph Henry Smith, *Appeals to the Privy Council from the American Plantations* (New York, 1950), 127–128; T 70/16, 38, and T 70/169, 7d–8d, cited in Davies, *Royal African Company*, 117.

24. "Legal Opinions of Thomas Corbett and Thomas Turnor," Calendar of State Papers, Domestic Series (SP) 29/398, 111, 115, 117, 119, 120, [December? 1677], National Archives, Kew.

joyed powerful support and suppressed a potentially competitive market, no scope existed for registering opposition using economic methods like purchasing from or selling to another corporation. Joint-stock monopoly companies were political phenomena whose property derived from monarchical fiat. Successful opposition to them had to employ political means. That was as true in the mother country as in the colonies, although the company enjoyed more political influence and power closer to the center of government in London. The first parliamentary petition against the African Company appeared in 1678, when the company's opponents had begun to congregate around the movement of Anthony Ashley Cooper, first earl of Shaftesbury, to exclude the duke of York from the succession. Four London merchants, Jeffrey Nightingale, William Dockwra, Richard Roe, and John Swinlowe, complained that the company "tends to the destruction of trade and navigation and prevents the employing of many thousand seamen and the building and employing many ships which would be built and employed were that trade again laid open." They asserted

> that for want of this liberty [to trade] the exportation of woollen manufactures is prevented and the prices brought so low that thousands of families are reduced to poverty, the rents of lands fallen and the customs lessened; that people are forced to take what the Company will pay for the manufactures they export and pay what they please for what they import; that notwithstanding their charter they do not hinder the Dutch.

The petition's description of the company's activities took on a more sinister note, explaining that they "had ships on that coast at a great distance from the Company's factory, which with their cargoes were taken and carried to Cape Corsoe, where the Company's factors (without any jury) confiscated them and kept their agents long in prison and murdered some of them." These allegations that the company limited trade and employment and failed to constrain international competition would become typical of later petitions. The constitutional power of the company's royal supporters, however, ensured that the merchants' call for redress would go unanswered, as the king dissolved the House of Commons in 1679.[25]

Opposition to the African Company's monopoly thus could not compete with the political influence of the African Company during the 1670s and 1680s. A long-standing colonial opponent of the company, Edward Littleton, explained that the company benefited, before 1688, from the support of "some

---

25. SP 29/442, 172, [January? 1678].

great Men . . . with whom we were not able to contend." One of these great men was the duke of York, the company's most assiduous political supporter. In February 1676, for example, he protected the company from political assaults from its opponents, dismissing a petition to the Privy Council protesting against the company's monopoly. A pamphlet avowed that a petition detailing the African Company's monopoly restricting the Suffolk woolen trade was submitted to "the King and Council" in the 1680s, "but the Duke of *York* being president of this Company, no Redress could be had."[26]

Political disputes about the African Company's monopoly also developed within a debate about the political arithmetic of labor within the early English Empire. Several writers of the final third of the seventeenth century began to question the received wisdom of the Elizabethan and Jacobean pioneers of the English Empire who viewed the American colonies as vents for England's excess population. Populousness now was regarded as a source of national wealth and greatness. Historical demographers have documented a decrease in England's population during this period, however, owing to the outbreak of plague, war, and migration to the colonies. Thus, by the Restoration, writers like Roger Coke, William Petyt, and Carew Reynell blamed this population decline on the American plantations. This argument became part of a critique of policy supporting the plantations. The decrease in population intensified calls for the use of enslaved African labor in the colonies to prevent further depopulation of England. The African Company attempted to buttress its political position by answering such calls. In 1668, the Company of Royal Adventurers celebrated that its trade in enslaved Africans had filled the breach in colonial labor when the 1665 plague had prevented migration. By 1680, the company had taken account of the prevailing view that the colonies weakened the domestic economy by absorbing too much of its labor force by suggesting that it had hindered "the exhausting [of] this Nation of its natural born subjects."[27]

---

26. [Edward Littleton], *The Groans of the Plantations* . . . (1689), 6. For the Suffolk woolen trade, see Roger Coke, *Reflections upon the East-Indy and Royal African Companies with Animadversions, concerning the Naturalization of Foreigners* (London, 1695), 10. See Albert O. Hirschman, *Exit, Voice, and Loyalty: Responses to Decline in Firms, Organizations, and States* (Cambridge, Mass., 1970), 33; Davies, *Royal African Company*, 106–107. At times, however, in these years, the monarchy moderated attempts to centralize control over its colonies by conceding to colonists' demands not to allow the African Company to impose prices on them. See, for example, Stephen Saunders Webb, *The Governors-General: The English Army and the Definition of the Empire, 1569-1681* (Chapel Hill, N.C., 1979), chap. 6.

27. "Answer of Sir Ellis Leighton, Secretary, by Order of the Royal Company to the Petition of the Representatives of Barbadoes," Jan. 23, 1668, in *CSPS*, V, no. 1680, 542–543; *Certain Considerations Relating to the Royal African Company of England* ([London], 1680), 5. See also Abigail Swingen, *Competing Visions of Empire: Labor, Slavery, and the Origins of the British Atlantic Empire* (New Haven,

In January 1685, the company's position received a further important political buttress from a common law court judgment that supported the monopoly of the East India Company. In *East India Company v. Sandys*, Chief Justice George Jeffreys, of the Court of King's Bench, ruled that the monarch could provide monopolistic charters and the means to enforce them. This ruling allowed the East India and Royal Africa Companies to indict the interlopers in their respective trades. The African Company interpreted this judgment as a huge boon to its operations. It noted the benefits of this judgment for their charter and business. A General Court minute summarized: "The Company have good grounds that the Sentence, in favour of Charters, will be advantageous to their trade by the discouragement: Interlopers must [have] from it."[28]

Thus, in the 1680s, the Royal African Company severely limited the activities of interlopers. Indeed, the African Company's close connection with James II enabled the company to use the Royal Navy to do so. The power of the company's supporters and its means of enforcing its monopoly made the company an effective slave-trading operation, undermining both the French and Dutch trades, both of which were managed by monopoly companies. From its foundation until 1688, the Royal African Company also dominated England's Atlantic slave trade, averaging a 75 percent market share of the trade in this period. It paid its investors 10 percent dividends between 1676 and 1688. The company's share price, as a result, performed well in these years in relation to other joint-stock companies. John Houghton stated in 1683, "The Guinea Company was as safe as the East India company." The company also enjoyed an impressive trade in gold, coining, on average, twenty-five thousand guineas a year between 1675 and 1688. Between 1683 and 1686, with the king as the company's governor and the governor of Barbados, Edwyn Stede, as the company's factor on that island, the company's market share improved to 86 percent. The assistants described these years as ones of "very great extraordinary Success."[29]

Conn., forthcoming); Keith Wrightson, *Earthly Necessities: Economic Lives in Early Modern Britain* (New Haven, Conn., 2000), chaps. 8–9. Promoters of the Virginia Company also advanced the view that the American colonies would be vents for England's growing excess population. See, as one of many examples, William Symonds, *Virginia: A Sermon Preached at White-Chapel* . . . (London, 1609), 19. On population decline, see E. A. Wrigley and R. S. Schofield, *The Population History of England, 1541-1871: A Reconstruction* (Cambridge, Mass., 1981), 207–215.

28. For *East India Company v. Sandys*, see "Pleadings and Judgments in the Case of the East India Company v. Thomas Sandys for Trading to the East Indies without License from the Company," Rawlinson Manuscripts, class C, no. 13034–238, Bodleian Library, Oxford. For the boon to the African Company's operations, see Minutes of the General Court, Jan. 14, 1685, T 70/101, 19.

29. Scott, *Constitution and Finance*, 21. See also *A Memorial on Behalf of the Royal-African-Company*

THE GLORIOUS REVOLUTION of 1688–1689 offered opponents of the African Company a new political context for the development of a political campaign to lobby against the company's charter and to escalate the slave trade. Even before the flight of James II, the company began to appreciate the precariousness of James's hold on power owing to his increasingly reckless attitude toward England's Anglican Church and markedly heavy-handed treatment of venerable institutions like the City of London corporation, whose charter was declared forfeit in 1683. In February 1688, the company informed one of its agents in the colonies, "We rather desire all seizure may be made by the Statute than by the power of our Charter," referring to the fourteenth-century statute that underpinned the workings of the Admiralty courts and the customs. After James II's departure in December 1688, all of the seizures the company had made under the terms of its royal patent in the 1670s and 1680s became subject to review by common law courts as lawyers and politicians began to chip away at every feature of royal prerogative, especially the civil law jurisdiction of the company's Admiralty courts. Interlopers began to bring suits against the company for seizure of their property, despite the judgment in *East India Company v. Sandys*. They argued that seizure was illegal because the company's power of forfeiture derived from the prerogative rather than from statute. These suits marked the beginning of the political movement to enlarge and develop the English slave trade.[30]

In June 1689, the interloping slave trader, Jeffrey Nightingale, who more than a decade earlier had petitioned Parliament on the commercial disadvantages the African Company imposed on the English economy, brought a suit against the company at the common law Court of King's Bench. Chief Justice John Holt turned this case into a trial of the legal powers of the African Company's vice-admiralty courts and the legality of their forfeiture power. Starting with this case, *Nightingale v. Bridges,* and then culminating in *Dockwra v. Dickenson* (1696), Holt used the common law to eradicate the company's forfeiture power but confirmed the legality of prerogative-sponsored monopoly companies:

> The King may create a corporation of merchants, and give them, by charter, an exclusive right to trade, and hold territories, within certain

---

Relating to Their Proposal Lately Given in to the Honourable House of Commons for the Better Establishment of That Trade: Together with Their Said Proposal Subjoin'd ([London, 1710]), 1.

30. Royal African Company to Christopher Robinson, Feb. 14, 1688, T 70/57, n.p. The fourteenth-century statutes underpinning the legal power of the Admiralty were: 13 Rich. II, St. 1, c. 5, and 15 Rich. II, St. 1, c. 5. See also Steckley, "Merchants and the Admiralty Court," *American Journal of Legal History,* XXII (1978), 137–175. For *East India Company v. Sandys,* see "Pleadings and Judgments," Rawlinson MSS, class C, no. 130, 34–238.

limits therein described; but a clause prohibiting others to trade within the said limits, "under pain of imprisonment, and the *forfeiture* and loss both of their ships and goods wheresoever found, *etc.* and giving power to enter into, search, and *seize* ships and goods," is void, for the King cannot by letters patent *create a forfeiture of,* or any way, by his own act, confiscate, a subject's property.

Holt forced the company to pay £4,300 in damages plus costs of £2 3s. 4d. to Nightingale but did not dispute the company's charter or its right to seek damages against interlopers. Holt forced the company to pay £2,650 12s. to William Dockwra in the later case.[31]

Holt's judgment in *Nightingale* sustained a dubious efficacy for the African Company's charter beyond 1689. As a result of the decision, during the early 1690s the company's revenue from the sale of licenses to trade in slaves remained buoyant. It allowed the African Company's charter to endure and, indeed, it would later be suggested that the company was the only state institution that could legally uphold a restriction on a subject's property rights. Nevertheless, depriving the company of the means to enforce its monopoly by threat of forfeiture in its own vice-admiralty courts appeared to some like an official endorsement of independent slave trading. Interloping slave voyages increased dramatically as a result.[32]

---

31. See Alexander Renton, ed., *The English Reports,* 178 vols. (London, 1900–1932), LXXXIX, 496–502 (1 Show. K.B. 135–1450) (hereafter cited as *ER*); W. Darrell Stump, "An Economic Consequence of 1688," *Albion,* VI (1974), 28. For Dockwra, see *The Case of E. H., W. Dockwra, J. Thrale, and T. Jones, Merchants, and Their Partners* ([London, 1695]); *ER,* I, 309–312, XC, 532 (Comberbach 367). Although the quotation is an accurate summary of the two cases (*Nightingale* and *Dockwra*), it is the nineteenth-century reporter's summary of the *Nightingale* case, not Holt's. Careful reading of the case law in this period shows that the African Company's *Nightingale* case was bound up with the broader issue of whether joint-stock monopoly companies in general could enjoy the power of forfeiture. The East India Company had been subject to a similar claim presided over by John Holt in *Beake v. Tyrell* in the spring of 1689. In this case, the company refused to admit that it had seized the goods of its interlopers with its legally controversial forfeiture power. Holt unequivocally undermined this power in *Beake v. Tyrell.* It seems likely that East India Company interests intercepted African Company representatives to warn them not to argue the validity of their vice-admiralty powers before Holt in *Nightingale* to prevent that power (and others) from being undermined for all companies. As a result, the African Company refused to instruct counsel for fear that the court would strike down more of the chartered company's power. This courtroom strategy saw the company receive the legal backing for its charter without the right to constitute its own vice-admiralty forfeiture courts. I am very grateful to Dr. George Van Cleve for invaluable discussions of this case. For *Beake v. Tyrell,* see *ER,* XC, 924 (Holt K.B. 47).

32. Royal African Company to Henry Carpenter and Thomas Belchamber, Mar. 10, 1691, T 70/57, n.p. See also Committee Minutes, Dec. 21, 1704, T 70/87, 190, which records how the Royal African Company settled out of court for £1,950 with Edward Searle and John Gardner, two prominent independent slave traders and lobbyists for a deregulated slave trade. For the com-

The *Nightingale* judgment thus led the Royal African Company to mount a political campaign to achieve parliamentary approval and statutory recognition for its discredited royal charter. A statute supporting the company's monopoly would supply unequivocal public support and power for the company's charter rights. The African Company's petition seeking the House of Common's endorsement of its charter arrived in the House on the last day of the Convention Parliament, January 27, 1690. This petition commenced the parliamentary deliberations about the slave trade, known as the Africa trade debates, that were to last on and off for almost a quarter century. The debates produced 206 parliamentary petitions. These petitions arrived from forty-nine locations covering the length and breadth of Britain and its Atlantic colonies, sporting perhaps seventeen thousand signatures. The debates also generated close to two hundred printed pamphlets circulated by the company and its opponents around coffeehouses in the capital, the provinces, and the colonies and in the lobby of Parliament.[33]

Parliamentary consideration of the African trade favored the African Company's opponents, who swiftly appeared to oppose the company's attempt to achieve statutory endorsement. In appealing to Parliament, the African Company exposed itself to a representative institution with new regulatory powers. After 1688, Parliament remained, as it had been from its creation, a vehicle for the representation of diverse interests unevenly spread throughout the kingdom. After 1688, however, Parliament's representative authority was subsumed within the functions of the state. Placing Parliament at the center

---

pany's post-1689 sale of licenses to independent traders, see Davies, *Royal African Company*, 125. Davies views the sale of licenses as evidence of the weakness of the company's position, but such sales can also be seen as evidence that the independent slave-trading merchants viewed the company's monopoly as legitimate. If the independent traders rejected the company's legitimacy, why would they need to purchase licenses?

33. These calculations of total signatories are based on extrapolations from transcriptions of a series of Africa Trade petitions preserved in T 70/175. The following are either petitions authored by the separate traders themselves or are petitions supporting deregulated slave trading: Jan. 17, 1709, 100, Feb. 1, 1709, 217, Dec. 8, 1709, 148, Dec. 9, 1709, 150–151, Dec. 13, 1709, 149, Dec. 20, 1709, 152, Jan. 10, 1710, 156, Jan. 12, 1710, 158, Jan. 12, 1710, 160, Apr. 19, 1711, 159, [date unclear], 168, [date unclear], 170, [date unclear], 173. The following are African Company petitions with signatories: Jan. 28, 1708, 66–67, Jan. 20, 1709, 147–148, 149–150, Feb. 1, 1709, 65–66, 83–84, Feb. 2, 1709, 31, 61–63, 80–81, Feb. 3, 1709, 68, 69, Mar. 26, 1709, 142–143, Mar. 30, 1709, 143, Apr. 8, 1709, 144–145, Dec. 15, 1709, 71, Jan. 11, 1710, 155, Dec. 3, 1710, 200–202, Feb. 27, 1711, 215–216, Dec. 3, 1711, 289–290, Feb. 12, 1712, 286, Apr. 12, 1712, 296, May, 5, 1712, 298, Dec. 12, 1712, 284–287. The Royal African Company printed about three hundred copies of its pamphlets; see T 70/58, loose fragment, 167. See also Tim Keirn, "Monopoly, Economic Thought, and the Royal African Company," in John Brewer and Susan Staves, eds., *Early Modern Conceptions of Property* (London, 1995), 458–466. For a full list of the parliamentary petitions in the Africa trade debates from 1690 to 1752, see Appendix 5, below.

of the state's means of regulating the economy diffused political initiative into the market. Previously disenfranchised representatives of the market, like the African Company's opponents, now had access to the regulatory apparatus of the state via Parliament to create, enlarge, and protect their economic interests. The structures and ideology behind political interventions in the economy altered, bringing different economic interests to the political forefront. The supremacy of Parliament allowed a platform for lobbying groups, like the African Company's opponents, determined to wrest open cozy relationships between the government and particular economic interests.[34]

Many of the most successful lobbies emerged from the Atlantic economy. During the second half of the seventeenth century, merchants developed the political means to resist metropolitan attempts to restrict their economy and centralize their political institutions. Strategies included the institution of colonial agencies in London and the shift from direct trade, in which merchants purchased colonial produce in America, to the consignment system, in which planters dispatched their goods to London correspondents who also represented the interests of their planter vendors within the metropolitan political process. The independent slave-trading opponents of the African Company cohered into an interest group that reflected their pan-Atlantic trading interests and political networks. Former interloping merchants-turned-litigants, like Jeffrey Nightingale and William Dockwra, combined with sugar importers, like John Gardner and John Bawden, to lead a parliamentary phalanx in favor of liberating England's slave trade from the African Company. The company's opponents formed a highly effective lobby that marshaled more petitions, developed a more appealing ideology that celebrated the role of the public's consent in deregulating the slave trade, and implemented a political strategy that better reflected the effects that constitutional change had brought to the mechanics of regulating overseas trade, especially Parliament's monopoly over the state's regulation of the national economy.

The company's financial position and its trade began to collapse as the parliamentary deliberations wore on. In 1689, the company's market capitalization was £263,736. By 1693, after three years of parliamentary discussion, the company's total value had fallen to just £93,759. The need to appeal to the re-

---

34. For the way in which government became a function of the legislature, see also Paul Langford, *A Polite and Commercial People: England, 1727-1783* (Oxford, 1998), 706. See also Jürgen Habermas, *The Structural Transformation of the Public Sphere: An Inquiry into a Category of Bourgeois Society*, trans. Thomas Burger (Cambridge, Mass., 1989), 58–59: the "parliamentiarization of state authority ... led ultimately to the point at which the public active in the political realm established itself as an organ of the state." See also Mark Knights, "John Locke and Post-Revolutionary Politics: Electoral Reform and the Franchise," *Past and Present*, no. 213 (November 2011), 78, 81.

formed Parliament drove the African Company into a vicious cycle in which the mutually reinforcing connection between its undermined political position and the decline of its trade as well as the deterioration in the value of its stock became publicly advertised and, as a result, compounded. The company's financial collapse helped its political opponents to argue that a reform of the Africa trade through a total deregulation (referred to as "free trade") or the institution of a regulated company (one open to all on payment of a small fee, referred to as "open trade") would replace the moribund company with a dynamic, expansive trade that would release the pent-up potential of the English merchant.[35]

In the 1690s, these largely metropolitan calls for the reform of the Africa trade were, to some extent, muffled in the colonies by a fear of the emergence of black majorities. Colonists sought to manage the ratio of white to black, worried that a black majority encouraged slave rebellion and made the colonies vulnerable to attack because foreign invaders could use a liberated slave population to attack the English. Hearing Parliament was about to break the company's monopoly and concluding such a move would have a dramatic impact on the racial mix in the colonies, one anonymous Barbadian wondered "whether we have not begun at the wrong end" by attempting to open the slave trade to all. We are "thus endeavouring to bring in a throng and multitude of Negroes, before we have by the means aforesaid, or by any other method, procured such a competent strength of whites as may be sufficient to oblige them to acquiesce in the condition they were born to."[36]

By the late 1690s, two complementary processes lessened colonists' concerns about black majorities. First, since 1660 colonial legislatures throughout America had conceived increasingly harsh punishments for slaves to reassure planters that the black population could be controlled. Jamaica, Barbados, and mainland American colonies began to codify racial difference in law by outlawing racial intermixture and protecting slaveowners' legal right to brutalize their slaves, including the right to murder them. By the early years of the eighteenth century, white settlers were sufficiently confident of their mastery over their slaves to arm them without fear of reprisal. Second, during the final third of the seventeenth century, the supply of white indentured labor began to decline as the English domestic economy expanded and as war with France absorbed men into the rapidly growing army and navy. Colo-

---

35. For the fall in the company's value over this period, see Minutes of the General Court, T 70/101, 24, 40.

36. Letter to the Barbados agents, Nov. 19, 1697, CO 28/3, 136. For evidence of colonial fears about black majorities during this period, see *CSPC*, XIII, no. 779, 241, no. 1041, 315–317, no. 1695, 522, no. 1700, 524, no. 1738, 531.

nies attempted legislation to encourage the importation of indentured servants, but the mother country ultimately resisted. Once it became clear that the supply of indentured servants from Europe had contracted and that colonial slave law would, despite initial concerns, substitute for the presence of a majority white overseeing caste, the transatlantic lobby to escalate the scale of England's slave trade gathered momentum. As fears about black majorities abated in the late 1690s, colonists became more prominent within the transatlantic parliamentary lobby against the Royal African Company, adding their voice in Parliament to the anti-African Company chorus led by transatlantic merchants. The politics of escalation unified the English Atlantic in a desire to end the company's monopoly. This unification received print support. Transatlantic pamphleteers like Edward Littleton, who sought to end the African Company's monopoly, collapsed the interests of the colonies and the mother country into an interdependent whole.[37]

This movement to combine the interests of the colonists and home-country merchants to expand the slave trade, however, contrasts starkly with the differing trajectories of English and American slave law. The Africa trade debates waged as English and colonial courts worked out their responses to slavery. American courts provided means to manage black majorities in favor of slaveowners. English courts, however, expressed profound ambivalence about the institution of slavery *within* England. The colonies and the mother country might have collaborated to enlarge the scale of the enslaved African population in the colonies, but the two legal jurisdictions remained separate when it came to the law of slavery. This contrast is all the more striking when considering the rulings of Chief Justice John Holt, the same judge who, in *Dockwra v. Dickenson,* had undermined the African Company's monopoly and, in doing so, helped to expand the slave trade. Between 1696 and 1706, Holt ruled in a series of cases that chattel slavery was contrary to English common law. In *Chamberlain v. Harvey,* he held that, under English law, a "negro cannot be demanded as a chattel." In this case, the court refused to base the slave's status in England on Barbados law. In *Smith v. Brown and Cooper* in 1706,

37. [Littleton], *The Groans of the Plantations,* 23. For the enactment of these racist codes, see, most recently, Christopher Tomlins, *Freedom Bound: Law, Labor, and Civic Identity in Colonizing English America, 1580–1865* (Cambridge, 2010), 428–458. For the contracting supply of white indentured labor, see Farley Grubb and Tony Stitt, "The Liverpool Emigrant Servant Trade and the Transition to Slave Labor in the Chesapeake, 1697–1707: Market Adjustments to War," *Explorations in Economic History,* XXXI (1994), 376–405. For the importance of transatlantic solidarity as expressed in the political process, see also William A. Pettigrew, "Historicizing Supply and Demand in Early American Economic History: The Importance of Transatlantic Politics," *William and Mary Quarterly,* 3d Ser., LXVIII (2011), 409–413.

Holt advised that the plaintiff ought to have pled his case in Virginia, where the legal system derived from the royal prerogative rather than the common law and would therefore endorse the rights of the owners of chattel slaves.[38]

The Africa trade debates thus concentrated on the legality of open slave trading, not on the legality of slavery. Although underpinned by colonial legislation to protect the interests of slaveowners, the Africa trade debates would have a far greater effect on the scale of the transatlantic slave trade and the size of the enslaved African populations in America than Holt's concern about slavery within England itself. The differing jurisdictions that defined the law of slavery as an inherently American concern would interact for the slave trade in a sequential, rather than a spatial, way. The same prerogative Holt argued supported slavery in the colonies would now be undermined at home and abroad to allow the slave population to increase. Common law might have disliked colonial slavery, but it favored the freedom of independent slave traders to supply slaves.

In 1698, the Royal African Company achieved a remarkable statutory victory. The increasing threat of French competition on the African coast (and the French capture of a company fort at Gambia in 1695), the prospect of a competitive Scottish Darien Company, the persuasiveness of the company's arguments (especially as a disinterested upholder of the state interest via the forts that Parliament persistently agreed were essential to the trade) as well as the company's continued political capital had all helped the African Company to achieve a compromise statute in its favor. After public deliberations throughout the 1690s, Parliament provided a reprieve for the African Company by recognizing its charter, but at the price of opening the slave trade to all English subjects for thirteen years. The 1698 act preserved the African Company but legalized independent slave trading on payment of a duty of 10 percent on all exports and imports for the trade between Cape Blancoe and Cape Mount (where the African Company forts were) and 10 percent on exports only between Cape Mount and the Cape of Good Hope (where the majority of the slaves were), with an exemption of duties on slaves and gold and payment of 5 percent only on redwood. The duties were payable to the company exclusively for the maintenance of the company's West African forts. The act also stipulated that individuals involved in slave trading could not serve in public office in the colonies. Having earlier conceded access to the Gold Coast and the slave coasts farther south in exchange for a 15 percent

---

38. For discussion of these cases, see George Van Cleve, "Somerset's Case and Its Antecedents in Imperial Perspective," *Law and History Review*, XXIV (2006), 616–618.

duty, the African Company's acceptance of a 10 percent duty through the 1698 statute suggests the separate traders' contribution to the act's terms.[39]

The African Company's calculation that it was better to receive statutory support, albeit partial, than to push for a monopoly backfired. Hundreds of merchants throughout England and the colonies responded by assembling cargoes of goods bound for Africa. The interloping slave traders became known as separate traders, or "ten per cent" men, in reference to the duty they paid under the terms of the 1698 act. A French official on the west coast of Africa, Andre Brue, observed the impact of the act:

> It is scarce possible to conceive what a Number of *English* Vessels this Permission brought to the *Gambra*. . . . Between *January* and *June*, 1698, these separate Traders exported no fewer than three thousand six hundred Slaves, by which Means they overstocked the Country with more Goods than they could consume in some Years.
>
> Nothing could be more imprudent than the Conduct of the *English* Company, who had better have received nothing from the Parliament for the Reparation of their Fort, than have accepted this Benevolence of Ten *per Cent*.

This expansion undermined the African Company's market share of the slave trade. In 1690, the African Company retained an 88 percent share of the English slave trade. By 1701, as a result of the deregulating statute of 1698, the company's share quickly reduced to 8 percent. Such was the stimulus that the statute provided for the noncompany trade that observers, like Brue, mistakenly assumed that independent traders had initiated the act.[40]

The 1698 statute led to a marked increase in the prices of slaves. The opening up of the slave trade made purchasing slaves on the African coast more competitive. The average price of a slave in America in 1689 was about fourteen pounds. By 1700, the price had increased to twenty-five pounds. The African Company's pamphleteers had predicted this increase. One of their arguments for monopoly was that it allowed English merchants to control the price of slaves on the African coast. But the price increase did not produce a reduction in demand. This circumstance may suggest that the racist colonial laws enacted during the 1690s and codified in the early years of the eighteenth century allowing plantation owners to discipline their slaves helped to make

---

39. See *Statutes of the Realm* (London, 1820), VII, 393–397 (Rot. Parl. 9 Gul. III, c. 26, 5, n. 2). For the company's earlier concession to the independent slave traders, see Minutes of the General Court, Jan. 10, 1698, T 70/101, 68.

40. *A New General Collection of Voyages and Travels* . . . , 4 vols. (London, 1745–1747), II, 78–79. For the African Company's changing market share of the slave trade, see Appendix 1.

demand for enslaved African labor less responsive to price. The increased price of slaves, however, also stimulated Britain's domestic economy as more of the goods that Britain exported to Africa needed to be exchanged for the more expensive slaves. The price inelasticity of slave labor suggests the effect that political factors had on the expansion of the trade.[41]

From 1705, the African Company began to argue that the act of 1698 did not suit its purposes because, despite the huge expansion of the trade, the duty did not raise enough money to pay for the company's forts. In 1700, the 10 percent duty raised £11,000, but after that it scarcely produced £4,000 a year because separate traders began to use their political power at home and in the colonies to habitually avoid payment. With its own trade depleted by the separate traders, the company turned to unwise financial contingencies. From 1702, the company began to pay dividends from its capital rather than from the profits of its trade. It also issued bonds to raise yet more money. In 1706, the company owed approximately £300,000 in bonds and £1,056,350 in stock. By relying on bonds rather than capital, and with the value of the company's shares hemorrhaging owing to the repeated obligations of its shareholders to advance money, the capital of the company was valued at far less than the loans that capital was meant to secure. As the utility of the company's dead stock—its forts—which provided the security for the company's loans, became publicly questioned, the company's shareholders and creditors became increasingly nervous about their investments. Political skill and the reputation of its management offered the only security for the company's investors once its capital and then its trade dried up.[42]

THE ROYAL AFRICAN COMPANY appealed to Queen Anne for redress in 1707 and mounted a second campaign to achieve parliamentary endorsement for its monopoly. The separate traders' lobby, much enlarged as a result of the expansion of the slave trade after 1698, continued to outmaneuver the African Company's political campaign. In this second stage of the Africa trade debates, the opinion of colonists would be placed at the center of deliberations

---

41. See David Eltis, "The British Transatlantic Slave Trade before 1714: Annual Estimates of Volume and Direction," in Robert L. Paquette and Stanley L. Engerman, eds., *The Lesser Antilles in the Age of European Expansion* (Gainsville, Fla., 1996), 152, table 6-1.

42. The African Company first reached the conclusion that the proceeds of the 10 percent duty did not cover the costs of the forts and that extra competition for slaves on the African coast raised the price of slaves; see Minutes of the Committee of Eight, Dec. 18, 1705, T 70/102, n.p. Its petition did not reach Parliament, however, until March 1708. Scott argued that "this mode of finance as well as the pressure of loans generally on the company at a critical period of its history was a more serious hindrance to its prosperity than the losses of the war or the competition of the separate traders" (*Constitution and Finance*, II, 29).

by a new Board of Trade, and a more sophisticated ideological dispute would emerge. The African Company received persuasive ideological backing from skilled and experienced writers like Charles Davenant and Daniel Defoe who, by this second stage, were government servants. These writers worried about the effects of the commercialization of English society, which the separate traders and the political power so clearly supported.[43]

In 1696, members of Parliament (MPs) had reconstituted the powerful Lords of Trade into the less powerful and more deliberative Board of Trade. Without access to the constitutional means to act unilaterally, the Board became an information-gathering body. Although it had been designed to preserve the monarch's traditional control over overseas trade revenues and remained technically a subcommittee of the Privy Council, the Board became almost from its inception a subcommittee of the House of Commons. The Commons regularly called upon the Board's commissioners, many of whom were MPs, to write reports and present them to the House and its various committees. The Board of Trade became a sounding board within a parliamentary framework for independent participants in the economy like the separate traders to Africa. It was therefore predisposed toward the cause of deregulation and, indeed, operated in the overseas economy as an alternative expression of state power to the old state-sponsored monopoly companies. From 1707, this new Board of Trade served as the umpire between the company and the separate traders and as an additional funnel for colonial opinion about the future of the Royal African Company.[44]

As fresh parliamentary deliberations continued in 1708, the separate traders received powerful support from the new Board of Trade. The Board's first report to the House of Commons into the Africa trade dispute, written in February 1708, read like a list of the separate traders' complaints against the company. Much of the separate traders' testimony appeared in the report verbatim. The commissioners unreservedly took the separate traders' side. For the Board, an institution charged with encouraging trade, the separate traders' superior trading record provided the ultimate recommendation. Its support for the separate traders severely damaged the company's credibility and shows that the infrastructure of the modern state offered a platform from which new

---

43. For the beginnings of the African Company's plan to appeal again to Parliament, see Minutes of the Committee of Eight, Jan. 10, 1706, T 70/102, n.p.

44. To take an important example, the Board's consultative, politicized format thwarted government attempts to resume the charters of several American colonies. In many instances, the Board of Trade appears to have gathered information for Commons inquiries on the basis of which the Commons, rather than the Board, made decisions. See Board of Trade Entry Books, May 14, 1713, CO 389/23, 256–266 (see also, 272–286).

ideas and new political groupings, like those assembled in favor of the deregulated slave trade, could fix on the company as a target for reform.[45]

The Board also helped to formalize colonial opposition against the company before a parliamentary audience. Believing its first report to lack the full weight of colonial opinion, Parliament requested in April 1708 that the Board of Trade embark on the first public inquiry into the transatlantic slave trade that would include testimony from all the Atlantic colonies. The report recognized the slave trade as the most important part of the Africa trade. The commissioners wrote to the governors of all Britain's Atlantic colonies:

> It being absolutely necessary that a trade so beneficial to the Kingdom should be carried on to the greatest advantage, there is no doubt but the consideration thereof will come early before the Parliament at their next meeting . . . the well supplying of the plantations and colonies with sufficient number of negroes at reasonable prices, is in our opinion the chief point to be considered in regard to that trade . . . we do hereby desire . . . you do inform yourself from the proper officers or otherwise . . . what number of negroes have been yearly imported directly from Africa . . . and that we may be the better able to make true judgement of the present settlement of that trade, we must further recommend it to you to confer with some of the principal planters and inhabitants within your government touching that matter, and to let us know how the negro trade was carried on [under Royal African Company's control and under the Act of 1698] . . . in what manner they think the said trade may best be managed for the benefit of the plantations.[46]

The Board of Trade's report asserted the separate traders' superiority as slave suppliers to the colonies. It accounted that the separate traders had supplied five times the number of slaves to Jamaica that the company had achieved, three times as many to Barbados, and nearly twelve times as many to the American mainland. The commissioners also concluded that the Royal African Company had not acted in the interests of the public and plantations

---

45. For the Board of Trade report, see Report of the Board of Trade for Parliament, Feb. 3, 1708, T 70/175, 7. For historians' alarm at the Board's conspicuous bias, see David A. G. Waddell, "The Career and Writings of Charles Davenant (1656–1714)" (D.Phil. thesis, University of Oxford, 1954), 233; and Steele, *Politics of Colonial Policy*, 109.

46. Minutes of the Board of Trade, Apr. 17, 1708, CO 391/20, 108. The commissioners sent this letter to the governors of Barbados, the Leeward Islands, Bermuda, New York, New Jersey, Maryland, New Hampshire, Massachusetts Bay, the president of the Council of Virginia, the deputy governor of Pennsylvania, the Lords Proprietors of Carolina, and the governors and Companies of Connecticut and Rhode Island.

and that it had hindered navigation. The report continued by recommending deregulated trade:

> Should so extensive a Trade be confined to an Exclusive joynt Stock, the Plantations may suffer for want of sufficient number of able Negroes at reasonable Rates, those Marketts being best supplyed where there are most Sellers. . . . We cannot but be sencible how prejudicial it must be to Trade in generall to have but one Buyer of all such Woollen and other Goods as are annually Exported for this Trade But one Freighter of so many Ships at home and but one buyer of the Plantation Commoditys abroad."[47]

The African Company would not receive a favorable reception at the Board of Trade. Its inability to develop a broad base of petitioning support in Parliament also hampered its prospects of obtaining a statute to support its monopoly and restart its trade. The separate traders, in contrast, gathered an impressive barrage of petitioning support from all corners of the British Atlantic world and consistently enjoyed the official endorsement of the Board of Trade.

THE SEPARATE TRADERS were able to use their breadth of support to prevent the Royal African Company from achieving a statute in its favor. Their lobbying tactics better understood the workings of the legislative process after the constitutional changes of 1688–1689. Because these changes ensured that Parliament enjoyed control of national economic regulation, the separate traders' prevention of a statutory African Company monopoly forced a total deregulation of the slave trade from 1712. As soon as the primacy of Parliament as regulator of the national economy became fixed, the logical implications of that arrangement also became apparent to merchants who favored deregulation. The improved powers of Parliament made the potential consequences of legislative failure greater because other branches of the constitution such as the monarchy and Privy Council could no longer be relied upon to resolve issues. If a statute to regulate the economy failed in the legislature, then a legislative vacuum would assist deregulation and produce "free" trade.

This regulatory context was itself partly initiated by independent slave traders. In 1692, in a discussion concerning the future of the East India Company, Gilbert Heathcote, the scourge of several monopoly companies during this period and a leading independent slave trader and lobbyist for a deregulated slave trade, complained to the Commons that ships had been hindered

---

47. See "Report on the Trade to Africa," Jan. 27, 1708/9, in Donnan, ed., *Documents*, II, 67.

from sailing to India by the Privy Council acting upon the company's representations. Heathcote achieved a nonstatutory motion in the House of Commons that it was the right of all English subjects to trade to the East Indies *unless* explicitly restricted by an act of Parliament. If a bill that attempted to monopolize a trade failed, then the legislative inertia would sustain deregulation.[48]

Such deregulation could be sustained with the help of another example of legislative inertia: the expiration of the 1662 Licensing of the Press Act in 1695. A counterpetitioning campaign based on the antimonopoly refrain prevented Parliament from replacing the old licensing statute. The expiration of this legislation allowed parliamentary deliberations about the economy to enter the extralegislative public sphere as participants printed reflections on parliamentary debates and circulated them in the lobbies of the Palace of Westminster, in the streets of London, in provincial towns, and around the peripheries of the British Empire. These pamphlets helped to form public opinion that would accept and endorse the implications left by legislative vacuums. Separate-trader writers began to restyle deregulation as the natural setting for the economy, with freedom to trade as a sacrosanct natural right. They encouraged filibustering, for example, on the grounds that it left regulation to the natural instincts that fueled the market. But extraparliamentary public opinion was not, on its own, sufficient. Deregulating parliamentary lobbyists, of which the separate traders to Africa were a pioneering example, had to employ the means to influence both public opinion and its representatives in Parliament to ensure the success of their proposals. They therefore encouraged parliamentary deliberation to legitimize their views—for example, by referring in pamphlets to points scored in parliamentary debates. By 1700, Parliament could not claim to monopolize the state's access to national means of representation. The increased use of petitioning and pamphlets provided alternative representations of the public sphere.[49]

48. For Heathcote's resolution, see Jan. 8, 1694, *Journals of the House of Commons,* I–LI (London, 1803), XI, 50 (hereafter cited as *Commons Journals*). See also *The Case between the African Company and the People of England* ([London, 1698?]), 1. The statute had, for some time, been seen in the colonies as the only means to restrict the economy; see George Frederick Zook, "A History of the Royal African Company, 1672–1713" (Ph.D. diss., Cornell University, 1914), microfilm (pagination obscured).

49. See Raymond Astbury, "The Renewal of the Licensing Act in 1693 and Its Lapse in 1695," *Library,* 5th Ser., XXXIII (1978), 301. See Mark Knights, *Representation and Misrepresentation in Later Stuart Britain: Partisanship and Political Culture* (Oxford, 2005) 127; and Rosemary Sweet, "Local Identities and a National Parliament, c. 1688–1835," in Julian Hoppit, ed., *Parliaments, Nations, and Identities in Britain and Ireland, 1660–1850* (Manchester, 2003), 50–51. See also Tim Keirn, "Parliament, Legislation, and the Regulation of English Textile Industries, 1689–1714," in Davison, Hitchcock,

Counterpetitioning lobbyists, like the separate traders, thus mounted campaigns to defeat regulatory statutes with increased frequency after 1688. Commercial interest groups began to lobby against statutory proposals to restrict the economy in order to ensure deregulation. The commercial interest group's counterpetition, therefore, became an important macroeconomic lever. In 1660, 1 percent of parliamentary petitions on economic matters were counterpetitions. In 1696, the figure was 20 percent; in 1705, it became 33 percent, and in 1713 it reached 65 percent.[50]

The separate traders' 1712 victory in Parliament proved to be a more resounding one by ensuring that the 1698 act expired without any statutory replacement, opening up the slave-trading market to all without any charges on the trade. This expiration, more than the 1689 and 1696 court judgments or the 1698 statute, represented the death knell for the Royal African Company's slave-trading operations. The separate traders had freed the slave trade from the bondage placed on it by the Royal African Company's monopoly and would enlarge Britain's slave trade and the African population of America still further.

THE ROYAL AFRICAN COMPANY used the political power of the restored Stuart monarch's royal prerogative to kick-start England's contribution to the transatlantic slave trade. But the polarized politics of the late seventeenth century helped independent merchants to develop a political case for their opposition. Constitutional changes in the 1680s and 1690s provided a platform for this campaign to succeed. The African Company's opponents, the separate traders to Africa, used a new transatlantic institutional playing field to make their case, especially in Parliament. They appreciated that legislative failure could devolve into trade deregulation. They mounted a campaign that combined counterpetitions and pamphlets, which articulated their natural right to trade in slaves as the best means to achieve their ends. In so doing, they developed a new commercial ideology. They thrived in an environment they had partly developed: an institutionalized British Atlantic empire within a political framework of competing lobbying groups pursuing their increasingly culturally legitimate self-interests. Their success massively expanded the capacity of Britain's trade in enslaved Africans.

Keirn, and Shoemaker, eds., *Stilling the Grumbling Hive: The Response to Social and Economic Problems in England, 1689-1750* (Stroud, U.K., 1992), 16.

50. This analysis of parliamentary petitioning derives from systematic examination of *Commons Journals*, VIII–XVII.

TWO

The Interests
"A Well-Governed Army of Veteran Troops"
versus "an Undefinable Heteroclite Body"
of "Pirates" and "Buccaneers"

In January 1690, when the African Company began its parliamentary appeal to obtain statutory support for its monopoly, its directors had every reason to be confident of success. The Hudson's Bay Company had recently received a statute to support its operation. The African Company had received the endorsement of the new monarch, William III, who had accepted the governorship of the company along with a thousand pounds of African Company stock. William proposed to use the company as part of his military strategy against the French. He charged the company with engaging in combat with French vessels and soldiers within the limits of its charter. The company's directorate and adventurers were also powerful and wealthy people. Edward Colston, the company's deputy governor, had made a fortune as an Atlantic trader and commanded great respect in commercial and political circles. Another director, Sir Benjamin Bathurst, who had served as an African Company director since 1677, was a City of London alderman and a prominent financier. Bathurst had also been a director of the East India Company since 1684. Other East India Company directors served the African Company at this time: Sir Thomas Cooke, George Bohun (Bathurst's nephew), and Sir William Hodges. Sir Peter Colleton, the influential lobbyist for the plantations and a director of the Hudson's Bay Company, and John Morice, who had vast experience of the Turkey trade as a director of the Levant Company, also lobbied for the African Company in the 1690 parliamentary session. Indeed, during its history, the Royal African Company was to benefit from 105 directors who brought experience from other companies.[1]

---

1. See Abigail Leslie Swingen, "The Politics of Labor and the Origins of the British Empire, 1650–1720" (Ph.D. diss., University of Chicago, 2007), 262. Twenty-seven percent of African Company directors served with other companies, compared to less than 5 percent for the sepa-

The entrenched power of the African Company would continue throughout the ensuing course of the Africa trade debates. During the period 1672–1752, thirty-eight directors of the company (or 10 percent) occupied positions in the government or court. Only twenty (or 2 percent) of the separate traders, on the other hand, held government offices. In fact, the company boasted sixty-five directors who were also members of Parliament (MPs), almost three times the number for the separate traders (twenty-four). The company also benefited from some heavy-hitting support from merchants, who commanded power with the most important business lobbyist in the land, the Corporation of the City of London. Directors like Sir John Fleet and Sir William Withers brought civic rank to the company's lobby as each served as lord mayor of London in the 1690s. The company's directors were far more likely to serve as officials within the City of London's governing corporation as aldermen, sheriffs, and lords mayor. Compared to less than 1 percent of the separate traders, almost 5 percent of the directors of the African Company enjoyed such offices, including twelve lords mayor. This kind of office holding helped to support the African Company's claim to act in the service of the state and for the good of the public.[2]

The African Company's corporate structure suited the task of parliamentary lobbying. The company was run by a deputy and subgovernor who were chosen from a directorate of major shareholders, the Court of Assistants. Its formal hierarchy of directors, officials, adventurers, and servants provided reliable parliamentary supporters for its cause. This group was large. It amounted to a potential constituency of well over one thousand individuals throughout the period of the Africa trade debates. The company also enjoyed a network of outposts and agents in the provinces, in Exeter and Bristol, and in the colonies of the Caribbean and the American mainland as well as several on the African coast (in addition to Africa House, its London headquarters on Leadenhall Street in the heart of the City of London). From these vantage

---

rate traders. The supplementary biographical information about the separate traders and the Royal African Company directors in this chapter derives from a trawl of the following databases from Gale Digital Collections: Seventeenth and Eighteenth Century Burney Collection Newspapers; State Papers Online; Eighteenth Century Collections Online; The Making of the Modern World.

2. African Company officials who also served as MPs include Sir Thomas Cooke, Sir Francis Dashwood, Sir Samuel Dashwood, Charles Godolphin, William Gore, Nathaniel Gould, Frederick Herne, Sir Nathaniel Herne, Edward Jeffreys, Jeffrey Jefferies, John Jeffreys, William Johnson, Richard Lockwood, Arthur Moore, Sir Benjamin Newland, John Nicholson, Sir William Prichard, Gabriel Roberts, Edward Rudge, Samuel Shepheard, Fisher Tench, Sir William Turner, Sir Thomas Vernon, and Humphrey Walcot. See Eveline Cruickshanks, Stuart Handley, and D. W. Hayton, eds., *The History of Parliament: The House of Commons, 1690-1715*, 5 vols. (Cambridge, 2002), I, 736.

points, the company's directors could cultivate its constituents from throughout the British Atlantic world to support its campaign in Parliament.[3]

The Royal African Company's joint-stock structure also assisted its lobbying efforts. Shareholders could influence key company decisions at an annual General Court. The company's stock provided a capital pool from which the company could divert cash to finance the authoring and printing of petitions and pamphlets and the various backhanders to parliamentary servants and lobbyists attending Parliament on their behalf. The African Company directors could, moreover, use political campaigns as an opportunity to request further subscriptions from shareholders. The company's directorate rightly believed that their cause looked more convincing to MPs when they enjoyed a sound financial footing. By advertising the effect that parliamentary establishment would have on its share price, the company could encourage shareholders to lobby on its behalf and attract new investment, increasing its capital at the same time it strengthened its political base. The Court of Assistants might also threaten to prevent adventurers from transferring their stock if they failed to comply with the company's lobbying strategy.[4]

In 1690, the independent slave traders' political capital was less impressive. Their interest group had to be formed from scratch. As far as it is known, there were no actively trading independent slave traders sitting in Parliament in 1690. Although it is difficult to assess the numbers of independent slave traders who interloped in the slave trade up to 1690, it is highly unlikely they represented a group close to a tenth of the size of the African Company's shareholders and creditors. They certainly did not enjoy the political connections or the preexisting hierarchical structure that so recommended the African Company as a lobbyist in 1690.

Thus, with its close relationship with the monarchy and the powerful and well-connected merchants on its board, a managerial structure well suited to and experienced in parliamentary lobbying, a broad base of support from powerful friends and investors, and a largely anonymous, uncoordinated opposition, the Royal African Company must have assumed that it could achieve parliamentary support for its monopoly. But it was not to be.

The Royal African Company's opponents developed a new and more

---

3. For a directory of the Royal African Company's directors from 1672 to 1752, see Appendix 4, below.

4. For details of the charges involved in lobbying, see Minutes of the Committee of Accounts, Aug. 30, 1711, Treasury (T), 70/112, 16, 34. For a separate trader's account of the African Company's strategy to force its investors to support its parliamentary campaign, see, *The Anatomy of the African Company's Scheme for Carrying on That Trade in a Joint-Stock Exclusive, on the Foot of New Subscriptions* ([London, 1710?]), 2.

powerful political base that gathered broad support from the seemingly unlimited beneficiaries of a deregulated trade. The company's appeal to Parliament exposed it to an opposition interest group that had been, since the 1670s, developing their political presence in Parliament. This group would prove itself, throughout the period of the Africa trade debates, better able than the company to innovate as lobbyists and to advocate more clearly for ideas that found favor with the legislature, thus thwarting the company directors' attempts to achieve statutory support for its monopoly. The directors failed to appreciate that the Glorious Revolution in 1688–1689 had created a new arena for the assertion of economic interests. From the 1690s onward, commercial lobbies, which represented the interests of individual merchants, jockeyed for position in a less restricted, parliamentary context. The directors of the African Company could corral a powerful base of mercantile support from those directly concerned in the African Company's stock, but, because of the company's strong associations with the displaced regime, its directorate would struggle to gather the breadth of support required to achieve legislative countenance. The company's opponents were able to depict themselves as the supporters of individual mercantile prowess and, according to the ideology of a commercial society, the protectors of a free, rich, and powerful polity. Such a vision proved more popular with legislators and with the public. This popularity proved critical to the development of a deregulated slave trade. It became the trade's legitimating foundation for the eighteenth century: slave traders could operate with the broadly conceived consent of the British national will as expressed through Parliament.

As one apologist for the independent traders put it in 1690, the African Company was about to unwittingly enter a lion's den of opposition that proved its political naïveté: "This is the first monopoly, that ever was brought to a Parliament to be confirmed. Parliaments do not use to confirm, or to support and encourage, illegal Projects; but rather to punish the Projectors. But these men have gone so long without punishment, that now they dare to pretend to favours." Inducing parliamentary punishment was easier than achieving parliamentary confirmation. The task facing the independent slave traders' lobby was different from that facing the African Company. The independent slave traders merely had to prevent the African Company from achieving a statute. Nonetheless, opponents of the African Company's monopoly would need to develop coherence as an interest group, to gather funds to lobby, to agree on a political strategy, to gather support and signatories for petitions, and author pamphlets that articulated a common worldview. To stand any chance of success in Parliament, the separate traders would have to achieve some measure of solidarity among disparate opponents of the African Company throughout England and its Atlantic holdings, from London to Whitehaven and from Port Royal to the Potomac.[5]

The following discussion focuses on the ways in which that solidarity was formed. The independent slave traders achieved this solidarity early enough in the 1690s to convince the African Company that it was worth moderating the proposal of full statutory confirmation of their charter to a compromise measure that liberated access to the trade in exchange for a 10 percent duty on the trade to finance the company's African forts. The resulting 1698 Act to Settle the Trade to Africa spectacularly backfired on the African Company and helped to broaden and strengthen the power and influence of the independent slave traders' lobby so that, by 1712, they could effect a complete deregulation of England's slave trade. Time and again during this period, the proponents of slave-trade escalation proved capable of thwarting the African Company's attempts to achieve a statute to endorse its charter. The movement to liberate the slave trade transformed itself from a handful of plaintiffs to a transatlantic phalanx of interests, from the grandest merchant oligarchs to provincial craftsmen and the retailers of the City of London, capable of raising a storm of petitions and pamphlets and deregulating an acknowledged pillar of Britain's commercial and martial prowess.

WHO WERE THE African Company's political opponents? The independent slave-trading opponents of the African Company remain more mysterious than the African Company's directorate and its shareholders. As traders with dubious legal backing (at least in the 1670s and 1680s), interlopers were well advised to conceal their activities. Historians have echoed contemporary commentators' complaints about the difficulty of establishing who the company's opponents were.[6] African Company pamphleteers, however, overstated the separate traders' mysteriousness for rhetorical reasons. Charles Davenant, the company's foremost propagandist, for example, stressed the difficulty of identifying the separate traders. Davenant wished to make their origins seem obscure in contrast to the well-established respectability of the company's management. As inspector general of imports and exports throughout his participation in the Africa trade debates, Davenant very likely knew at least who the prominent separate traders were. Davenant meant to undermine the separate traders' political legitimacy. He portrayed the separate traders

---

5. *The Case between the African Company and the People of England* ([London, 1698?]), 2.
6. See K. G. Davies, *The Royal African Company* (London, 1957), 148. Some advance has been made by Nigel Tattersfield in *The Forgotten Trade: Compromising the Log of the Daniel and Henry of 1700 and Accounts of the Slave Trade from the Minor Parts of England, 1698-1725* (London, 1998) and the compilers of *The Trans-Atlantic Slave Trade Database (Voyages Data Set)*, http://www.slavevoyages.org.

as an irresponsible, anonymous, and amateur horde, "an undefinable heteroclite body" of "pirates" and "buccaneers," bringing chaos and indignity to the trade. Davenant depicted the African Company in Ciceronian terms as the upholders of the public good. He described them as a "well-governed army of veteran troops, supported with an inexhaustible treasure." It is nevertheless possible to identify the separate traders (in both their trading and their lobbying guises) and to make conclusions about how they became involved in slave trading and how they sustained their interest group to achieve parliamentary victory.[7]

From 1672 to 1688, when the African Company's monopoly was easiest to enforce, interloping slave traders sailed throughout the British Atlantic world. This group combined Londoners, provincials, and merchants resident in the colonies, small-scale and grand merchants; it included litigants against the company and experienced lobbyists who cultivated and channeled support from provincial and colonial petitioning interests. From the 1670s onward, interloping slave traders often revealed themselves by becoming litigants against the company. The 1678 petition against the company listed a group of interloping merchants who had been victimized by the company's courts. These men included the London merchants Jeffrey Nightingale and William Dockwra. Dockwra, who was a sworn enemy of the company's governor, James, duke of York, would later found the London penny post service as a distribution mechanism for the earl of Shaftesbury's Whig opposition ideology.[8]

Company observers on the west coast of Africa in the 1680s pointed to the prevalence of slave traders based in the Caribbean, especially Barbados. These traders included Colonel John Hallett, John Bawden, and John Gardner. Hallet, originally from Lyme in Dorset, developed a large trade in London and then lived in Barbados from the 1660s to the 1690s. Bawden, along with

---

7. Charles Davenant, *Reflections upon the Constitution and Management of the African Trade, etc.*, in Charles Whitworth, ed., *The Political and Commercial Works of That Celebrated Writer, Charles D'Avenant, LL.D. . . .* , V (London, 1771), 144, 237, 239 (hereafter cited as Davenant, *Reflections*). Unlike Daniel Defoe, there is no evidence that Charles Davenant was paid to write on behalf of the Royal African Company. For Defoe's payments, see Tim Keirn, "Daniel Defoe and the Royal African Company," *Historical Research*, LVI (1988), 243–247. This interest group cannot be understood without appreciating the market that the group sought to maintain and expand. I therefore distinguish between "commercial" separate traders—whose participation in the African trade can be documented—and "lobbying" separate traders—who acted politically on behalf of the cause of independent slave trading. There is, of course, some overlap between the two groups. Accounting for the sometimes uneven relationship between the traders and the lobbyists provides important insights into the determinants of political action in this case.

8. For Dockwra, see T. Todd, *William Dockwra and the Rest of the Undertakers: The Story of the London Penny Post, 1680–82* (Edinburgh, 1952), 10.

Gardner, operated one of the largest sugar commission businesses in Barbados. He was also, like William Dockwra, an interloper in the East India Trade. In addition, Bawden was active as a lobbyist for Caribbean interests in London. He set up a lobbying group called the Gentleman Planters of Barbados, which met from 1671 (every Friday at the Cardinal's Cap Tavern on Cornhill) to oppose Charles II's attempt to tax trade with Barbados more heavily. An agent attended Privy Council meetings to assert the group's views. Such lobbying appears not to have achieved much. John Gardner was a Barbadian sugar trader, a former shareholder in the African Company, and one of the merchants who elected to purchase a license from the African Company to trade independently. He imported Barbadian sugar on a truly vast scale. In 1686, he brought in £28,394 from the West Indies. The Whig journalist John Oldmixon observed, "The opening the *African* Trade was . . . more owing to his [Gardner's] Contrivance and Industry than any other Person or Persons whatsoever." According to Oldmixon, the Gardner and Bawden firm worked hard to prevent Dalby Thomas, spokesman for the plantation interest before becoming the African Company's governor on the coast of West Africa, from creating a company that would monopolize all trade from Barbados to London. The interlopers of the 1670s and 1680s, then, were a group of established, wealthy, and powerful merchants who often traded and lobbied in support of the broader campaign for trade outside that of the long-distance enterprises like the Royal African and East Indian Companies. Far from being a band of pirates and buccaneers, the majority of these men were prominent and successful merchants with great political as well as commercial experience.[9]

The independent slave traders' lobby came into being partly from the need to bring suit in the courts. During the 1690s, anti–African Company petitions arrived in Parliament primarily from individuals whose interloping African cargoes had been seized by the company during the 1670s and 1680s, men such as Thomas Byfield and John Thrale. Byfield was a prominent Dissenting London merchant with trading interests throughout the Atlantic. He excelled in the tobacco trade. He also interloped in the East India trade and invested in

---

9. On the prevalence of Barbadian interlopers, see Robin Law, ed., *The English in West Africa, 1681–1683: The Local Correspondence of the Royal African Company of England, 1681–1699*, pt. 1 (Oxford, 1997), 6, 30. For John Hallett, see Jacob M. Price, "The Tobacco Adventure to Russia: Enterprise, Politics, and Diplomacy in the Quest for a Northern Market for English Colonial Tobacco, 1676–1722," in American Philosophical Society, *Transactions*, LI, pt. 1 (1961), 107. On Bawden and Gardner, see Nuala Zahedieh, *The Capital and the Colonies: London and the Atlantic Economy, 1660–1700* (Cambridge, 2010), 61, 105; Davies, *Royal African Company*, 67; [John Oldmixon], *The British Empire in America* . . . , 2 vols. (London, 1708), II, 43, 47, 53 (Bawden was Oldmixon's uncle); Minutes of the Committee of Accounts, Jan. 7, 1693, T 70/17, n.p.; John Gardner, *The Appellants' Case* ([London, 1690?]), 1.

the 1698 tobacco adventure to Russia. He appears to have enjoyed especially close trading relations with the Carolinas. Thrale had been James II's agent for receiving customs duties at Barbados and the Leeward Islands. Such men were likely to command the attention of MPs.[10]

The lobby also reflected the breadth of sincere, spontaneous political opposition to the African Company that existed throughout the English Atlantic. This opposition found new means to express itself by 1690. Thereafter, the English state related to its Atlantic colonies in a different way. Gone were the prerogative-sponsored attempts to centralize control of the empire. A more deliberative style led to the increased involvement of colonial testimony in Parliament, often offered in petition form or in person. Parliament's need to involve colonial opinion provided another opportunity to solidify the anti-monopoly interest group. The first group of lobbyists for an independent slave trade took advantage of these changes. These powerful merchant grandees cultivated and directed parliamentary petitions throughout England and its colonies. Domestic, provincial interest groups well used to appealing to Parliament, like the "Clothiers of *Suffolke* and *Essex*" and the "Mayor, Aldermen, and Common Council and Inhabitants of the City of *Exeter*," spoke in opposition to the company alongside colonial interests, like the "Merchants and Planters, trading to, and interested in, the Island of *Barbadoes*" and Jamaica. Despite arriving from different parts of the country, the wording of the Suffolk and Exeter petitions strongly suggests that the documents were authored together, probably in London, before being sent to the provinces for signing. The other petitions, including those from the colonies, represent spontaneous, uncultivated opinion that doubtless appeared in Parliament via metropolitan mediation but probably without the intervention of the interests from Essex, Exeter, or Suffolk.[11]

In February 1694, a House of Commons select committee's investigation into the workings of the African trade provided the independent slave traders' lobby with another platform that helped them to greater coherence. The records of this committee identified a group of anti–African Company lobbyists. Robert Harley, a rising star of the House of Commons, chaired a committee that provided an official London voice for a long-established opposition bent on defeating the African Company's parliamentary campaign. On March 2, 1694, Harley's committee invited a group of early opponents of the

---

10. For these petitions, see *Journals of the House of Commons*, I–LI (London, 1803), X, 382, 393 (hereafter cited as *Commons Journals*); Zahedieh, *Capital and the Colonies*, 60. For Byfield, see Price, "The Tobacco Adventure to Russia," in APS, *Trans.*, LI, pt. 1 (1961), 105.

11. For these petitions, see *Commons Journals*, X, 382, 383, 449.

African Company to appear before it; the group included Edward Littleton, Gilbert Heathcote, John Gardner, and Melisha Holder. All were wealthy merchants and experienced lobbyists.[12]

Edward Littleton, a Caribbean sugar trader, had earlier put forward a case for colonial resistance to James II's attempts to increase taxes on colonial sugar importation in England. Littleton also associated James's fiscal designs with the price-fixing effects of the African Company's monopoly. In *The Groans of the Plantations,* Littleton complained about the control that the company exerted over the prices of slaves and its policy of seizing the property of independent slave traders, which, for Littleton, meant being treated like "forrainers, taken in open War." His previous commentary on the Africa trade made him a useful witness for Harley's subcommittee. Gilbert Heathcote became the wealthiest and most powerful merchant of his day, with trading interests in Jamaica, the North American mainland, India, Russia, the Baltic, and, from the 1690s, the slave trade. He served as agent for Jamaica from 1693 until 1704. Heathcote and Gardner were also partners in slave-trading voyages from the colonies. Melisha Holder was an affluent and influential Barbadian merchant and, along with Edward Littleton, agent for Barbados in the 1690s. Gardner, Heathcote, and Holder, like Littleton, were well informed about the African trade, especially its American slave-trading aspect, and had well-established and strong opinions about it.[13]

By 1698, mainland American interests began to assert their opposition to the African Company in Parliament (perhaps confident in their ability to manage black majorities). On May 24, 1698, the bill to partially deregulate the Africa trade reached the House of Lords. During the next several days, the first colonial interests to designate themselves as planters as well as merchants petitioned the House of Lords for the chance to appear in person to discuss the bill. These petitions came from the "Planters of *Virginia* and *Maryland* and the Merchants tradeing thereunto" (May 25) and "the Planters and Merchants concerned in the Island of *Jamaica,* in Behalfe of themselves and others the Planters in the said Island" (May 26). On May 27, a petition in support of the African Company's bill appeared from "Planters and Merchants of

---

12. Harleian Manuscripts, no. 3710, 149–260, British Library, London.

13. [Edward Littleton], *The Groans of the Plantations* . . . (London, 1689), 6, 7. Later on, according to Robert Harley's notes, Sir Samuel Barnardiston, the Whig MP for Suffolk and a former deputy governor of the East India Company in the 1670s, appeared against the company alongside Timothy Mascall, a Barbadian sugar trader, Thomas Woodfine, an African trader, Colonel Beckford a Jamaican planter, and a "Mr. Waite" (who is likely to have been James Wayte, a prominent separate trader to the Chesapeake under the terms of the 1698 act) as well as a few other men who remain unidentified, including Samuel Sherrin, Tudor Thomas, John Dawkins, Mr. Murrells, and Mr. Sutton. See Harleian MSS, no. 3710, 241.

PLATE 1. *Sir Gilbert Heathcote*. By Michael Dahl I. Oil on canvas. Courtesy, Bank of England

His Majesty's *Cariby Islands* in *America*." Two petitions from planters of Barbados appeared on May 30 arguing against the bill. Both of these Barbadian petitions mourned the "great duty" that the bill would impose on the slave trade and contended that it would be "prejuditiall" to the trade of the island and of England. There is a great deal of overlap in the wording of these petitions. They were almost certainly compiled by a single interest and then distributed around London to be signed. Unlike most of the Africa trade petitions, the signatories for these petitions survive. The Jamaican petition continued the involvement and leadership of Gilbert Heathcote, whose signature appears first. Thomas Byfield also signed as well as the large-scale sugar importer, Bartholomew Gracedieu. The first of these anti-African Company petitions from Barbados on May 30 was led by another litigant against the company, Sir William Booth, a plantation owner in Barbados and a former naval officer under Charles II. Melisha Holder also signed.[14]

The petition from the Chesapeake marks the first entry of a constituency that would be critical to the overall movement: the opponents of the African Company who had interests in the mainland colonies but whom the company had done least to satisfy. The signatories were not all planters or residents of either Virginia or Maryland, despite describing themselves as such. Eleven of the eighteen signatories (Benjamin Brain, Edward Carleton, both John and Thomas Cary, Thomas Corbin, Isaac Milner, Christopher Morgan, John Munday, Micajah Perry, John Sail, and Thomas Taylor) were tobacco merchants. Four of the signatories (John Corbin, Fred Jones, Benjamin Harrison, and Henry Hartwell) were permanent residents of Virginia, and the latter two were members of the Governor's Council in Virginia. Edward Chilton was not a permanent resident but lived in Virginia from 1682 to 1694, serving as attorney general of the General Court; once back in England, policymakers viewed him as an expert on Virginian affairs. The Chesapeake lobby at this time, then, was first and foremost a Virginian interest combining London tobacco merchants with a handful of influential Virginia expatriates and resident planters.[15]

---

14. For these petitions, see *Journals of the House of Lords* (London, 1767–1830), XVI, 297, 299, 300, 305. The signatures on the Chesapeake petition appear in the following order: Edward Carleton, Edward Chilton, Benjamin Harrison, Jr., Fred Jones, Isaac Milner, John Corbin, Henry Hartwell, Benjamin Brain, Thomas Cary, John Munday, Christopher Morgan, Charles Ridgley, John Cary, Thomas Taylor, John Sail, Thomas Corbin, Micajah Perry, and Nathaniel Rous. Several of the signatories on the Jamaican petition, including Heathcote and Gracedieu, would go on to become slave traders: Lawrence Galdy, Nathaniel Micklethwaite, Henry Sherwin, John Warman, and Benjamin Way. In addition to Booth and Holder, signing the Barbados petition was an assortment of Barbadian assemblymen (including Samuel Barwick) and planters (such as Nathaniel Blakiston and Richard Guy). Samuel Barwick was the only known slave trader. A merchant petition from Bristol also followed the Chesapeake petition. In addition to the mayor of Bristol, John Bubb, several slave traders signed the petition: John Baker, John Corseley, John Day, John (later Sir John) Hawkins, Abraham Hook, and Francis Rogers. For the Bristol petition, see Leo Francis Stock, ed., *Proceedings and Debates of the British Parliaments respecting North America*, II (Washington D.C., 1927), 240. All of these interests objected to the bill's tax on the slave trade.

15. See Thad W. Tate, "Chilton, Edward," in Sarah B. Bearss, ed., *Dictionary of Virginia Biography*, III (Richmond, Va., 2006), 212–215. I am grateful to Professor Tate for bringing this information and his article to my attention. For evidence of tobacco trading, I consulted Dr. Perry Gauci's unpublished database of mercantile petitions. For evidence that Chilton, Corbin, Harrison, Hart-

As with Edward Littleton, John Cary had previous form as an anti–African Company pamphleteer. Cary authored the famous *Essay on the State of England, in Relation to Its Trade* in 1695 in which he advocated an open slave trade. He described the African trade as being "of the most Advantage to this Kingdom of any we drive" and went on to argue that "to advise a Government to monopolize, and consequently to lessen this Trade, by confining it to a limited Stock, is the same as to advise the People of *Egypt* to raise high Banks to confine the River *Nilus* from overflowing, lest it should thereby fertilize their Lands." Cary was one of the largest tobacco importers in the 1690s. Similarly conspicuous in the list is Micajah Perry, the lynchpin of the British Atlantic tobacco business until the 1720s. Isaac Milner originated from Whitehaven from a nonconformist family. Several of these men went on to become prominent commercial and political separate traders including Carleton, Milner, Munday, Perry, and Nathaniel Rous.[16]

Although domiciled in Virginia, Henry Hartwell, Benjamin Harrison, and Edward Chilton were, at the time of signing the petition, in the imperial capital on official business. They were members of commissary James Blair's delegation to London to secure the dismissal of Virginia's then governor, Sir Edmund Andros (who had been an African Company shareholder). They had previously been active in soliciting officials in London to support the proposed College of William and Mary, which had been chartered in 1693. Benjamin Harrison also sought promotion for himself, securing, on this trip, the position of attorney general of Virginia. Chilton and Hartwell coauthored *The Present State of Virginia and the College* with Blair in 1697. This tract represented a critique of what Blair, Chilton, and Hartwell believed to be an overconcentration of power in the office of royal governor in Virginia. They also sought, in writing this pamphlet, to persuade the Board of Trade to encourage the formation of towns and a more mercantile economy in the Old Dominion. Their desire to prevent the African Company from obtaining a duty

---

well, and Jones lived in Virginia, see [Henry] Hartwell, [James] Blair, and [Edward] Chilton, *The Present State of Virginia and the College* . . . (London, 1727), xxxii–xxxv. For Jones, see *Virginia Magazine of History and Biography*, II (1894), 6. For Corbin, see Richard Beale Davis, ed., *William Fitzhugh and His Chesapeake World, 1676-1701: The Fitzhugh Letters and Other Documents* (Chapel Hill, N.C., 1963), 331. For Harrison and Hartwell's councillorships, see "Genealogy: Harrison of James River (continued)," *VMHB*, XXXI (1923), 283; and Correspondence of the Board of Trade, Colonial Office (CO) 5/1308, no. 18, National Archives, Kew. For Corbin's and Perry's arrangement with the Royal African Company, see Charles L. Killinger III, "The Royal African Company Slave Trade to Virginia, 1689–1713" (master's thesis, College of William and Mary, 1969), appendix. For the group's slave-trading interests, see T 70/1198. For Carleton as a separate trader, see Stock, ed., *Proceedings and Debates*, II, 239.

16. John Cary, *An Essay on the State of England, in Relation to Its Trade* . . . (Bristol, 1695), 74, 76.

on the slave trade became part of their reforming mission in the metropolis. Chilton, Hartwell, and Blair had sought, throughout the 1690s, to enhance their control over settler society in Virginia. Creating a college to educate ministers and the elite in Virginia, securing the position of attorney general, and opposing the power of the royal governor were all part of Virginia's push for greater control of its fortunes. Achieving greater control over the supply of enslaved Africans was also a crucial part of this plan.[17]

Later in the summer of 1698, one of the Chesapeake delegates, Benjamin Harrison, Jr., appeared in person before the Lords select committee charged with examining the African trade. Accompanying him was John Gardner, the leader of the cause for free trade, and Melisha Holder. Alongside Gardner, Harrison, and Holder, Peter Paggen, a London-based tobacco and firearms trader, lobbied against the African Company's proposed regulation of the African trade.[18]

In the 1690s, then, the African Company's political opponents based their argument for slave-trade deregulation on a constituency that integrated the interests and political capital of many of the trading constituencies of England with the growing wealth and power of all the English American colonies. This political movement against the Royal African Company combined the clothiers of Berkshire, Devon, Essex, Gloucester, Norwich, Somerset, Southwark, Suffolk, Wiltshire, and Yorkshire, who resented the African Company's restrictions on their exporting of cloth; the cutlers of Hallamshire, who resented the company's control of the supply of ivory for their knives; the civic authorities of Exeter and Bristol, who represented their various merchant constituents; and, predominating, the planters and traders of Jamaica, Barbados, and the Chesapeake, who wished for an improved supply of enslaved Africans directly from Africa. The African Company, by contrast, received the support of isolated weaving interests in Witney, Kidderminster, and Shrews-

---

17. See Hartwell, Blair, and Chilton, *The Present State of Virginia and the College*, xxxii–xxxv. The association between the desire to reform the governance of Virginia and the desire to liberalize the slave trade is indicated by the support that Gawin Corbin, the African company's agent, offered to Governor Francis Nicholson. For Gawin Corbin's support for Nicholson, see J. M. Sosin, *English America and Imperial Inconstancy: The Rise of Provincial Autonomy, 1696-1715* (Lincoln, Nebr., 1985), 66. In December 1698, the Maryland assembly had also instructed leading separate trader Peter Paggen to monitor Francis Nicholson, whom the Assembly believed to be in London "upon some private sinister account"; see N. Blakiston, N. Greenberry, Thomas Tench, John Court, and Thomas Brooke to Peter Paggen, Dec. 21, 1698, Egerton Family Papers, MssEL 9572, Huntington Library, San Marino, Calif. See also William A. Pettigrew, "Transatlantic Politics and the Africanization of Virginia's Labor Force, 1688-1712," in Douglas Bradburn and John C. Coombs, eds., *Early Modern Virginia: Reconsidering the Old Dominion* (Charlottesville, Va., 2011), 279–299.

18. See Trade to Africa Bill, in *The Manuscripts of the House of Lords*, n.s., X, 1712-1714, ed. Maurice F. Bond (London, 1953), no. 3019, 167–168 (hereafter cited as *Lords MSS*).

bury and generic interests in the smaller Caribbean colonies of the Leeward Islands.[19]

Thus, with colonial demand for slaves increasing year after year beyond the African Company's ability to satisfy that demand, independent slave trading represented an obvious opportunity for English-Atlantic merchants and ship captains. The overlap between these groups suggests a cabal of leaders for the lobby from all of the sizable Atlantic colonies that included John Gardner, Benjamin Harrison, Jr., Gilbert Heathcote, and Melisha Holder. This interest group of merchants (and, in the case of Harrison, a Virginian planter), although small in scale, was nonetheless remarkable because it integrated diverse Atlantic and English provincial interests: Jamaican and Barbadian sugar and Chesapeake tobacco, planters and merchants. The independent slave traders' parliamentary lobby included men who served as official representatives of the colonies, like Heathcote, and, like Littleton and Cary, who had written pamphlets on the management of the Atlantic economy that espoused the advantages of a deregulated slave trade. Because of their formal role as agents of colonies and because of the size of their American trades, Gardner, Heathcote, Holder, and Littleton likely cultivated the Barbadian and Jamaican petitions against the company. Indeed, their established leadership suggests the provenance of many of the colonial petitions to Parliament that opposed the African Company. Moreover, the similar wording found in all the colonial petitions—"... prejudiciall to the said plantations and to the trade of England"—indicates that particular individuals, including Gardner, Holder, and Heathcote, organized the petitioning campaign. The important role played within the lobbying group by Virginia colonists Benjamin Harrison, Edward Chilton, and Henry Hartwell perhaps implies that the African Company had produced sincere and spontaneous ire from colonists, who then elected to join their metropolitan allies to mount their campaign to liberate the slave trade. These expatriate lobbies also might have sought to improve their standing with London's merchant elite to help them achieve their broader aims for the Virginia colony. The desire of all of these men to produce and sustain a united colonial and domestic front against the African Company, however, is beyond doubt.[20]

THE AFRICAN COMPANY'S compromise strategy and the strength of its political connections enabled it to achieve the partial deregulation statute of

---

19. For the petitions, see *Commons Journals*, XI, 100, 486, 639, XII, 166. The third group (the civic authorities of Exeter and Bristol) might have had a connection with the leader of the West Country faction in Parliament at this time, Sir Edward Seymour, who presented the petitions from his constituency of Exeter.

20. Stock, ed., *Proceedings and Debates*, II, 236–238, 240–241.

1698. The large population of independent slave traders that this legislation produced, however, demonstrates the dynamism of the English trading community at the end of the Nine Years' War (also known as the War of the Grand Alliance) and the independent slave traders' sense of the boundless possibility of deregulation. The provisions of the 1698 act together with the public deliberations that had produced it advertised the commercial opportunities that slave trading offered and encouraged many merchants to participate in human trafficking. Because the company collected a duty on the deregulated trade and recorded the names and cargoes of those who paid it from various ports, identification of this founding generation of separate traders is possible. The company listed the investors in slave cargoes, who were not always the masters, or captains, of the ships bound for Africa. This data reveals 1,038 individuals between 1698 and 1712 (the terms of the 1698 statute) who directly participated in independent slave trading.[21]

What can be said of this founding generation of independent slave traders? The separate traders emerged overwhelmingly from the community of Atlantic traders. Of those whose previous trading interests can be established (382), 93 percent (357) had experience in the Atlantic. On the whole, the separate traders had trafficked in Atlantic commodities such as sugar or tobacco. Diversifying their businesses into human cargoes allowed the separate traders, whose colonial correspondents informed them of the extent of colonial demand for slaves, to integrate and augment their Atlantic businesses. They also

---

21. By "separate traders," I mean all those who invested in a cargo bound for Africa. These people typically traded in slaves, but not all African cargoes sought to ship enslaved Africans. Many wished only to trade in gold, ivory, or redwood on the African coast. I refer to the trade in all three as "African trade" to distinguish it from slave trading. Technically, a separate trader was anyone who assembled what could be distinguished as an African cargo and paid the mandatory 10 percent duty. It is unclear whether "separate" in "separate trader" meant noncompany or was some pejorative reference to individual trading and self-interestedness from a society not entirely rid of the authority of corporatism. The separate traders themselves used the phrase to describe their group, so it seems unlikely that it was pejorative. The data concerning the total population of independent slave traders derives from several sources: T 70/1198–1199 and T 70/349–356; *Voyages*, http://www.slavevoyages.org; Tattersfield, *Forgotten Trade;* and David Richardson, *Bristol, Africa, and the Eighteenth-Century Slave Trade to America*, I, *The Years of Expansion, 1698–1729*, Bristol Record Society, *Publications*, XXXVIII (Bristol, 1986). I have only included those for whom we have a clear forename and surname. If there were two entries with the same surname and one has no forename, then the second entry assumes the first name of the other. Because investment in slave-trading voyages was often as diffuse as a thirty-second share and because merchants often simply consigned certain goods typical for an African cargo, this figure greatly surpasses the number of slave-trading voyages during this period. Because I am interested in the individuals involved, I have broken down partnerships and conglomerates into individual contributions. Eight of the independent slave traders were female. For a full directory of these separate traders, see Appendix 2, below.

believed, as colonial interests frequently attested, that a deregulated slave trade would expand the entire Atlantic economy. This population became increasingly enfranchised by a new political culture that strengthened the relationship between business and the political process and celebrated behavior that took advantage of this opportunity. The changing balance of power in the British Atlantic empowered (ideologically and institutionally) merchants with experience of Atlantic trade to use political means to lobby against metropolitan pockets of economic privilege.[22]

In striking contrast to the elite separate traders' almost exclusively Atlantic profile, Iberian, Levant, and East India merchants dominated the Royal African Company's directorate. Of the 168 directors of the company during the years 1698–1712, the prior trading interests of 61 can be identified. Of these, only 26 percent operated Atlantic trades compared to 93 percent among the separate traders as a whole. Seventy-four percent plied non-Atlantic trades mostly in Europe but also in the Levant and in the East Indies compared to 6 percent among the commercial separate-traders group. The company's initial subscription had included many individuals with Atlantic interests, but, by the time of the Africa trade debates in Parliament, several of these figures had either sold out or defected to the separate traders.[23]

Merchants joined this group of separate traders for a number of reasons, in addition to the desire to integrate their Atlantic trading interests. Some shifted into independent slave trading after service with the company. A few turned to slave trading as other trades diminished owing to the interruptions of war. Economic impulses pushed others to elaborate on their trading connections and experience by shifting into slave trading from unrelated trades. For many, independent slave trading provided a new source of trade and enabled merchants from the fringes of England and from outside London's elite clique of merchants to prosper and, in turn, become powerful merchant oligarchs. Human trafficking became a means to social mobility.

Dalby Thomas claimed that the separate traders enjoyed more success in the African trade than the company because the separate traders had more experience: "The 10 per cent men have one advantage over us: their masters are old traders and your honours have often men unknowing in the trade." Many

---

22. I have established the prior trading interests of the separate traders according to their other lobbying activities by using a database of contemporaneous mercantile petitions compiled by Dr. Perry Gauci. It was possible for an Atlantic trader to trade substantially with Europe (separate trader Gilbert Heathcote offers an excellent example).

23. K. G. Davies, "Joint-Stock Investment in the Later Seventeenth Century," *Economic History Review*, 2d Ser., IV (1952), 298–299; Davies, *Royal African Company*, 67.

of the interlopers of the 1670s and 1680s and the independent traders of the 1690s continued as separate traders after 1698.[24]

Experience of the African trade also derived from employment with the Royal African Company. Overlap between the populations of separate traders and African Company directors and officials is revealing. Of the separate traders active during the period of the act of 1698, thirty-three had previously been members of the African Company. Service with the African Company before the 1690s had taught several individuals that there was more money to be made from trading slaves on private account than there was from a company salary. Charles Davenant, the African Company pamphleteer, argued that what little experience and credibility the separate traders had they had gathered using underhanded means from former African Company employees or, as he referred to them, "some deserters, who have been debauched and seduced out of the company's service." Overseas monopoly companies had often struggled to command the loyalty of their employees once they were stationed abroad. But the slow growth in the scale of demand for enslaved Africans from the early 1690s and the rapid growth after 1698 compounded the frustration that many felt with the constraints the company imposed on the trade. Entrepreneurial individuals wished to take advantage of this growing demand, and many did so beyond the company's authority.[25]

Robert Heysham, who was to become the most successful separate trader in the early eighteenth century and the movement's most important parliamentary lobbyist, and his brother, William, had both worked for the Royal African Company. Born in Lancashire, Robert became a London sugar merchant on a vast scale, and he also transported wine and other goods across the

24. Sir Dalby Thomas to the Royal African Company, Mar. 26, 1706, T 70/26, n.p.

25. Ann M. Carlos and Jamie Brown Kruse, "The Decline of the Royal African Company: Fringe Firms and the Role of the Charter," *Economic History Review*, 2d Ser., XLIX (1996), 291–313; Davenant, *Reflections*, 161, 273. Chief among Davenant's deserters was Abraham Houlditch, who had been agent-general at Cape Coast in 1672 and used the expertise he obtained to become a separate trader. He represents the only example of a merchant who integrated his transatlantic trading portfolio from slave trading to colonial produce (in this case, Jamaican sugar), rather than the other way round, as most separate traders did. Together with Robert Brook, Houlditch operated a partnership in the Jamaican and African trades. The Houlditch and Brook partnership shipped slaves throughout the period of the Africa trade debates and regularly used the provincial outports as places of departure. Houlditch and Brook also became ruthless and effective parliamentary lobbyists against the African Company. The company alleged that Houlditch had appeared on several occasions in parliamentary debates about the Africa trade and could be relied upon to set "himself up upon all occasions to seek their utter ruin" (John Perry to John Yeamans, Aug. 31, 1708, T 70/44, n.p.). For Houlditch's employment with the Royal African Company, see George Frederick Zook, "A History of the Royal African Company, 1672–1713" (Ph.D. diss., Cornell University, 1914), microfilm (pagination obscured). See also Tattersfield, *Forgotten Trade*, 373.

Atlantic. Most of his business was in commission trading. In 1696, he was the largest sugar importer to England after the Royal African Company with an annual turnover of £11,400. He regularly appeared at the African Company's board meetings in the late 1690s and supported the company in Parliament during the first stage of public consideration of the Africa trade issue. By the early eighteenth century, though, Robert Heysham would become an exemplar for the independent, deregulated nature of the Atlantic trade, avoiding directorships of joint-stock companies and using political means to sustain his considerable interests in the Atlantic. His slave-trading business became the core of his commercial operation from the early years of the eighteenth century. Between 1702 and 1712, he consigned African cargoes with a total sworn value of £33,920, greatly in excess of any other separate trader.[26]

Several separate traders experimented in independent slave trading because the trades in which they had experience had declined. Many merchants were persuaded by the act of 1698 to engage in human trafficking for the first time, which is suggested by the changing profile of the anticompany lobbyists as well as the increased volume of England's slave trade after 1698. The shifting fortunes of trade in Europe during the Nine Years' War and the War of Spanish Succession led individuals to assemble cargoes bound for Africa. Humphrey Morice, another prominent separate trader and a future pillar of the separate traders' interest group, began his career as a merchant trading to the Iberian Peninsula but expanded his interests to Jamaica and then to slave trading—thanks to the 1698 act—during the European trade depression of the early years of the War of the Spanish Succession.[27]

Other separate traders switched to slave trading from enterprises that the enlarged African trade was designed, in part, to replace. Both William Heysham and Peter Paggen switched to slave trading once the supply of white labor from England began to dry up during the Nine Years' War. Others marketed goods to Africa that they had already traded across the Atlantic. Paggen along with Isaac Milner had traded firearms to Maryland throughout the 1690s. They then turned to trading in guns with slave vendors in Africa.

---

26. For Robert Heysham's appearance at the African Company's Court of Assistants, see Minutes of the Court of Assistants, October 1699, T 70/85, n.p. For his pro-company testimony in Parliament, see Harleian MSS, no. 3710, 234. All consignment totals derive from Davies, *The Royal African Company*, appendix vi, 372–373.

27. Humphrey Morice to Thomas Wood, Apr. 22, 1703, Mar. 1, 1705, Aug. 20, 1706, Letterbook of Humphrey Morice, Humphrey Morice Papers, Bank of England Archive, London. A slump in the wine trade with France because of the Nine Years' War encouraged, in much the same way, wine merchants to interlope in the East India trade. See D. W. Jones, "London Overseas-Merchant Groups at the End of the Seventeenth Century and the Moves against the East India Company" (D.Phil. thesis, University of Oxford, 1970), 317.

PLATE 2. *Humphrey Morice*. By Godfrey Kneller. Oil on canvas.
Courtesy, Bank of England

Firearms became an integral part of the African trade because of the role they played in inciting intertribal conflict and thereby facilitating a steady supply of the enslaved.[28]

28. For William Heysham's involvement in the trade in indentured servants, see W. Noel Sainsbury et al., eds., *Calendar of State Papers, Colonial Series, America and West Indies* . . . , 44 vols. (London, 1860–1969) (hereafter cited as *CSPC*), XVIII, no. 41, 31. For Peter Paggen's involvement in shipping white soldiers to the colonies, see Gilbert Heathcote to William Blathwayt, May 10, 1701, Blathwayt Manuscripts, vol. 341, Huntington Library, San Marino, Calif. A pamphlet on the

Most merchants became separate traders to integrate their existing Atlantic businesses. As noted previously, Isaac Milner, of Whitehaven, had been a considerable tobacco merchant before 1698, and he was also a lobbyist for the independent slave trade in 1698. He appears to have served a trading apprenticeship to Peter Paggen. Milner went on to become a slave trader on a large scale. From 1698, he oversaw twenty-four Guinea ventures with an aggregate cargo value in excess of twenty-four thousand pounds. When Milner was not shipping slaves himself, many Virginia planters purchased slaves with bills on his account. His influence in the Chesapeake became, as a result, considerable. His shift into slave trading clearly helped to develop his tobacco businesses.[29]

Independent slave trading also offered trading opportunities that attracted merchants on the fringes of the City of London's mercantile establishment. The career of Peter Paggen is especially instructive in this regard. Born in 1651, Paggen was a Huguenot immigrant from the Low Country who began his trading career as a ship captain in the Chesapeake tobacco trade. He soon was one of the most considerable London tobacco merchants of his day, becoming free of the Brewer's Livery and a sheriff of the City of London. In addition to a vast tobacco trade, Paggen was a specialist in human cargoes moving soldiers during the Nine Years' War and then enslaved Africans. He also served as an informal agent for interests from Maryland. Along with Gilbert Heathcote and John Cary, Paggen was part of the parliamentary opposition to the East India Company that had lobbied from 1696. Cary and Paggen became directors in the New Company (a rival to the East India Company founded by a syndicate of interlopers) in 1698. His oppositional stance to the African Company reflected his belief that the East India Company's directorate ought to be opened to commercial outsiders like him. Clearly, Paggen's opposition to monopoly was opportunistic rather than principled, but his success against both companies and his own origins outside London's commercial elite suggest

---

Africa trade described how the government's tightening up on "spiriting" of indentured servants increased the demand for slaves; see *The African Companies Considerations on the Late Act of Parliament for Settling the Trade to Africa; Answer'd Paragraph by Paragraph* (London, 1708), 1. For the part played by firearms in assisting the supply of slaves in West Africa, see Kwame Yeboa Daaku, *Trade and Politics on the Gold Coast, 1600-1720: A Study of the African Reaction to European Trade* (Oxford, 1970), 19. Daaku also notes the effects of such importations on political structures: "The greatest single disintegrating force in politics was the importation of firearms" (19). Charles Davenant also associated the independent slave traders with illegal gun running; see *Reflections*, 194, 320; see also *That the Trade to Affrica, Is Only Manageable by an Incorporated Company and a Joynt Stock, Demonstrated in a Letter to a Member of the Present House of Commons, by a Gentleman in the City* (London, 1690), 3.

29. For Isaac Milner's apprenticeship to Peter Paggen, see Francis Nicholson to Board of Trade, Aug. 20, 1698, CO 5/174, no. 52. See also John Sheffield to Thomas Starke, Aug. 2, 1699, Records of the Exchequer (E) 219/446, National Archives, Kew.

that the movement against both companies owed much to the desire to break open the control that a traditional commercial elite had enjoyed by virtue of prerogative-sponsored monopoly trading companies.[30]

Many others who previously had been excluded from London's mercantile elite benefited from a deregulated market, including West Countryman Benjamin Way. Way descended from the Dissenting Way family of Bridport, close to Lyme on the Dorset coast. He was the younger brother of the prominent Bristol separate trader, Joseph Way. Benjamin became a substantial Jamaica sugar and wine merchant as well as a slave trader. The Burridge family of Lyme Regis also fit this mold. John Burridge, Junior, was born in 1681 in Lyme Regis. He was the scion of a prominent Dissenting merchant family in Lyme who had plied a trade to the Chesapeake for some years. Along with his father, John, he persistently assembled cargoes for the slave trade, succeeding his uncle of the same name. William Clayton of Liverpool was also in this group of provincial separate traders, and he played a critical part in developing that city's slave trade. He began his trading career as a tobacco merchant and lobbyist and then became a prominent slave trader, transporting cargoes to Africa in four consignment years. Large numbers of Bristolian separate traders, including the prominent local politician, Abraham Elton, Junior, and local MP, Joseph Earle, and those from other provincial outports, such as Samuel Eyres of Falmouth, George Barons of Plymouth, John Cross of Portsmouth, William Penneck of Topsham, and Thomas Lutwidge of Whitehaven, also appear among the population of separate traders after 1698.[31]

The provincial bias of the separate traders was reflected in their base of petitioning support. Almost half of their petitions came from the provinces, a quarter from the colonies, and almost a fifth from the metropole, whereas the African Company's support was distributed equally among provincial, colonial, and metropolitan interests. Although only two of thirty African Company petitions came from the southwest of the country, 40 percent of the separate traders' petitions derived from there. With its Atlantic coastline, the southwest benefited from the expansion of Atlantic trading more than other regions of the country. The decentralization of regulatory initiative to the provinces from the 1690s thus allowed provincial lobbyists, like those from the southwest, to make their case for free trade.[32]

---

30. For Peter Paggen's (and Isaac Milner's) involvement in gun trading, see Minutes of the Council of Maryland, CO 5/714, no. 52, 386. See also *Post Boy* (London), May 15, 1712; *Supplement* (London), Apr. 15–18, 1709.

31. For Benjamin Way, see Tattersfield, *Forgotten Trade*, 241–242, 247–248. For William Clayton's backing of the tobacco trade, see Board of Trade Correspondence, CO 5/1315, no. 7.

32. See Appendix 5, below.

London-based merchants, however, dominated these early stages of the independent slave trade. The majority of the separate traders (607, or 58 percent) assembled cargoes in London. Londoners were also the most persistent separate traders, assembling 80 percent of voyages in more than six years and 100 percent in more than nine years. There were 106 African voyages (10 percent) that originated from Bristol and just 44 others (4 percent) that commenced in other, smaller outports. The rest were independent slave traders from the English American colonies. Who were these Londoners? The 1698 statute allowed merchant grandees to experiment with or expand their existing slave-trading operations. The upper echelons of London's commercial elite seemed to have stirred the lord mayor in 1699, Sir Richard Levett, into independent slave trading, albeit tentatively. The builder of Kew Palace, Levett assembled African cargoes in 1703 and 1704 (as well as in 1693). Levett was married to Elizabeth Crispe, the daughter of Sir Nicholas Crispe, who had been the proprietor of the English forts on the west coast of Africa during the middle years of the seventeenth century, and a brother-in-law to Sir John Holt, the judge in *Nightingale v. Bridges* whose ruling discouraged the African Company's monopoly in 1689. Levett's slave trading perhaps suggests that familiar concerns encouraged him to diversify from his successful Chesapeake tobacco and cloth businesses into slave trading.[33]

One pro-company pamphleteer divided the capital's community of separate traders into "Two Sorts": "Several Worthy merchants"—grandees such as Richard Levett and Gilbert Heathcote, "Men of Unquestionable Reputation and Great Estates, [who] have Houses in Jamaica, Barbadoes, and other places where the Slaves are sent, where they are concern'd as Factors"—and a sec-

---

33. That the majority of separate traders' cargoes were assembled in London reinforces James A. Rawley's assertion that London continued to dominate the slave trade until the 1730s; see Rawley, "The Port of London and the Eighteenth-Century Slave Trade: Historians, Sources, and a Reappraisal," in *London, Metropolis of the Slave Trade* (Columbia, Mo., 2003), 18–39; and T 70/1198. There were also three voyages listed as commencing in Lisbon. Minor outports include Cowes (five traders), Dartmouth (six traders), Exeter (one trader), Falmouth (four traders), Liverpool (eleven traders), Plymouth (six traders), Portsmouth (twelve traders), and Whitehaven (one trader). The most persistent Londoners included the firm of Abraham Houlditch and Robert Brook (thirteen years), Daniel Jamineau (thirteen years), Joseph Martyn (thirteen years), Peregrine Brown (twelve years), Anthony Tourney (twelve years), James Wayte (eleven years), Richard Harris (ten years), Thomas Merrett (ten years), and Edward Searle (ten years). Robert Heysham and Isaac Milner (who had both been born outside London) assembled African cargoes in all fourteen years of the 1698 act. I derive numbers of consignment years from the database compiled from T 70/349–356, 1198, 1199. Nicholas Crispe appeared before Parliament at the height of the Africa trade dispute stating his claim to the company's territory; see *Commons Journals*, XVI, 180. A company pamphleteer described how he was a pawn of the separate traders; see *The Unavoidable Consequences of a Trade to Africa, in a Regulated Company, as Proposed by the Separate Traders, Demonstrated* ([London, 1712]), 2.

ond group of "Shopkeepers, who trade with the aforesaid Merchants; So it's their Interest to have an open Trade, and they cannot be to eager in soliciting, Several Selling India Goods, referring to themselves that pleasant and profitable Article of Draw Back." The upstart cockney retailer became an early stereotype of the independent slave trader. More than a third of the separate traders worked, as the pamphlet suggested, as retailers. Many separate traders imported East India goods, men like Robert Atkins. Nearly a quarter of the forty-four London slave traders whose addresses can be established operated from Cornhill, one of London's central retail districts, where John Bawden's antimonopoly meetings started in the 1670s. Another anti–African Company pamphleteer indicated that separate traders tended to be cloth retailers and alleged that a monopolized African trade would lead to the ruin of many "linnen-drapers shops between Aldgate and Temple-Bar."[34]

Retailers, although conspicuous enough to encourage Davenant and others to dismiss the separate traders as lowborn amateurs, did not dominate the total population of slave traders. Almost half of the separate traders were ship captains, including Captain Peregrine Brown and Captain Robert Cruickshank. The African Company's directorate worked in different sectors; far fewer were ship captains. Of the ninety-five African Company directors whose other employment can be established, 17 percent were army officers (not one separate trader served in the army during this period). The close connections between the African Company's directorate and the military operations of Charles II and James II blended the two constituencies beyond 1688. Only six African Company directors worked in retail. The differing caste of the African Company's directors helped company apologists make the case that the African Company was better placed to manage the African trade in the interests of the British state rather than the balance sheets of the countinghouses of Cornhill. But the collective commercial jostling of Cornhill coffeehouses proved able to develop a slave-trading operation that could better defend the national interest than the politically isolated directors at Africa House, a few hundred meters away at Leadenhall Street.

---

34. For the petition mentioning shopkeepers, see "Petition of Divers Shipwrights, Ropemakers, Sailmakers, Anchor-smiths, and Divers Other Tradesmen, in Behalf of Themselves, and Many Others, Inhabitants of London, Wapping, Limehouse, etc. and Places Adjacent, Employed in Naval Architecture, and Manufactures relating Thereunto," Jan. 29, [1709], *Commons Journals*, XVI, 75. For "Article of Draw Back," see *A Letter to a Member of Parliament, Setting Forth the Trade to Africa* (n.p., [1709?]), 1–2. For Atkins, see Royal African Company to Robert Atkins, Mar. 26, 1741, T 70/48, 101. Separate traders who operated from Cornhill include: Ben Howell (*Daily Courant*, Sept. 25, 1711); John Morton (*Post Boy*, Dec. 31, 1709–Jan. 3, 1710); and Matthew Snablin (*London Gazette*, Mar. 15–19, 1715). For "linnen-drapers shops," see *Some Remarks on a Pamphlet, Call'd, Reflections* . . . , quoted in Davenant, *Reflections*, 259.

Beyond London, a remarkable number of independent slave traders assembled cargoes in the colonies. As many as 284 (or 27 percent) of the post-1698 slave-trading voyages originated in the colonies with men such as Humphrey Primate of Barbados, John Pym of Jamaica, John Pratt of Carolina, Robert Plumstead of New England, Frederick Philipse of New York, Daniel Owley of the Chesapeake, and John Rock of Antigua. Many separate traders detected the extent of demand for slave labor in the colonies during residence there. Conspicuous among them for their persistence as slave traders are Joseph Martyn, Stephen Godin, and Richard Harris. Joseph Martyn, of Love Lane in London, appears to have been resident for a time in Nevis and subsequently specialized in sugar imports from Nevis, Antigua, and Jamaica. Martyn was, with Robert Heysham, one of only two private merchants in 1696 that approached the Royal African Company's import turnover of sugar (£16,326) with a turnover of £10,221. Like Heysham, Martyn became a high-volume slave trader, assembling, between 1702 and 1712, cargoes of export goods to Africa valued at £19,359. Stephen Godin was a permanent resident of South Carolina and provides a rare example of a prominent separate-trader lobbyist resident in the colonies. Godin assembled African cargoes between 1702 and 1712 totaling £1,189. Richard Harris developed an interest in slave trading because of his residence in Jamaica. Harris became one of the largest consigners of African goods. Between 1702 and 1712, Harris made nine consignments to Africa valued at £25,121.[35]

Of the dominant population of Atlantic traders within the population of separate traders, 69 percent traded with the Caribbean islands, with the remaining 33 percent trading primarily with the American mainland (including

---

35. Eight traders were from Antigua, ninety-three from Barbados, two from Boston, eleven from Carolina, nine from unspecified West Indies colonies, ninety-two from Jamaica, one from Leeward Islands, five from Maryland, four from Montserrat, fifteen from Nevis, five from New England, seven from New York, one from Newport, Rhode Island, two from Saint Christopher, and seven from Virginia. In the 1690s, Edward Lascelles was a sizable wine merchant trading between Madeira and Barbados. A resident of Bridgetown in Barbados in the 1680s, he relocated to London around the beginning of the eighteenth century, joining the Grocer's Company (a livery with strong connections to colonial trade) in July 1701. He sustained his stake in the Atlantic sugar trade as a merchant, as an owner of a transatlantic vessel, and as a banker to West Indian businesses, granting loans to planters and acting as executor and trustee. He also began to develop an interest in the slave trade, consigning, between August 1703 and October 1709, six cargoes valued at £2,997 18s. For more information about Edward Lascelles, see S. D. Smith, *Slavery, Family, and Gentry Capitalism in the British Atlantic: The World of the Lascelles, 1648-1834* (Cambridge, 2006), 46–50. For the size of Martyn's sugar-importing business, see Jones, "London Overseas-Merchant Groups," 204. For Joseph Martyn, see Colonial Papers of the Privy Council, July 12, 1683, CO 1/49, no. 131. For Stephen Godin, see Copies of Affidavits and Information, 1698–1712, Jan. 24, 1706, T 70/1434, n.p.

Newfoundland). In terms of numbers of consignment years, the smaller colonies made a more tentative inroad into the slave trade. Separate traders who traded to the larger colonies, including the previously undersupplied mainland colonies, proved more persistent and successful. Of those separate traders who assembled cargoes in more than six years in this period, 42 percent traded with the Chesapeake.[36]

On a number of occasions, commentators remarked that merchants tended to support an open slave trade, whereas planters favored the Royal African Company's monopoly. An African Company agent reported, "The traders are generally of their [the separate traders'] side." A comparison of the total petitions in favor of the Royal African Company and of the separate traders supports this association between the company and the planters and the separate traders and the colonial merchants. Of the cultivated petitions for the company, half were from manufacturing interests, and a third were from colonial planter interests. The rest were trading interests. Interests that opposed the company proved to be overwhelmingly mercantile. Of the anticompany petitions, twenty-one were either authored by separate traders themselves (three) or by trading interests (eighteen). Only five arrived from planting interests. The great majority of the company's petitioning supporters were planters (nine), with just two coming from traders. The colonies from which the company and the separate traders received their petitions also suggest a tendency for traders to favor deregulated trade and planters to favor the African Company. Including both phases of parliamentary consideration, the company received two petitions from Barbados, two from Montserrat, three from generic Caribbean interests, three from Nevis, and one from the Leeward Islands. The Leeward Islands had fewer and smaller trading centers and, as a result, a smaller community of traders. All petitions from Montserrat and Nevis favored the company, and all came from resident planting interests.[37]

The company remained popular with planters because it provided credit, unlike the separate traders, who preferred payment in cash or colonial produce. Indeed, the African Company repeatedly justified its monopoly and its track record with reference to the credit that it had extended to planters in the colonies. A petition from the "Planters of his Majesty's *Leeward Caribee Islands*" that appeared before the House of Commons on March 19, 1698, ar-

---

36. Of the Caribbean traders, 42 percent traded with Jamaica, 27 percent traded with Barbados, and 17 percent traded with the Leeward Islands. On the mainland, 46 percent traded with the Chesapeake colonies of Virginia and Maryland, and 12 percent traded with Carolina. Nineteen percent traded with New England and New York, and 23 percent traded with Newfoundland.

37. For the African Company comment that the separate traders received support primarily from merchants, see Thomas Stewart to Royal African Company, Mar. 10, 1713, T 70/8, 146.

gued that the African Company had been at "great Charges" to extend credit to them. John Hussam, the African Company's agent at Nevis, explained, "The Inhabitants of those Islands wish the Trade might be Settled in the Company's Favour being assured of a More Generous Credit from the Company than Private Traders have or can give." The House of Lords committee concluded that the planters supported the company "because the company trusted them." According to traditional accounts of the African Company's demise, such trust proved to be the company's undoing because the company failed to collect much of its colonial credit. By the 1690s, the company measured its debts in the colonies at £170,000, a large proportion of its capital and trade. The company, however, willingly extended such credit for two political reasons. First, the credit enabled the company to portray itself as a public-spirited venture that helped to develop the plantation economies of the Caribbean Islands. As Charles Davenant would later articulate, the company served a pseudo-public purpose in offering banking facilities to the colonists. It did not expect to retrieve colonial debts in the short term, and its long-term perspective ought to have been, and was, an encouragement to some investors. Second, the company's debt provided a source of political capital for the company in the colonies. Debtors could be relied upon to support the company.[38]

There was clearly substantial overlap in practice between the interests of planters and of merchants. The separate traders often succeeded in integrating these interests, but the attempts to reify them, often by the company, reflected either the financial munificence or the political impotence of the company in the colonies. The broad association between planters and the Royal African Company, on the one hand, and merchants and the separate traders, on the other, helps to prevent the impression that there existed a simple conflation between colonial interests and opposition to the company. It also suggests the important part played by "deterritorialized" merchants—that is, those who enjoyed commercial and political constituencies throughout the British Atlantic world—in effecting the deregulation of Britain's transatlantic slave trade.

The population of active independent slave traders was thus opportunistic.

---

38. For Royal African Company petitions celebrating its provision of credit to the colonies, see, as one example, *Commons Journals*, X, 34. For the petition from the Leeward Islands, see ibid., XII, 166. See also [William Cleland], *The Present State of the Sugar Plantations Consider'd; but More Especially That of the Island of Barbadoes* (London, 1714), 29. For Hussam's comment, see John Hussam to Royal African Company, Nov. 16, 1710, T 70/8, 108. For the scale of the colonists' debts to the company, see Minutes of the General Court, T 70/101. The company recorded the levels of debts in the colonies at its annual report in January. The company's credit in the colonies oscillated between a half and a third of its market capitalization. For the importance the company attached to its credit provision, see Davenant, *Reflections*, 137.

Its members often had previous trading experience and sometimes were involved with the African Company itself. Typically, they were from the margins of the merchant establishment, whether in London, the provinces, or the colonies. Most important, they were representative of the burgeoning unregulated Atlantic economy. Extending their business into slave trading represented a form of vertical integration. Such a move could make the separate traders' businesses more efficient and less risky as it helped to improve the steady supply of the plantation crops they sold in England by assisting the supply of labor. The deregulated slave trade helped to ensure that the alignment of economic interests was transatlantic and not adversarial between colony and metropole. The lobbyists for deregulated slave trading followed this transatlantic model of economic interests because MPs and ministers wished, by the second stage of the debate, beginning in 1707, to support transatlantic interests when making decisions.

THE INDEPENDENT SLAVE traders produced a political interest group that labored in Parliament, before the Board of Trade, and in print on their behalf. Institutions, personal connections, and trading interests helped to shape this group's membership. The Board of Trade and Parliament often gave it coherence. The Board inquiry in 1708 allowed the first show of strength from the interest group after the 1698 statute. Of the independent slave traders' 1690s interest group, Peter Paggen and his apprentice Isaac Milner continued to lobby, but the Board of Trade's need for information about the ways in which the Atlantic economy functioned would bring other individuals into the separate traders' lobby. The information the Board possessed about the separate traders' activities determined which separate traders the Board's commissioners would summon for further intelligence. Using this information, the Board galvanized opposition to the company by uniting domestic disapproval with the contempt that planters in the colonies had for the company. The Board of Trade thus helped to cement the separate traders as a transatlantic interest group. These inquiries by the Board also helped determine the separate traders' political leadership. Once a separate trader had provided information for the Board, that person typically continued acting on the separate traders' behalf. In this way, the Board's summons, as with those of parliamentary subcommittees of the 1690s, helped to impart a clearer identity to an often disparate group of Atlantic merchants.

Two additional institutional features of the developing Atlantic political economy became important to the formation of the separate traders' political lobby: the emergence of colonial agencies and the shift from direct trade to consignment trade. The rise of the colonial agencies from the 1670s provided colonists with an official means to influence political events in London. A number of separate traders served as colonial agents. Gilbert Heathcote, William Heysham, Joseph Martyn, Peter Paggen, and Nathaniel Rous all had acted as agents for colonial assemblies (Heysham and Rous for Barbados, Heathcote for Jamaica, and Martyn and Paggen for the Leeward Islands and Maryland, respectively). Their own slave-trading operations doubtless influenced their sympathy for deregulated trade; an agency position, however, necessitated that they use political means to advance their economic interests and those of their constituents.[39]

The shift from direct trade (in which English firms purchased colonial produce via factors in America) to the consignment trade (in which the colonists dispatched their produce to commission merchants in London) provided colonists with correspondents in London and elsewhere in England who could act politically on their behalf. A large proportion of the separate traders ran London commission houses. The transatlantic business partnership between Robert and William Heysham enabled the Heyshams' commission business to manage the commercial and lobbying sides of their enterprise. These networks provided a means for the separate traders to learn of and respond to colonial demand for African labor as well as to cultivate planter and metropolitan support for their cause.[40]

A core group of separate traders, however, had known each other and worked together as merchants before the Board of Trade's inquiry. The separate traders' lobby expressed the commercial changes wrought by the deregulation of the trade since the 1690s as much as it reflected the concurrent changes in transatlantic politics. Trading, apprenticeship, and familiar connections also help explain the formation of the interest group that deregulated the British slave trade. Before appearing before the Board of Trade or at Parliament together, Humphrey Morice, Isaac Milner, and Peter Paggen enjoyed longstanding trading connections. In February 1705, Morice wrote excitedly to Thomas Wood, his contact in Jamaica, about his plans to begin a slave-trading operation with Milner's help, whom he described as "my sure friend to assist mee always in any such enterprise." (As noted previously, Milner had served as apprentice to Paggen.) Morice also discussed the possibility of needing Paggen's assistance (which could be obtained via Milner). Morice had mar-

39. *CSPC*, XVIII, no. 981, 717 (Rous), XIII, no. 1192, 348 (Martyn), XVII, no. 1255, 619 (Heysham), XVIII, no. 911, 641 (Paggen); Francis Nicholson to Paggen, Dec. 21, 1698, Egerton Family Papers, MssEL 9572, Huntington Library, San Marino, Calif.

40. See Jacob M. Price, *Perry of London: A Family and a Firm on the Seaborne Frontier* (Cambridge, Mass., 1992), 30–32; and K. G. Davies, "The Origins of the Commission System in the West India Trade," Royal Historical Society, *Transactions*, II (1952), 89–106.

ried Judith Sandes, the niece of a prominent separate trader, John Browne. He would later marry Paggen's daughter, Katherine.[41]

Participation in other commercial interest groups also brought politically active separate traders together. Prior crusades for deregulation, in particular, helped to compel separate traders to lobby against the African Company. Prominent 1690s slave-trade lobbyists Gilbert Heathcote, Bartholomew Gracedieu, Edward Littleton, and Peter Paggen had been involved with the opponents of the Old East India Company during the 1690s.[42]

The separate traders' political activities took several forms. First, they signed petitions to Parliament explicitly designating themselves as separate traders. Second, traders, like Humphrey Morice, Edward Littleton, and William Wood, authored reports and pamphlets in support of free trade for Parliament or the Board of Trade. Third, they appeared in person to lobby the Board of Trade and Parliament. Lastly, separate traders signed petitions that purported to be from disinterested bodies. On these terms, two hundred individuals can be classed as politically active separate traders. Of these, slightly below half, ninety, were interested separate traders who had a proven slave-trading record.[43]

---

41. See Humphrey Morice to Thomas Wood, Aug. 7, 1705, Humphrey Morice Papers; James A. Rawley, "Humphrey Morice: Foremost London Slave Merchant of His Time," in *London,* 43. Morice's papers at the Bank of England report his personal and business connections to the following separate traders: Edward Lascelles, Peter Hollander, William Wood (who was his agent in Jamaica), Abraham Houlditch and Robert Brook, Nathaniel Rous, Cornelius Deane, Robert Heysham, John Burridge, Thomas Lloyd, Stephen Godin, Robert Atkins, and Edward Dodd.

42. For the opposition of Heathcote, Gracedieu, Littleton, and Paggen to the Old East India Company, see Jones "London Overseas Merchant Groups," 356.

43. An "interested" separate trader was one who acted as part of the lobby and had a proven slave-trading record. Political actions were recorded for only those individuals explicitly documented as separate traders. During the period of the 1698 act, there were 323 political actions. A significant majority of these actions (197—or 61 percent) were signatures on primary separate-trader petitions. The remaining 39 percent were divided between the remaining three forms of political activity: authoring pamphlets and reports, lobbying before Parliament and the Board of Trade, and signing petitions from disinterested groups, or "secondary" petitions. Appearing in person before Parliament or the Board of Trade was evidence of trading commitment and was the sole preserve of the interested separate trader. I have included as political actions only actual appearances by separate traders before these bodies and have excluded those instances in which separate traders were merely invited or scheduled to appear. For interested separate-trader petitions, see T 70/175, 100 (Jan. 27, 1709), 148 (Dec. 8, 1709), 217 (Feb. 1, 1709). Petitions by interested separate traders were often distinguished by subregion, for example, "separate traders to Virginia and Maryland." "Secondary" separate traders signed petitions that either directly supported specific traders or supported the cause of independent slave trading in general. Secondary petitions could count as interested if evidence exists that the signatories traded in slaves. There are 130 such petitions during this period. We have signatories for 11 of these petitions, nearly eleven hundred signatories in total. For petitions from secondary separate traders, see, from Barbados, Dec. 9, 1709,

Within this group, there was a strong correlation between the extent of interest in the African trade and the extent of political activity. Of the politically active separate traders, 81 percent assembled cargoes in more than one year and more than half did so in more than three years. Of those separate traders who assembled African cargoes in more than eight years, 80 percent were politically active.

Those who paid the 10 percent duty on the outward journey from London predominate among the group of politically active separate traders. They were primarily triangular traders, as opposed to bilateral traders such as Elias Abenaker and John Pratt who did not transport slaves to the colonies but either traded in nonhuman cargoes or sold their slaves to other traders on the African coast. Those who had a prior Atlantic trading interest were also more likely to act politically. Although nearly a quarter of the Atlantic traders acted politically in support of the separate trade, only 12 percent of those slave traders who devoted the majority of their commercial energies to European trades supported the separate traders politically.[44]

A small number of the most committed Africa traders of this period showed no interest in lobbying against the African Company. Two of the most commercially active separate traders, Daniel Jamineau (thirteen consignment years) and Anthony Tourney (twelve consignment years) made no political effort to safeguard their involvement in the African trade. Nine addi-

---

T 70/175, 150-151, Jamaica, Mar. 5, 1711, CO 388/14, 8(1), Dartmouth, Dec. 13, 1709, T 70/175, 149, Liverpool, Dec. 20, 1709, T 70/175, 152, Exeter, Jan. 10, 1710, T 70/175, 156, Whitehaven, Jan. 12, 1710, T 70/175, 158, Plymouth, Apr. 19, 1711, T 70/175, 159, Bridgewater, Jan. 12, 1710, T 70/175, 160, Birmingham, [date unclear], T 70/175, 168, Shipwrights of London, [date unclear], T 70/175, 170, Packers of London, [date unclear], T 70/175, 173. For a full directory of politically active separate traders, see Appendix 3, below.

During the second phase of parliamentary consideration, from 1707 to 1714, eighty-six MPs engaged directly with the Africa trade debates. Nine commercially active separate traders served as MPs between 1690 and 1714: John Burridge, Senior, and John Burridge, Junior, of Lyme Regis, William Clayton of Liverpool, Joseph Earle of Bristol, Sir Bartholomew Gracedieu of St. Ives, Sir Gilbert Heathcote, Robert Heysham of Lancaster, William Heysham of Lancaster, and Humphrey Morice of Newport. But thirteen MPs whose direct involvement in the slave trade cannot be established also lobbied for the cause of independent slave trading: John Bromley II, Sir James Campbell, Sir Alexander Cumming, Sir Robert Davers, Gilfrid Lawson, William Farrer, Richard Lloyd, James Lowther, George Montague, Thomas Onslow, John Pulteney, Samuel Shepheard, and Robert Yate. Evidence of this activity appears in the *Journal of the Commissioners for Trade and Plantations* . . . , 14 vols. (London, 1920-1938), I-III; *Commons Journals*, XI-XVI; and various miscellaneous commentaries of these debates, typically pamphlet commentary or reflections in Royal African Company correspondence.

44. Among the politically active Atlantic traders, 69 percent traded with the Caribbean, and 31 percent traded with the mainland. The largest proportions of politically active traders were from Jamaica (34 percent), the Chesapeake (22 percent), and Barbados (12 percent).

tional individuals active in at least seven consignment years are conspicuous in their absence from separate-trader petitions and lobbies. Tourney, Sir William Benson, and James Berdoe primarily shipped iron to Africa. Because they usually sourced the ore from Northern Europe, they operated outside the Atlantic constituency of trading interests that formed the bedrock of the separate traders' political movement.[45]

Benson, Jamineau, and Abraham Lodge had good reason not to publicly attack the African Company. Although they operated independently, they also on occasion shared cargoes with the Royal African Company and so were unlikely to jeopardize this trading relationship. Similarly, Jeffrey Jefferies and Thomas Coalthurst had served as African Company directors and continued to hold shares. Their contacts with the African Company operated alongside their independent slave-trading businesses. Both brought them profits. Publicly favoring either group might upset this lucrative balance.[46]

Sustaining the separate traders' interest group represented a significant challenge. Disputes about the Madeiran consulship, the tobacco adventure to Russia, the need to work with the African Company in other contexts, colonial rivalries, and party differences might have divided the men who became separate traders. Persistent separate traders, for example, disagreed about the best means of governing British interests in Madeira. Three of the separate traders played a part in the movement to create a Russian market for British American tobacco, John Goodwin, Isaac Milner, and Micajah Perry. Two other prominent separate traders, Peregrine Brown and John Brown, opposed the Russian tobacco adventure.[47]

---

45. The separate traders who did not lobby against the company were Thomas Carter (nine consignment years); Thomas Coalthurst, Robert Diamond, Laurence Hollister, John Travers, Joseph Way (eight consignment years each); and Sir William Benson, Lewis Casamajor, and Sir Jeffrey Jefferies (seven consignment years each).

46. See Appendixes 2 and 4, below.

47. Such was the importance of Madeira to English Atlantic trading interests that a movement gathered pace to establish a separate consulship there to defend English trading interests. Separate traders that backed this proposition were Joseph Jackson, Edward Lascelles, Isaac Milner, Peter Paggen, Francis Sitwell, and James Wayte. Certain traders, however, preferred the old arrangement in which the ambassador in Lisbon remained responsible for English interests on the wine island. Isaac Milner's cousin, John Milner, was consul at Lisbon, and several separate traders representing both tobacco and sugar interests (Humphrey Morice, John Burridge, Nathaniel Rous, Joseph Martyn, and Robert Heysham) sought to avoid Madeira's acquiring its own consulship, presumably to prevent further interference in their trade. John Goodwin also lobbied the Board of Trade in 1707 to arrange convoys to Madeira. See David Hancock, *Oceans of Wine: Madeira and the Emergence of American Trade and Taste* (New Haven, Conn., 2009). For separate-trader involvement in the dispute over the proposed Madeiran consulship, see Additional Manuscripts, 61510, 120, and 61620, 127, British Library, London. For Goodwin, see Correspondence of the Board of Trade, CO 5/1315, no. 63. For the tobacco adventure to Russia, see "Virginia Tobacco in Russia,"

The fluid allegiances and complex structures of commercial society in the reign of Queen Anne also saw politically active directors of both the separate traders and the African Company work together for common causes. Richard Harris, the most politically active of all the lobbyists for the separate traders, was appointed to the Lieutenancy of the Ward of Tower Hamlets alongside Joseph Jorye and Fisher Tench, both of whom had lobbied to end independent slave trading only months before. At the height of the parliamentary dispute between the African Company and the separate traders, Peter Paggen served as a director of the East India Company and the Royal African Company, as did Urban Hall, Sir William Withers, Samuel Shepheard, Sir John Fleet, Sir James Bateman, and Sir John Andrews. Clearly, lobbyists on both sides pursued other interests when it suited them.[48]

The refusal of large-scale separate traders to act politically against the company, the memory of older commercial disputes between the separate traders, and the willingness of politically active separate traders to work alongside African Company directors in different contexts complicates the simple narrative of two mutually exclusive groups (procompany and anticompany) railing against one another until monopoly succumbed to free trade. In certain contexts, at certain times, the struggle between company and separate traders could be clearly demarcated, but the distinctions between the two factions did impose restrictions on how members of both lobbies would relate to other issues.

Certain broader commercial interests, however, would encourage nonslave traders to become politically active separate traders. Fifty-eight separate traders acted politically but do not have a proven slave-trading record. Of these actions, the majority were signatures on petitions, but several individuals could be relied upon to fight in the separate traders' corner in public. Sir Robert Davers appeared on the separate traders' behalf on three occasions before the Board of Trade and eight times before Parliament. Although Davers was the absentee owner of a Barbadian plantation, there is no evidence that he participated in slave trading himself. He unofficially represented the plantation interest before Parliament, and his appearance as a lobbyist for the separate traders suggests that the lobby emerged in concert with what became known as the plantation interest—a group of traders who purported to uphold the interests of merchants and their planting contacts. Much the same

---

VMHB, IV (1896–1897), 60; and the transcript of the Library of Congress manuscript in "Tobacco Trade in Russia, 1705," *William and Mary Quarterly*, 2d Ser., III (1923), 251.

48. For the appointments to the Lieutenancy of the Ward of Tower Hamlets, see *St. James's Post* (London), Aug. 12, 1715. For Paggen's involvement in the East India Company, see *Supplement*, Apr. 15–18, 1709.

can be said for John Bromley, Francis Mitchell, and Thomas Onslow, who also defended Caribbean interests in Parliament.[49]

The tobacco interest was even more conspicuous in the separate traders' defense. Several of the politically active separate traders whose trading activity cannot be documented were men who had lobbied on behalf of the tobacco interest in general. Men such as Benjamin Bradley and Godfrey Webster supported the separate traders with signatures to their petitions but did not diversify from tobacco into slave trading. Both Bradley and Webster boasted success as lobbyists against the Russia Company. Many of the most vociferous opponents of the company in Parliament were linked to the tobacco trade but otherwise had no connection to the slave trade. MPs representing tobacco-trading areas, like Gilfrid Lawson, MP for Cumberland, and James Lowther, MP for Carlisle, were interested in the tobacco-trading activities of nearby Whitehaven and so supported the open slave trade as a means to develop the tobacco trade. Similarly, Richard Norris and William Clayton, both members for Liverpool, also regarded a free trade as a means of enlarging the tobacco trade. As with other Liverpudlians, Clayton began to develop slave-trading interests of his own. As a prominent politician in the town, Clayton aided the separate traders' cause and gathered petitions from the borough against the Royal African Company. The established tobacco lobby proved a powerful ally to the cause for open slave trading.[50]

The differing commercial interests of the separate traders can be seen in their leadership. Of the thirty-two elite identifiable separate traders whose repeated political involvement and trading record can be established, ten operated predominantly as Chesapeake tobacco merchants. Nine were primarily Jamaica sugar merchants. Six were Barbados merchants, three operated primarily with the Leeward Islands, and one traded to Carolina. All were London-based (although many had not been born in the capital), apart from Stephen Godin and John Baker, who resided in Carolina and Jamaica, respectively, John Day and Francis Rogers, who were both Bristolians, and William Clayton, who was Liverpudlian. They divided, therefore, primarily into Chesapeake and Jamaican "circles." The predominance of tobacco merchants matches the percentage increase in slave trading to the American mainland that the deregulation had helped to produce. The Caribbean Islands, however, and especially Jamaica, continued to receive more slaves than the main-

---

49. Robert Davers was elected unofficial representative in Parliament for the West Indies in 1699; see Andrew J. O'Shaughnessy, "The Formation of a Commercial Lobby: The West India Interest, British Colonial Policy, and the American Revolution," *Historical Journal*, XL (1997), 71–95.

50. William Clayton traded in four years. Richard Norris traded in two. See also Appendix 3, below.

TABLE 1. ELITE SEPARATE TRADERS, 1690–1712

Name	Trading years	No. of political actions	Base	Primary trading zone
Arnold, William	5	2	London	Barbados
Baker, John	4	2	Jamaica	Jamaica
Brown, Peregrine	12	3	London	Chesapeake
Burridge, John, Jr.	5	5	London	Jamaica
Clayton, William	4	2	Liverpool	Chesapeake
Cruickshank, Robert	2	1	London	Chesapeake
Day, John	5	2	Bristol	Barbados
Dodd, Edward	3	1	London	—
Godin, Stephen	4	2	Carolina	Carolina
Goodwin, John	3	2	London	Chesapeake
Harris, Richard	10	28	London	Jamaica
Heathcote, Gilbert	2	1	London	Jamaica
Heysham, Robert	14	13	London	Barbados
Holmes, Richard	2	2	London	—
Houlditch, Abraham	13	6	London	Jamaica
Kent, Charles	6	4	London	Jamaica
Lascelles, Edward	6	2	London	Barbados
Levett, Richard	4	2	London	Chesapeake
Martyn, Joseph	13	7	London	Leeward Islands
Milner, Isaac	14	13	London	Chesapeake
Morice, Humphrey	4	22	London	Jamaica
Nelthorpe, George	2	3	London	Chesapeake
Paggen, Peter	7	6	London	Chesapeake
Perry, Micajah	3	2	London	Chesapeake
Rogers, Francis	7	2	Bristol	Leeward Islands
Rous, Nathaniel	6	3	London	Barbados
Sitwell, Francis	2	2	London	—
South, Humphrey	5	1	London	Barbados
Waterhouse, David	4	2	London	Leeward Islands
Way, Benjamin	7	2	London	Jamaica
Wayte, James	11	7	London	Chesapeake
Wood, William	4	2	London	Jamaica

Sources: *Journals of the House of Commons*, I–LI (London, 1803), X–XII, XV–XVII; T 70/175; T 70/1198–1199; T 70/349–356; *The Trans-Atlantic Slave Trade Database (Voyages Data Set)*, http://www.slavevoyages.org; Nigel Tatersfield, *The Forgotten Trade: Comprising the Log of the Daniel and Henry of 1700 and Accounts of the Slave Trade from the Minor Parts of England, 1698-1725* (London, 1998); David Richardson, *Bristol, Africa, and the Eighteenth-Century Slave Trade to America*, I, *The Years of Expansion, 1698-1729*, Bristol Record Society, Publications, XXXVIII (Bristol, 1986).

land. The shared leadership of the deregulation movement between mainland American and Caribbean interests proved long lasting and effective.

Tension between these subgroups of separate traders was rare. One example deserves mention. In February 1712, fearful of the Harley ministry's support for the African Company, two Jamaican separate traders, Humphrey Morice and Richard Harris, moderated their proposals in a Board of Trade hearing. They agreed to pledge themselves to a minimum export value of one hundred thousand pounds on goods bound for Africa and a maximum price for slaves and conceded to allow a regulation of the trade that would finance African forts and British consuls on the African coast. Morice and Harris also agreed to raise a deposit from the Bank of England to act as security to reassure planters that independent traders would continue to supply the plantations when trading conditions limited profits. They acceded to a higher charge of 15 and then 18 percent on the trade. On March 12, 1712, another group of separate traders, including Sir Robert Davers, Robert Heysham, Gilfrid Lawson, Thomas Onslow, and Thomas Lowther, indicated that they had been misinformed about Morice's and Harris's concession: "[Davers et al.] acquainted their lordships that there was a report on the Exchange, as if they had come into an Exclusive Joint Stock which was never their intention, and therefore if Mr Harris and Mr Morrice had agreed to anything of that nature it was without their knowledge and consent." Davers and company explained that they could not, contrary to what Morice and Harris had allowed, submit to any regulation in relation to the price of slaves and would not concede that forts were necessary for the trade. The separate traders' consistent solidarity had been fractured for the first (and only) time because of the strength of the African Company's support in the ministry and in the Board of Trade between 1710 and 1712. In the end, nothing was done in Parliament to support the company apart from a means for its creditors to purchase the company. The 1698 statute expired in the summer of 1712, effectively liberating the slave trade entirely from all duties and charges.[51]

On the whole, however, the separate traders enjoyed a remarkably cohesive political leadership. Sharing the responsibility were Richard Harris, Robert Heysham, Isaac Milner, Joseph Martyn, Humphrey Morice, Peter Paggen, and James Wayte. As noted previously, all had prior experience in different Atlantic trades. Harris and Morice traded to Jamaica; Heysham traded with Barba-

---

51. For Morice and Harris, see Transcription of Board of Trade Minutes, Mar. 12, 1712, T 70/175, 295. See also *A Specimen of the Falsehoods, Absurdities, and Contradictions Contained in Some Late Papers, Publish'd by the Separate Traders to Africa* ([London, 1711]), 1.

dos; Milner, Paggen, and Wayte traded to the Chesapeake; and Martyn traded with the Leeward Islands. All also trafficked in slaves on a vast scale.

Throughout the period of the 1698 statute, however, Richard Harris was the most politically active of all the elite separate traders, signing petitions, authoring reports to the Board of Trade, and appearing in person before the Board. The Board of Trade regarded Harris as the separate traders' leader. Harris also became a key conduit through which petitions, expertise, and finance flowed against the company. He forwarded the opinion of the merchants and planters of Jamaica to the House of Lords inquiry in June 1713, which proved to be important anticompany testimony. The Bristol Society of Merchant Venturers contributed £150 to the separate traders' parliamentary campaign against the company through Harris's company books. He also authored pamphlets that were often adaptations of his reports written during Board of Trade inquiries about the African trade. In December 1708, Harris also gathered anticompany testimony from former Royal African Company employees detailing the company's attempts to ruin the independent trade, contrary to the spirit of the 1698 act. A pamphleteer recognized the depth of Richard Harris's knowledge: "Mr Richard Harris, a Merchant . . . no Body understands this [slave] trade better, or is more to be credited."[52]

The extent of Humphrey Morice's political activity was second only to that of Richard Harris. He also authored pamphlets, signed petitions, and appeared before the Board. Isaac Milner also became a regular witness before the Board of Trade to provide evidence against the Royal African Company. Robert Heysham can be designated as the separate traders' leader in the House of Commons. Heysham served as MP for Lancaster from 1698 to 1715. He was also the Barbadian assembly's agent between 1700 and 1702, a position that influenced much of his parliamentary activity during this period. Robert's brother, William, was also an MP. Whereas Harris, Morice, and Milner dominated the separate traders' crucial representations to the Board of Trade, Robert Heysham was their Parliamentary protagonist. He appeared before Parliament and the Board of Trade to promote the separate traders' case. He also cultivated pro–separate trader petitions. He was the key parliamentary orchestrator for the separate traders. He dominated parliamentary committees charged with authoring bills to regulate the African trade and was a teller for the votes in favor of the separate traders.[53]

52. James A. Rawley, "Richard Harris, Slave Trader Spokesman," in *London*, 57–81 (quotation on 60, from [Richard Rigby], *An Answer to a Calumny* . . . [London, 1728], 29). See also Richard Harris to Board of Trade, Nov. 10, 1713, CO 388/11, and Merchant Venturers' Hall Book, 16, Bristol Records Office.

53. For Robert Heysham's cultivation of petitions, see drafting committees on Mar. 17, 1709,

THE HIGH PROPORTION of triangular traders within the politically active separate traders, the predominance of traders with prior Atlantic interests, the role of an embryonic plantation interest within the disinterested separate traders, and the link between avoidance of political activity and non-Atlantic trade combine to provide the most important insight into what motivated separate traders to trade in slaves and to lobby to advance the cause of a deregulated slave trade. The large group of politically active separate traders who did not deal in slaves underscores the extent to which the separate traders' political concerns represented the broader issues of the Atlantic world market. That such a disparate group of Atlantic traders operated so consistently together is significant and underscores the importance of Atlantic trade in general as a force in opposition to monopoly. The predominance of the tobacco interest to the separate traders' cause during the second phase of parliamentary consideration between 1707 and 1713 also suggests that London provided the arena in which separate traders with differing commercial concerns could cement intercolonial alliances. Transatlantic institutions with new, more deliberative styles of operation, like the Board of Trade and colonial agencies, helped to cement the separate traders together during this second phase, but, on the whole, they derived their bond from the experience of Atlantic trade and that trade's emergent political voice.

These separate traders sought to advance their individual interests, but they did so collectively. They assembled networks to assist their lobbying; from Cornhill coffeehouses where they authored petitions and pamphlets to the lobby of the House of Commons and the anterooms of Whitehall Palace, these individual traders gathered together to develop their cause and their case. They worked to create a huge constituency of supporters throughout the Atlantic world. They enjoyed the institutional momentum provided by colonial agencies as well as the transatlantic ties forged by commission trading to bring planter and merchant together. They also brought their own political experience and service to bear to ensure that their campaign would make an impact and liberate the slave trade.

The separate traders' interests and constituencies encompassed every corner of the British Atlantic world, from London to the Atlantic colonies to the provincial outports on the Atlantic rim. Signing a separate-trader petition might evidence support for the expansion in colonial produce trading since

---

Feb. 18, 1710, Feb. 20, 1710, Mar. 31, 1712, and May 2, 1713, T 70/9. For Morice's authorship of separate-trader pamphlets, see Humphrey Morice to Nicholas Morice, Mar. 25, 1709, Letterbook, Humphrey Morice Papers. For Morice's parliamentary career, see Cruickshanks, Handley, and Hayton, eds., *House of Commons*, IV, 935–936.

the act of 1698, or the expansion in the exporting of English manufactures, or the reexporting of Indian or Dutch commercial goods to Africa. As a political interest group, the separate traders represented not only the interests of slave trading but also the broader concerns of the Atlantic commodities economy that now relied on African slave labor.

Identifying the separate traders' Atlantic interests and their transatlantic constituency and recognizing the coherence of their political leadership does not wholly explain the separate traders' success over the African Company's formidable lobby. It does, however, begin to clarify what was at stake for the company and its free-trading opponents. Atlantic interests formed the basis for the separate traders' entry into slave trading. Their Atlantic constituency provided crucial support for their public lobbying, which helped them to sustain that trade and to protect their interests from the African Company. The company itself sought to uphold the interests of its beneficiaries: management, shareholders, and creditors. These were, of course, economic interests, but they mediated through a changing ideological and political framework. The politicization of the slave trade required the separate traders and the African Company to provide, in public, ideological justification for their respective interests. The separate traders promoted ideas that celebrated the national benefits of a self-regulating commercial society. The African Company celebrated monopoly as the best guardian of the state's interest. Each side claimed to advance liberty, each believed its position was the most British. These ideological positions would offer both groups the means to translate their interests into favorable regulatory outcomes. It is to these ideological positions that we now turn.

THREE

The Ideas
Challenging the "Tales of . . . Mandevil"

The conspicuous emergence of a population of independent slave traders and their wish to associate themselves with certain areas of the country and particular ideas led contemporary observers of the Africa trade debates to develop a stereotype of the independent slave trader. Thomas Southerne's slave-trading archvillain, Captain Driver, in his 1699 dramatization of Aphra Behn's novel, *Oroonoko,* was callous, hardheaded, upwardly mobile, and a stickler for unthinking graft: "There's nothing done without it, Boys. I have made my Fortune this way." The better-bred Widow Lackitt railed against the Captain: "You forget your self as fast as you can; but I remember you; I know you for a pitiful paltry Fellow, as you are; an Upstart to Prosperity; one that is but just come acquainted with Cleanliness, and that never saw Five Shillings of your own, without deserving to be hang'd for 'em." More famous was the eponymous hero of Daniel Defoe's pioneering 1719 novel *Robinson Crusoe,* who had embarked on his merchant career as an independent slave trader in the 1680s. Crusoe epitomized the separate-trader profile as a provincial trader from an immigrant family who sought quick profits to better himself socially. He exhibited a new, intense individualism on his desert island that exemplified the rugged, intrepid capitalist determination of the separate trader.[1]

Society's stereotyping of the separate traders according to their driving economic and social ambitions reflected the separate traders' and the Royal African Company's own attempts to depict themselves within broader ideological categories. Pamphlets and petitions placed the narrow debate between the company and the separate traders in the context of larger issues to grab the attention and support of disinterested parties, legislators, and the public at large. These ideological depictions helped both sides legitimize their interests and were a central part of their respective political campaigns. They reveal

---

1. Tho[mas] Southerne, *Oroonoko: A Tragedy* . . . (London, 1699), 13; Daniel Defoe, *The Life and Strange Surprizing Adventures of Robinson Crusoe* . . . (1719), ed. J. Donald Crowley (London, 1972), 3, 16.

important features of the mentalities that cultivated and embraced slave-trade expansion in the British Atlantic at the beginning of the eighteenth century.

Independent slave traders appeared to be especially sensitive about liberty. Like William Wilkinson, Thomas Phelps, an independent slave trader, embarked in August 1685 on an interloping slave-trading voyage only to be captured, not by the African Company, as Wilkinson and others were, but by Barbary corsairs. The experience of captivity made Phelps acutely appreciative of his personal liberty:

> Liberty and Freedom are the happiness only valuable by a Reflection on Captivity and Slavery, they who are unacquainted with, and have not notice of the Miseries of the latter, will never put a due Value and consideration upon the former.... Here the Government secures every Man in the possession and enjoyment of what Gods blessing and his own industry has allow'd.[2]

By the Africa trade debates, it is clear that reflection on captivity could derive from the experience of slave trading as well as from the experience of captivity (whether the captors were the African Company or North African rulers). Phelps's separate-trading antecedents, most of whom had not experienced captivity, developed their view of the world and their appeal to the public with frequent (and, to our eyes, perverse) references to freedom and to liberty and the various ways in which the company inhibited the enjoyment of these rights. The separate traders launched their campaign to develop the slave trade as a crusade for English liberty. The African Company responded by noting that the separate traders' attachment to liberty did not produce a trade that was suitable for upholding the interests of the British state in Africa and in America, and they later co-opted the separate traders' rhetoric by citing the company's freedom to enjoy property and the ways in which monopoly could best uphold national liberty. Although the two parties disagreed about the determinants and ramifications of liberty, they both deployed the syncretic rhetoric of liberty and freedom as a means to compel all observers to rally to their cause. The ideological dispute between separate traders and the company became, as one pamphleteer put it, a "paper counter scuffle" about liberty.[3]

---

2. Thomas Phelps, *A True Account of the Captivity of Thomas Phelps, at Machaness in Barbary and of His Strange Escape in Company of Edmund Baxter and Others, as Also of the Burning Two of the Greatest Pirat-Ships Belonging to That Kingdom, in the River of Mamora; upon the Thirteenth Day of June 1685* (London, 1685), unpaginated [preface, i–ii].

3. Charles Davenant, *Reflections upon the Constitution and Management of the African Trade, etc.*, in

There were important areas of agreement between the separate traders and the African Company. Both sides saw the particular value of the African trade, without deviating significantly from the balance-of-trade formula and, most remarkably, without (after the 1680s) challenging the Navigation Acts or the morality of slavery. As Daniel Defoe tersely put it, the African trade was the most important that Britain participated in because it "exports nothing but what we can spare, and brings Home nothing but what we cannot be without—That sets our Poor to Work . . . and extends our Dominions. . . . That barters Gold for Glass Beads, and the Riches of *Africk,* for the Baubles of *Europe.*" The slave trade was, as Nuala Zahedieh writes, a "mercantilist's ideal." Both sides noted the value of African slaves over white indentured labor and subscribed to the view that England's settler colonies improved the domestic economy by stimulating manufactures. Both sought to promote the state interest and defend it against the encroachments of French and Dutch rivals, though the African Company was more likely to dwell upon the prospect of Dutch competition.[4]

The following discussion focuses on the ways in which the public political disputes between the Royal African Company and the separate traders generated a conflict of ideologies. It shows that late Stuart politics forced both sides to justify their interested positions and their very different constituencies in ideological terms. These ideologies reflected both sides' interpretation of how the political context changed during the dispute. The attack and response between the two interests, who often referred to themselves as "parties," produced a dialogic impetus to the formulation of a new nexus of ideology. This debate hinged (with changing emphases as it wore on) on the determinants of several features of the elastic notions of freedom and interest. Which version of the slave trade best satisfied the "national interest" and therefore offered the best guarantees to uphold the nation's liberty (in a Machiavellian sense)? For the African Company, the self-interested trading activity of the separate traders was socially corruptive, and it enervated national liberty. The nation depended upon a corporate, organic hierarchy. A monopoly company would express that hierarchy and assert the interests of the state abroad to uphold English liberty against barbarous Africans and the competition of rival European states. For the independent traders, national liberty and economic growth was best achieved by the economic contributions of individual sub-

---

Charles Whitworth, ed., *The Political and Commercial Works of That Celebrated Writer Charles D'Avenant, LL.D. . . . ,* V (London, 1771), 147 (hereafter cited as Davenant, *Reflections*).

4. *Review of the State of the British Nation,* Mar. 6, 1711, 589–592; Nuala Zahedieh, *The Capital and the Colonies: London and the Atlantic Economy, 1660–1700* (Cambridge, 2010), 248.

jects. It was the entrepreneurial spirit of these "free" merchants, like themselves, that provided the fiscal basis for the English victory over Louis XIV.

These conflicting images of the determinants of national economic growth, happiness, and freedom involved differing views on the workings of the English constitution and especially the legitimate source of regulatory power within it. Again, these conflicts debated the meaning of liberty and freedom. Ought not the arbiter of national regulation be the Parliament (and therefore the consent of the public), as the separate traders desired? The Glorious Revolution created a more deliberative style of politics in which print discussions mediated between political interests and strategies and legislative outcomes. After 1688, the Royal African Company could no longer promote its interest exclusively with reference to the ideological power of the royal prerogative (though the company continued to celebrate its royal associations as well as its prefix). The company thus sought to justify its goals with reference to a broader "national" constituency. But the company implied the regulatory sovereignty of a state that operated without the restrictive influence of the people, the public, or the subject. This debate pitted the freedom to consent to the regulatory mechanisms of the state via Parliament against the liberty to enjoy monopolistic property without molestation from the parliamentary process.

The separate traders' position also changed as the public debates raged on. Their traditional antimonopoly argument with an absolutist government, which dated from the 1670s, would by the 1690s evolve into a celebration of the ancient political rights and freedoms (as upheld by a Parliament with regulatory sovereignty) that William III had defended, and then, after 1707, into a call for a transatlantic nation of individual free traders whose collective effort, as consecrated by Parliament, would generate national economic growth and safeguard national power and freedom. Such was the attachment of the separate traders to the parliamentary arena that they asserted that Parliament had the right to countenance legislative inactivity as much as statute; if Parliament made no regulatory statute, no equivalent method of regulation could be offered by rival branches of the constitution. Without alternative constitutional means to regulate the national economy after 1689, the trade in slaves would default as open, allowing the enterprising independent trader to flourish—a legislative outcome implicitly endorsing the natural right to trade in slaves.

OPPOSITION TO THE African Company's monopoly was as old as the monopoly itself. Freedom figured early on as a focal point for opponents. Resistance to the Royal African Company's monopolistic predecessor, the Company of Royal Adventurers Trading to Africa, derived from a Barbadian group who dressed their interests with the Grotian language of "freedom." This group had, since the 1650s, opposed the Navigation Acts, which had forced the colonists to cease trading with non-English merchants. In December 1667, the group petitioned Parliament against the company's monopoly, portraying it as an absolutist innovation that withheld and undermined English freedoms such as trial by jury. This idea of free trade meant free access to trade within a specific market and free access to any market.[5]

Elias Leighton, the company's secretary and a staunch supporter of James, duke of York, responded to this petition by declaring that the company was "in its Constitution National"—that is, it could satisfy the interests of the state and the national economy at large. He appealed for the king's support by celebrating the royal prerogative as the surest means to uphold that interest, at home and overseas. Leighton argued that the national interest of England could only be sustained with the help of forts on the African coast, and these could only be maintained with the help of a joint-stock company supported by "Royal Authority." He depicted the petitioners as colonial usurpers who had used their control over "dilatory" Barbadian courts to prevent the company from recovering its debts from them. For Leighton, the colonists' "free trade" argument was nothing more than a shallow attempt to disguise their self-interest and would not therefore satisfy Parliament and the Privy Council—institutions designed to uphold the national good over and above the base and selfish instincts of individual planters. During the Privy Council examination of these petitions early the following year, Leighton quipped:

> That open markets and free trade are best for those that desire them is certain and so it is to buy cheap and sell dear, and most of all to have commodities for nothing and if all his Majesty's dominions and plantations were made only for Barbadoes it might be expedient; but since it is conceived that his Majesty will have regard to what may preserve the trade of the nation, and not only to what will gratify Barbadoes, [the Privy Council] think their [Barbadian] desire of free trade will

---

5. This petition is quoted in the Royal African Company's response, *An Answer of the Company of Royal Adventurers of England Trading into Africa, to the Petition and Paper of Certain Heads and Particulars Thereunto Relating and Annexed, Exhibited to the Honourable House of Commons by Sir Paul Painter, Ferdinando Gorges, Henry Batson, Benjamin Skutt, and Thomas Knights, on the Behalf of Themselves and Others Concerned in His Majesties Plantations in America* ([London], 1667), 1. For colonists' free-trade arguments, see Christian J. Koot, "A 'Dangerous Principle,' Free Trade Discourses in Barbados and the English Leeward Islands, 1650–1689," *Early American Studies*, V (2007), 132–163.

prove as impractable and pernicious to themselves as destructive to all other public interests.⁶

Leighton's articulation of the company's position was to remain the bedrock of the company's self-justification throughout the 1660s and 1670s. His emphasis on the superiority of "Royal Authority" as the best constitutional means to uphold the national interest on the African coast was reiterated in the company's new name and its motto. Designed as a tool for the ruling dynasty's control of imperial policy, the company was reestablished as the Royal Africa Company in 1672, and its motto, *"regio floret patricionio commercium, commercioque regum,"* made explicit the perceived link between royal patronage and commercial prosperity. The royal prerogative remained the nucleus of the power of the state until 1689, especially in the context of international trade and empire.⁷

The mid-1670s argument against the company saw pamphleteers combine an earlier promotion of free trade with more concerted objections to the company's absolutist use of the royal prerogative to enforce its monopoly. In 1674, Carew Reynell argued against prerogative management of overseas trade and empire in general: "If his Majesty desires to advance his Empire, it is but granting more priviledge to Trade, and security to mens persons, and properties from Arbitrary power." In 1675, Roger Coke wrote that monopoly trading companies like the African Company "render the Ingenuity and Industry of many people useless" and were "the pre-emption of Freemen." Carew's and Coke's development of an antimonopoly position born of the constitutional rights of the subject (or freeman) and associated with parliamentary action and "ordinary Discourse" would prove influential for later separate traders.⁸

The company responded to such complaints by styling interlopers as self-interested, as it had done under Leighton's leadership. In 1680, a pro-African Company pamphlet stated: "While every single Person pursues his own particular Interest, the Publique is deserted by All, and consequently must fall

6. *An Answer of the Company of Royal Adventurers,* 17; and "Answer of Sir Ellis Leighton, Secretary, by Order of the Royal Company to the Petition of the Representatives of Barbadoes," Jan. 23, 1668, in W. Noel Sainsbury et al., eds., *Calendar of State Papers, Colonial Series, America and West Indies . . . ,* 44 vols. (London, 1860–1969) (hereafter cited as *CSPC*), V, no. 1680, 542–543.

7. A similar exchange took place between Governor Sir Jonathan Atkins and the Royal African Company in 1675, and the company was targeted in Pariliament by interlopers using similar ideas in the late 1670s. An approximate translation of the motto is: "Business is flourishing due to royal patronage and the kingdom is flourishing due to business." See Davenant, *Reflections,* 263.

8. Carew Reynell, *The True English Interest . . .* (London, 1674), 9, 71–72; Roger Coke, *England's Improvements; in Two Parts; in the Former Is Discoursed, How the Kingdom of England May Be Improved . . . ; in the Latter Is Discoursed, How the Navigation of England May Be Increased, and the Soveraignty of the British Seas More Secured to the Crown of England . . .* (London, 1675), 66, 67.

to Ruine. For which Reason, the Crown hath Erected and Established Fraternities or Companies of Merchants." The common law Court of Kings Bench upheld this position in 1683 by stating that royally sponsored monopoly companies were most important when the trade brought English subjects into contact with heathen peoples. In *East India Company v. Sandys,* Judge George Jeffreys ruled that the English interest should employ a prerogative-sponsored monopoly company because a fixed society provided the only means for the English kingdom to uphold its commitment to Christianity.[9]

Placing Christianity to one side, the emerging dispute between the African Company and its interloping opponents focused on a disagreement about the determinants of national prosperity. Interlopers viewed prosperity emanating from individual, private enterprise, which was best developed under "free trade." The African Company sought to prove that national prosperity derived from royal patronage. This disagreement had important strategic corollaries for both lobbies. It encouraged interlopers to pursue their economic interests outside the scope of the royal prerogative and its sovereign repository. Once the prerogative had been formally undermined in 1689, the interlopers would use the legislative branch of the constitution to promote private economic initiatives. The acknowledged defeat of absolutism by the 1690s saw the separate traders' arguments acquire a popular sanction that buttressed the antimonopoly cause in ways impossible in the 1660s, 1670s, and 1680s.

THE GLORIOUS REVOLUTION would drastically change the strategies, ideologies, and fortunes of the respective disputants in the Africa trade debates. Interlopers, like Jeffrey Nightingale and William Dockwra, who earlier, in 1678, had questioned the validity of the African Company's charter in a petition to Parliament, reintroduced their cases, believing that the royal prerogative and all that had emanated from it, including the African Company's right to use forfeiture to prevent incursions on its monopoly property, would be null and void. A series of court hearings helped to cement that view, without declaring the African Company's monopoly to be illegal. These hearings would force the company to seek statutory support for its monopoly and thus justify its monopoly in an entirely different way.

In Nightingale's 1689 case, *Nightingale v. Brydges,* the interlopers' prosecuting barrister, Sir Bartholomew Shower, helped to develop one of the separate traders' earlier ideological positions—that their vision of free trade ex-

---

9. See *Certain Considerations Relating to the Royal African Company of England* . . . (n.p., [1680]), 1; *The State of the Trade to Africa, between 1680 and 1707, as Well under the Management of an Exclusive Company, as under That of Separate Traders, Impartially Considered* . . . ([London, 1708]), 1.

pressed their ancient constitutional rights as Englishmen. In so doing, Shower formulated a common law manifesto for independent slave trading. Shower explained why the statutory limitation of property was preferable to restrictions derived from the prerogative: "Each subject's vote is included in whatsoever is there done: an Act of Parliament hath the consent of many men, both past, present, and to come." "The Kings of England," Shower continued, "have always claimed a monarchy royal, not a monarchy seignoral; 'under the first . . . the subjects are freemen, and have a propriety in their goods, and freehold in their lands, but under the latter they are villains and slaves.'" English common law, as a result, "gives a true property in contradistinction to the superintendant power, and for this purpose it distinguishes between bondmen, whose estates are at their lord's will and pleasure, and freemen, whose property none can invade, charge, or take away, but by their own consent; a several property in the subject is so sacred as nothing more."[10]

Shower based his case on the constitutional tradition that Englishmen were never held as villains or slaves under feudal tenure to the king. Free from slavery themselves, they were protected in their right to develop their property in other human beings. Shower cited the famous Hampden case of the 1630s, which established the subject's right to consent to all forms of taxation, and therefore implicitly invoked sections of the Declaration of Rights, which prevented the monarch from taxing subjects without their consent. Shower thus grafted the rhetoric of the Glorious Revolution onto Coke's earlier position that monopolies trampled on the ancient rights of English "freemen." Without their consent, Englishmen could not be deprived of their freedom to prosper from an expanded slave trade. The future of the slave trade would hinge on the will of the English majority. Monopolistic restrictions on the trade were tyrannical. Using eminent legal authorities such as *Bracton,* Shower grounded access to an enlarged slave trade in Englishmen's ancient freedoms.[11]

The right to trade in slaves, then, became equivalent with such sacred English rights as the right to political representation and the right to habeas corpus. The Africa trade debates became, at heart, about which version of the Africa trade the people of England would consent to. The African Company sought the parliamentary means to limit the right to trade in slaves to their

---

10. Harleian MSS, no. 3710, 238, British Library, London. Since the African Company declined to instruct counsel, Shower only recorded what he was "prepared to argue." Shower's argument is in Alexander Renton, ed., *The English Reports,* 178 vols. (London, 1900–1932), LXXXIX, 498 (1 Show. K.B. 137, 138) (hereafter cited as *ER*). These arguments closely resemble those developed by John Locke in his *Two Treatises of Government* . . . (London, 1690), 263.

11. *ER,* LXXIX, 498. *Bracton* prescribed the laws of legitimate kingship. See *De legibus et consuetudinibus Angliae* (1569), ed. and trans. Samuel E. Thorne (Cambridge, Mass., 1977).

charter. The separate traders opposed them. Because the right to trade derived from the right to political representation, political means provided the best methods of sustaining the right to economic self-interest. The separate traders used every means possible to demonstrate that the British people would not consent to a monopolistically organized slave trade.

In the 1690s, the separate traders' ideology therefore advanced a constitutional argument for slave-trade deregulation that associated their cause with the revolutionary settlement of 1689. As part of this strategy, the separate traders caricatured the African Company's monopoly—because of the strength of its ties with the displaced regime—as the product and expression of the lascivious courtly corruption of the later Stuart kings. They alleged that the company misused the royal prerogative to compel people to invest in a scheme that many feared gave the company too many arbitrary powers:

> Through the Countenance of the then Duke of *York* their Governour, and the strong Influence of the Beams of the then Prerogative, a Brood at length came forth to engage in a Design so apparently opposite to the Laws of the Land, so destructive of the Native Liberty and Freedom of the Subjects of *England,* and so contrary to the true Interest of the Nation, with respect to its Commerce.

They reinterpreted certain aspects of the company's charter—most notably its stipulation that company personnel could seize the goods of interloping African traders and prosecute their captains and crews in company-sponsored Admiralty courts—as representative of the Jacobite tyranny from which William III had liberated England. Whenever antimonopolists advanced these arguments, they helped to associate the slave trade with national pride. The separate traders' constitutional argument thus shifted from one opposing the arbitrary violation of English rights to one that asserted the popular political will. A free trade in the enslaved became emblematic of the liberties of the people.[12]

One of the judges at the King's Bench who was involved in weakening the company's monopoly, Sir John Somers, later explained corollaries of anti–African Company judgments in *Nightingale v. Bridges* and *Dockwra v. Dickinson*. Because of the constitutional right to use political means to sustain access to trade, petitioning became an invaluable means to object to the African

---

12. *The Case of the Late African Company, and the Trade to Guiny, and Other Parts within the Said Company's Patents* (n.p., [1694]), 1. For examples of pamphlets that reinterpreted the company's charter as emblematic of Jacobite tyranny, see William Wilkinson, *Systema Africanum* . . . (London, 1690), 3. See also Wilkinson, *An Answer to the Book Written by the Guiney Company in Their Own Defence, for the Management of Their Trade in Africa* (London, 1690).

Company's proposal to limit slave trading to their monopoly. A non–Africa trade pamphlet justifying the right to petition asserted: "Wherever therefore any Government is established, there the natural Right which People had to secure what was their own, must be so far at least continued, as to allow them a liberty to petition for what they think their Right, because this is a Privilege which they could not give up, when they enter'd into Society." Early-eighteenth-century conceptions of society involved the acceptance of political representation and the part played by representation in the management of economic opportunity. This acceptance naturalized political participation in government. The separate traders sought to style their goals in the language of the revolution to depict their aims as conversant with and conducive of the restoration of an ancient constitution, which the later Stuarts (and their "brood") had undermined with the help of their tyrannical "Royal company."[13]

The need to gather parliamentary support for its cause and the power of the separate traders' constitutional argument led the African Company to alter its ideological position in the 1690s. Just as the monopolists in the African trade had noted in the 1660s the self-serving features of freedom of trade arguments, so pamphleteers for the African Company in the 1690s noted that the separate traders' constitutional arguments catered to narrow, private interests. The interlopers, according to one pamphleteer, "while they pursue nothing but their private Interest, do cover themselves with the Mantle of pretended Zeal for publick Liberties and Rights."[14]

The company began to detach itself from its patrician image by celebrating the capaciousness of its monopoly and how it could serve to further the interests of the individual subjects to whom the separate traders' constitutional argument sought to appeal. In response to an early separate-trader petition from the "Merchants and Planters of the Island of Barbadoes," delivered October 30, 1690, an African Company pamphlet styled the company as a public servant with an ever-watchful eye for the needy colonists, especially those who operated on a smaller scale. One African Company correspondent claimed that the company offered a service to the less affluent, "meaner" planters. Echoing this argument, another pamphlet explained that a deregulated trade only served the interest of the grander plantation owners:

---

13. [John Somers], *Jura Populi Anglicani, or, The Subjects Right of Petitioning Set Forth; Occasioned by the Case of the Kentish Petitioners* . . . (London, 1701), 33.
14. *That the Trade to Affrica, Is Only Manageable by an Incorporated Company and a Joynt Stock, Demonstrated in a Letter to a Member of the Present House of Commons, by a Gentleman in the City* ([London, 1690]), 1.

> The Rich *Planters* having liberty to fetch *Negroes,* may furnish themselves with the best, and then to oblige those *Planters* that are poor and needy, to take off the worst upon such terms, as they shall think fit to sell them. . . . So we may be sure, that how careful soever the rich Planters will be to provide for, and to furnish themselves with a multitude of lusty hands; yet they will not judge it for their Interest to supply their poor Neighbours.[15]

The African Company's monopoly, so its pamphleteers argued, provided a means to manage the slave trade for the benefit of all ranks of American society. Their monopolistic version of the trade allowed rather than prevented broad participation in the Africa trade via its joint-stock format and stressed the joint-stock corporation's traditional deliberative and associational structure:

> [A separate-trader victory] will be so far from rendring it [the African trade] more enlarged and National, that it will reduce it into fewer hands than it now is in. . . . For while it is supported and carryed on by a *Joynt Stock,* Persons of all Qualities, Sexes, and Ages, are capable of being Adventurers in it, and of having equal Advantage by it with the very *Managers* themselves; whereas upon the exchanging this way of management into the Method of a *Regulated* Company, not only all *Females, Children* and *Persons of great Figure and lofty Title,* must be shut out, but it must immediately lapse into a few hands, and those such who are both the most wealthy and opulent, and whose alone *Province* is Traffick and Commerce.

Responding to the constitutional arguments of the independent slave traders after 1688, the African Company suggested that its joint-stock format provided the surest means of protecting the atomized economic concerns of planters, merchants, and investors.[16]

THE PARLIAMENTARY DISPUTE between the separate traders and the Royal African Company entered a second stage from 1707 to 1714. During this time, the ideological positions adopted by both sides began to acquire greater

---

15. Ibid., 5–7; Royal African Company to Edwyn Stede, Benjamin Skutt, and William Harding, Nov. 11, 1690, Treasury (T) 70/57, n.p., National Archives, Kew ("meaner"). For the petition, see *Journals of the House of Commons,* I–LI (London, 1803), X, 456 (hereafter cited as *Commons Journals*).
16. *That the Trade to Affrica,* 6–7. For the corporation's deliberative structure, see Philip J. Stern, *The Company-State: Corporate Sovereignty and the Early Modern Foundations of the British Empire in India* (Oxford, 2011), 94.

sophistication. The dialogue intensified as each side interpreted the causes of the greatly expanded slave trade after the 1689 and 1698 deregulations. The dialogue also reflected a more varied ideological context, which stemmed from the shifting political fortunes of the political parties. Much of the richness of the debate emanated from discussions about the possibilities and perils of a commercialized society. The separate traders expanded on their 1690s constitutional opposition to the company. This argument had originally fixated on the idea of a national economy that was extrinsic to the wealth of the crown. From 1707 onward, the separate traders developed a vision for this economy that exhibited a distinctly modern cast, one that celebrated freedom to trade and open competition as surer buttresses to national wealth and greatness than an arbitrary state. Their 1690s argument had espoused the constitutional right to destroy economic restrictions. Their post-1707 argument, reflecting on the huge growth of the slave trade, argued for the economic expansion that destruction would have for the nation and the empire. The African Company responded via the writings of the political economist Charles Davenant. Davenant channeled growing concern about the corrupting effects of wealth into a criticism of deregulated trade that deployed Machiavellian language. The substance of the debate between the African Company and the separate traders reveals differing perspectives on national economic goals. The separate traders' political victory suggests that economic modernity arrived with the political modernization of interests.[17]

A 1707 Board of Trade inquiry provided disputants from both sides with the opportunity to develop ideological positions. In December 1707, the London separate trader Richard Harris submitted a written response to the Board's request for testimony about how the trade ought to be managed. Harris deployed a popular metaphor to illustrate the superiority of the separate traders' constitution for the trade—the beehive. This metaphor had been used by seventeenth-century English writers to represent Dutch frugality, discipline, and commercial success. In 1705, Bernard Mandeville had published *The Grumbling Hive*. Mandeville hoped to demonstrate that the wealthy leaders of the hive's attachment to "golden age" republican ideas would, if implemented, restrict the hive's economy and lessen its power. Harris's depiction of the beehive combined both approaches.

Harris compared two scenarios for the hive: one impersonating the African Company's vision for the trade and the other, the separate traders' vision. The African Company's hive involved the detachment of "25" elite bees to

---

17. For the resurgence of Machiavellian language, see J. G. A. Pocock, *The Machiavellian Moment: Florentine Political Thought and the Atlantic Republican Tradition* (Princeton, N.J., 1975), 423–461.

"provide hony for the subsitance of the whole community." Although the "25" succeeded in fattening themselves, they failed to get enough for "others in their custody" so that "the whole might starve for all them." Harris then depicted the separate traders' version of the hive: "Suppose the whole hive went out and must starve unless each got enough for him self"; "Which is most likely to get the most hony . . . tho the 25 did their duty . . . they would not fix on so many flowers as 200." These twenty-five "drones," Harris went on, "will take no pain" to uphold the good of the hive: "Why truly they must assuredly cundone and starve while the bees of foreign hives gather the hony." Harris, like Mandeville, compared the power of individual interest (here characterized as "pain" and articulated as the desire to avoid starvation) to the dronish duty of social elites like the directors of the African Company. For both, individual interest would gather more wealth ("hony") for society; that wealth would be better distributed within the society (to two hundred rather than twenty-five) and would better guarantee the state's national interest by preventing rival nations from collecting the wealth. Here was an ideological vision for the deregulated African trade that took the separate traders beyond their 1690s celebration of the right to oppose monopoly to an acclamation of deregulated trade as the handmaiden for an open, rich, and powerful society. In his application of this vision to the Africa trade dispute, Harris preempted the company riposte of self-interestedness by declaring, "The managers of all company[ies] have their own ends and private designs before the good of the whole or the nation, not taking the pains in trade as private person do who have no thoughts but of making good voyages for themselves and their country."[18]

The Board of Trade inquiries compelled Charles Davenant to begin pamphleteering against the separate traders in early 1709. He would develop a sharp critique of the Harris position that was infused with "Country" ideology—the view that self-interested commercial activity erodes society's traditional lifeblood and virtue and, if unregulated, could compromise the freedom of the state by making it vulnerable to outside attack. Railing against the celebration of individual, vicious interest that was the prime mover in Harris's hive, Davenant offered, in classical terms: "The general good of mankind being the great end of all government, the humours, liberties, yea, and private interests too, of particular persons, must always yield and give way to the common safety and general interest of the whole system of rationals." For Davenant, as for African Company apologists before him, the trade ought to

18. Richard Harris to Board of Trade, [December 1707?], Colonial Office (CO) 388/11, no. 16, National Archives, Kew.

be managed for the good of the state and the whole, not to advance the selfish interests of individuals or colonial cliques. The national interest, they believed, was the province of the state, especially so in the context of international competition for trade. Company pamphleteers therefore invoked the national interest to gain state approval for their proposals and to deflect accusations that their concerns did not extend beyond their own self-interest.[19]

Unlike his predecessors, Davenant made explicit precisely how this state-sponsored trading entity would work. He compared the African trade to a state whose "constitution" ought to be perfected. And the correct constitution for such a state enfranchised all members of the social elite. He deftly avoided the thorny issue of the source of the state's legitimacy—the people. As a civic humanist, Davenant loudly proclaimed the importance of parliamentary deliberation to the integrity of the state, but such views had already been appropriated by his opponents. For Davenant, the interests of the British state were far better advanced by a joint-stock monopoly company that could combine within its shareholders the expertise of merchants, landowners, policymakers, and officials than by a swirling mass of self-interested traders. Davenant summarized: "Any society of trade, consisting of a mixture of noblemen, gentlemen, and merchants, is much more likely to answer the ends of an united and joint management, in matters of trade, than if it consisted of merchants only." As a permanent body, this pool of expertise could be securely conveyed between generations.[20]

Davenant supported a public utility model of the company that produced slaves according to demand, exported sufficient British goods to maintain employment, and extended generous credit to the colonists to develop the

---

19. Davenant, *Reflections*, 148. See also Paul Slack, "Material Progress and the Challenge of Affluence in Seventeenth-Century England," *Economic History Review*, LXII (2009), 583. Charles Davenant had been a lobbyist for the East India Company in the 1690s. He wrote *An Essay on the East-India-Trade* . . . (London, 1696) in which he espoused a conventional "balance of trade" argument, which celebrated the East India Company for ensuring that England exported more than it imported. Davenant developed these arguments in greater detail once he began to write in support of the African Company. Davenant had been overlooked a number of times for positions on the Board. He was repeatedly scathing of their activities, and their report about the African trade he dismissed as "political . . . computations" (96). For Davenant's preoccupation with national defense when writing about trading matters, see David A. G. Waddell, "The Career and Writings of Charles Davenant (1656–1714)" (D.Phil. thesis, University of Oxford, 1954), 163.

20. Davenant, *Reflections*, 140, 269. The inclusion of landowning elements within the Royal African Company's membership was often cited as an argument in favor of joint-stock organization; see *Proposals for Raising a New Company for Carrying on the Trades of Africa and the Spanish West-Indies, under the Title of the United Company* (London, 1709), 7. Andrea Finkelstein characterized Davenant's thought as "civic humanist" in *The Harmony and the Balance: An Intellectual History of Seventeenth-Century English Economic Thought* (Ann Arbor, Mich., 2000), 225.

plantations' export and import economies. To preempt the accusation that the extent of the company's uncollected debts in America confirmed the weakness of its position, Davenant portrayed the African Company as a sympathetic, public-spirited banker for the colonies and implied that the separate traders were too rapaciously self-interested to allow the development that the African Company's generous credit had produced in America:

> One substantial Creditor is always much more indulging, and encouraging to a Debtor, than an indefinite Number of several petty Creditors can be supposed to be; because each of these having different Views, as well as separate Interests do commonly strive who shall outdo the other in Diligence for recovering Payment . . . till they ruin the Common Debtor, and render him uncapable of doing Justice to either: Whereas, were he concern'd only with one Society of discreet Persons, they would, for their own Interest, have a generous and compassionate regard to his Circumstances; and, by a reasonable Forbearance, enable him to pay themselves; and to continue a Correspondence and Dealing with them; and to improve his own Plantation into the Bargain.[21]

Alongside his depiction of the company as a generous banker to the colonists, Davenant chose to focus his readers' attention on the company's sovereignty over its eastern Atlantic, African domain, rather than its West Indian markets. Davenant justified the company's monopoly with reference to its forts on the West African coast. These forts became the central focus of the African Company's appeals in Parliament. They would embody, so the African Company argued, the strength of the British state in view of the barbarous "Natives" and the ruthless representatives of European rivals who swarmed the coast of Africa. Interlopers, by definition, without "pre-concerted Rules of Management" could not convey any of the legitimating force of government to heathen peoples and, therefore, could not serve as a conductor for the "coercive power" of the state, as Davenant prescribed. The African Company's monopoly also allowed it to assert the interests of the British state against the intense competition of other European nations on the coast of Africa.[22]

21. [Davenant], *Essay on the East-India-Trade*, 7; Davenant, *Reflections*, 138, 144, 306. For Davenant's portrayal of the company as a kindly banker for the colonies, see [Charles Davenant], *Several Reasons Proving, That Our Trade to Africa, Cannot Be Preserved and Carried on Effectually by Any Other Method, Than That of a Considerable Joint-Stock, with Exclusive Privileges* ([London, 1710?]), 3. Earlier company pamphleteers had resented American opposition to the company in light of the generous credit that the company had extended to them: "That is it unjust to complain of that, as an injury, which they desired as a favour"; see *That the Trade to Affrica*, 5, 6.

22. Davenant, *Reflections*, 144, 239; for Davenant's fixation with the "coercive" power of the state, see 131. For "pre-concerted Rules of Management," see *A Memorial Touching the Nature and*

An African Company petition of January 20, 1709, noted that the "unbounded liberty" of the separate traders created a "divided interest" on the African coast that ruthless African vendors exploited to increase the price of slaves. Davenant suggested that this divided interest lessened the British state's effectiveness when competing on the African coast: "There is a Maxim of Policy which holds good among Companies for Trade, as well as Kingdoms and States; That where-ever any Power or Force is to be exercised, the more contracted and united that Power is, the more prevalent will be the Effects thereof." The African Company believed its restored monopoly would provide this contracted, united power.[23]

Between February and April 1709, a separate-trader pamphleteer took issue with several of Davenant's arguments in *Reflections*. The starkly contrasting interpretations of what best constituted the nation's interest that emerged from these dialogues helped to generate new ideological positions. These exchanges are worth quoting at length. In *Some Remarks on a Pamphlet, Call'd, Reflections,* the anonymous author replied to Davenant about "whether it is not for the Nation's Interest to carry on the Trade by excluding the separate Traders, and commit the Charge to a Collective Society" by asking his urban, trading audience in London "whether it is reasonable to shut up all the Linen-Drapers Shops between *Aldgate* and *Temple-Bar,* and commit the Charge of that Trade to one Person only." What would happen to the national economy if Parliament reduced the management of all of London's clothing retailers to a single organization? By the same logic, what effect would the African Company's monopoly have on the British Atlantic economy as a whole?[24]

Davenant responded in part 3 of *Reflections* by driving a wedge between the separate traders' and the company's conceptions of the national interest. For Davenant, the national interest was something upheld overseas. For the author of *Some Remarks,* the national interest referred to the collective economic opportunities of merchants within England. Davenant suggested that a properly constituted African trade should favor the projection of British power on the African coast over the development of the British economy at home: "Pray what affinity has the linnen-drapers shops between Aldgate and Temple-Bar to the nature and uncommon circumstances of the trade on the

---

State of the Trade to Africa (London, 1709?), 4. For the unsuitability of private individuals' managing trade with "Natives," see *A Few Remarks Proper to Be Regarded in the Establishment of the African Trade* ([London, 1709?]), 1; and *A Few Remarks upon the Royal African Company, in respect to Their Trade and Settlements* ([London], 1713), 2.

23. *Commons Journals,* XVI, 64; [Davenant], *Several Reasons Proving,* 2.

24. *Some Remarks on a Pamphlet, Call'd, Reflections, on the Constitution and Management of the Trade to Africa . . .* ([London], 1709), 5.

coast of Africa? Have the French, Dutch, Danes, Brandenburghers and Portugueze any forts and castles between Aldgate and Temple-Bar?" It was essential for the British to maintain a united front against European trading rivals. For the author of *Some Remarks,* the African Company's interpretation of the national interest threatened Britain's true interest because it led the company to use its "coercive power" to oppress independent British traders and prevent them from generating the wealth that made Britain happy and powerful. He viewed the national interest in terms of the interest of the people, not the state. The African Company "hath committed to [its] Charge a sort of military Power over him [the separate trader], by means of Soldiers, Forts and Castles, etc., whereby he is enabled to oppress and abuse such his Fellow-Trader in what manner he pleases, and hinder him from trading, tho he don't trade himself."[25]

This exchange demonstrates the widening gulf in the two sides' interpretations of the national interest. For the company, national interest was equivalent to state interest. For the separate traders, the interest of the state was inseparable from the interest of the people; only the people could determine the national interest. Here, then, was the beginning of a "neo-Roman" argument for slave-trade deregulation to match Davenant's civic humanist concern about the corrupting social effects of self-interest.

THROUGHOUT THE PAMPHLET debates of 1710 and 1711, the separate traders continued to develop their conception of the national interest, which drew on traditional antimonopoly rhetoric, the constitutional arguments of the 1690s, Richard Harris's hive analogy, and the wish of the author of *Some Remarks* that the trade be managed for the interests of the people, not those of the state. An important innovation was their effort to define the national interest with reference to breadth of participation in the trade rather than the strategic interests of the government overseas. This strategy responded to Davenant's humanist concern that celebrations of individual self-interest would undermine the liberty of the state; separate-trader writers emphasized that participation in trade would uphold Britain's liberty by expanding its economy and improving its military might. Freedom of trade was seen as the surest way to encourage imperial expansion and the discovery of new markets. They argued, in petitions and pamphlets, that naval frigates, financed by a buoyant national economy, would be far better at defending British interests on the African coast than the company's profligate forts. They also encouraged the accommodation of the colonial periphery and contested the supremacy of

---

25. Davenant, *Reflections,* 131, 260; *Some Remarks on a Pamphlet, Call'd, Reflections,* 28.

the royal prerogative as the absolute law of Britain's American dominions. In direct contrast to the African Company, which had connected royal patronage with the prosperity of the realm, the separate traders believed prosperity emanated from the aggregate enterprise of private merchants. This emanation entailed political manifestations of private interests that were separate from the crown's sovereign repository.[26]

To the supporters of deregulated trade, the African Company's monopoly represented the most pernicious species of state intervention in the economy. It undermined the national interest because it prevented breadth of participation in the African trade. In the separate traders' most dramatic invocations, the African Company's monopoly came to represent an engrosser of the entirety of a trade that Atlantic merchants increasingly regarded as inherently deregulated:

> To erect an *African* Company exclusive, is to subject the Trade of one half of the World, the Trade of *Africa* and *America*, and the Navigation depending thereon, to but one Person; which would prove a Monopoly, in every respect, the most grievous to the Subject of any in the worst of times, being effectually three Companies under one Denomination, a Woollen Manufacture Company at home, a Negroe Company in the Plantations; and in short, a general *West-India Company*, who would have the Power of laying what Excise they pleased on the Productions of our Plantations, consumed at home and abroad.[27]

For the separate traders, the national interest was the interest of each individual subject, regardless of their profession or where in the kingdom they lived. The 1707 Act of Union with Scotland and its codification of universal access to pillars of the English and Scottish economies within Britain encouraged the deployment of this rhetoric. Their notion of the national interest evolved from deliberations between government and interest groups, rather than from the state, and it focused on those who via taxation financed the government, rather than on the interests of the government itself. In essence, the separate traders understood the national interest in terms of the breadth of the benefits that would accrue to the national community of traders. The phrase "national interest" came to embody a mixture of concerns: full employment (in both the manufacturing and agricultural sectors), sufficient

---

26. For frigates as protectors of the African trade, see *A Letter from a Merchant in Bristol, Touching the Trade to Africa, as It Relates to the Out-Ports of Great Britain* ([London, 1711]), 1. For the encouragement of the colonial periphery, at least in the Atlantic, see [John Oldmixon], *The British Empire in America* . . . , 2 vols. (London, 1708), I, xxvii.

27. *The Case of the Separate Traders to Africa* . . . ([London? 1709]), 1–2.

national income to sustain military campaigns abroad, and, increasingly, the growth of the economy evenly spread across the kingdom. As one separate-trader petition put it on January 29, 1708, the trade ought to be managed in such a way "as may turn to the Advantage of the *British* Nation in general."[28]

With breadth of participation in trade, believed the separate traders, came a proportionate increase in the scale of the economy, and from a large economy came a strong state. The liberated slave trade would stimulate the economy as a whole because the economy would grow in proportion to the number of men involved in the trade. "As a Nations Riches consists in the Diffusiveness of them," wrote one pamphleteer, "so Trade, the Source of Riches, ought to be as extensive and diffusive."[29]

Defining the national interest as breadth of participation was, as indicated previously, a response to Davenant's arguments in *Reflections*. Separate-trader pamphleteers proved intellectually agile in co-opting the company's republican language for their own ends. One argued that open trade put the good of the national economy ahead of the interest of the individual merchant better than the African Company's monopoly: "When Trade is distributed into many separate Hands, it cannot answer each particular Man's private interest so much, as if he was the sole Proprietor of the Trade; but yet the Nation gains more by such a Distribution." As much as domination of their markets represented the ideal for independent traders, a deregulated trade would better advance the national interest as a whole.[30]

By 1711, the separate traders also began to express their support for the national interest by emphasizing the geographical breadth and diversity of their trading area, as opposed to the African Company's focus on London. Provincial cities were proving more successful at asserting themselves on the national political stage in this period. Petitions to Parliament from provincial towns and cities increased by a factor of twenty. The separate traders branded themselves the friends of the outports and the supporters of nonmetropolitan

---

28. "Petition of the Merchants and Planters, Separate Traders to Africa, Interested in, and Trading to the Plantations of Virginia and Maryland," Jan. 29, 1708, *Commons Journals*, XVI, 75. Daniel Defoe noted the separate traders' exploitation of some of the terms of the Act of Union; see *An Essay upon the Trade to Africa* . . . ([London], 1711), 48.

29. The conceptualization of a national economy was also assisted by political arithmetic and the compilation of national economic statistics. See Mary Poovey, *A History of the Modern Fact: Problems of Knowledge in the Sciences of Wealth and Society* (Chicago, 1998), 126. For the connection between broad participation in trade and trade expansion, see *A Letter to a Member of Parliament concerning the African Trade* (n.p., [1709?]), 3.

30. *An Answer to Several Pretended Arguments, Proving, That Our Trade to Africa Cannot be Preserved and Carried on Effectually by Any Other Method Than That of a Considerable Joint-Stock, with Exclusive Privileges* (n.p., [1710?]), 2.

trade. The African Company's monopoly was contrary to the national interest, they argued, because it prevented the economy outside London from developing. One pamphleteer complained, "Are not we of the Out-ports Fellow Subjects of *Great Britain?* Where are our Liberties?" Another worried, "But what availeth the so long desired Peace, if Trade is to be locked up [in London]"? According to the separate traders' conception of the national interest, taxation revenues derived from trade had helped to finance the nation's war with France, because that war enlarged and extended trading opportunities for all during peacetime. Such ideas received additional support from the perceived contribution the commercial economy made to the war effort during the Nine Years' War and the War of Spanish Succession. Apologists for a commercial society attributed England's hard-won victories to an abundance of trade. These wars helped to increase the social appeal of commercial activity and the ideology that supported it as more and more pamphleteers connected victory, and therefore liberty, to national wealth.³¹

The separate traders' focus on nonmetropolitan trade and the individual merchant as keys to advancing the national interest included extolling the honest provincial trader over and above the "monied" speculator of the nefarious capital. They worked hard to associate the African Company with the corrupt practices of "Stock-jobbing" financial speculators in the City of London. One pamphleteer referred to the company's political strategy as "Stock-jobbing Politicks" because he believed that the company lobbied to achieve short-term increases in its share price rather than to secure the interests of the nation as a whole. The separate traders also proposed to advance the interests of the ordinary provincial craftsman over the metropolitan dilettantes. The African Company, wrote another pamphleteer, discriminated against "the experienc'd Merchants of *Bristol* and the Outports, in favour of the Unskilled at *London*." The ingenuity of the ordinary trader far outweighed social rank, which the African Company persistently favored. One separate trader looked forward to a time when the coast of African was run by "Souldiers instead of Generals." The legislature would recognize the worthiness of their cause, believed the separate traders, because it articulated benefits to the population as a whole.³²

---

31. *A Letter from a Merchant in Bristol, Touching the Trade to Africa, as It Relates to the Out-Ports of Great Britain* (n.p., [1711?]), 2 ("Where are our Liberties?"); *The Case of the City of Bristol, and All the Outports, in respect to Trade, Especially to That of Africa* (n.p., [1713]), 2 ("Trade is to be locked up"); Slack, "Material Progress," *Econ. Hist. Rev.*, LXII (2009), 594. For the increase of provincial petitions, see Perry Gauci, *The Politics of Trade: The Overseas Merchant in State and Society, 1660–1720* (Oxford, 2001), 214–215.

32. *Reasons for Vesting the Settlements on the Coast of Africa in the Crown: and the Dangers of an Exclusive*

The separate traders buttressed their ambition to spread access to slave trading to all ranks of society with political tactics that involved broad support. At the beginning of the eighteenth century, political disputes increasingly resembled popularity contests. Moving with the times, the separate traders placed more value on the number of signatures on their petitions than the status of their signatories, in contrast to the African Company. Sensitive to their parliamentary audience, a pamphleteer warned that a revamped monopolistic Royal African Company could, as the East India Company had in the election of 1700–1701, "have such an Influence in many Burroughs of *England* in their Elections, that deserves Gentlemen's Consideration." The separate traders contrasted their popular mandate with the belief that a restored African Company monopoly would have the power to subvert political liberties.[33]

The African Company's pamphleteers disputed, as in earlier stages of the debate, the claims of the independent slave traders to represent the interests of the mass of ordinary traders. The company challenged the separate traders' claims about being representative of a large, burgeoning Atlantic market. They questioned whether free trade would necessarily enlarge the scale of Britain's slave trade. The company accurately stressed the oligarchic profile of the separate traders' elite political leadership, men like Sir Gilbert Heathcote, Robert Heysham, and Micajah Perry, to draw a contrast with the African Company's many hundreds of shareholders and creditors. A pro-company pamphleteer turned a separate-trader allegation on its head by arguing that a victory by the separate traders in the dispute would engross the African trade "in the hands of ten or twelve Separate Traders." Another suggested that the separate traders were a "set of Men, who suffer themselves to be led by the Caprice, Humour, and unaccountable Designs of Two or Three Persons" who displayed "gross Ignorance of the *African* Trade." And a third portrayed them as a group of "Arbitrary" oligarchs who were determined to engross the trade in a manner far in excess of the company.[34]

Company Demonstrated ([London, 1712]), 2 (Stock-jobbing Politicks"); *Some Remarks on a Pamphlet, Call'd, Reflections,* 31 ("Souldiers instead of Generals").

33. See Mark Knights, *Representation and Misrepresentation in Later Stuart Britain: Partisanship and Political Culture* (Oxford, 2005), 137. For emphasis on the importance of the "Publick," see *Considerations upon the Trade to Guinea* (London, 1708), 26. For the importance of appeasing the "people," see *The Case between the African Company and the People of England* ([London], 1698?). For the separate traders' scaremongering about the company's possible interference in elections, see *Reasons for Vesting the Settlements on the Coast of Africa in the Crown,* 3. For the East India Company, see Robert Walcott, "The East India Interest in the General Election of 1700–1701," *English Historical Review,* LXXII (1956), 223–239.

34. *The Case of the Royal African Company* ([London? 1710]), 3 ("hands of ten or twelve"); *In*

The separate traders' conception of the national interest as the interest of the people enabled them to depict the individual trader as the lifeblood of society whose political rights ought to be protected and upheld. With this idea, their post-1707 ideology closely resembled that advanced with reference to the constitution in the 1690s. As the second stage of debate waged on, the separate traders more frequently collapsed the right to pursue political means to assert their economic self-interest into that most elastic of all eighteenth-century motifs, "freedom."

The campaign to liberalize the slave trade thus became a cause that championed freedom over slavery. To rally their cause, the separate traders celebrated the right to trade as an inherent feature of the national character. One pamphleteer wrote, "Freedoms of trade . . . [are] the fundamental point of English liberty." "Liberty" continued to invoke the legal privilege of individuals and groups, whereas "freedom" shifted from an aggregated description of the national economy and of national autonomy to an individual right. More than a third of the parliamentary petitions seeking to deregulate the slave trade referred to the desire to have the trade "freed" or to the inherent right to "freedom" of trade. Separate traders depicted monopolies, as a result, as stains on the national character. Without any appreciation of the irony of the language, one pamphlet asserted that monopolies are "the Badges of a slavish People. . . . If this so beneficial a Trade was but freed from that Nest of Drones, the *African* Company, and Industry left at liberty farther to improve it, the Nation would quickly be convinced that nothing hitherto but an English Freedom has been wanting to extend the Trade."[35]

The separate traders therefore began to deploy both of the early modern conceptions of freedom: they continued to assert that Parliament was the arbiter of the national interest, and they fastened the cause of slave-trade escalation to the neo-Roman theory of free states. They applauded the potential that the parliamentary system provided for merchants to translate their political rights into enlarged economic opportunity for all and the part played by this enlarged opportunity in defending Britain's interests internationally. By 1710, the separate traders also began to celebrate their personal freedom to trade without the restraint proposed by a statute to support monopoly. They

---

Some Short Remarks, on Two Pamphlets Lately Printed; the One Entituled Considerations upon the Trade to Guinea; the Other Entituled Proposals for Raising a New Company, for Carrying on the Trades of Africa and the Spanish-West-Indies, under the Title of the United-Company ([London, 1709?]), 1 ("set of Men"); *The Unavoidable Consequences of a Trade to Africa, in a Regulated Company, as Proposed by the Separate Traders, Demonstrated* (n.p., [1712?]), 4 ("Arbitrary").

35. *An Abstract of Several Cases relating to the Trade to Africa* (n.p., [1714]), 3 ("freedoms of trade"); *Letter to a Member of Parliament*, 3 ("Badges of a slavish People").

thus naturalized the freedom to trade; deregulated trade (that is, one not governed by statute) became the default approach for the national economy.[36]

To blend these understandings of freedom and liberty, the separate traders noted how the removal of trading constraints for individual subjects would benefit the national economy as a whole. The individual right to access the economy had "Publick" connotations. This change invigorated the ideological challenge to monopoly trading companies. One Bristolian separate trader explained, "Of all Cases relating to the Publick, none is more destructive to the Subjects Liberty, and renders them more uneasy, than the Establishment of Monopolies in Trade, which were always esteem'd the greatest Badges of Slavery and Oppression." A proposal to regulate the national economy became subjected to the increasingly interchangeable interests of the "Subjects Liberty" and the "Publick." This interchangeability helped self-interested behavior receive the cultural endorsement of venerable constitutional language. The residual belief (upheld in public by Davenant and the African Company) that the pursuit of self-interest could have socially destabilizing effects obliged separate-trader pamphleteers to perpetrate an ingenious subterfuge: the social benefits of the ideology of interest would be expressed, unlike the national interest, with the help of that older political language—the language of the liberty of the subject.[37]

The campaign by the separate traders to enlarge the slave trade thus saw them blend several discrete ideological positions: the constitutional freedom to representation; the right to use politics in an interested way; the more abstract notion of freedom as the absence of legal constraint; and that great intellectual achievement of the eighteenth century, the belief that individual self-interest could benefit the economy as a whole. This blending of ideas provided the ultimate means of combining the separate traders' interests with their evolving ideology and their political tactics. Few lobbies examined and used the connections between these various expressions of freedom at the beginning of the eighteenth century more than the separate traders to Africa. Fewer still deployed arguments for freedom with such sophistication to achieve an enlargement of unfreedom on this scale.

BY 1711, the African Company's writers had begun to challenge the sincerity of the separate traders' liberty crusade. The company's pamphleteering apologists noted that the separate traders' rhetorical connection between liberty

---

36. For these differing conceptions of freedom and their rivalry, see Quentin Skinner, *Liberty before Liberalism* (Cambridge, 1998), 10, 17.

37. *Case of the City of Bristol*, 1.

and slave-trade escalation had "deceiv'd many well meaning persons" into supporting the cause of a deregulated slave trade. They characterized the separate traders' attachment to liberty as intoxication, referring to their having "taken their Swill of Liberty." Pamphleteers began to associate the separate traders' version of the trade with the social criticisms of commerce, which had earlier been voiced by the Society for the Reformation of Manners. The African Company helped to replace the seventeenth-century explanation for vice—luxury—with what would become the eighteenth century's equivalent—excess of liberty.[38]

For the African Company, liberty referred to the sanctity of property. Petitions repeatedly referred to the company's rights as a "body politick," especially during the parliamentary sessions in the spring of 1712, when the company came close to being dissolved. One apologist believed free trade would tyrannically dispossess the company of its property: "The company humbly conceive, they are purchasers, and that it's hard, their territories, so purchased and fortified at their immense charges, should be invaded and violated by their fellow-subjects, under the notion of free and open traders." Separate traders responded with examples of Parliament's intervening to compulsorily purchase property for the public good, a process one compared to the demolition of a private house to build a new street. For the company, its charter represented its property. And property was as exclusive for the company as the right to trade was universal for the separate traders. "If the Company have such Property," a company propagandist declared, "it must of Consequence be an Exclusive Property: for if it be common to all, it can be no Property." Property was, then, according to one Royal African Company formulation, antithetical to the widening of economic opportunity. A pamphleteer neatly summarized: "For, tho' Liberty and Property are very desirable Things, when they go Hand in Hand; yet 'tis hop'd that the one will never be indulged to destroy the other."[39]

---

38. *An Answer to the Reasons against an African Company Humbly Submitted* . . . (London, 1711), 23 ("well meaning persons"); Robert Bleau, *A Letter from One of the Royal African-Company's Chief Agents on the African Coasts* ([London? 1713]), 1 ("Swill of Liberty").

39. *The Case of the Royal African-Company and the Plantations* ([London, 1714]), 2. For the petitions, see *Commons Journals*, XVII, 181, 184. For the separate traders' comparison of the dissolution of the company to the tearing down of a private house to build a new street, see *A Second Letter to a Member of Parliament, Relating to the Settling the Trade to Africa* (n.p., [1710]), 1. See also *The Case of About One Thousand African-Creditors Now United with the Company, by Virtue of the Late Act of Parliament* (n.p., [1713]), 2; *Property Derived under Charters and Grants from the Crown of England, Not Inferior to Property Derived under Grants from the Subjects of England* ([London 1713?]); *Particulars Wherein the Bill for Laying the Trade to Africa Free and Open, Takes Away and Destroys the Property of the African-Company and Their Creditors, Now United by an Act Passed in the Last Session of Parliament* (n.p., [1713]), 1 ("Exclusive Property"); *Reasons against the Bill for the Better Improvement of the Trade to Africa, by Establishing a Regulated-Company* (n.p., [1709]), 1.

One pro–African Company author proposed to deconstruct the word "liberty" to discredit the separate traders as the harbingers of political chaos and promote the company as the backbone of an ordered, stable society. This author drew a distinction between natural and civil liberty. Natural liberty could have no practical relevance in a debate about the future organization of the slave trade because it

> is only another name for *Anarchy* and *Confusion,* and in such a sense the Arguments drawn from the Birth-right and Liberty of the Subject, plead equally against all the Corporations of *Great Britain* and against all Orders and Distinctions of Men, as against a Joint-Stock Constitution; which I hope no honest Member of any Society would think of, without Horror and Detestation.

The company apologist went on to illustrate how joint-stock monopoly companies would advance civil liberty and a harmonious society:

> But if by Liberty, be meant a *Civil Liberty,* such as is most agreeable to, and best adapted for promoting the Common Interests of the whole *Community,* then, I humbly conceive the Advocates for a Joint-Stock, are most truly and sincerely desirous of such a Liberty. For, if a new Joint-Stock be subscrib'd, as large as the Trade can bear, and all and every of her Majesty's Subjects of *Great Britain* and the Plantations, who shall or may be inclined to trade to *Africa,* be admitted to subscribe, or buy what share of that Common-Stock they think fit, and thereby be set upon an equal foot with all the rest of their fellow Subjects; and entitled to a share of the profits of the Trade, in proportion to their respective Adventures: I confess, I can see no reason to surmise, that such a Constitution would be in the least repugnant to the Civil Liberty of the Subject; nay, I hope I have already made it appear, that our Civil Rights and Liberty to the Trade cannot be preserved and secured, but by such a Joint-Stock Constitution.[40]

The separate traders' persistent claim to extend economic opportunity to the nation as a whole allowed the African Company to regroup around a vision of an ordered, harmonious society. The natural-law arguments that

---

40. See *Answer to the Reasons against an African Company,* 23–24. Eight of the thirteen nontrading separate traders who supported open trade in Parliament hailed from borough corporations, and all nine of those separate traders who sat in Parliament themselves represented borough corporations. Such men, however, vigorously denied that joint-stock organization of the Africa trade provided the best means to encourage "civil liberty" in this context. See also, for example, *An Answer to Several Pretended Arguments,* 2.

the separate traders advanced in favor of the escalation of the slave trade portrayed a large constituency who might benefit from deregulation. For the company, such arguments provided an opportunity to stress their ideological preference for an ordered, more humane society that promoted social responsibility:

> [Joint-stock monopoly companies] . . . have not only the Discoveries, Observations, and Experience of their Predecessors standing always upon Record before them, by a continued Series of journals, etc. (But as in the Body Natural) so even the weakest Member of such a Society may, in some respect or other, be made Useful to the common Interest of the whole Body Politick; yea and partake too, in some Measure, of the Knowledge, Understanding and Judgement of those other Members whom God has bless'd with a more than ordinary Portion thereof.

Here was an old, medieval argument for the corporation rehashed for a rapidly commercializing society. The company's monopoly would provide the glue to repair the social fracturing brought about by deregulated trade that the company depicted either as a Hobbesian nightmare or referenced, by 1714, as derivative of the "tales of . . . Mandevil." The company would also provide what Daniel Defoe repeatedly described as "Security" for the slave trade—that is, guarantees that the trade would continue regardless of prevailing trading conditions.[41]

By the final years of the Africa trade debates, before the complete deregulation of the slave trade, separate-trader pamphleteers disputed the African Company's accusations that an unregulated trade would create an uncertain, unreliable trade. They did so by articulating ideas that would become pillars of economic theory. One writer argued that free trade would offer a vent for every citizen's natural and insatiable desire to truck and barter. The market appeared as a system that operated with more certainty and more efficiency than a state-run trade. Individual interest would provide a more reliable basis for trade than state fiat.

> There can be no greater Security of the Continuance of any Branch of our Foreign Trade, than the absolute and everlasting necessity thereof, as is the Case of the Trade to *Africa*, by reason of its being founded

---

41. For the comparison with "the Body Natural," see [Charles Davenant], *Several Arguments Proving, That Our Trade to Africa, Cannot be Preserved and Carried on Effectually by Any Other Method, Than That of a Considerable Joint-Stock, with Exclusive Privileges* ([London, 1712]), 3. For "tales of . . . Mandevil," see *A Letter to a Separate Trader to Africa* ([London, 1714?]), 1. See Defoe on "Security," in *Review*, Feb. 22, 1709, 565–568.

on the Commutation of Cloths, and other Merchandize necessary to Human Life, for Gold, Negroes, Elephants Teeth, Dye-woods, and other useful Commodities produced in *Africa*. So that till Men cease to wear Clothes and rather chuse to go naked; till the Planters cease to cultivate their Lands, and rather chuse to starve; till Gold becomes out of Esteem, and Mankind cease to seek farther after it; till our Sheep cease to produce Wool, and our Poor chuse to perish rather than work; in short, till there is an end of all Commerce in the World, there is a greater Certainty of the Continuance and Security of our *African* Trade, than of any other Branch of foreign Trade whatever.[42]

A deregulated trade also allowed the market to induce competition between independent traders that produced important, national, public benefits. The political right to trade, and to lobby to guarantee that right, produced economic benefits. These benefits resulted from the free rein that deregulated trade offered to each individual trader's ingenuity and industry. One pamphleteer argued the African Company's monopoly power would inhibit its ability to innovate in the trade, whereas the "different Genius" of the independent slave traders

> will direct them daily to new Experiments for extending the Trade, who will thereby transmit down more Observations and Experiences than any one Body of Men can do going on in the same dull Track of their Predecessors, and wedded to their Errors perhaps for want of attempting new Experiences which might discover them.

Another separate trader added: "'Tis an undoubted Truth, that nothing conduces so much to the Increase of Trade, as Emulation among Traders; and to that Point chiefly we owe our greatest Discoveries and Improvements in Trade, which cannot be in an Exclusive Company, who have no Rivals."[43]

For these separate-trader pamphleteers, independent trade brought competition, which involved social emulation. This emulation would provide a surer means of transmitting trading expertise to participants in the British economy than any emphasis the company might place on "Discoveries, Ob-

---

42. *The Argument Touching Security Necessary to Be Given for Carrying on the African Trade, Demonstrated to Be Groundless and Ridiculous* (n.p., [1711?]), 1. See also *The African Company's Property to the Forts and Settlements in Guinea, Consider'd; and the Necessity of Establishing the Trade in a Regulated Company, Demonstrated* ([London, 1709?]), 1.

43. *An Answer to Several Pretended Arguments*, 4; *Reasons against Establishing an African Company at London, Exclusive to the Plantations, and All the Out-Ports, and Other Subjects of Great Britain* (n.p., [1711]), 2. Henry Martyn had used similar language in support of emulation in *Considerations upon the East-India Trade* (London, 1701), 165.

servations and Experience of their Predecessors standing always upon Record before them, by a continued Series of Journals." The separate traders proposed an adversarial model of social interaction as the best means to develop the national economy, one that contrasted directly with the African Company's hierarchical model.[44]

Daniel Defoe, on the other hand, insisted on a unified, controlled African trade. He argued, "The Effect of Rivals in Trade is always lessening the Trade first, then lessening the Profits by under-selling to ruin one another, and at last both are undone." Likewise for Thomas Phipps, another African Company pamphleteer and servant; security of property represented a surer encouragement of industry and growth than competition: "The Field that lies common for all People, is always begger'd and neglected, it is Property that incites Industry, and Perpetuity that gives Encouragement for Improvements for future Generations." The company's charter represented a public property that if dissolved would jeopardize the collective economic incentives and commercial expertise of the trading populace.[45]

For the separate traders, however, deregulated trade produced national economic and military benefits because it transferred responsibility for trade away from government and to "those animal Spirits, those Springs of Riches which have enabled us to spend 100 Millions for the sake of our Liberties, in a long and bloody War." The growing sense that a trader's desire to profit would guarantee the security of trade, that competition between traders was good for customers, and that the market would operate regardless of the state helped to make it easier for the state and for the public to countenance the separate traders' lobbying victory—the complete deregulation of the trade.[46]

THE SEPARATE TRADERS' ideological case for deregulation involved a public celebration of the Englishman's natural right to trade in slaves—a right

---

44. [Davenant], *Several Arguments*, 3. The argument that the African Company achieved some efficiencies by virtue of its superior retention and distribution of information, especially about customer preferences, has been made by historians; see Kwame Yeboa Daaku, *Trade and Politics on the Gold Coast, 1600-1720: A Study of the African Reaction to European Trade* (Oxford, 1970). See also Ann M. Carlos, Jennifer Key, and Jill L. Dupree, "Learning and the Creation of Stock-Market Institutions: Evidence from the Royal African and Hudson's Bay Companies, 1670-1700," *Journal of Economic History*, LVIII (1998), 318–344.

45. *Review*, Feb. 17, 1709, 557–560; *Mr. Phipps's Speech to a Committee of the Honourable House of Commons, concerning the African Trade, March the 27th 1712* (London, 1712), 12.

46. *Letter to a Member of Parliament* ("animal Spirits"), 3. See also *Mr. Phipps's Speech*, 4; [Pieter de la Court], *Extract of Divers Passages relating to Exclusive Joint-Stock Companies, Taken from Monsieur De Witt's Treatise of the True Interest and Political Maxims of Holland and West-Friesland, Published by the Authority of the States General, and Translated into English in the Year 1702* ([London, 1713?]), 3.

as inherent to being English as the rights to trial by jury and political representation. This right derived from a political tradition and a political language and had efficacy before economic thinking endorsed the macroeconomic effects of self-interested lobbying. Arguments in favor of free trade were typically advanced according to rights better characterized as political than economic, or they referred to unregulated trade as the English economy's state of nature, without espousing economic theory. For the separate traders, freedom primarily involved the political right to defend individual economic self-interest, which included the right to use politics to pursue a deregulated market. Supporters of free trade did not, on the whole, formulate arguments based upon the efficiency of unregulated markets. When such arguments were deployed, their authors intended them as justifications for deregulation after the fact. The separate traders achieved that deregulation by celebrating the natural and politically constituted right to trade, rather than the economic measures that came to recommend access to that right.

The African Company built its case for statutory endorsement around its suitability as a vessel for the coercive power of the British state against barbarous heathen Africans and ruthless European rivals. For its opponents, the African Company represented all that appeared outmoded and pernicious about the old political system. Breadth of participation in the economy, both geographically and socially, defined free trade and thus supported the national interest. The separate traders' fixation with the deliberative, public, popular definition of the national interest would endear their version of the trade to a parliamentary and extraparliamentary audience who would embrace the legislative vacuum that their persuasive political ideas and successful lobbying tactics would help produce.

Each side fixated on liberty when seeking to persuade the public of its legitimacy. For the separate traders, the liberty to trade would expand the economy and produce benefits for the nation as a whole. The political liberty to influence the British state's style of regulation via parliamentary lobbying was also important to their ideology (and their strategy). For the African Company, liberty meant the enjoyment of the full benefits of their property, their monopoly. This attempt to co-opt the separate traders' rhetoric suggests the extent to which the African Company's earlier arguments that its monopoly would provide a surer vehicle for the coercive power of the state had been discredited by the impressive enlargement of the African trade that the separate traders' political campaign had produced.

To match their largely Atlantic personnel, the separate traders began to formulate ideas that would become strongly associated with the British Atlantic context: the freedom to trade, the right to political representation to assert that freedom, the belief in market deregulation, and the unsuitability of monopolies for the Atlantic world market where they, so one separate trader put it, "hath crampd and crippled the Plantations in a grievouse manner." "It hath been a mere canker upon them, and hath eaten them out: it hath suck'd the marrow out of their bones."[47]

If the interests and ideas of the separate traders and the African Company are considered together, the differences between the two suggest an ideological bifurcation on West Indian (for the separate traders) and East Indian (for the African Company) lines. The African Company's fixation on the interests of the British state in Africa was the cornerstone of its justification for its joint-stock monopoly. Its mistaken belief that it had as much right to its charter territories as the separate traders had to their plantation houses forced separate traders to spell out the realities of Atlantic trade: "But supposing the Company's Title to the Land of *Africa* was as good as those of the Planters of *Barbadoes* or other Colonies, Do any of those Colonies hinder any Body from Trading there?" For the separate traders, the Atlantic was to be a mare liberum. Their Atlantic outlook and their distinctive association of Atlantic trade with deregulation also helped them to accommodate the East India Company into their vision of Britain's trading empire (in response to the African Company's apologists, who had been encouraged by the rising fortunes of the East Indian Company's monopoly after 1708):

> The Reason for doing the one [monopolizing the East India trade], is the true Reason for not doing the other [the African trade]; because the Exports to India being Bullion, and the Imports from thence consisting of such Commodities as very much interfere with the Manufactures of Great Britain, therefore such a Trade ought to be confined to but one Exporter and one Importer.... But in the African Trade, the Exports consisting of the Woollen and other Manufactures of Great Britain, and the Imports consisting of Gold, Elephants Teeth, and Hands absolutely necessary for raising the Productions of our Plantations, of much more Advantage to us than Gold or Silver, 'tis better, doubtless, to open such a Trade to ten thousand Exporters and Importers, than confine it to one Person or Company exclusive.[48]

47. One separate-trader pamphleteer noted how the Atlantic was a disproving ground for monopolies with reference to the Virginia Company; see *Observations on D. T's Considerations on the Trade to Africa, Humbly Offered to the Honourable House of Commons, Relating to the Bill Now before Them* (n.p., [1698]), 1. For "marrow out of their bones," see *Case between the African Company and the People of England*, 1.

48. *The Case of the National Traders to Africa* ([London? 1713]), 2, 3; *Case of the Separate Traders to*

The African Company's principal ideological faux pas was to mistake its West Indian customers for its African clients. It elected to treat its American customers and rivals with the same barbarism as its African vendors. But, unlike the African vendors and the East Indian Company's customer base in South Asia, the African Company's plantation customers enjoyed representation within the metropolitan political system, one that increasingly adjudicated how Britain's overseas economy was regulated. Institutional changes would ensure that these customers would seek and achieve revenge on the African Company by destroying its monopoly and expanding the scale of Britain's transatlantic slave trade. The African Company's ideological campaign failed because it could not reconcile its East Indian ideology with the West Indian ideology of its customers and competitors. The separate traders were able to disconnect their activities from the state, whereas the East India interlopers were bound ever tighter to the state by becoming a critical source of government finance. But this was as much a story of differing political strategies as one of contrasting ideological posturing.

Africa, 3 ("true Reason for not doing the other"). For the East India Company's closer relationship with the state, see Stern, *The Company-State,* 162.

FOUR

The Strategies
"As Witches Do the Devil"

Daniel Defoe left the public gallery of the House of Commons late on March 17, 1709. As he hurried past chamber porters whose pockets stretched with bribes, into the Court of Requests filled with tireless lobbyists, printers, petitioners, and beleaguered members of Parliament, and out into a cold Westminster evening, his reflections on the day began to anger him. What Defoe had observed, and at times recorded for his newspaper, *Review of the State of the British Nation,* about the political strategies of both sides in the Africa trade debates greatly concerned him. Throughout his coverage, Defoe supported the Royal African Company against the separate traders because the vicissitudes of a deregulated trade could not guarantee that the strategically important Africa trade would be continued regardless of trading conditions: "No Men; or Sett of Men in the Nation, ought to be trusted with, or engag'd in the Trade to *Africa,* but such as can give to this Kingdom a certain Security, that the Trade shall be preserv'd to the Nation."[1]

The African debates provided more for Defoe's journalistic antennae than a sectional conflict. They confirmed his worst fears about what the Glorious Revolution had done to English politics. The Africa trade debates, protracted since January 1690, dragged on for a further four sessions of Parliament. Defoe believed that their inconclusiveness indicated a new inadequacy in the political process. Participants in the dispute, Defoe declared, "seem to give over Disputing for Conviction of one another, and labour to possess other Men, with the Reasonableness of their respective Pretensions." Defoe believed that, in attempting to court popular support for a particular position, participants discarded the need to agree to a perfect solution; he went on about "the unhappy Custom of the Age, *viz.* Of appearing for or against, as Parties, Preju-

---

1. *Review of the State of the British Nation,* Feb. 22, 1709, 565–568 (quotation on 566). As with all aspects of the *Review,* Defoe's interest was steered by Robert Harley, an expert in the African Trade, who wished to see some important commercial and governmental role for the Royal African Company.

dices, Friendships, Examples, or Interests Guide us, rather than by the true Method of Enquiring into the Bottom of Things, and Impartially Judging, according to the Weight of their proper Merit." In other words, truth for Defoe existed independently of the opinions of those involved in the dispute. So often a champion of the people's importance to politics, Defoe had become concerned about the unsettling interventions of the mob when campaigning in favor of the Act of Union between England and Scotland, which was agreed in 1707. By the time of the Africa trade debates, Defoe argued that effective government would be undermined by the need to court the multitude. Parliamentary deliberation had sacrificed the ends of debate for the means. Defoe ended by expressing his "hope the Time may come again, when Men of Sense shall judge Things as they are, rather than as Men of Art would make them seem to be." By art, Defoe meant the art of political strategy.[2]

As he crossed Whitehall, Defoe encountered another Africa trade pundit, who, unlike Defoe, appeared "all in Joy." The man, whom Defoe did not name, began to boast about the achievement that day of a parliamentary resolution. This resolution supposed that a regulated company (one open to all traders on payment of a small membership fee) provided the best means to finance the African Company's forts. Defoe repeatedly objected to this idea because he believed that a regulated company could not ensure the "Security" of the Africa trade as effectively as a joint-stock monopoly company could. Defoe assumed that the man must be an opponent of the Royal African Company because the resolution favored the dissolution of the old joint-stock company and the formation of a new regulated company.[3]

Defoe's discovery that the man was an African Company supporter provided the most interesting insight of the day. Defoe continued, "Being inquisitive of the Reasons and Foundations of his Joy, he told me, because the Committee had resolv'd upon establishing that Trade just as the Company desir'd." Defoe expressed bemusement at this seeming contradiction. The man supported his statement by explaining that the House's resolution "determines for the Company's Proposal; for it is impossible, the separate Traders can offer any thing that can provide for the preserving the Trade by maintaining Forts and Castles." African Company supporters, so Defoe inferred, had engineered parliamentary resolutions that, if passed, would threaten the company's exis-

---

2. [Daniel Defoe], *An Essay upon the Trade to Africa* . . . (n.p., 1711), 3–4.
3. *Review*, Mar. 17, 1709, 605–607 (quotation on 605). A regulated African Company had been proposed as early as November 1680; see Records of the Royal African Company, Colonial Office (CO) 268/1, 81–87, National Archives, Kew.

tence. But such resolutions would also undermine the separate traders' position. As Defoe acknowledged, the separate traders' proposals could not gain parliamentary approval because they failed to support the African Company's forts, and therefore the interests of the British state and the security of the trade. Defoe's initial misidentification of the man suggests that Defoe believed the separate traders would welcome resolutions in favor of a regulated African Company. But, owing to the joyful man's declarations, Defoe began to understand the subtle mechanisms of the early-eighteenth-century British Parliament more fully and the effective lobbying strategies of interests within it.[4]

Had he encountered a separate-trader lobbyist on that evening, however, Defoe would have been confronted with the same joyful pleasure at the day's outcome. By 1711, he had come to comprehend the separate traders' lobbying strategy: "They car'd not whether the Parliament did any Thing or no, provided they did but delay the Company; for then they knew the Thing would fall into their Hands of Course, the Company not being able to stand of themselves, without some Act was passed in their Favour, which they had nothing to do but to prevent." The African Company required a statute in its favor to resurrect its monopolistic charter. The separate traders could operate freely in a legislative vacuum as soon as the act of 1698 expired, which it did in 1712. Their lobbying strategy of filibustering parliamentary deliberations worked to their advantage as long as they used parliamentary discussions to develop the impression of sincere and broad public enthusiasm for a deregulated trade. Defoe was familiar with this style of politicking. He had used the press during the "standing army" controversy in the late 1690s to influence parliamentary deliberations by creating the impression of public support for a disbanded military. What angered him about the separate traders' deployment of this political technique was their success in gathering support from what Defoe would characterize from 1708 as the hellish "legions" of the masses.[5]

But the separate traders' political strategy worked. Its success hinged upon political circumstances brought about by the constitutional changes of the late 1680s. Greater traction for public opinion in Parliament in the 1690s, Parliament's legislative supremacy over economic matters, and the increas-

---

4. *Review*, Mar. 17, 1709, 605–607 (quotations on 605).

5. [Defoe], *Essay upon the Trade to Africa*, 25. See also *A State of the Trade to Affrica and the Royall Affrican Company of England and of the Forts and Castles on the Coast of Guinea since anno 1671*, Stowe Manuscripts 9, 32, Huntington Library, San Marino, Calif., in which the anonymous author notes that the separate traders preferred to block African Company attempts to achieve a statute rather than promote their own legislative outcomes. For Defoe's use of "legions," see Daniel Defoe, *Legion's New Paper: Being a Second Memorial to the Gentlemen of a Late House of Commons* (London, 1702).

ing tendency of pamphleteers to associate economic benefits with deregulation all encouraged the separate traders to generate the impression of broad public support for independent slave trading, thus justifying parliamentary inaction and the complete deregulation of the trade. The Africa trade proceeded from 1712 according to a legislative vacuum engineered by a political strategy that fastened, in a pioneering way, core tenets of liberal politics—the importance of public deliberation and the people—with prophetic features of liberal economics—the belief that economies grow in the absence of state intervention. The separate traders' more acute understanding of the early-eighteenth-century legislative process allowed them to ensure that Britain's slave trade would proceed, from 1712, without any form of regulation by the British state.

Compared below are the political strategies of the separate traders and the African Company: their respective political actions, mediated by political ideologies and in response to changing political and constitutional circumstances, which sought to engineer regulatory outcomes to satisfy their different interests. The principal structural change in this period was parliamentary supremacy over state regulation of the national economy. Because the monopolistic African Company expressed the monarchical dominion and the separate traders expressed the use of parliamentary influence, the shift overwhelmingly favored the separate traders' campaign to deregulate the slave trade. Once the Africa trade debates began in Parliament from 1690, the separate traders appeared as a reactive interest group, one that had to respond to the flawed strategy of the company. The separate traders' strategy did not discourage parliamentary deliberation or public interest in the Africa trade dispute. By the early years of the eighteenth century, both factions worked hard to develop political support for their lobbies. On the contrary, the Africa trade dispute produced more petitions and more pamphlets than any other issue relating to overseas trade policy during the first quarter century after 1688. The length of the Africa trade deliberations (from 1690 to 1713) and the extent of public participation helped to discredit the company in the public's imagination and cement the idea that slave-trade deregulation represented the sense of the nation. The separate traders also used their public support and the scale of their expansive trade to generate political capital in the colonies, which enabled them to supplant the African Company's entrenched creditor power there and helped them to evade payment of the 10 percent duty the 1698 statute had imposed on the trade. From the changes to transatlantic lobbying to the nuances of statutory regulation, the separate traders exposed the difficulties that the company faced in attempting to adapt to a new political environment. Their superior appreciation of the new interdependence of political and economic interests would ensure that the slave trade would become one of the very first of Britain's overseas trades to be made free.[6]

THE SEPARATE TRADERS' political strategy was to cultivate the broadest base of public support possible and express that support in petitions to block the African Company's attempts to achieve statutory confirmation of its monopoly. Once the 1698 statute ended, they would lobby for parliamentary resolutions and support from the Board of Trade to develop public approval for the deregulated trade. This strategy aligned with their avowed ideology: that the national interest, as arbitrated by their primary constitutional friend, Parliament, was best defined by the participation of the populace, not by the ministry, the crown, or the state. Petitioning and lobbying in person were the perfect expressions of the constitutional right to protect free trade, which the separate traders often celebrated. They connected the publicly authorized legislative vacuum that precipitated free trade with a right to trade that they increasingly articulated as "natural"—and that reflected their broadly based interests.

From the early 1690s, the English legislative process became more responsive to the interests of an increasingly assertive constituency in the provinces and on the colonial periphery. Many on this periphery opposed the Royal African Company's monopoly. The increased use of petitions to record grievances and legitimize requests for parliamentary sanction thus saw the Royal African Company under siege from numerous interests cultivated by and sympathetic to the separate traders. The separate traders enjoyed the support at one time or another during the debates of forty different petitioning locations, whereas the company received support from just eleven. The separate traders obtained sixty-one petitions from the English provinces, compared to eleven for the company. Similarly, the Act of Union and the expectations it produced among Scottish commercial interests encouraged Scottish merchants to lobby Parliament when they believed the capital engrossed economic opportunity. Scottish boroughs submitted nine petitions against the company, citing that a monopolistically organized slave trade would contravene articles 4 and 21 of the Act of Union (which referred to the free-trade area that the union created and the ancient rights of Scottish boroughs). The separate traders' ideological commitment to satisfying the national interest

---

6. Comparably, the leather trade saw the presentation of more than 150 petitions from more than 100 different locations between 1697 and 1699 in their two-year campaign to have the leather duties repealed; see John Brewer, *The Sinews of Power: War, Money, and the English State, 1688-1783* (New York, 1989), 233.

TABLE 2. ORIGINS AND INCIDENCE OF PETITIONS DURING
THE AFRICA TRADE DEBATES, 1707–1713

1707–1708		1708–1709		1709–1710	
ST	RAC	ST	RAC	ST	RAC
Barbados		London	Barbados	London	Barbados
London		Exeter	London	Barbados	Nevis
Bristol		Chesapeake	Nevis	Dartmouth	London
Exeter		Montrose	Exeter	Bristol	
Birmingham		Edinburgh	Montserrat	Liverpool	
		Jamaica	Kidderminster	Exeter	
		Bristol		Birmingham	
		Birmingham		Plymouth	
		Dundee		Whitehaven	
		Whitehaven		Bridgewater	
		Inverness			
		Aberdeen			
		Liverpool			
		Chester			
		Taunton			
		Glasgow			
		Barbados			

Note: Petitions are in support of either the separate traders (ST) or the Royal African Company (RAC); petitions directly from the Royal African Company are not included. Each location appears in the order in which a petition from that location was submitted to Parliament. Multiple petitions from the same location in the same year are not included.

Sources: Journals of the House of Commons, I–LI (London, 1803), XV–XVII.

with breadth of participation, rather than through appeals to the state interest, as was the company's strategy, saw support for deregulated trade achieve a remarkably broad platform. They were committed to politicking and building a political constituency. Parliament had become the recognized champion of the national interest, and the separate traders understood the importance of matching the tone of their campaign, and its actions, with the vogue for parliamentary politics both inside and outside the chambers of Parliament.[7]

7. For the rising importance of petitioning, see David Zaret, "Petitions and the 'Invention' of Public Opinion in the English Revolution," *American Journal of Sociology,* CI (1996), 1497–1542. For the increased incidence of provincial petitions, see Perry Gauci, *The Politics of Trade: The Overseas Merchant in State and Society, 1660–1720* (Oxford, 2001), 214–215: "The twenty-fold increment in provincial petitioning in the reign of William is unmistakable proof that extra-London forces were striving hard to influence policy in the Commons, and this momentum was maintained in

1710–1711		1711–1712		1712–1713	
ST	RAC	ST	RAC	ST	RAC
Edinburgh	London	London	London	London	London
Scotland	Kidderminster	Barbados	Nevis	Bristol	
London		Bristol	Westbury	Ashburton	
Jamaica		Birmingham		Kingsbridge	
Birmingham		Liverpool		Crediton	
Bristol		Exeter		Modbury	
Liverpool		Minehead		Liverpool	
Exeter		Westbury		Lancaster	
Lyme Regis		Carolina		Birmingham	
Carolina					
Whitehaven					
Dartmouth					
Taunton					
Totnes					
Ashburton					
Minehead					
Plymouth					

The barrage of petitioning on behalf of the separate traders was partly cultivated by the separate traders' political leadership and partly sincere, spontaneous reaction to the African Company's attempts to achieve statutory support for its monopolistic charter. The separate traders appreciated the need

the succeeding reign." During the 1690s, the company received support from wool-producing areas such as Witney, Kidderminster, Shrewsbury, and from Montserrat. The separate traders benefited from petitions from Suffolk, Essex, London, Jamaica, Barbados, Hallamshire, Berkshire, Wiltshire, Southwark, Norwich, York, Gloucester, Devon, Virginia, Maryland, Plymouth, Bristol, Exeter, and Somerset. In the second stage of debate, the company received petitions from London, Exeter, Barbados, and Kidderminster, whereas the separate traders cultivated petitions from Jamaica, Barbados, the Leeward Islands, Bristol, Exeter, Devon, Birmingham, Virginia, Maryland, Wapping, Montross, Edinburgh, Dundee, London, Whitehaven, Inverness, Liverpool, Aberdeen, Chester, Glasgow, Dartmouth, Plymouth, Bridgewater, Lyme Regis, Carolina, Taunton, Totnes, Ashburton, Minehead, Westbury, Kingsbridge, Crediton, Modbury, and Lancaster.

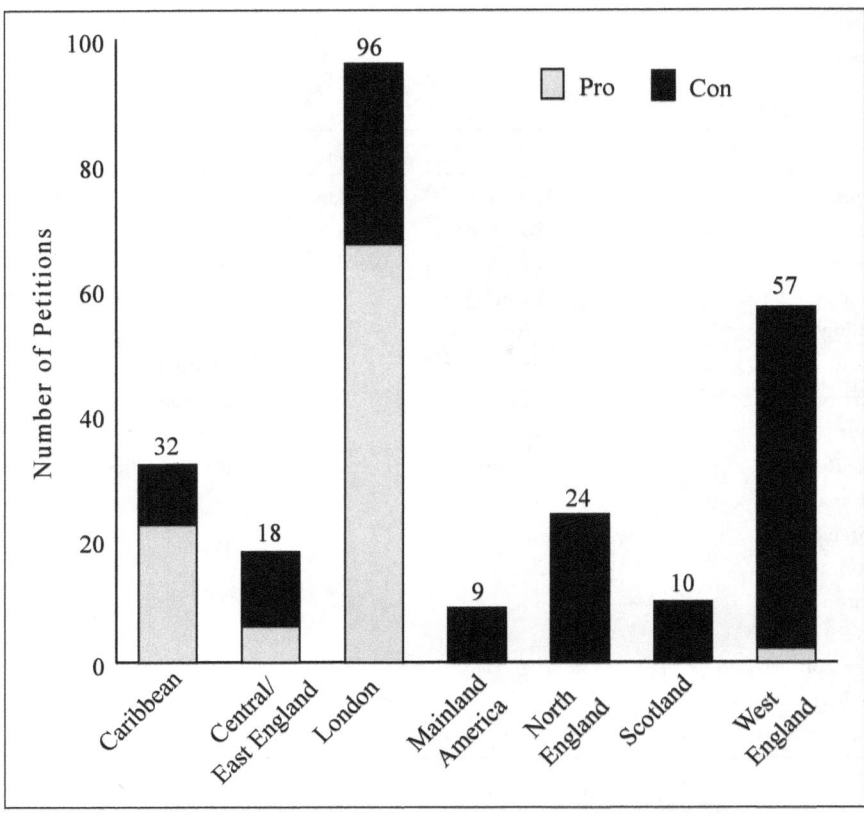

FIGURE 4. Petitions for and against the Royal African Company's Monopoly by Location during the Africa Trade Debates, 1690–1752. *Journals of the House of Commons,* I–LI (London, 1803), X–XII, XV–XVII, XIX, XXI, XXIV–XXVI; *Journals of the House of Lords* (London, 1767–1830), XVI, XIX.

to actively cultivate support in their political campaign. Unlike the African Company, they had no scruples about pursuing their own interests through political maneuvering. The mobilization of political support was good politics, the new politics, which, in turn, legitimated their interest as the public interest.

The separate traders' Westminster lobby also proved responsive to outside interests. Powerful mercantile groups, like the Bristol Society of Merchant Venturers, that were likely to resist attempts by metropolitan interests to represent them often sent their members to monitor the progress of the Africa trade debates. The Bristol Society provided the Bristol member of Parliament (MP), Joseph Earle, with "a butt of sherry wyne" to be distributed in Westminster to further the interests of the company's opponents. Provincial petitions purported to be responses to reports of African Company attempts to achieve a monopolizing statute. Local MPs often notified provincial interest groups of the African Company's activities in Parliament.⁸

Separate traders themselves often raised the alarm of monopoly in the provinces. The process of accruing provincial signatories for petitions reveals much about the delicately weighted balance of power between the cultivators of petitions and those who signed them. The Tory MP for Liverpool and a separate trader, William Clayton, gathered Liverpudlian signatories for a petition from his constituency before forwarding the petition to London, where he hoped still more people would sign. Jasper Mauditt, the company's agent in Liverpool, described that "their Member of Parliament have sent downe a Peticon to be Signed against the Company's proceedings in Parliament." A petition from Liverpool duly appeared before Parliament on February 11, 1709. Later that year, the Tory separate trader, Robert Heysham, the separate traders' parliamentary protagonist, wrote to provincial MPs, including Clayton, to arrange petitions supporting the deregulation of the slave trade. In late January 1709, Mauditt informed Africa House "that this post Mr Heysham has written to Captain Clayton to Get a petition from that Town against the Company." Heysham also wrote to several other MPs and obtained a petition from Chester in February 1709. His brother, William, had also supervised the collection of signatures for a Barbadian petition. Such lobbying helped the separate traders to recruit sympathetic MPs to their banner while gathering supportive petitions. It also saw their often national political networks assist in the achievement of a broad petitioning platform.⁹

The separate traders' independent support was essential for a good parliamentary reception because the larger the constituency of beneficiaries of free trade the more difficult it was for the African Company's pamphleteers to argue that the separate traders' movement served private interests. Such accusations, however, proved less of a problem because appeals to private interests could be connected to celebrations of the national interest and thus part of a legitimate justification for public redress.¹⁰

---

8. Jacob Reynardson to Royal African Company, Feb. 26, 1713, Treasury (T), 70/45, n.p., National Archives, Kew. See also Records of the Society of Merchant Venturers, Merchant Venturers Hall Books, Jan. 4, 1709, Nov. 10, 1713, Bristol Record Office.

9. Jasper Mauditt to Royal African Company, Jan. 28, 1709, T 70/9, n.p.; Mauditt to Royal African Company, [late January 1709], T 70/9, n.p. In the latter citation, Mauditt describes Clayton as Captain Clayton, his namesake, despite earlier referring to William Clayton the MP.

10. Charles Davenant, *Reflections upon the Constitution and Management of the African Trade, etc.*, in Charles Whitworth, ed., *The Political and Commercial Works of That Celebrated Writer Charles D'avenant, LL.D. . . .* , V (London, 1771), 130 (hereafter cited as Davenant, *Reflections*). See also Tim Keirn, "Parliament, Legislation, and the Regulation of English Textile Industries, 1689–1714," in

To match the breadth of interests of their petitioning support, the separate traders sought to ensure that each petition received broad endorsement. As with the growing importance of making a claim to influence policy based upon satisfying the national interest, this aspect of the separate traders' political strategy reflected the growing currency of proposals based upon the recorded involvement and interest of larger numbers of people. Although far from democratic, the reformed, late Stuart political system involved unprecedented participation levels. Parliamentary proposals benefited, as a result, from breadth of support. The separate traders valued the number of signatures over the social status of the signatories. Excluding the separate traders' own petitions, those petitions that supported free trade contained approximately eight thousand signatories, compared to the company's twenty-five hundred supporting their monopoly. The separate traders' political repertoire better suited the post-1688 political climate in which appeals to broadly based public opinion legitimized proposals for change.[11]

The African Company, on the other hand, concentrated on dragooning its own membership to support its campaign in Parliament. It preferred to author its own petitions than to gather support, fielding forty-four of its own petitions to the thirty it cultivated, whereas the separate traders sent only five petitions from under their own name. This was a deliberate strategy on the company's part, whose directors were ideologically opposed to the new, deliberative public politics, which they believed involved the worst kind of political trickery. The separate traders, they suspected, shanghaied signatories and imposed on provincial politicians. In February 1709, the company expressed surprise that a London merchant, Heysham, could have orchestrated Liverpool's MP Clayton to gather a petition from its corporation, "a thing very uncommon." The African Company observed the separate traders' cultivation of petitions with a suspicion that reflected their desire to rise above the fray of this new politics and that, in the end, limited their lobbying success. Awed by the separate traders' success as a mobilizing force, Daniel Defoe associated the separate traders' lobbying methods with a form of black magic. He watched with amazement "the Clamours of the Petitions which they have rais'd, *(as Witches do the Devil)* from the several Counties of *England,* and made the poor People say any Thing they bid them." The African Company's apologists revealed their superciliousness in believing petitioners—in this case dis-

---

Lee Davison et al., eds., *Stilling the Grumbling Hive: The Response to Social and Economic Problems in England, 1689-1750* (Stroud, 1992), 15.

11. See Mark Knights, *Representation and Misrepresentation in Later Stuart Britain: Partisanship and Political Culture* (Oxford, 2005), 5, 96, 137. These figures represent extrapolations from transcriptions of a series of petitions on the Africa trade debate preserved in T 70/175.

missively described as "poor People"—to be passive participants in the political system.¹²

Defoe's assertion that the separate traders manipulated those who submitted petitions from the provinces suggests that the African Company was especially keen to benefit from sincere and spontaneous petitions, again, to deflect charges of self-interest during parliamentary proceedings. The company's campaign to gather its own petitions disputes this claim. The African Company relied upon its provincial and colonial agents to gather signatories for its petitions. These interests typically needed persuading about the advantages of an Africa trade managed by joint stock. The company wrote letters and circulated pamphlets to colonial contacts to convince planters that it represented their concerns and suggested that planters send their own petitions to Parliament, because the company, unlike the separate traders, did not receive any spontaneous petitions from civic bodies. This strategy proved fruitless. The company began to send its own petitions, for which it hoped its colonial and provincial agents would gather signatures, but these officials often prioritized the "quality" of signatories—or the social status of those signing—over their quantity. One particular episode deserves note. In September 1709, the Royal African Company's agents in Barbados, Raynes Bate and Thomas Stewart, enclosed a petition "of the Best Characters and Estates in the Island and are now owners of 2//3 of the Land and Negroes." The agents went on to recount how the governor bowed to the interests of separate trader William Heysham and had his militia officers rally their "common soldiers" to sign a separate-trader petition that was "Kept out of Town and signed by Servants and Such." "Had we thought," they went on, "the number of hands and not the quality we could easily out done them . . . [and] could had all the sailors in the five men of war which are [not] in much better circumstances than [r]ough servants hardly a degrees above slaves." Bate and Stewart wished to lampoon the separate traders' desire to recruit as many people as possible to support the cause of a liberated slave trade to discredit them in the eyes of Parliament.¹³

Convinced of the importance of appearing to cultivate rather than coordinate petitions, a company official chastised one of its agents for failing to alter the text of a number of petitions, which, because of their similar wording,

---

12. *Review*, Mar. 22, 1712, 626–628; Royal African Company to Jasper Mauditt, Feb. 8, 1709, T 70/44, n.p. "The Petition of the Mayor, Aldermen . . . etc. of Liverpool" appeared in Parliament on Dec. 20, 1709. William Clayton's was the first signature on the petition. See T 70/175, 152.

13. Raynes Bate and Thomas Stewart to Royal African Company, Sept. 3, 1709, T 70/8, 95 ("of the Best Characters" and "common soldiers"); "Extract of a Letter from Messrs. Raynes Bate and Thomas Stewart, Dated Barbadoes, Sept. 1709," Sept. 3, 1709, Rawlinson Manuscripts, class A, no. 312, no. 5, 7, Bodleian Library, Oxford ("Had we thought").

appeared to lack sincerity. The letter explained, "We thank you for procuring hands to the address we rec'd bye captain foor and wish some small alterations had been in the words that it maight not have appeared to have been verbatim with that from Barbados." The texts of the separate-trader petitions from various locations reveal that they had no such compunction about encouraging diverse interests to subscribe to a centrally authored petition.[14]

To support further the impression of disinterested support, the great majority of the petitions that the African Company sent to the colonies to be signed did not explicitly support the company but, instead, argued that the 1698 act raised the prices of slaves and reduced their supply. A petition from Montserrat in February 1709 offers an example of one of these seemingly neutral petitions. It pointed out "that they have not, for several Years past, been sufficiently supplied with Negroes by the Royal *African* Company, and the separate Traders together, who have not imported above an Hundred in a Year" and pleaded "that the *British* Interest on the Coast of *Africa* may be preserved, and the Trade put on such a Foot, that a sufficient Number of negroes may be had, at moderate Rates." The company hoped that concentrating on the increasing prices of slaves since the liberation of the trade in 1698 (despite the extent of the company's involvement in this legislation) would be more help in bringing the supporters around to the company's cause than criticizing the separate traders directly.[15]

Although the Royal African Company put considerable energy into cultivating petitions, its requests fell largely on deaf ears. Its anachronistic determination to deflect accusations of self-interest led its management to author neutral petitions that shied away from making policy proposals and therefore, in the end, undermined the company's lobbying aims. Because the benefits of a deregulated slave trade could be deemed limitless and because the separate traders more directly cultivated provincial and colonial petitions, the separate traders enjoyed far more success as a petitioning lobby. The African Company's lobbying style impersonated, to some extent, the unilateralism of its absolutist creators, whereas the separate traders' more diffuse and flexible or-

---

14. Royal African Company to John Hussam, June 17, 1714, T 70/58, 501. See, for example, *Journals of the House of Commons*, I–LI (London, 1803), X, 456, 459 (hereafter cited as *Commons Journals*).

15. "A Petition of the Planters and Inhabitants of Her Majesty's Island and Colony of Mountserrat," Feb. 2, 1708, *Commons Journals*, XVI, 83. See also "Petition of the Planters and Inhabitants of Barbados," March 1708, T 70/58, 330; Royal African Company to John Stewart, Sept. 6, 1715, T 70/58, 549: "We are sorry the people of your island should not see their interest in signing such a petition as that sent in ours of the 14th December since that does ask for any thing but a right establishment of the trade without pointing expressly at the method."

ganization reflected the political decentralization that proved critical to their success in Parliament.

THE SEPARATE TRADERS' successful political strategy was even more apparent in the arena of transatlantic politics. They mounted a strategy that better understood and took advantage of the altered relationship between the mother country and the colonies brought about by the Glorious Revolution. Like the new political culture it produced in Britain, the revolution encouraged a more deliberative, consultative style to the imperial relationship. The reformed Board of Trade deferred the initiative for imperial policy to merchant practitioners, providing representatives of the deregulated Atlantic market, like the separate traders, with a louder and more influential political voice in Westminster.

The African Company had commanded considerable influence in the colonies from the 1670s onward. Company officials often held high political offices. From 1683 to 1686, for example, Edwyn Stede was governor of Barbados as well as the Royal African Company's agent on the island. Moreover, when, after 1688, the English state offered less direct support for the company in the colonies, the company turned to its colonial debts as a source of influence there. Since its creation, the African Company had provided slaves to colonists without receiving payments up front for those slaves. The extent of these debts (totaling £170,000 by 1691) and the threat of foreclosure on them coerced obedience from many American planters and became the means for company officials to entrench themselves within colonial government. In 1695, Governor Francis Russell of Barbados wrote:

> The Agents of the African Company carry such a sway here as almost to stop any proceeding, for if a man does not vote as they would wish for a Vestryman or Assemblyman they proceed against him for what he owes them for negroes. . . . If the African Company be continued I hope you will oblige them not to employ or countenance such men as principals, for if such be encouraged it must be the Company and not the King's Governor that will govern here. For although some will be honest, the majority will let interest carry the balance.

Less impartial commentators, such as the prominent independent slave trader Gilbert Heathcote, complained about the alignment of company and gubernatorial power to Robert Harley's parliamentary subcommittee charged with examining the Africa trade dispute in 1694: "By making the Governors of the Plantations (who are Judges of the Courts of Equity) their Factors for selling their Neggroes and recovering in their Debts, . . . no releife could be had ag't their Oppressions."[16]

Colonial interests, including Heathcote, thus began to cultivate particular MPs and petition the House of Commons to end the company's monopoly and creditor power. These petitions formed part of a broader colonial opposition against the company. During the 1690s, nineteen colonial petitions in favor of open trade were submitted, in contrast to the four received that explicitly favored monopoly. The company's parliamentary opponents specifically targeted its monopoly power using legislation, and they succeeded in inserting a clause into the 1698 Africa trade act that prevented those involved in the sale of slaves from holding public office or serving on colonial courts.[17]

This clause in the 1698 statute proved controversial. In a letter to the Board of Trade in February 1699, Governor William Beeston of Jamaica argued that this provision would greatly unsettle the colony and royal authority there because slave trading had been lucrative for so many with political ambitions and because government office brought comparably few benefits. Beeston's comment also speaks to the uncertain legal environment for the company's charter, despite the statutory support it received in 1698. The act

> has put us in such disorder that I see nothing to the contrary but that law and justice must cease among us, and by consequence his Majesty's authority, if there be no officers to support it, for severall have laid down already; and the rest when they please will make it an argument

---

16. Gilbert Heathcote, quoted in Elizabeth Donnan, ed., *Documents Illustrative of the History of the Slave Trade to America*, 4 vols. (Washington, D.C., 1930–1935), I, 158. See also "Representation of Gilbert Heathcote and John Gardner," Feb. 13, 1693, Harleian Manuscripts, 7310, 207, British Library, London. For details of the African Company's debts in the colonies, see Minutes of the General Court, T 70/101, n.p. The company recorded the levels of debts in the colonies in its annual report in January. For an example of a Royal African Company petition that referred to the company's public-spirited provision of credit to the colonies, see "Petition of the Inhabitants of Mountserrat," Mar. 19, 1697, *Commons Journals*, XII, 166. See also W. Noel Sainsbury et al., eds., *Calendar of State Papers, Colonial Series, America and West Indies* . . . , 44 vols. (London, 1860–1969) (hereafter cited as *CSPC*), XIV, no. 1930, 524–529; John Cary, *An Essay on the State of England in Relation to Its Trade, Its Poor, and Its Taxes, for Carrying on the Present War against France* (Bristol, 1695), 83. African Company officials noted that debtors would be a first port of call for company agents in the colonies collecting sympathetic signatories for company petitions to Parliament; see Royal African Company to Edward Parsons and Samuel Horne, Mar. 5, 1697, T 70/57, n.p.

17. *Commons Journals*, X–XII; *Journals of the House of Lords* (London, 1767–1830), XVI. See also Appendix 5. For the dissatisfaction of a London-based group of Atlantic merchants with the political and judicial positions held by the African Company's agents in the colonies, see Egerton Family Papers, MssEL 9610, 1, Huntington Library, San Marino, Calif. This manuscript copy was printed as *Amendments Humbly Proposed to the Bill, for Settling the Trade to Africa, with the Reasons Thereof* (n.p., [1698]).

that they serve those offices for no reward, and therefore not knowing how soon their friends in England may concern them in a ship of Negroes they will not part with that which may be a profit, for that which they are sure is none, but trouble and charge; besides it frightens them all that an information shall lye against them in Westminster hall, where any envious people may informe against them, and judgement be given before they know anything of it.

The Board of Trade informed Beeston that "other plantations do think it no inconvenience but rather an advantage to them." The agents for Barbados had written to the Board in the same year praising the act's provisions because the island had experienced public officials' using their office to advance their vested interests. Beeston confirmed that the act forced officials from their positions, although he did not specify whether these officials supported the company or deregulated trade. Raynes Bate, the company's agent in Barbados, where the company enjoyed a brisk trade, stepped down from the island's council. Bate mourned his resignation and explained that he had sought public office solely to further the company's interests. Bate believed that the African Company's future depended upon its entrenchment in colonial government.[18]

The separate traders, however, who were also subject to the act's prescriptions, held onto their offices and used them to prevent the African Company from expanding its support. In 1700, government officers in Barbados who supported the separate traders or wished simply to avoid settling their debts to the African Company minimized the frequency and duration of court sittings to prevent the company from pursuing its debtors. The company's inability to collect the huge debts owed to it by colonial planters became a political liability rather than a source of political power as it had been before 1698. The independent slave traders' strategy of separating slave trading from judicial responsibility undermined the African Company's pseudopublic credentials and helped cut off some of its political life support, forever altering its power in the colonies. With their creditor power now severely constrained and recognizing the extent of colonial support for the separate traders during the first phase of parliamentary consideration in the 1690s, the African Company sought to improve its profile in the colonies by courting (as opposed to compelling) colonial support.[19]

18. Sir William Beeston to Board of Trade, Feb. 20, 1699, Board of Trade's response to Beeston, Oct. 12, 1699, Jamaica Entry Books, CO 138/9, n.p. See also "Letter from Barbados Agents to the Board of Trade," Oct. 11, 1699, Barbados Entry Books, CO 29/6, 342–344.
19. King William III to Barbados, Apr. 8, 1700, T 70/170, 24.

The company began to develop a transatlantic base by gathering influential spokesmen for the plantation interest to its cause. Around the time of the 1698 legislation, the company appears to have turned Dalby Thomas, an articulate spokesman for the plantation interest, from the "chiefe manager" of the independent slave traders' lobby to the African Company's chief agent on the African coast. Company directors also elected Thomas Pindar as deputy governor from 1703 to 1710 (with stints as subgovernor from 1705 to 1706). Pindar was one of only a few Atlantic merchants represented in the directorate of the company, and his appointment, alongside that of Dalby Thomas, records the company's strategy to improve its understanding of colonial affairs so that it could better solicit support from its transatlantic customer base. In March 1706, the company wrote to Robert Davers, an influential parliamentary spokesman on colonial affairs and a powerful representative for Barbados in London, and enclosed a pamphlet. It hoped that Davers would include extracts from it in his next letter to Barbados

> to indeavour to influence your friends to consider the necessity of finding out some expedient to prevent the continuance of the heavy burthen that lies upon the plantations by the extravagant prices of Negroes which cannot be otherwise whilst they are so extravagantly dear upon the coast whereby the whole advantage arises to the natives of Guinea and the sole prejudice to her majesties subjects and most especially those of the plantations.

Davers, however, chose to serve the interests of the separate traders in Parliament.[20]

The separate traders' transatlantic power grew stronger, however, as the second stage of debate commenced in 1707. Their cause received the persistent endorsement of the Board of Trade because the separate traders understood the predilections of that body toward the interests of deregulated trade. As an information-gathering, deliberative body that reported to Parliament (and responded to the same styles of lobbying), the Board of Trade relied on the opinion of independent merchants with Atlantic connections, exemplified by the separate traders, when formulating its policy for the Atlantic, including its policy for the management of the slave trade. The Board and the

20. Royal African Company to Sir Robert Davers, Mar. 28, 1706, T 70/44. The details about Thomas Pindar's service to the Royal African Company are derived from Minutes of the General Court, T 70/101, n.p. Other Atlantic merchants interested in the directorate of the Royal African Company included Robert Bristow, James Gohier, Sir Jeffrey Jefferies, Colonel Joseph Jorey, and Colonel Charles Long. See, for Bristow, CO 5/1313, no. 4; for Gohier, CO 28/12, no. 16; for Jefferies, CO 5/1314, no. 56; for Long, CO 137/10, no. 20.

African Company, on the other hand, had a rather dysfunctional relationship. They clashed as two different impersonations of transatlantic imperial policy: the Board was deliberative and accommodating of colonial testimony; the company was either coercive or dismissive of colonial testimony and, by the second stage of the Africa trade debates, almost inactive in transatlantic trade.

Separate traders with transatlantic interests understood the new Board of Trade's reliance on mercantile opinion presented an opportunity to further their interests, and they used every opportunity to push their agenda, for example, when asked by the Board to comment on tobacco trading. In November 1707, after discussing an act relating to the gauge of tobacco hogsheads, the Board's commissioners diverted the conversation to the slave trade and asked tobacco merchants Micajah Perry and Isaac Milner for their opinion on how that trade should be continued. Perry and Milner replied, "The separate traders . . . furnished . . . above 800 negroes annually, since the passing the late Act, and . . . the company had sent none to Virginia or Maryland since, nor seaven years before." They added that "the separate traders . . . paid to the company . . . more by the ten percent than the . . . company have laid . . . upon their forts . . . [and they] have received all the discouragement imaginable from the company's factors there." Although the Board's commissioners scrutinized such testimony, this exchange provides an excellent example of the Board's reliance on Atlantic merchant opinion as well as the political value of the separate traders' commercial range. Like many other Atlantic merchants, both Perry and Milner also operated as separate traders. Such men answered the Board's call for colonial expertise with opinion grounded both politically and commercially in personal interest.[21]

The African Company could not influence the Board of Trade in this way. Its formal association with the coast of Africa and the narrower commercial reach of its directors restricted the opportunities for them to shunt a pro-company argument into a broader discussion of overseas trade. The company's pseudostate authority (or, by 1707, aspiration) also saw it clash with

---

21. *Journal of the Commissioners for Trade and Plantations* . . . , 14 vols. (London, 1920–1938), I, 430. The first report in favor of the separate traders showed a particularly strong influence from the tobacco interest: "The greatest part of the Negroes furnished to Virginia, Maryland, Carolina and New York has been by the Separate Traders, and that not above two Hundred have been sent to those Parts by the Company since their Establishment. Which not having been contradicted by the Company We must observe upon it that those Plantations so profitably supplyd by the Separate Traders, near one halfe of the Tobacco cou'd not have been produced and brought hither, and that much that would have lessen'd her Majesty's Customs and the Navigation of this Kingdom We need not mention" (CO 390/12, 172–282). These conclusions reached the Board's report before the receipt of any testimony from the Chesapeake, suggesting again that tobacco merchants resident in England exerted considerable influence over the Board.

the Board's jurisdiction. The Board's commissioners looked on the company's directors with political and constitutional distaste. Most important, the dwindling commercial interest of the company in the Atlantic made them less relevant as merchant practitioners than the separate traders. By 1708, the African Company understood the Board's tendency to rely on information provided by independent, Atlantic merchants and pleaded with the Board: "The Company humbly hope their Lordships will not incourage any Persons that are utter Enemies to them and their Trade maliciously to misrepresent them." The company, it seemed, suspected a bad press from Atlantic interests. Their fears were to be realized.[22]

The Board's transatlantic inquiry into the workings of the slave trade in spring 1708 provides further evidence of the strength and sophistication of the separate traders' transatlantic lobbying. The inquiry placed colonial evidence at the heart of the dispute and explicitly highlighted the slave trade as more important to the African trade than the export of English manufactures. Both emphases favored the separate traders. Even before the results had been gathered, the inquiry represented a blow for the Royal African Company because the company preferred to focus the public's attention on the coast of Africa, where it could more easily make the case for its forts and thus for a joint-stock organization of the African trade. In short, the Board's inquiry forced the company to account for its activities against West Indian criteria rather than its suitability as a representative of the British state on the African coast.

Appreciating the extent of the separate traders' support in the colonies and at last understanding how important willing as opposed to coerced support was to the parliamentary audience for the Africa trade debates, the African Company responded to the Board's inquiry by intensifying its efforts to cultivate colonial support. As with the company's responses to the separate traders' ideological case for deregulation, its effort to emulate the separate traders' lobbying strategies proved the power of those strategies. In March and April 1708, Thomas Pindar commissioned several pamphlets to be written, printed, and circulated throughout London, the provinces, and the colonies. He wrote a letter to accompany the pamphlets as part of the company's attempts to compete with the separate traders' transatlantic propaganda machine and prevent them from increasing their foothold in the colonies. In it he declared:

22. Charles Davenant's responses to the Board of Trade's 1708 report are contained in [Davenant], "Some General Observations and Particular Remarks on the Report Made by the Lords Commissioners for Trade and Plantations the 3rd February, 1708 Touching the Contents of the Royal African Company's Peticion to Referred to them by her Majesty," T 70/175, 87–96.

> It is supposed the Enemys to the Company may have sent to your Colonyes the Scurrilous and false Pamphlets they distributed and they have the vain expectation and hopes to prevail on your Planters that they will joyn with them to prevent the Company as being further able to support the interest they have gained. . . . I am of the opinion the same Persons will give the same unreasonable obstructions the next as in the last Parliament and that it will be difficult to preserve this Trade unless the Plantations make application that it may be done.

Pindar's assessment went beyond the metropolitan expectation that colonists should intervene in the formulation of imperial policy to the assertion that colonial input would be critical if Parliament was to resolve the Africa trade debates.[23]

Pindar's letter, which was circulated to Nevis, Montserrat, Jamaica, Barbados, and Virginia, summarized the sensitivities of the company's potential Atlantic constituency. Pindar listed the beneficial effects for the colonies that a parliamentary establishment of the Royal African Company would have on the trade: African traders would be brought back under the control of the company's forts, and slaves would be both cheaper and healthier. He contrasted this situation with the consequences of the Royal African Company's failure to achieve a statute in support of its monopoly: increased slave prices, with the "natives" controlling quality as well as price, and other European nations' taking control of the forts. In short, a separate-trader victory would "be the occation of great Scarcity of Negroes in the Plantations, and of their extravagant high prices and be so much discouragement to their Planters and Inhabitants, as will in all probability reduce their flourishing Estates in a few yeares to a Very inconsiderable Vallue." Pindar saved his most frightening portent for last: the Dutch using a foothold in Africa to undercut the British West

---

23. The pamphlets that Thomas Pindar circulated around the colonies in April 1708 were "Considerations of the Late Act for Settling the Trade to Africa" (published as *Some Considerations on the Late Act of Parliament, for Setling the Trade to Africa* [(London, 1709)]); "The British Interests on the Coast of Africa" (published as *The British Interest on the Coast of Africa Consider'd, with the Interest of Other Europeans, and the Politicks They Used for Carrying on That Trade* [(London, 1708)]); "The Falsities of the Private Traders" (published as *The Falsities of Private Traders to Africa Discover'd . . .* [(London, 1708)]); and "The Political Arithmetick of the Private Traders Deteacted" (published as *The Scandalous Political Arithmetick [as They Term It] of the Private Traders Detected* [(London? 1708?)]). Thirty of each were printed for Barbados, twenty for Antigua, ten for Montserrat, twenty for Nevis, ten for Saint Christopher, twenty to Jamaica, and thirty for Virginia. The African Company financed the printing of three hundred documents in total. See T 70/58, loose fragment, 167. For Pindar's quote, see Royal African Company to Gawin Corbin et al., Apr. 20, 1708, T 70/58, 333. Pindar is mentioned as a merchant with an interest in the trade to the Leeward Islands in *Journal of the Commissioners for Trade and Plantations*, I, 548.

Indian plantations, despite the British company's own concerted and continuing attempts to establish these operations:

> The Climate being proper for Sugars, Indigo, Cotton and Ginger, and the Dutch once gaining the Possession of the Country will have the Natives under their direction and ground for nothing and may soone make Considerable Colonies there, by the multitude of hands and import to all Europe sufficient quantities of those Goods at much lower prices, than can be afforded from the British Plantations, none of which can be done provided there be a Brittish Company with a Joint Stock able to maintain an Equall Power on the Coast with them.

The deputy governor ended by shrewdly asserting that he had more interest in the colonies than he did in the company. Pindar's strategy reflects the company's new belief that it was better to defer to colonial interests than to domineer them. At the same time, he maintained the African Company's traditional concern to appear public-spirited: "With regard to the Publick good of the Islands in which I shall injoy a much greater proportion of advantage than from the small Concern I have in the company which allso Considered, may remove the Jealousy of every person from suggesting that my private interest in the Company does in any degree byass me against the publick good." Pindar's bid to court colonial support would fail as the last vestiges of the company's creditor power were eroded by the 1698 act and by an impressive power grab by the separate traders in the colonies.[24]

The restarting of public deliberations about the future of the company appears to have compelled a further round of enforcement of the 1698 act's provision that slave trading be separated from government or judicial office. Many company supporters in the colonies resigned their offices, believing a position with the African Company either superior to or the equivalent of public office. As mentioned previously, the company's factor in Barbados, Raynes Bate, had resigned from his position on the council in 1707. In Jamaica, Colonel Peter Beckford resigned his factorage to sustain his council position but assured his African Company correspondents that he would "on all occasions promote the Company's Interest in that Island." That the African trade debates led to stricter enforcement of this aspect of the 1698 act is evidence of the separate traders' desire to isolate the African Company from political power in the colonies to prevent what company apologists, such as Charles Davenant, wished to see—the trade operating with the state's coercive power.[25]

---

24. Royal African Company to Corbin et al., Apr. 20, 1708, T 70/58, 334.
25. Bate to Royal African Company, Aug. 6, 1707, T 70/8, 47: "The . . . council having made

If the company's political power had waned in the colonies by 1708, some haughtiness remained alongside a constitutional suspicion of the Board and a disdain for gubernatorial power. When Daniel Parke, the governor of the Leeward Islands, had approached Edward Chester, the company's factor on Antigua, about the Board's inquiry, Chester offered

> proud Answer that he had no orders from the Royall Company to obey my orders. . . . I told him what orders I had, he said he had nothing to Do with the Committee for Trade. I told him he was very Impertinent, and in Returne he told me he would not change his Post for mine, for that he got twice as much mony, and had less to do, and was not obliged to the fateigue of goeing from Island to Island.

Chester's dismissal of the authority of the "Committee for Trade" in favor of the "Royall Company" records one influential figure's perception of the political resources that the company pretended to in the West Indies compared with the limited power of the more recently formed, though explicitly state-sponsored, Board of Trade. The two organizations competed in Chester's mind and in reality as alternative versions of metropolitan-sanctioned state authority.[26]

Chester's truculence might also suggest the political frustrations and sensitivities brought by his employers' diminishing market share of the trade in enslaved Africans. The stipulations of the 1698 act to create a conflict of interest between good government and slave trading proved to be a highly effective tactic for the separate traders. It lessened the company's creditor power and provided vacant political positions from which the separate traders could develop and exploit their own creditor power. Combined with the 1698 act's more dramatic effect—the growth it produced in independent slave trading—the separate traders' improved market share eclipsed the company politically in the colonies.

By 1708, the separate traders used this political influence in the colonies to intimidate potential supporters of the company. Separate traders on Nevis prevented the Royal African Company from petitioning against them because

---

exceptions against his being of the council because of the Act to settle the trade to Africa which forbids any agent of the company to be judge in any court which they of the council are and his design in being of the council being to serve the company he has wholly quitted those thoughts and promises to apply his time wholly to the company's service." For Peter Beckford, see Colonel Beckford to Royal African Company, July 11, 1709, T 70/8, 94. See also Davenant, *Reflections*, 306.

26. For Chester's disputes with Parke, see Donnan, ed., *Documents*, II, 46. See also Philip J. Stern, "'A Politie of Civill and Military Power'": Political Thought and the Late Seventeenth-Century Foundations of the East India Company-State," *Journal of British Studies*, XLVII (2008), 253–283.

several separate traders held council positions. In 1709, when the company approached Virginian tobacco planters for support, its agent, Gawin Corbin, claimed that planters refused to sign any public petitions for fear of offending their merchant creditors, many of whom operated as separate traders—including, most notably, Micajah Perry and Isaac Milner—or the powerful anticompany faction in the colony's legislature. Corbin recounted, "Cannot get a Petition to the Parliament the people being afraid (through fear or ignorance) to put their hands to any thing that may appear in publick."[27]

The separate traders' creditor power in Barbados was even more conspicuous. William Heysham had served as an African Company agent on Barbados from 1695 until 1700. Heysham switched the creditor power of the company for that of his own commission business (which he shared with his brother, Robert). William would use the scale of his commission business to command the allegiance of the governor of Barbados to the separate traders' cause. In September 1709, company agents noted that Heysham had disabused Governor Mitford Crowe of his pro-company sympathies and compelled him to force the militia to sign a petition in support of the separate traders: "The Officers of the Militia who were put in by the Governor (who is wholly in Mr Heysham's Interest and Never a favourer of the Company's) have obliged their Serjeants and Common Soldiers to sign a Petition against the Company." William also used his political capital to sidestep colonial officers charged with collecting the 10 percent duty on behalf of the African Company. According to a disinterested contemporary, "The Heyshams, both Parliament men for Lancaster town, had defrauded the companie of at least £80,000." For once, the African Company's political methods were adopted by the separate traders, rather than the other way around.[28]

---

27. For Nevis, see John Hussam to Royal African Company, Aug. 19, 1708, T 70/8, 99: "Advising of the Readiness of the Inhabitants of that Island to Sign a Petition in favour of a Joynte Stock Company has a petition from them, and could have had one from the Governor's Council and Assembly had it not been for 3 Separate Traders who are of the Councill." See also Corbin to Royal African Company, Sept. 14, 1709, T 70/8, 97. Micajah Perry, the unofficial leader of England's tobacco industry, assembled African cargoes in 1702, 1704, and 1707; see T 70/1198.

28. "Extract of a Letter from Messrs. Raynes Bate and Thomas Stewart," Sept. 3, 1709, Rawlinson MSS, class A, no. 312, no. 5, 7. The Royal African Company's agents also alleged that William Heysham withheld records of the slave trade to Barbados during his tenure to prevent the company from calling in its debts (Bate to Royal African Company, Apr. 24, 1707, T 70/8, 38). For the Heysham brothers' fraud, see Nicholas Morice to Humphrey Morice, Mar. 25, 1709, Letterbook of Humphrey Morice, Humphrey Morice Papers, Bank of England Archive, London. For William Heysham's Barbadian agency for the Royal African Company, see Royal African Company to Nicholas Prideaux, [July 1695], T 70/57, n.p. On William Heysham as agent for the island of Barbados, see "Minutes of Council in Assembly of Barbados," May 14, 1700, CSPC, XVIII, no. 437, 253–254.

When the replies to the Board of Trade's inquiry into the slave trade reached the Board's commissioners in December 1709, the separate traders continued to use their favorable position with the Board to ensure that the testimony was conducive to their cause. Micajah Perry was on hand to dispute the figures that the Barbadian governor Crowe submitted to the Board. Two separate traders to Jamaica, Benjamin Way and Richard Harris, presented a memorial against the African Company to the Board only moments before conveying Jamaican governor Thomas Handasyd's anticompany response. The separate traders' dominance of Jamaica allowed them to submit the island's responses to the Board's inquiry via Harris and Way. Such mediation clearly undermined the Board's impartiality, but it also formed an important part of the mechanics of a functioning British Atlantic polity, one that encouraged a presence for colonial interests in the metropolis. The separate traders took advantage of the switch from direct trade to consignment or commission trading, ensuring their transatlantic constituency. Separate traders serving as agents for colonies were well placed to mediate between the preferences of planters and the concerns of the government. The Board's report again supported the separate traders in resounding terms.[29]

As the Africa trade debates waged on in London, colonial support for the African Company began to wane still further. By 1711, the company's traditional heartland, the Leeward Islands, began to withdraw its support for monopoly. The African Company's agent on Nevis, John Hussam, reported that he found "the Planters very Cold and Indifferent about signing an address in the Company's favour." Similarly, in Antigua, the company's agent, Edward Chester, reported (in a remarkable *volte face* that indicates the extent to which the political positions of the separate traders and the Board of Trade on one hand and the African Company on the other had switched) that the planters on that island "are mostly for an open Trade." Chester informed Africa House that he could not "restrain [interloping] vessels from trading without a letter to the gentlemen from the Queen or the Lords C[ommissioners] of T[rade]." Jamaica, Barbados, and the mainland American colonies, however, remained steadfast in their opposition to the African Company's monopoly.[30]

A new political context and great commercial success had thus allowed the separate traders to develop a model of political power partly inspired by the

---

29. For separate-trader mediation of anti–African Company testimony from the colonies before the Board of Trade, see K. H. Ledward, ed., *Journals of the Board of Trade and Plantations*, 14 vols. (London, 1920–1938), I, Nov. 23, 1708, 546–558, Dec. 6, 1708, 558–571. For the Board of Trade's report in late January 1709, see CO 390/12, 172–282.

30. Hussam to Royal African Company, Sept. 16, 1711, T 70/8, 116; Edward Chester to Royal African Company, June 23, 1713, July 30, 1713, T 70/8, 135, 138.

company's political heyday in the 1680s. The political control that the separate traders' creditor status conferred allowed them to prevent their planter debtors from supporting the company. They also used the creditor status that slave trading offered them to augment their political and commercial positions in the colonies. That colonial opponents of the Royal African Company began, from the beginning of the eighteenth century, to use political tactics made notorious by the company suggests the extent to which the deregulation of the slave trade saw the political center of gravity in the colonies swing away from the African Company and toward the separate traders. The separate traders, however, would be careful to combine their creditor power with the legitimacy derived from courting public opinion to their cause. In this, their methods differed markedly from the lobbying strategies of the Royal African Company.

WITHOUT BROAD transatlantic support and in the face of the separate traders' entrenched power in the colonies and their public support in the mother country, the Royal African Company relied on a traditional lobbying strategy. It envisioned the Africa trade as best managed with the help of the coercive power of the state. The African Company had been brought into being by the royal prerogative and attempted to cement its relationship with the monarchy by distributing company shares to William III and, later, Queen Anne. After 1688, the company concentrated on developing its relationship with the government via the monarchy or the ministry. Hoping to mimic the proximity of the monied companies, such as the East India Company and the Bank of England, to the government, the African Company saw appeals to the state's power, rather than that of the public sphere, as a more efficient means to achieve favor.[31]

The company intensified its appeal for ministerial support after the change in government in 1710 and adjusted to the different political context. Two features of this context helped to sentimentalize the monarchy in ways that the company exploited. First, the Whig ministry's impeachment of the firebrand Anglican vicar, Henry Sacheverell, for castigating Whig principles of government and Dissenting religion led to an upsurge of opposition to the

---

31. For the African Company's gift to William III of company shares worth one thousand pounds, see Minutes of the General Court, Jan. 16, 1689, T 70/101, 23. For its gift to Queen Anne, see Minutes of the Court of Assistants, Dec. 7, 1714, T 70/89, 91. The African Company experimented with gathering breadth of support, but only out of desperation. It instructed its agent in Exeter, Matthew Barrett, "If the Governing part of the city will not joyn with the Company[,] gett the hands of the workmen concerned in you manufactures and return it"; see Royal African Company to Barrett, Mar. 1, 1711, T 70/44, n.p.

Whig government and a landslide election victory for Robert Harley, who was forced to incorporate Tory views into his government from 1710. Despite the part played by popular opinion in bringing down the Whigs in 1710, Sacheverell, like Daniel Defoe, worried that broad-based, popular movements ("legions," in Defoe's language) like the separate traders would erode the power of the monarch. Second, the leading separate trader and governor of the Bank of England, Sir Gilbert Heathcote, advised the queen against changing ministries because it would destabilize the nation's credit; this audacious move led many Tory writers to suppose that merchants had begun to talk out of turn and that the monarchy ought to be protected by the government and by public opinion.[32]

By the summer of 1711, the company was in no position to celebrate its commercial achievements and connect them to the support of the monarchy. Instead, it dramatized the weakness of its position on the African coast to create a sense of national emergency that monarchical and ministerial sympathy could more easily translate into a state response than could the slow-moving, deliberative Parliament. Thomas Pindar explained that such a strategy was designed to enlist ministerial support:

> This day and last week [I] have attended a committee of lords of the cabinet and the lords commissioners for trade, and have now so concerted measures, as I hope will rebound to the great benefit of the company and all concern'd with them. The ministry agree pursuant to the address of parl[iament] to give some assistance for preservation of the settlements in Africa, and In conjunction with the company are directed to send out the produce of the duty arising by the African act appropriated for that end, and at the meeting of the parliament, to represent the whole in order to a speedy and effectuall support and settlement of the trade.[33]

The following year, the strength of the African Company's political position and the expiration of the 1698 statute (as well as the passage of an act allowing the company's shareholders to unite with their creditors) encouraged the company to revert to associating itself with the royal prerogative. It posted "advertisements" on the pillars of the Royal Exchange and circulated them throughout the British Atlantic world:

---

32. See Henry Sacheverell, *The Perils of False Brethren, both in Church, and State: Set Forth in a Sermon Preach'd before the Right Honourable the Lord-Mayor, Aldermen, and Citizens of London, at the Cathedral-Church of St. Paul, on the Fifth of November 1709* (London, 1710), 34.

33. Pindar to George Mason, July 26, 1711, T 70/44, n.p.

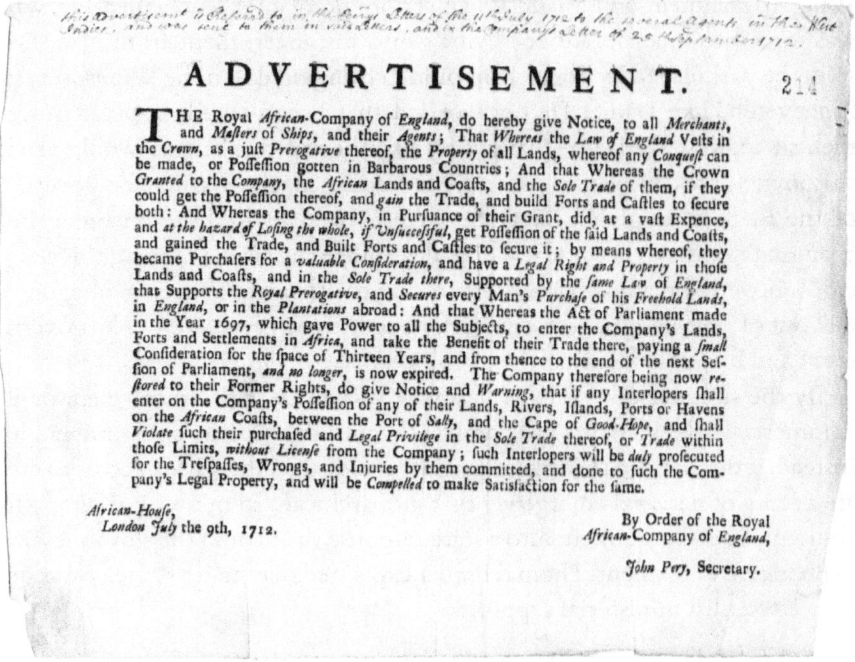

ADVERTISEMENT.

214

THE Royal *African*-Company of *England*, do hereby give Notice, to all *Merchants*, and *Maſters* of *Ships*, and their *Agents*; That *Whereas* the *Law of England* Veſts in the *Crown*, as a juſt *Prerogative* thereof, the *Property* of all Lands, whereof any *Conqueſt* can be made, or Poſſeſſion gotten in Barbarous Countries; And that Whereas the Crown *Granted* to the *Company*, the *African* Lands and Coaſts, and the *Sole Trade* of them, if they could get the Poſſeſſion thereof, and *gain* the Trade, and build Forts and Caſtles to ſecure both: And Whereas the Company, in Purſuance of their Grant, did, at a vaſt Expence, and *at the hazard of Loſing the whole, if Unſucceſsful*, get Poſſeſſion of the ſaid Lands and Coaſts, and gained the Trade, and Built Forts and Caſtles to ſecure it; by means whereof, they became Purchaſers for a *valuable Conſideration*, and have a *Legal Right and Property* in thoſe Lands and Coaſts, and in the *Sole Trade there*, Supported by the *ſame Law* of *England*, that Supports the *Royal Prerogative*, and *Secures* every Man's *Purchaſe* of his *Freehold Lands*, in *England*, or in the *Plantations* abroad: And that Whereas the Act of Parliament made in the Year 1697, which gave Power to all the Subjects, to enter the Company's Lands, Forts and Settlements in *Africa*, and take the Benefit of their Trade there, paying a *ſmall* Conſideration for the ſpace of Thirteen Years, and from thence to the end of the next Seſſion of Parliament, *and no longer*, is now expired. The Company therefore being now *reſtored* to their Former Rights, do give Notice and *Warning*, that if any Interlopers ſhall enter on the Company's Poſſeſſion of any of their Lands, Rivers, Iſlands, Ports or Havens on the *African* Coaſts, between the Port of *Sally*, and the Cape of *Good-Hope*, and ſhall *Violate* ſuch their purchaſed and *Legal Privilege* in the *Sole Trade* thereof, or *Trade* within thoſe Limits, *without Licenſe* from the Company; ſuch Interlopers will be *duly* proſecuted for the Treſpaſſes, Wrongs, and Injuries by them committed, and done to ſuch the Company's Legal Property, and will be *Compelled* to make Satisfaction for the ſame.

African-Houſe,
London July the 9th, 1712.

By Order of the Royal
African-Company of *England*,

John Pery, Secretary.

PLATE 3. "Advertisement by Order of the Royal African-Company of England," July 9, 1712. From Treasury 70/58, print mark 214, National Archives, Kew

> The Law of England Vests in the Crown, as a just Prerogative thereof, the Property of all Lands, whereof any Conquest can be made, or Possession gotten in Barbarous Countries; And that Whereas the Crown Granted to the Company, the African Lands and Coasts, and the Sole Trade of them . . . and have a Legal Right and Property in those Lands and Coasts, . . . Supported by the Same Law of England, that Supports the Royal Prerogative, and Secures every Man's Purchase of his Freehold Lands.

The company could now claim some legal basis for its attachment to the royal prerogative and, therefore, its monopolistic charter. For the first time since the Glorious Revolution, the Royal African Company would offer a rejoinder to the independent slave traders' constitutional argument that monopolistic trading companies deprived subjects of their right to consent to taxation and, thus, the protection of their property.[34]

34. "Advertisement by Order of the Royal African-Company of England," July 9, 1712, T 70/58, print mark 214. The African Company believed that after the expiration of the 1698 act the man-

The African Company's attempts to enforce its monopolistic charter after 1712 ended in failure, however. The constitutional settlement of 1689 and the countenance it had received since then would not be so easily dismissed. The company required a statute to endorse its monopolistic charter, whereas the separate traders' slave trading did not. Despite courting the ministry and attempting to court the monarch, no African Company bill received the favor of the sort of personnel who could guarantee its success. After repeated lobbying, Queen Anne refused to intervene on the African Company's behalf, relaying to the company's management that she "did not think fit to meddle in it." To achieve public success, the African Company would need to mount a parliamentary campaign that demonstrated that its monopoly satisfied the broad-based, national interest as much as the separate traders' model of the trade. A campaign that nestled up to ministers and monarchs endorsed the separate traders' stereotype of the company, that it exemplified the corruptions of a bygone overbearing monarchy. The company's political strategy failed to court a parliamentary interest and demonstrated either its inability to understand or refusal to acknowledge the changing institutional landscape wrought by the Glorious Revolution. Unable to use the reformed constitution to its advantage, the Royal African Company turned itself into an anachronism by seeking to depend on a monarchy still powerful but no longer sovereign in matters relating to overseas trade regulation.[35]

THE SEPARATE TRADERS had consistently won the battles to secure broad support for a liberalized slave trade. In every session, they achieved more signatories on more petitions from a wider variety of constituencies throughout the British Atlantic world. How did this broad support assist the separate traders' victory in the Africa trade debates? How did broadly based consent connect to slave-trade escalation? After all, the separate traders did not deregulate the slave trade with the help of a parliamentary statute. A typical route to parliamentary resolution included appealing to the ministry or the monarch to compel a governmental intervention in Parliament's proceedings. The African Company deployed this tactic but did not succeed in obtaining a statute. Another common method of resolving a parliamentary dispute of this kind took place within the chamber itself, voting. Votes occurred on several

---

agement of the slave trade ought to revert to its charter because the ruling in *Nightingale v. Bridges* had been by default.

35. For Queen Anne's refusal to intervene in support of the Royal African Company, see Minutes of the Court of Assistants, June 8, 1714, T 70/89, 34. For the company's concession of defeat in the quest to gather parliamentary support, see *Resolutions of a General Court of the Adventurers of the Royal African Company, Held on Thursday the 26th February, 1712/13* ([London, 1713]).

occasions in the Africa trade dispute—in 1709, 1712, and 1713—and, overall, the African Company and separate traders were evenly matched, but such votes mattered far less for the separate traders than they did for the African Company because of the company's need for a statute. The separate traders used victory in such votes as an endorsement for deregulated trade without the taxation inherent to any form of statutory intervention in the trade.

Knowing that, since *Nightingale v. Bridges,* the common law courts would not support the vice-admiralty enforcement powers of prerogative-sponsored monopoly companies and would encourage free competition in the slave trade, the separate traders implemented a political strategy that developed broad support to defeat rather than to achieve a statute. The formal process of legislating a statute, then, was less important to the resolution of the Africa trade dispute than the informal means of using pamphlets and petitions and parliamentary discussions to engineer a public opinion sympathetic to free trade. This strategy ensured that, when the slave trade deregulated—and the breadth of support for this outcome ensured that it would—it did so *completely* and received the endorsement of a more amorphous but more powerful constituency than a ministry, a monarchy, or Parliament: national public opinion. The separate traders understood that a total deregulation would best advance their interests. They deployed an ideology that celebrated the natural right to trade in the enslaved, a right that should not be impeded by regulatory statutes. They appreciated that the breadth of their support in Parliament could prevent the company from achieving any of the statutes they attempted to buttress their monopoly. A legislative vacuum was what they aimed for, and the strategy helped to transform their interests into ideology as free trade became a natural law that could only be overturned by statute. For free traders in enslaved African men, women, and children, as with the freedom of the press, parliamentary statute would be regarded as an intrusion on liberty—a liberty nevertheless formed and celebrated through public discussion of the slave trade.

Parliament's supremacy within the English constitution after 1689 and the newfound control over economic matters that supremacy allowed helped to limit the economic significance of statute. Because Parliament's regulatory supremacy ensured that no other branch of the constitution could be permitted to legislate if Parliament failed to agree to a statutory solution, legislative vacuums became possible. Lobbyists, like the separate traders to Africa, who sought deregulation therefore often worked only to block attempts to regulate via statute, producing regulatory inertia and, with time, a public acceptance of deregulation. Parliamentary deliberations and public pamphlet discussions nonetheless helped to legitimize that deregulation. Pamphlets espousing the market as a self-regulating mechanism fostered toleration of the legislative vacuum. Economic ideology was, then, the rationalization of a structural phenomenon—legislative failure. The separate traders' espousal of protoeconomic ideas to legitimate the ensuing legislative vacuum helped attain approval for economic thinking as the eighteenth century progressed.

Pro-African Company pamphleteers understood the separate traders' lobbying strategy but could not gain enough public support to thwart it using a regulating strategy. One writer explained in 1713: "The Company have a *Right* and *Property* in the Coasts, Forts and *Sole* Trade, *or they have not. If they have not;* then what need have the Separate Traders of an Act of Parliament to give 'em a Liberty they have already without an Act?" The Royal African Company's need and quest for a statute helped, therefore, to ensure that its failures to achieve one would pave the way for free, as opposed to merely open, trade. The company's opponents only reacted to the African Company's political initiatives. Time and again, separate-trader petitions responded to African Company proposals to support its monopoly with a statute. By 1712, the ambiguities surrounding the slave trade in 1689 had been replaced by well-rehearsed public support for free trade.[36]

How had the separate traders developed this political strategy? Sir John Holt's judgment in *Nightingale v. Bridges* had undermined the African Company's charter to the extent that the company sought Parliament's endorsement. Holt implied that the courts would not countenance monopolistic charters' powers of enforcement without statutory support. The separate traders' political strategy was also informed by an awareness of the expansive potential of deregulation in the trade. Holt's decision helped the separate traders to associate independent slave trading with natural rights. As one anonymous company pamphleteer explained:

> As the impunity of such practices [independent trading] did incourage the authors to persevere for some time in such like courses: so others taking their views and measures from the seeming success of the former [separate traders], without any regard to the consequences of trading in that manner, join'd in an out-cry against the privileges of the company, as a monopoly inconsistent with the liberty of the subject, and not establish'd by act of parliament; and that therefore they

---

36. *Objections to the Bill for Establishing the Trade to Africa, in a Regulated Company* (n.p., [1712]), 3. There are numerous examples of such slave-trade petitions. See, especially, "A Petition of Divers Clothiers of Suffolke and Essex," Apr. 21, 1690, *Commons Journals,* X, 382.

would exercise their natural right of trading to Africk, as well as the company.³⁷

Moreover, the independent slave trader Gilbert Heathcote achieved a parliamentary resolution in January 1694 that saw Parliament confirm Holt's position. Parliamentary endorsement for free trade enabled, according to one pro-company pamphleteer, the separate traders to fix their strategy on sustaining a legislative vacuum that would prove beneficial to their trade:

> Ever since the Parliament Voted that it was the undoubted Right of all the Subjects of *England* to Trade to Foreign Parts — none of those Free Traders have ever brought to the Parliament a Bill to settle this Trade, but still opposed what was offered by the Company.... because those Free Traders... had just cause to believe that under such a Regulation, whatsoever it should be, they must Pay towards what by the Parliament should be thought necessary for the general Interest of that Trade — whereas if they could continue that heavy load upon the *African* Company only by opposing this Bill, they should then enjoy their Trade without that Expence.

Indeed, the separate traders initiated proceedings in Parliament in only three of the sixteen sessions of the Africa trade debates. When they did so, they sought to filibuster Royal African Company measures through those proceedings. The company noted the separate traders' filibustering in a petition to Queen Anne on December 3, 1710:

> Some few Private Traders for selfish and particular ends had the art of propogating and imposing impractical notions on some members of the legislature in such a manner and possessing them with very groundless prejudice against the Company, that both the sessions terminated without any actuall care being taken for the preservation of the Trade.³⁸

---

37. *An Account of the Rise and Progress of Our Trade to Africa, Preceding the Year 1697*, in *A New General Collection of Voyages and Travels* . . . , 4 vols. (London, 1745–1747), I, 666.

38. *Considerations Relating to the African Bill* ([London, 1698?]), 3. Gilbert Heathcote's resolution of 1694 was in relation to the East India trade (see Jan. 8, 1693, *Commons Journals*, XI, 50). The years when the separate traders initiated proceedings were 1710, 1712, and 1713. An adviser to the duke of Chandos in the early 1720s made a similar assessment of the separate traders' strategy: "And in Truth the separate Traders themselves after they had gained their Ends by disappointing the Affrican Company of an exclusive Trade neglected prosecuting this new Bill" (Stowe MSS 9, 32). See also "Petition to the Queen," Dec. 3, 1710, T 70/175, 200–201.

These "impractical notions" included bills to deregulate the trade. The repeated failure of regulated company bills became a motif for the Africa trade debates. Daniel Defoe explained the failure of a regulated company bill in 1712 by characterizing the separate traders' proposals as fantastical: "I cannot say the Vigour of the Company has gain'd the Victory; but the Difficulty, or rather Impossibility of the Chimerical Settlements some Men have proposed, has given the dead Blow to all their Attempts." Defoe neglected to appreciate that there was strategy behind these chimeras. When anti–African Company proposals appeared in the 1690s, seldom did they advocate statutory alternatives to the company's monopoly, instead using such vague terms as "advantageous Regulation," "a better, more beneficial, and equal Establishment," and "Liberty, and Freedom of Trade." Later, separate-trader petitions became explicitly antiregulatory. In 1708, one petition pleaded to "be relieved from the heavy duty of ten per cent." In 1709, the language had changed to: "[trade] may be continued free and open to all the Subjects of *Great Britain,* discharged from such Part of the £. 10. *per Cent.* Duty." Calls for regulated company statutes typically emerged from cross-party drafting committees, which hoped to legislate through compromise measures, rather than from separate-trader petitions, which preferred to argue in favor of an ill-defined notion of "free trade" or simply for parliamentary consideration. Separate-trader petitions deliberately complicated legislative proposals to the extent that they failed.[39]

Encouraging parliamentary deliberation but discouraging statutory resolution became the separate traders' lobbying modus vivendi. They cultivated extraparliamentary opinion and steered a middle course in Parliament to achieve nonstatutory parliamentary rulings that would modify public opinion in favor of free trade and ensure that the legislative vacuum was tolerated. These rulings accrued more public significance the more interest in Parliament increased after 1688. The rulings were meaningful because of the ritualized nature of parliamentary deliberation. Once a legislative proposal had reached a certain stage, it gathered legitimacy even if the proposal ultimately failed.

39. *Review,* June 8, 1710, 121–123. For the 1690s petitions, see "Petition of Divers Clothiers of Suffolke and Essex," Apr. 21, 1690, *Commons Journals,* X, 382, "A Petition of the Merchants and Planters, Trading to, and Interested in, the Island of Barbadoes," Apr. 22, 1690, X, 383. For the petitions that wished to be relieved from the 10 percent duty, see "Petition of Merchants, and Planters, Separate Traders in Africa, and Interested in, and Trading to Barbadoes, and the Other Leeward Islands," Mar. 16, 1708, *Commons Journals,* XV, 612, "A Petition of the Merchants and Planters, Separate Traders to Africa, in Behalf of Themselves and Divers Others, Interested in and Trading to, the Island of Jamaica," Feb. 1, 1709, XVI, 77, "A Petition of Divers Merchants of London, Traders to Africa," Dec. 8, 1709, XVI, 235.

Because the African Company required the legal authority of a statute, such nonstatutory parliamentary rulings were of less use to the company and were, because of the weakness of their parliamentary lobby, less frequent. But, once it became clear that the separate traders enjoyed sufficient support to block the African Company's attempts at legislation to support its monopoly, the company sought parliamentary rulings that supported its forts, confident that the separate traders would not endorse these rulings. These rulings secured the survival of the forts and the company in the short term, but they could not ensure the immediate means to finance their operation; that would require regulation, which would, by definition, require a statute.

Nonstatutory parliamentary rulings in favor of free trade appeared in several forms. First, and perhaps most important, was the precedent established by the act of 1698 itself, which could be deemed nonstatutory after its expiration in 1712. The act proved that open trade expanded British exports to Africa, enlarged imports of enslaved Africans to America, and increased the size of the Atlantic colonial commodity trades. One separate-trader pamphlet argued that this act had been designed to prepare the way for unregulated trade. Despite the company's role in achieving it, the 1698 act was clearly an essential stepping-stone to total deregulation of the British slave trade.[40]

The Board of Trade's reports to Parliament offer another example of a nonstatutory parliamentary ruling. Charles Davenant noted that the Board's findings in early 1709 provided much needed legitimacy to the separate traders' cause and "the Transcribing them by way of report and intermixing them with such accounts as were demanded of the Royal African Company, has happened to give them some more seeming authority than can reasonably be supposed to have been ever intended by the Lords Commissioners." Davenant believed that such legitimacy proved influential with public opinion and helped, in turn, to influence the political process, "for the Separate Traders have taken occasion, from thence to print certain paragraphs of there [sic] own base allegations by way of Extracts out of the said report, as vouchers to gain Credit to the very same allegations again without doors." Davenant's complaint represented more than sour grapes. A separate-trader pamphlet acknowledged that the Board's report reflected a deliberate lobbying strategy:

> The Report is drawn up with such Exactness and Impartiality, that whensoever the Parliament will please to call for it, I dare take upon me to say, it will justify my present Undertaking, and verify the most,

---

40. For the pamphlet that viewed the 1698 act as an important precedent for free trade, see *The Case of the Separate Traders to Africa . . .* ([London? 1709]), 1.

if not all the Suggestions and Allegations here laid down, and give Such a Light and Insight into the whole Matter, that the Publick will be kept no longer in the dark about it.

The Board of Trade's rulings thus played another important part in informing public deliberations about the slave trade.[41]

The various stages that each legislative proposal reached provide a third category of nonstatutory parliamentary rulings: from points scored in debate, to votes and resolutions, to bills. Pamphleteers referred to the perceived outcome of parliamentary debates or to testimony deemed trustworthy because of submission in the House of Commons. One colonial representative of the African Company informed his superiors, "The inhabitants think it in Vain to Sign Any More Papers in favour of the Company Since the Parliament Countenance the Separate Traders." One separate trader disputed the utility of the company's forts, not through any investigation or reasoning on the part of the author, but "because it hath often been made appear at the Bar, that most of the Negroes brought from *Africa* are loaden where we have no Settlements." Pamphleteers relayed the perceived outcome of parliamentary debates to undermine their opponents. The same was true of parliamentary votes. The Royal African Company often circulated these votes—in effect, summaries of nonstatutory parliamentary resolutions—to colonial agents to gather support for its proposals. Parliamentary votes also affected how the economy functioned. A separate-trader pamphlet described the way in which a vote in favor of a regulated company bill led to expansion in the trade: "Since the vote of the honourable House of commons about eight years ago, that the trade thither was best to be managed by a regulated company, there has been a greater trade driven thither, notwithstanding all the difficulties at home, and hazards of war, than ever was carried on in times of peace."[42]

Parliamentary resolutions—unlike, at this stage, the content of the debates

---

41. Charles Davenant's responses to the Board of Trade's 1708 report are contained in [Davenant], "Some General Observations and Particular Remarks on the Report Made by the Lords Commissioners for Trade and Plantations the 3rd February, 1708 Touching the Contents of the Royal African Company's Petition Referred to Them by Her Majesty," T 70/175, 87–96. See also *Considerations upon the Trade to Guinea* (London, 1708), 26.

42. William Fry to Royal African Company, July 25, 1710, T 70/8, 106 ("in Vain"); *An Answer to a Paper Called, Short Remarks on the African Trade* (n.p., 1711) ("appear at the Bar"); Lewis Galdy to Royal African Company, Oct. 8, 1711, T 70/8, 116: "Has rec'd the Votes of the House of Commons against the African Trade, several of their Planters much against the Company." See also Royal African Company to Edward Chester, July 17, 1711, T 70/58, 402; *Reasons Humbly Offered by the Merchants and Traders to Guinny and the West-Indies, against a Bill for Settling the Trade to Africa* ([London? 1698]), 1.

themselves (outside partisan pamphlets)—were often printed, which made them more influential outside the chamber. They conferred some legitimacy for parliamentary proposals in the absence of a statute. A petition from Exeter, for example, cited that a resolution in favor of a regulated company in a previous session had "so far encouraged the Petitioners, that it gave a new Life to their Trade, and some Thousands of Pieces . . . made more than usual, and the Price advanced from Eleven Shillings and Six-pence *per* Piece to Fifteen Shillings and Six-pence *per* Piece." Parliamentary resolutions suggested, especially when originating from the committee of the whole House, that there existed broad parliamentary approval for the proposed scheme and that its translation into statute was undone by disagreement over the legislation's fine print (a disagreement that was in the separate traders' interest to develop). One pamphlet complained that the company's assumption that the law of the African trade would revert to its 1672 charter after the expiration of the 1698 act proceeded

> without any Regard to the many Resolutions of this Honourable House repeated last Session, *viz. That the African Trade ought to be free and open to all her Majesty's Subjects,* the said Company ordered Advertisements to be fixed on the Pillars of the *Royal Exchange,* and other Publick Places, wherein they threaten to sue any Person that should presume to trade in *Africa* any longer. . . .'Tis true the Bill for the National Trade did not pass last Year, but even the Adversaries thereto did agree, 'twas not because they were against an open Trade, but that some Clauses in that Bill were excepted against.

This pamphleteer believed a nonstatutory parliamentary ruling from the reformed Parliament commanded more public authority than a charter derived from royal prerogative. Another believed that a resolution from a parliamentary committee of the whole House in favor of free trade had more authority than a resolution in favor of the company's forts from a private parliamentary committee.[43]

---

43. "A Petition of the Mayor, Aldermen, and Common Councilmen of the City of Exon, and Also of the Merchants, Serge-Makers, Fullers, and Other Trading People, Employed in and about the Woolen Manufactory within the Said City and County of the Same, and Parts Adjacent," Dec. 9, 1691, *Commons Journals,* X, 579. The belief that anticompany legislation failed for reasons other than a lack of support was commonplace. See also *The Present Case of the African Trade Truly Stated, with Reasons for the Bill for Establishing the Same Now Depending* (n.p., 1711), 1; *The Case of the National Traders to Africa* (n.p., 1713), 1; *The Anatomy of the African Company's Scheme for Carrying on That Trade in a Joint-Stock Exclusive, on the Foot of New Subscriptions* ([London? 1710?]), 2. The author of the following pamphlet would have disagreed about the primacy of statute over prerogative, as late as 1713: *Property Derived under Charters and Grants from the Crown of England, Not Inferior to Prop-*

The open-trade bills themselves offered further evidence of parliamentary support and provided some information about how the trade might function without a statute. Pamphleteers deemed previous bills to be binding on future parliamentary deliberations: "Who but this Company would come to Parliament to ask an Exclusive Trade, when but 7 or 8 Months before the House passed a Bill for a Free and Open Trade?" The separate traders also used their bills on the African coast to persuade African traders not to deal with the company:

> We believe the Separate traders' captains and officers may impose on you and the rest of our servants by magnifying the pretended advantages they gained this parliament, but we must observe to you, that tho' they had prevailed to far as to have the liberty of offering a bill to the House in order to lay open the trade to Africa, the House did not think fit to pass that bill but adjourned it from day to day until the session was ended.[44]

The separate traders' victory was to convince the public at large that they could operate the trade without statutory approval. These nonstatutory parliamentary rulings proved invaluable in achieving this outcome. Their triumph over the company resulted from a lobbying strategy that reflected an astute appreciation of the post-1688 legislative and regulatory processes. The separate traders combined an impressive breadth of public support with a constitutional notion of free trade that depicted parliamentary statute as an intrusion on the natural right to trade.

THE SEPARATE TRADERS and the African Company thus mounted differing political campaigns that pursued distinctive lobbying strategies and reflected their own institutional structures and ideologies. The separate traders' campaign, in the end, proved successful in effecting the deregulation of the slave trade.

An unregulated trade might have defaulted to the mechanics of the mar-

---

erty Derived under Grants from the Subjects of England ([London? 1713?]). For two more separate-trader petitions citing the efficacy of previous parliamentary resolutions to the management of the trade, see "A Petition of Divers Merchants of London, Traders to Africa, and Thence to the Plantations, in Behalf of Themselves, and Many Others Concerned in the Said Trade," Apr. 21, 1713, *Commons Journals*, XVII, 297, "A Petition of the Merchants and Traders of the City of Bristol," Apr. 21, 1713, XVII, 297–298. For the pamphleteer comparing resolutions from different parliamentary committees, see *Remarks on the Supplement to the African Company's Case* (n.p., [1730?]), 2.

44. *The Anatomy of the African Company's Scheme*, 2 ("who but this Company"); Royal African Company to Sir Dalby Thomas, May 5, 1709, T 70/52, 223; Royal African Company to William Hickes, May 5, 1709, T 70/52, 226.

ket, but that does not diminish the importance of the separate traders' political campaign to achieving deregulation. Within a market that featured a monopoly company, however impotent that monopoly was, full deregulation of the market required a concerted political campaign to oppose that monopoly company. The separate traders understood that parliamentary sovereignty over national economic regulation created an opportunity for reactive interest groups to deregulate trade. They used political means to guarantee legislative failure that in turn ensured legislative inertia, which the separate traders repackaged as the natural liberty to trade in the enslaved. They therefore convinced the public to embrace the deregulation of Britain's transatlantic slave trade. Their success ensured the transportation of perhaps an additional million and a half Africans to the New World and forced the African Company to reconsider its future. The separate traders' out-of-doors campaigning both resulted from and expanded the public's involvement in political considerations. It led the public not just to countenance deregulation but also to endorse or embrace an expanded, open slave trade as a public good and a right to which every Englishman was entitled.

This public support of deregulation was crystal clear, but the position of the Royal African Company after 1712 was not. Robert Harley's political support allowed the company to endure, and the company started a new chapter in its history with the help of a government concerned about how the separate traders' legislative vacuum short-circuited the state's management of trade. The dialogic impetus between the company and the separate traders would continue to dominate the slave trade after the victory of the separate traders. In seeking new political means to support its operations, the African Company would combine its old suspicion of unregulated commercial activity with a new sentimental treatment of African commerce to provide an institutional setting in which antislavery opinion gathered public traction as part of a public reinvention of the humanitarian imperatives of commercial regulation.

Part Two
Re-regulation, 1712–1752

FIVE

The Outcomes
Tropical Burlesques

In the summer of 1712, the Africa trade appeared in a confused state. Each side in the slave-trade debates claimed that the expiration of the 1698 act favored its cause. The expiration seemed to favor the separate traders because the 10 percent duty had expired with the act. In June 1712, however, the African Company secured a statute authorizing its many creditors to obtain three-quarters of the company's assets in return for canceling their company bonds. Company supporters argued that this Act for Making Effectual Such Agreement as Shall Be Made between the Royal African Company of England and Their Creditors (known as the Creditors' Act) offered clear parliamentary legitimation of its charter, and therefore its monopoly, and, as one company apologist declared, put an end "to the late toleration [enjoyed by the separate traders] . . . of ranging licentiously in their neighbours [the Royal African Company] dear bought inclosure." Daniel Defoe was especially adamant that the Creditors' Act settled the trade in favor of the Royal African Company: "Upon this Act, as upon a steady Foundation, the present New Building of the Company stands fixt, and to the Disappointment of the Enemies of our Commerce it is like to stand, and perhaps is at this Time in a greater Prospect of flourishing than in the best of its former Circumstances could be said of it."[1]

The African Company concurred and dispatched warnings to separate traders not to interlope in the African trade without first purchasing a license from the company that increased the 1698 statute's duty from 10 to 15 percent of the value of an African cargo. African Company directors remained determined to manage the trade via their charter. In February 1713, they proposed that bills of exchequer be used to prevent separate traders who were assembling African cargoes from departing for the African coast. The separate traders' resounding political victory in the parliamentary dispute about the slave trade and legal challenges to the enforcement powers of the com-

---

1. *Some Remarks on a False and Scurrilous Libel, Intituled, The Case of the National Traders to Africa* (n.p., 1713), 2; Daniel Defoe, *A Brief Account of the Present State of the African Trade* (London, 1713), 18.

pany's charter, however, meant that this represented the most extreme form of wishful thinking.²

The following discussion assesses the outcome of the Africa trade debates. It analyzes the nature of the separate traders' victory and the meaning of Parliament's and the state's backing for deregulated slave trading up to the middle of the eighteenth century. The Africa trade debates concentrated on the problem of who ought to have access to the slave trade. The separate traders had conclusively won that issue. The aftermath of their victory ensured a huge expansion in the capacity of the British American slave trade, a greatly increased enslaved African population in America, and the continued development of provincial slave-trading centers, first Bristol and then Liverpool.

Political consideration of the slave trade would not end with the separate traders' victory, however. Both lobbies continued, though their strategies, ideas, and interests changed significantly. The political context also shifted. In particular, the separate traders' legislative vacuum posed a conundrum for the British state, which sought regulatory means to improve its financial position. The state experimented with disastrous legislative attempts to use public enthusiasm for slave trading to solve its financial problems via Robert Harley's South Sea Company. This company would satisfy the asiento contract to supply slaves to the Spanish Americas. The Africa trade debates had confirmed public support for slave trading, and Harley understood that the perceived commercial benefits of the asiento would compel investment in the South Sea Company. These investments would provide a prop for the Harley government's weak financial position as Harley designed to convert government debt into South Sea stock. Regulated slave trading would be, for Harley, the pillar of government finance. With Harley's support (and the arguments of his propagandist, Daniel Defoe), the African Company was able to position itself alongside the South Sea Company. This political maneuvering provided important protection for the African Company and a potential lucrative contract to supply the South Sea Company with slaves. Moreover, the courtship of subsequent ministries in the 1720s, 1730s, and 1740s—as a promoter of trade with the African interior under the leadership of the duke of Chandos and

---

2. For the African Company's warning to interlopers, see Royal African Company to Raynes Bate and Thomas Stewart, July 11, 1712, Treasury (T) 70/58, 418–419, loose sheet, print mark 214, National Archives, Kew. For a separate traders' claim that the company's threat of seizure in 1712–1713 was tyrannical, see *The Case of John Leadstone, a Private Trader Residing in Africa* (n.p., [1713]), 1. See also *An Account of the Ships Employed in the African Trade, from the Ports of London and Bristol, Belonging to the Separate Traders to Africa; with the Value of the Said Ships and Cargoes, and the Number of Negroes Usually Carried by the Said Ships* (n.p., [1713]), 1; and *An Abstract of Several Cases Relating to the Trade to Africa* (n.p., [1714]), 1.

then as a holding company for state subsidies for its forts—ensured that the African Company survived intact throughout the first half of the eighteenth century.

The British state could not deny the separate traders' argument that open access to slave trading was a natural British birthright endorsed by broadly based public opinion. The legislative vacuum and the natural right to trade in slaves that it protected provided the backdrop for a series of statutory pronouncements involving key lobbyists for the separate traders that protected the legitimacy of slave trading and the interests of independent slave traders into the second half of the eighteenth century. The political capital of the separate traders continued beyond the Africa trade debates to strengthen the status and power of slave trading and slaveowners within the British Empire.

THE SEPARATE TRADERS scoffed at the African Company's claim that the expiration of the 1698 act allowed the trade to revert to the company's charter. They responded to the African Company with a final open trade bill in Parliament in 1713. This bill represented the separate traders' last calculation that continued public deliberation was necessary to silence the African Company's talk of using their charter to monopolize the trade. After that, they did not see the need to appeal to Parliament to gain public countenance for their deregulated trade.

An African Company pamphlet indicates the effects of a separate-trading explosion on the coast of Africa after the expiration of the 1698 act in 1712. The failure of the 1713 open trade bill was inconsequential because "these Gentlemen [the separate traders] have, . . . made a full Experiment what they can do for the Nation and Themselves, even as much as if they had had their Darling Act." A quarter century of deregulated slave trading and of public deliberations about the management of the slave trade had confirmed that a liberalized slave trade provided more slaves to the colonies and that free trade enjoyed widespread support. By the summer of 1712, it became apparent that the Royal African Company was in no position to enforce its monopoly.[3]

The expiration expanded the slave trade in a more sustainable way than the expansion brought about by the 1698 act. Raynes Bate, a company official, reported in June 1713 that there appeared on the African coast "more interlopers and other ships than have been known at one time, that they were neither encouraged nor molested by the factors." Other Royal African Company agents in the colonies reported that the separate traders had vowed to continue

---

3. Robert Bleau, *A Letter from One of the Royal African-Company's Chief Agents on the African Coasts* (n.p., 1713), [1].

trading without license from the company owing to "encouragement from England" that consisted of the incontrovertible backing of national public opinion generated by twenty-three years of public deliberation. Later commentators believed that there was parliamentary intention in the lapsing of the 1698 statute: "The Legislature have let this duty drop, which they would not have done, had they thought that forts and settlements were in anywise necessary." Another agreed: "Experience shewing that this Duty depressed a growing Trade it was sufferd to expire in 1712."[4]

A company pamphlet confirmed the benefits of the expiration for the separate traders: "SINCE the Expiration of that Act, which was in the year 1712; all others his Majesty's Subjects have traded *freely to* Africa, without contributing any thing to the said charge; And the Company have born and defrayed the Whole of that Expence; and by this means the separate Traders have reaped the whole Profit of this Trade." Investors began to abandon the company. By June 1714, company stock dropped to "37p which is lower that at any time hither to it has been and declining." The African Company's market capitalization shrunk to as little as £21,500. After more than forty years, the company appeared to be on the brink of bankruptcy and total collapse.[5]

After 1712, the separate traders continued to use their political capital to protect their interests. They persisted in supporting deregulation, but their lobbying took on a new anticolonial guise. In response to various colonial attempts to regulate the slave trade through taxation on slave imports, separate traders—including, most vocally, Richard Harris—offered resistance. Throughout the 1720s, Harris helped to block colonies' attempts to increase the duties levied on imported slaves. He helped secure in 1717 a prohibition from the crown that prevented colonial assemblies from taxing imported slaves. The separate traders also blocked the South Sea Company's attempt to monopolize the slave trade with Jamaica. Once the apologists for the colonies, British-based separate traders like Harris and Humphrey Morice became, as with many Atlantic merchants, resistant to colonial attempts to regulate their interests and, as did the Royal African Company before them, began to tire of the colonists' habitual refusal to settle their debts to British merchants. In

---

4. Bate et al. to the Royal African Company, Mar. 26, 1713, T 70/8, 128 ("encouragement from England"), June 30, 1713, 135 ("neither encouraged nor molested"); *Journal of the Commissioners for Trade and Plantations* . . . , 14 vols. (London, 1920–1938), Apr. 29, 1726, V, 248 ("duty drop"). See also duke of Newcastle's report, Additional Manuscripts, 33053, 293, British Library, London. It is important to acknowledge that the expansions in slave trading in 1698 and 1712 were both assisted by the onset of peace. The expansion after 1712 proved more sustainable.

5. *An Abstract of the Case of the Royal African Company of England* ([London, 1729]), 1. For the drop in share price, see Royal African Company to Richard King, June 3, 1714, T 70/45, n.p.

1724, a leading separate trader, Stephen Godin, despite a long period of residence in the colonies, proposed that "it were better to have no colonies at all unless they be subservient to their mother country." Harris and Morice agreed and led the campaign to make colonial property liable to debts owed to British merchants. They succeeded in 1732, when Parliament passed a statute that enforced uniform imperial treatment of slave property for the purposes of debt recovery in Britain and its colonies, overriding all contrary colonial laws.[6]

Under this law, the Debt Recovery Act of 1732, Parliament classified enslaved Africans in the colonies as property for the purposes of debtor-creditor relations. The act confirmed the legality of slave property in the empire. Along with the 1733 Molasses Act, which taxed the importing of French colonial produce into British territories (which Harris also supported), the Debt Recovery Act marked a sea change in the relationship between the colonies and the mother country. It also shows that the separate traders' leadership began, as it did during the Africa trade debates, to respond to that changed relationship. The decentralization of imperial initiative to the American periphery from which the separate traders had drawn benefit at the beginning of the eighteenth century would now reverse; separate traders and the British state and Parliament began to use statutory means to tighten the mother country's economic and fiscal controls over the British American colonies. This act provided one of the first statutory expressions of the British government's increasingly centralizing initiatives toward the colonies—a tendency that, broadly interpreted, would lead to the Stamp Act of 1763. The separate traders, in short, helped to create a firm national consensus that the slave trade was legitimate and that it enjoyed the public's approval and deserved the state's protection. They had created a public platform that ensured the government would perform its strategic, military role, which the African Company had often proposed to do.[7]

With their political power thus unquestioned after 1712, the separate traders continued to prosper. Their later careers show that they persisted in using Parliament to uphold their economic interests. This use of parliamen-

6. James A. Rawley, "Harris, Richard (d. 1734)," in *Oxford Dictionary of National Biography* (Oxford, 2004), accessed May 14, 2013, http://www.oxforddnb.com/view/article/47571; Stephen Godin, quoted in Charles M. Andrews, "Colonial Commerce," *American Historical Review*, XX (1914), 45; James A. Rawley, "Richard Harris, Slave Trader Spokesman," in Rawley, *London, Metropolis of the Slave Trade* (Columbia, Mo., 2003), 71 (Virginia duties), 81 (Jamaica duties); Jamaican Letters to the Board of Trade, Colonial Office (CO) 137/17, 25–27, National Archives, Kew. For Morice's and Harris's involvement in the Creditors' Act campaign, see Correspondence of the Board of Trade, CO 324/11, 246, 247.

7. For the Debt Recovery Act, see George William Van Cleve, *A Slaveholders' Union: Slavery, Politics, and the Constitution in the Early American Republic* (Chicago, 2010), 21.

tary politics to expand the British economy had repercussions beyond the trade in enslaved Africans. Since the mid-1690s, Parliament had serviced the national debt with the help of the Bank of England. As a two-time governor of the Bank of England (1709–1711, 1723–1725) and an influential politician within the Corporation of London and in Parliament, Sir Gilbert Heathcote shifted his lobbying activities after 1712 away from the expansion of trade to the protection of national credit, watching with some satisfaction as the Tory's counterpoise to the Bank of England, the South Sea Company, failed in the early 1720s. He died in 1733, at the age of eighty-one, and was reputed to be the richest commoner in England, with a fortune of seven hundred thousand pounds.[8]

Robert Heysham and Richard Harris continued to use the lobbying techniques they had pioneered as separate traders. Heysham remained an active parliamentary lobbyist on trading matters, opposing the 1713 French Commerce Bill. He died in 1727 with landed investments in Hertfordshire, Essex, and Lancashire valued at £26,000, a personal estate amounting to £19,960 net per annum, and a house at Billiter Square. He expired resplendent and surrounded by goods suitable for export to Africa. Harris continued to be active on the Board of Trade and as a slave trader. Between 1718 and 1733, Harris embarked 1,931 enslaved from Africa. Along with Humphrey Morice, he was regarded by the 1720s as one of Britain's chief experts on the African trade. James Rawley concluded, "At his death in 1734, Richard Harris probably had exerted more influence over British slave trade policy than any other person in the first three decades of the eighteenth century. . . . [He] was an unacknowledged legislator for the transatlantic slave trade."[9]

Peter Paggen became a pillar of the London trading establishment. He purchased Wandsworth Manor House from the Royal Family and lived there in great splendor. His loutish hunting expeditions upset the local residents of nearby Battersea, who disputed his pious reputation and highlighted his commercial background, sarcastically quipping in a letter to the *Weekly Journal*: "that truly religious, pious, modern, Protestant Saint, Capt. Peter Pagan." Paggen died in 1720.[10]

---

8. Jacob M. Price, "Heathcote, Sir Gilbert, first baronet (1652–1733)," *ODNB*, accessed May 14, 2013, http://www.oxforddnb.com/view/article/47571.

9. Rawley, "Richard Harris," in Rawley, *London*, 80–81. For Heysham's legacy, see Will of Robert Heysham, Common Serjeant's Book, VI, box 49, fol. 114b, no. 3263, Corporation of London Records Office, London Metropolitan Archives. See also Eveline Cruickshanks, Stuart Handley, and D. W. Hayton, eds., *The History of Parliament: The House of Commons, 1690–1715*, 5 vols. (Cambridge, 2002), IV, 354–358.

10. *Weekly-Journal; or, Saturday's Post*, Feb. 1, 1718.

The later life of Humphrey Morice, in particular, exemplifies the separate traders' intermixture of political and trading interests. Having married Paggen's daughter, Katherine, in 1722, Morice spent much of his time at Wandsworth Manor House. Between 1718 and 1732, he dispatched fifty-three voyages to Africa for slaves. In total, he transported 11,443 Africans in ships he owned that were named after his daughters. A witness before the Board of Trade in 1750 asserted, "Mr. Morris [sic] imported more Gold Coast negroes into our Colonies in two or three years about twenty-eight years ago, than all the merchants of Bristol and Liverpool." The experience of lobbying together seems to have led to a lasting friendship between Morice and Richard Harris. By the 1720s, Morice and Harris owned and operated ships together. He and Harris also went foxhunting together at Morice's Chiswick estate.[11]

Despite the huge profits slave voyages generated for Humphrey Morice and the clear endorsement they provide for his skills as a merchant, Morice's career ended in failure. His later years perhaps show that the Africa trade debates had led him to favor the political means over the economic ends of trade. His political campaign to guarantee the freedom to trade in the enslaved assisted his career in the City of London. By 1727, he had secured the most prestigious political position of all: governor of the Bank of England. In Morice's case, however, his political profile failed to solve some financial worries. His belief that political power could sustain economic success proved illusory and led him into crime and then suicide. Morice abused his position as governor and began to embezzle bank funds, siphoning them into trust funds for his daughters. Unable to conceive of a public fall from grace and a private life of upward struggle, Morice poisoned himself in 1737. The legacy he left, along with Harris, Heathcote, Heysham, and his father-in-law, Paggen, was as leader of the political movement that produced the largest forced intercontinental forced migration in world history.[12]

FROM 1712, the Royal African Company continued to deploy political methods to develop trading opportunities, which prevented it from fading into obscurity. The company's lobbying strategy since 1710 of courting ministerial support had been gaining ground. In 1710, Robert Harley, a longtime expert on the African trade, became Queen Anne's chief minister. The scale of the government's debt presented Harley with his most serious challenge. Because

---

11. James A. Rawley, "Humphrey Morice: Foremost London Slave Merchant of His Time," in Rawley, *London*, 43 ("Mr. Morris"). For evidence of Harris and Morice as a hunting partnership, see Humphrey Morice Papers, Oct. 8, 1714, Additional Manuscripts, 48590 B, British Library, London.

12. Cruickshanks, Handley, and Hayton, eds., *House of Commons*, II, 277.

of his expertise, and partly because of African Company lobbying, Harley appears to have considered using the Royal African Company as a vehicle to restore the public finances. He obtained a legal opinion from the attorney general supporting the sale of the monarch's right to two-thirds of the value of any gold mines developed by the Royal African Company so that the company's African territories could be used to encourage investment as well as for a revamped slave-trading operation. He also employed Daniel Defoe to promote the African Company in his newspaper, the *Review,* from 1709 to 1713.[13]

In the end, however, Harley opted for a different course. Partly owing to the Africa trade debates' persistent description of the huge economic benefits of the transatlantic slave trade and owing to the widespread public dissatisfaction with the Royal African Company, he proposed a new slave-trading company and created in 1711 the South Sea Company. This company proposed to improve the government's credit by exchanging discounted government bonds for stock in the new company. To give the company credibility as a trading entity, it was charged in 1713 with satisfying the asiento to supply slaves to Spanish America (a key term extracted by Britain during the peace negotiations at Utrecht to end the War of Spanish Succession). The South Sea Company thus represents the ministry's renewed attempt to use the slave trade, as it did with the East India trade, to benefit government finance. As such, it was a response to the separate traders' legislative vacuum, which allowed independent slave trading to be conducted outside the purview of state regulation.[14]

Harley's decision to create a new corporate entity to manage the asiento in place of the African Company suggests the extent to which year after year of parliamentary deliberations had discredited the African Company in the public's eyes. Harley elected to support the African Company, however, because he saw a role for it as a potential slave supplier to his South Sea scheme and because the company and their supporters had worked hard to influence him. The African Company therefore became associated with a Tory policy. Propping up the African Company became part of the Tories' pro–South Sea Company position. The South Sea Company also entertained a proposal from the separate traders to supply it with slaves, but the awarding of that contract,

---

13. See Sir Edward Northey to the Right Honourable earl of Oxford, n.d., Oxford, Bodleian Library, MS. Clar., XC, 192–195. Harley had been supportive of the African Company since the 1690s. He had presented a pro-African Company petition to the House of Commons in January 1694; see Petitions to the King, T 70/169, 204. Daniel Defoe argued that the 1710 government limited the chances for the separate traders to achieve government support (*Review,* June 8, 1710). Sir Gilbert Heathcote had confronted Queen Anne and argued that a change of ministry would ruin the nation's credit. Such presumptive behavior might have affected the separate traders' standing.

14. For a recent discussion of the formation of the South Sea Company, see Carl Wennerlind, *Casualties of Credit: The English Financial Revolution, 1620–1720* (Cambridge, Mass., 2011), 197–234.

in 1713, to the African Company underlines the extent to which the company had successfully positioned itself within the Harley ministry's affections.[15]

This contract between the South Sea Company and the Royal African Company represented a possible economic lifeline for the African Company. It also offered a means for the African Company to improve its political position because the South Sea Company's directorate could be relied upon to lobby against legislation that might intrude on both companies' shared trading opportunities. Many African Company directors became South Sea Company directors. The African Company explained its strategy to one of its agents: "We now advise you that the Assiento contract for selling Negroes in the Spanish west indies being fix'd in the South Sea Company, we have agreed with that company to provide them with Negroes. . . . By this interest we have now acquired you may rest assured no act of Parliament will ever pass in favour of interlopers for an open trade." Sure enough, in June 1713, when a bill to deregulate the slave trade reached the House of Lords, the management of the South Sea Company "resolved, that the sub Governor, deputy Governor, . . . to wait on the Lord High Treasurer and acquaint his lordship that it is the opinion of this court that it will be for the advantage of this company that the bill to settle the trade to Africa do not pass this session." Later that month, Charles Montagu, earl of Halifax, the lord treasurer, presided over the Lords select committee that stalled discussion of the 1713 anti–African Company bill to protect the company from dissolution. The African Company thus successfully developed a government-sponsored interest via its connection to Robert Harley and then its contract with the South Sea Company to ensure its survival in 1713.[16]

---

15. The plan to use trade with the Spanish empire to raise the Tory party's reputation in trade and finance emerged as early as 1709 in *Proposals for Raising a New Company for Carrying on the Trades of Africa and the Spanish West-Indies, under the Title of the United Company* (London, 1709). See also *A Letter from a West-India Merchant to a Gentleman at Tunbridge . . .* (London, 1712), 29. Maximillian E. Novak, *Daniel Defoe: Master of Fictions, His Life and Ideas* (Oxford, 2001), 183, claimed that Defoe himself, along with William Paterson, had formulated the plan to develop a trading company to South America, ahead of his employment by Harley. Defoe's support for the Royal African Company thus might have been more sincere than that of a hired pen for Harley. The South Sea Company initially concluded that neither the African Company nor the separate traders could supply any advantage to the South Sea Company. By October 6, 1713, the South Sea and Royal African Companies had reached an agreement. See "An Account of the Proceedings of the Court of Directors of the South Sea Company from Their First Institution in Relation to Trade," Kings MS, no. 73, 24–30, British Library. This Tory revival harks back to that which prevented the resumption of Pennsylvania's charter; see I. K. Steele, *Politics of Colonial Policy: The Board of Trade in Colonial Administration, 1696–1720* (Oxford, 1968), 80.

16. Royal African Company to John Clark, Aug. 14, 1713, T 70/52, 332; "Records of the South Sea Company," June 30, 1713, 129, Add. MSS, 25495, British Library. For Halifax's potential role in

The contract would become a poisoned chalice for the African Company. In August 1713, the South Sea Company contracted with the Royal African Company to supply forty-eight hundred slaves on the coast of Africa. Confident that the agreement would solve its financial problems, the Royal African Company hardly watched as the separate traders, buoyed by broad public support, destroyed its market share. To make matters worse, the South Sea Company's contract with the Royal African Company began to cause the latter some concern. In May 1714, the South Sea Company owed the Royal African Company £7,695. The company began, once again, to apply to Parliament for a statute in support of its monopoly. Such was the widespread recognition of the company's commercial, financial, and political humiliation over the past quarter century that they were unable to find a member of Parliament (MP) to present their petition during the 1714 parliamentary session. By June 1714, the Africa Company petitioned the queen about the "deplorable state" of their trade and proposed that she either support their campaign for parliamentary establishment or let them sell their forts. The company made one final attempt to gather extra funds from its shareholders on condition of a statute in summer 1714. This campaign failed, and many of the Royal African Company's old guard of directors jumped ship, one assumes, fatigued by association with the company. Queen Anne died in 1714, and the arrival of the Hanoverian monarchs and the change of government it brought about severed the African Company's personal link with the ministry. In October 1714, a Royal African Company official claimed that "the change of the ministers of state had fallen the African and South Sea stocks and frustrated the Company's expectations." As Britain's independent slave trade expanded, the company appeared to enter an inane retirement.[17]

Defeated in the slave trade by the separate traders, the company attempted to reinvigorate its stock by developing plantations near its African forts as well as a profitable trade with the inland parts of Africa. It wished to concentrate its commercial efforts where it had always focused the attention of potential political supporters—on Africa itself. These wishes reflected long-held ambitions for the company. Both Charles Davenant and Daniel Defoe

---

stalling anti–African Company legislation, see Trade to Africa Bill, June 23, 1713, in *The Manuscripts of the House of Lords*, n.s., X, *1712-1714*, ed. Maurice F. Bond (London, 1953), no. 3019, 173.

17. Minutes of the Bye Committee, [May 27, 1714], T 70/141, 22; Royal African Company's Petition to Queen Anne, June 6, 1714, T 70/170, 154–155; Gerrard Gore et al. to the Royal African Company, Oct. 9, 1714, T 70/5, n.p. For the company's inability to find a presenter for their petition, see Royal African Company to William Cleland, Apr. 13, 1714, T 70/45, n.p. For the company's attempt to gather funds from its shareholders, see Subscriptions Book, Feb. 25, 1714, T 70/178, 3; and Minutes of the General Court, Feb. 18, 1714, T 70/101, 160–161.

had celebrated the inland trade of Africa as one of the opportunities for Britain that the African Company provided. Davenant described the development of plantations to grow indigo, pepper, and cotton on the African coast as something of a "very great national advantage" because "none can pretend that our Western Plantations are capable of furnishing this nation with sufficient quantities of these commodities." Defoe echoed Davenant by declaring, "It is the undoubted Advantage of this Nation to plant, raise, or produce any Commodity, tho' now growing in our own Colonies, while our said Colonies are not able to produce the Quantity we want, and that we are oblig'd to buy it in other Countries for our ready Money."[18]

For Davenant and Defoe, the full rewards of an inland commerce with Africa, or of plantations there, was only possible with the complete support of the state and a corporation. If the state's interests were properly upheld by the company, the state could begin to develop its territorial holdings in Africa and reap the huge benefits of gold mining and the trade with the continent's vast and unknown interior. Davenant believed the joint-stock format provided the best means to gather sufficient capital to mine gold. The company, so its petitions advised, offered the only means for the British interest on the coast of Africa to be maintained. The separate traders, as their epithet implied, were too detached from the interests of the British state to successfully advance them. An African Company pamphlet in 1713 declared that a financially restored African Company would exist "to improve the *British interest in Africa,* to get knowledge of the more *Inland* Countries, thereby to promote the greater Consumption of *British Manufactures.*" Another in the same year argued in similar terms: the company would assist the state in "Penetrating into the Inland Parts where, beyond Controversy, are as *Great Treasures* of *Gold* as are found in *Brazile,* or in any other Parts of *America,* and which can *never* so much as be *attempted* in an open Trade."[19]

---

18. Charles Davenant, *Reflections upon the Constitution and Management of the African Trade, etc.,* in Charles Whitworth, ed., *The Political and Commercial Works of That Celebrated Writer Charles D'Avenant, LL.D. . . . ,* V (London, 1771), 319 (hereafter cited as Davenant, *Reflections*); *Review,* Mar. 12, 1709.

19. *The Present State of the Royal African Company* (n.p., [1713]), 1; *A Proposal for Settling the Trade to Africa, Wherein the Ends Professed to Be Aimed at, Both by the Separate Traders, and the Company; and Also by the North Britains, Out Ports and Plantations, and Likewise by the Manufacturers, Are Effectually Provided for* (n.p., [1713]), 2; Davenant, *Reflections,* 260. The African Company never fully renounced its aim of establishing sugar and indigo plantations on the coast of Africa. This further fueled colonial opposition. See W. Noel Sainsbury et al., eds., *Calendar of State Papers, Colonial Series, America and West Indies . . . ,* 44 vols. (London, 1860–1969), XIII, no. 2530, 1. For the African Company petition that spoke of the British interest, see *Journals of the House of Commons, I-LI* (London, 1803), XVI, 242.

Such a trade would, of course, require large-scale investment and, thus, political capital. Because of the African Company's public humiliation since the 1690s, such capital would be difficult to assemble. The African Company saw an opportunity to ingratiate themselves with the new Hanoverian dynasty. The support of the new monarch, George I, would help to improve the company's political position without having to resort to another parliamentary appeal. In July 1715, the Royal African Company's subgovernor, William Paston, earl of Yarmouth, and several directors appeared before the king with some of the fruits of the African interior: "a tyger, civet cat, guinea hens, green birds, and lumps of gold . . . which his majesty was pleased to receive very graciously and admitted all the gentlemen present to kiss his hand." The company positioned itself before the king as the victim of the bullying South Sea Company, which had strong links with the previous ministry:

> That since the expiration of the . . . act of Parliament the interlopers have assumed the name of free and open traders and have entred the company's lands and possessions in Africa with such numbers and force that cannot be resisted or repressed without the aid and protection of the government. . . . And as an addition to the injuries and oppression the company groans under, they complaine of the South Sea Company for acting like interlopers and now attempting to send a great number of shipps to invade this company's territories and take from them the benefit of their dear bought trade on those coasts. . . . The African Company therefore (who are not able to contend with the great power of the South Sea Company) humbly resort to yr Maj as supreme moderator.

The African Company pledged to make such moderation worth the king's while by proposing a scheme by which the company would lend the monarch one-third of a million pounds at 5 percent interest. The company would be restyled as the British African Company, with representatives from the South Sea Company and the provincial outports of Liverpool and Bristol.[20]

---

20. For the company's courtship of George I, see Minutes of the Court of Assistants, July 5, 1715, T 70/89, 136. The animals were sent to the Tower of London; see *Weekly Packet* (London), July 2, 1715, and (for the text) Minutes of the General Court, Oct. 21, 1714, T 70/101, 164. For the details of this scheme, see Minutes of the Bye Committee, Apr. 23, 1715, T 70/141, 24. Other similar schemes appeared in 1716 and 1718. In 1716, a proposal to use the African Company to raise one million pounds emanated from Arthur Moore and was passed onto Robert Walpole by the duke of Chandos. For Moore's scheme, see Duke of Chandos to Robert Walpole, Oct. 27, 1716, Stowe Manuscripts 57, XIV, 242, Huntington Library, San Marino, Calif.

By 1716, the company indicated its formal desire to favor commercial contacts with the African interior over its participation in the slave trade. The minutes of the General Court recorded: "It is obvious that the Royal African Company have lost great sums of money by the trade; their exports, for many years pass'd have been very small, their charges great; and their disappointments in the negroe trade, many and various."[21]

The African Company persisted in its courtship of the royal family by entering the fray during the feud between George I and the Prince of Wales in 1717 (father and son disagreed about how to share the more tedious features of royal protocol). The king's Civil List debts had mounted, which weakened his financial position. Noting the extent of these debts and thrust out of office, Robert Walpole began to cultivate various corporations for loans that would secure the monarch's personal finances in exchange for a form of state sponsorship. Success for Walpole would help him rebound into the ministry. The African Company became a possible candidate. Not since the reign of James II had there been the prospect that the company could provide financial support for the monarchy. The duke of Chandos, one of the most notorious embezzlers and projectors of the eighteenth century, began, as a result, to invest in the company.[22]

As paymaster general under James Churchill, first duke of Marlborough, during the War of Spanish Succession, James Brydges, first duke of Chandos, had amassed an estate of six hundred thousand pounds. The most notorious pillager of public funds, Chandos began to pour his vast wealth into an ostentatious aristocratic lifestyle and corporate adventures. His route to investment in the African Company seems to have been through familiar and personal connections. In 1696, Chandos had married Mary Lake, the daughter of Sir Thomas Lake, an African Company director and the sister of Sir Bibye Lake, who would become the company's deputy governor in 1722. Charles Davenant, who lived with the duke until his death in 1717, most likely supplied much of the inspiration for the duke's outlook on the African trade. By 1720, Chandos had become a director of the African Company and was its principal investor and visionary.[23]

By investing in the African Company, Chandos tapped into a buoyant European stock market. The late 1710s were good years for publicly traded

21. Minutes of the General Court, May 16, 1716, T 70/101, 173.
22. Account Books, Aug. 23, 1719, Stowe MSS 12, III, 1.
23. For details of the duke of Chandos's biography, see C. H. Collins Baker and Muriel I. Baker, *The Life and Circumstances of James Brydges, First Duke of Chandos, Patron of the Liberal Arts* (Oxford, 1949), 12, 44–62, 83.

corporations. John Law's Mississippi Scheme in France had instigated a vast boom in European share prices. Companies of all sorts appeared and floated on the stock exchanges of Paris and London. The principal vehicle for the overheating of the London stock market was the South Sea Company. The government enthusiastically welcomed this stock market boom. The African Company's royal charter and its long pedigree must have made it appear venerable as an investment in comparison to the hundreds of new companies that appeared in these years. Companies sought the comparative advantage born of legitimacy that a seventeenth-century royal charter would provide. Funds gathered by the burgeoning insurance industries flocked to established corporations like the African Company. In the summer of 1718, the Royal Exchange Assurance began to invest in the Mines Royal and the Mineral and Battery Works. Insurance companies, such as Onslow's and Chetwynd's, which had tried and failed to become incorporated, began to invest huge sums in the African Company so that the company's charter might protect their businesses. These newly wealthy companies entered the bidding war for state favor as the issue of financing the new king's Civil List went unsolved. Chandos and others, including the directors of insurance companies, began to invest greater sums in the African Company to take advantage of rising interest in the African Company and in equities in general.[24]

For Chandos, there were two pillars to the African El Dorado. The prospect of helping to finance the monarchy and the political rewards that would bring combined with a steadfast belief that there were huge sums of money to be made trading with the interior of the African continent. The extent of the stock boom in the 1710s led Chandos to see that the time was right to make an investment in deepening Britain's commercial ties with Africa: "Reflecting, that the carrying-on Trade in the piddling Manner they had done for some Years past, would never answer their great capital Stock, [Chandos] advised them to make some Attempt for opening a Trade into the Inland Parts of *Africa*." By the following year (after the stock market bubble had burst), Chandos himself declared: "I am so fully perswaded of the advantages which may accrue from this trade, that I shall not despair of having Africa become so beneficial to England as America is to Spain." From 1720 onward, the company, under Chandos's leadership, would reinvent itself, and thus the British presence in Africa, as a territorial entity and an agent of inland penetration and conquest, of gold mining, and of plantations. The duke of Chandos's in-

---

24. Barry Supple, *The Royal Exchange Assurance: A History of British Insurance, 1720-1970* (Cambridge, 1970), 18; Ron Harris, *Industrializing English Law: Entrepreneurship and Business Organization, 1720-1844* (Cambridge, 2000), 61, 66, 67.

volvement with the Royal African Company would represent the company's final trading flourish.²⁵

The company, hoping to strike gold on the stock market and in Africa, completely overhauled its financial structure. The scheme involved engrafting 15,696 new African Company shares to the old African Company's capital at a discount of 25 percent. The funds raised from these new shares would provide eighty thousand pounds to cover the old company's outstanding debts. The proprietors of the old stock were to be paid a dividend of ten pounds upon each of their shares, with the new shares providing a trading stock for the benefit of the old and new owners of the company. Joseph Taylor, Chandos's attorney and a shadowy figure in London's financial scene, became the public mastermind of the financial mechanics of the scheme. Taylor had already proven himself a versatile and socially astute lawyer. He had defended Robert Harley during his impeachment in 1715. He then became clerk of Bridewell and the Bethlehem Hospital. These activities shrouded a highly profitable private practice, which served some of the wealthiest clients in England, such as the Child family, the descendants of the East India Company supremo, Sir Josiah Child, including Sir Richard Child, Josiah's heir and the future Lord Castlemain. This practice brought him into contact with Chandos, whose aunt was Josiah's third wife. Taylor became one of Chandos's lawyers and a financial confidante and fixer. His experience, contacts, and expertise made him an ideal person to manage the 1720 reconstitution of the Royal African Company.²⁶

The scale of Chandos's investments in the scheme, his behind-the-scenes management of early subscribers, and his control over other investors' holdings suggest that he shared the responsibility for the new company with his cousin, Humphrey Walcot, and with Joseph Taylor. By March 1720, Chandos admitted to having a share of £400,000 in the new adventure. He celebrated

---

25. Bartholomew Stibbs, *A Voyage up the Gambra, in 1724, for Making Discoveries, and Improving the Trade of That River* . . . , in *A New and General Collection of Voyages and Travels* . . . , 4 vols. (London, 1745–1747), II, 193–194; Chandos to James Phipps, Jan. 6, 1721, Stowe MSS 57, XVII, 314.

26. The mechanics of the engraftment were described later in *An Antidote to Expel the Poison Contained in an Anonymous Pamphlet, Lately Published, Entitled, A Detection of the Proceedings and Practices of the Directors of the Royal African Company of England, etc.* . . . (London, 1749), 14. For Joseph Taylor as the clerk of Bridewell, see Chandos to Lord Guildford, Mar. 18, 1720, Stowe MSS 57, XVIII, 8. For Taylor's service to the Child family, see Outward Letter Books, Stowe MSS 57, XVIII, 8. For Brydges' relationship with Taylor, see Chandos to Joseph Taylor, Dec. 6, 1723, Mar. 4, 1724, Stowe MSS 57, XXIII, 108, 322. Historians have failed to identify Taylor and describe his relationship with Chandos; see Ann M. Carlos, Karen Maguire, and Larry Neal, "Financial Acumen, Women Speculators, and the Royal African Company during the South Sea Bubble," *Accounting, Business, and Financial History*, XVI (2006), 225.

the enthusiasm of key ministry figures such as Henry Boyle, earl of Carlton, and Peter Methuen. The subscription proved tremendously popular. Chandos's correspondence is full of apologetic letters informing wealthy punters that their application for stock had been unsuccessful. The subscription for the new African Company shares raised, according to Chandos, in excess of £2 million. Taylor poured in resources from his "friend at Wansted," Sir Richard Child. Lady Child also invested substantially. Two courtiers close to the Baroness Gemmingen, who was the nanny for the prince of Wales's children and a close friend of the king's mistress, also made sizable investments that restored the connection the separate traders had often made between the bedchamber intrigues of the court and the Royal African Company's capital. After the old company's shareholders and their creditors had been paid and the various intermediaries who had managed the deal received their fees, £147,967 remained for the new African Company's trade. A new group of directors, many of whom enjoyed considerable prestige, came to serve the African Company at this time, including Martin Bladen, a Board of Trade commissioner, Richard Lockwood, a prominent Turkey merchant and one of the duke's principal financiers, as well as Edward Waller, the chancellor of the Exchequer's financial go-between. Directorships of the new company proved so desirable to the powerful that both Charles Spencer, third earl of Sunderland, and Charles Townshend, second viscount Townshend, failed to achieve favor.²⁷

As a result of the engraftment of 1720, the African Company had been reborn as a powerful and wealthy corporation that Chandos proudly noted had been transformed, at his initiative, from "the most despicable and ruin-

---

27. For evidence of Chandos's control over the stock of others, see Chandos to Richard Lockwood, Jan. 13, 1721, Stowe MSS 57, XVII, 322. Chandos informed Lockwood that John Drummond, Daniel Hayes, and the earl of Clarendon were happy to become African Company directors and added, ". . . and therefore will you be so good as to desire [advise?] Mr. Taylor to transfer to Lord Clarendon as much stock as is wanting to [Qualify] him to be a Director out of the 3,000 to Cap he hath of Mr. Coz Brydges." For Chandos's admission of the scale of his involvement, see Chandos to Taylor, Mar. 18, 1720, Stowe MSS 57, XVIII, 7. For Carlton and Methuen, see Outward Letter Books, Stowe MSS 57, XVIII, 31. Chandos wrote to Colonel Martin Bladen, "I have discoursed with Lord Carlton about this affair, and find him perfectly disposed to support the Scheme" (Chandos to Taylor, Mar. 18, 1720, Stowe MSS 57, XVIII, 7). For "Friend at Wansted," see Chandos to Taylor, Dec. 6, 1723, Stowe MSS 57, XXIII, 108. For Lady Child's investment, see Chandos to Taylor, Mar. 18, 1720, Stowe MSS 57, XVIII, 7. For the involvement of the baroness, see Chandos to Sir Matthew Decker, Apr. 15, 1720, Stowe MSS 57, XVIII, 23. For the financial side of the engraftment, see Ann M. Carlos, Nathalie Moyen, and Jonathan Hill, "Royal African Company Share Prices during the South Sea Bubble," *Explorations in Economic History*, XXXIX (2002), 61–87. For the disappointment of Sunderland and Townshend about not being made African Company directors, see Chandos to Mr. Hutchinson, May 21, 1720, Stowe MSS 57, XVIII, 48.

ous Condition that any body of Men ever found themselves in." Contemporaries noted that Chandos's energetic involvement with the African Company "made some Noise in the World, and their Stock rose considerably, when all the rest were sunk." Robert Walpole, the future prime minister, who made perhaps nine thousand pounds from African stock, encouraged separate trader Humphrey Morice's involvement with the new African Company. Both Morice and then Richard Harris declined to be involved, however. Later, Chandos would suggest to Walpole that the African Company's relative durability as a corporation after the bursting of the South Sea Bubble might recommend it to the government as a vehicle to manage the public debt. Under Chandos's guidance, the African Company entered a new period of optimism and assiduity.[28]

The fresh capital generated by the engraftment produced the company's most impressive trading phase, during which it assembled record numbers of cargoes, filled its warehouses, repaired its forts, and built a new fort at Angola. The *London Journal* reported, "The African Company are now sending all sorts of Goods fit for their Guinea Trade." Chandos had sought advice from experts in the African trade, including present and former officials of the African Company as well as two African princes that were guests at extravagant dinner parties at his stately mansion, Cannons, in Edgware, north of London. Chandos explained that, after questioning the princes over dinner, he had become convinced that their expertise could assist him "to take hold of the opportunity to make what discoveries they can of the Products of those Parts of the World." For Chandos, the principal opportunity was gold mining. By the summer of 1722, Chandos concluded that "the slave trade is a losing trade" and that the business of the company ought to be with "home returns"—goods traded back to England, especially gold.[29]

---

28. For Chandos's assessment of the part he played in restoring the African Company's fortunes, see Chandos to Sir Nicholas Laws, Sept. 23, 1720, Stowe MSS 57, XVII, 180. For the positive effect this restoration had on the company's share price, see James Houstoun, *Dr. Houston's Memoirs of His Own Life-time* . . . (London, 1747), 126–127. For Morice's courtship of Chandos, see Chandos to Mr. Purcell, July 11, 1720, Stowe MSS 57, XVIII, 80. For Morice's appeal to Walpole for assistance with African affairs, see Chandos to Robert Walpole, Oct. 18, 1720, Stowe MSS 57, XVII, 233; see also Chandos to Lockwood, July 14, 1721, Stowe MSS 57, XIX, 115. For Walpole's African Company windfall, see J. H. Plumb, *Sir Robert Walpole: The Making of a Statesman* (London, 1956), 309. For Chandos's attempts to involve the African Company in state finance, see Chandos to Walpole, Dec. 1, 1720, Stowe MSS 57, XVIII, 200: "I hear you're close to restoring credit. Can the African Company scheme not share in it?"; and again in James Brydges to Walpole, July 3, 1721, Cholmondeley Manuscripts, Cambridge University Library.

29. For the African Company's fort at Angola, see *An Antidote to Expel the Poison*, 15. See also *London Journal*, July 2–9, 1720. For Chandos's belief that the princes would help him find gold

Most impressive about Chandos was the extent of his commercial imagination and vision and the relentless energy he deployed attempting to realize that vision. The duke carefully researched all of his business ventures. Besides gold mining, Chandos proposed the cultivation of cotton, indigo, and pepper on the African coast as well as the manufacturing of "Callicoe and Muslin," wood for "wainscoting," "Barbary Matting," and walking canes. He advised his contacts in Africa of various tropical products that would fetch a good price in London, including gum to make "dragon's blood powder that sells for a crown an ounce," the stone of a "Bezoar Monky" extracted from its intestine, and the "civett" of a cat, a "very valuable commodity at Sierra Liono." He proposed that African agents market English fashions in Africa and that African textile designs be sent to Manchester for copying and the resulting products sold in England and the colonies. He wrote to Hans Sloane about African crops that might be delivered and used as medicines. He gathered a team of Cornish miners and transported them to the African coast to begin digging for gold. He assembled histories of Africa and journals to research the continent's geography and commercial potential as well as manuscript copies of seventeenth-century excursions to Africa, including one transcribed by Robert Hooke. His vision for the Royal African Company's trade with Africa was nothing less than an amalgamation of all of Britain's imperial experience up to that point; it combined the development of a market for English goods and a resource for extracting precious metals and importing valuable raw materials for the British and European markets.[30]

DESPITE CHANDOS's undeniable energy and vision, his scheme to develop the African Company's trade had, by 1725, utterly failed. The company struggled to disassociate itself from the financial irregularities of the South Sea Bubble and of Chandos's own personal history of financial impropriety. In March 1721, the *London Journal* reported a refinancing deal for the company, and it

---

mines, see Chandos to Captain Paul, Jan. 26, 1722, Stowe MSS 57, XX, 88. For Chandos's conclusion that the slave trade was a losing trade, see Chandos to Mr. Baldwyn, July 7, 1722, Stowe MSS 57, XXI, 22.

30. For cotton, indigo, pepper, calico, and muslin, see Chandos to Mr. Baldwin, Mar. 3, 1722, Stowe MSS 57, XVIII, 386. For wainscoting, Barbary matting, and walking canes, see Chandos to Mr. Plunkett, Oct. 29, 1721, Stowe MSS 57, XIX, 242. For dragon's blood powder, see Chandos to Phipps, Aug. 4, 1721, Stowe MSS 57, XVIII, 254. For the "Bezoar Monky" and the "civet" of a cat, see Chandos to Mr. Glynn, Jan. 12, 1723, Stowe MSS 57, XXII, 160. See also Chandos to Mr. Tinker, Dec. 1, 1724, Stowe MSS 57, XXV, 46; Chandos to Sir Hans Sloane, Dec. 4, 1721, Sloane Manuscripts, 4046, 152, British Library (I am grateful to Dr. Lindsay O'Neill for showing this letter to me); Chandos to Phipps, Jan. 6, [1721], Stowe MSS 57, XVII, 314; "Copy of a Journall up the River Gambia Found amongst Dr. Hooks Papers," Stowe MSS 9, 1.

was "reckon'd that the Company have lost Ninety Five Thousand Pound Sterling by the Bargain." Two other forces conspired to undermine the company's renaissance. The company's restored trade provided rich and easy pickings for pirates. One newspaper estimated that the African Company's losses reached two hundred thousand pounds by the summer of 1720. Some of the Cornish miners that the company had dispatched to the African coast to assist with the gold mines mutinied and began to steal from the company in the summer of 1722. The miners joined pirate ships prowling the west coast of Africa. The others remained, wrote James Houstoun, but in a deplorable state: "I found, at my Arrival, most of them dead, and those alive were now and then a digging of little Holes or Pits in the Ground by the Sea-side, and searching that Earth for Gold; which appeared to me to be rather a Burlesque than any real Enquiry."[31]

The possibility of any European power establishing gold mines on the west coast of Africa or asserting themselves independently of their African hosts was remote. For, as Houstoun continued to explain about the Cornish miners, "They durst not venture the Miners out of the reach of the Castle Guns, lest the *Negroes,* who certainly took them for Conjurors, should make Incursions on them, to the Hazard of their Lives." Houstoun summarized why Chandos's mining adventure had failed: "The Scarcity of Provisions for Subsistance, and the Resistance that necessarily must be made by the Natives, are Reasons of the Impossibility of the Project of discovering and possessing their Mines." His explanation for Chandos's failure received further support in early 1722, when the African Company received the "disagreeable News, . . . that the Natives of Angola, assisted by a Portuguese Man of War, had burnt the Company's Guard-Ship, call'd the Royal Africa, . . . and destroy'd their Settlement at Cabenda." This event devastated Chandos's plans to use the company as a vessel for British interests in the African interior.[32]

The African Company again looked to the South Sea Company for an im-

---

31. *London Journal*, Mar. 4, 1721. For the company's financial irregularities, see also John Atkins, *A Voyage to Guinea, Brasil, and the West-Indies* . . . (London, 1735), 267. For the Cornish pirates, see Chandos to Mr. Payne, July 9, 1723, Stowe MSS 57, XXII, 275. For newspaper reports of the company losses owing to the pirates, see *Weekly Journal; or, Saturday's-Post*, July 9, 1720. For "Burlesque," see James Houstoun, *Some New and Accurate Observations Geographical, Natural, and Historical; Containing a True and Impartial Account of the Situation, Product, and Natural History of the Coast of Guinea* . . . (London, 1725), 23.

32. Houstoun, *Some New and Accurate Observations*, 23, 24; *Daily Journal*, Feb. 10, 1723–1724. To make matters worse, by 1723 the attorney general, Philip Yorke, having responded to an inquiry from Chandos, gave his opinion that the company's charter could not be used to enforce the company's monopoly; see "Philip Yorke's Legal Opinion on the Company's Charter November 23rd, 1723," Stowe Brydges Papers, STB Legal, box 1, 1640–1729/30.

provement in its fortunes. News regularly spread that the South Sea Company would merge with or purchase the African Company. Such rumors were designed solely to improve the African Company's share price, but they were futile. The separate traders' well-established lobbying machine repeatedly blocked the South Sea Company's attempts to monopolize or even dominate the slave trade to Jamaica just as they had blocked the African Company's earlier attempts.[33]

Beleaguered by continued misfortunes and the strength of the competition and despite his best efforts to understand and communicate a new basis for the African trade, the duke of Chandos conceded defeat in February 1725. He declared, "Ever since I have had the misfortune to know any thing of the Company, disappointments vexations and loss have been all the fruits we have reapt from our care and application." Chandos's ambitious engagement with the trade ended in disaster. He lost £110,000 in his African adventures, compounding his huge losses in the South Sea Bubble. As he explained to Lord Bolingbroke in September 1721, "I have lost in this month above five hundred thousand pounds." The results of his investment in the company soon brought public ridicule. Jonathan Swift quipped about Chandos's career: "All he got by fraud is lost by stocks." One pamphleteer lampooned his obsession with gold mining and his experiments adjacent to Cape Coast Castle: "Their Trading-Stock was soon spent; no Gold was found; and a great Hole in the Side of a Hill alone remains, as an everlasting Monument of their Industry." Rapacious pirates, the low reputation of corporate finance, and the irrefutable power of the African states to prevent Europeans from imposing their commercial will on the African continent all conspired to thwart Chandos and his new African Company.[34]

WITHOUT CHANDOS'S INVOLVEMENT, the company soon foundered. It became vulnerable once again to attack in Parliament and in the Board of Trade. As it requested state support, a phalanx of separate traders convinced the

---

33. For the African Company's hot and cold relationship with the South Sea Company in the 1720s and 1730s, see Chandos to Sir John Eyles, Apr. 20, 1723, Stowe MSS 57, XXII, 237. See also *Newcastle Courant* (Newcastle upon Tyne), Dec. 26, 1724; and *Echo; or, Edinburgh Weekly Journal*, Jan. 14, 1730.

34. Chandos to Mr. Lynn, Feb. 24, 1725, Stowe MSS 57, XXV, 245; Chandos to Bolingbroke, Oct. 5, 1720, Stowe MSS 57, XVII, 206. For the scale of his financial losses, see Chandos to Dr. Stewart, Apr. 3, 1725, Stowe MSS 57, 316. For the quotation from Swift, see Jonathan Swift, "The Dean and Duke," in *The Works of Dr. Jonathan Swift, Dean of St. Patrick's, Dublin* . . . (Dublin, 1765), XIII, 333. For the pamphlet, see *A Detection of the Proceedings and Practices of the Directors of the Royal African Company of England* (London, 1749), 9. For Chandos's letter to Bolingbroke, see John Robert Robinson, *The Princely Chandos: A Memoir of James Brydges* . . . (London, 1893), 181.

Board that a supported African Company would restrict the scale of Britain's overseas trade. The differences between the political positions of the African Company and the separate traders in the 1720s had only hardened since the 1710s. The separate traders' natural rights argument had become more strident. One of their lobbyists representing the Bristol and Liverpool separate traders summarized:

> The said separate traders have an equal and natural right to trade to those parts. That by our constitution no one should be constrained in his right, unless it were for a public good. That the question is at present, whether the benefit of this trade should be dispersed over all the kingdom, or monopolised by a few of His Majesty's subjects. . . . That by our constitution the King had not a power, without consent of Parliament, to exclude any of his subjects from trading to any parts of Africa.[35]

The African Company's response to the modern politicking of the separate traders continued to express suspicion of petitioning interests and appealed to a society led by disinterested, genteel experts. As the African Company secretary, Francis Lynn, put it: "There are Cart Loads of Petitioners ready to be presented against Us."

> Though, It be Our happiness That the Meanest person in the Kingdom, may be allowed to petition, when He Thinks himself aggrieved; your Lordships known likewise That Petitions are never allowed to judge of themselves and considering the Arts by which Such Petitions may be obtained, and the Capacity of Those who generally speaking, are most forward to sign them, we think we have no Reason to apprehend any Danger from them. It is to those, who have the honour to be entrusted with the Care of Publick affairs are able to judge impartially between such Petitioners and Us, that We address our Selves; . . . That alone with competent Judges will weigh infinitely more than Numbers of Petitions, sign'd by Persons who with regard to the Nature and Circumstances of the Trade to Africa can hardly be allowed to know their Right Hand from their Left.[36]

The strength of the separate traders' connection with the prime minister, Robert Walpole, and the influence of men like Humphrey Morice would trump any appeal the African Company might make. The African Company's

---

35. *Journal of the Commissioners for Trade and Plantations*, I, 252.
36. "Petition of the Royal African Company," Feb. 7, 1727, T 70/172, 77.

attempt to develop and then monopolize Britain's trade with the African interior had done nothing to undermine the separate traders' growing slave-trading operation, and their interest group remained a force to be reckoned with.

As a result of the separate traders' entrenched political influence and the African Company's petitioning weakness, the company's opponents were able to exploit public disapproval of trading corporations since the South Sea Bubble and brand any political appeal by the company as a trap for unwary investors. The Chandos episode had not helped the company in this regard. African Company directors, such as Richard Lockwood, had their campaigns for election tainted by association with the ruinous financial schemes of the company. John Perceval, first earl of Egmont, witnessed a parliamentary debate in February 1730 during which the pro-company faction argued that the company's forts were soon to fall into the hands of a foreign power. The separate traders responded, without having to resort to the company's unimpressive trading record, that "this is only a job to flurry up the actions of the African Company, that some may sell out, and draw other unwary persons to buy, which may be the ruin of many families." Egmont went on to explain, "The majority [of MPs] were apprehensive such a countenance given it would cause a rise in the African Stock and render it a bubble to the deceiving unwary people, who would imagine the House intended to favour the Company, when they do not, and buy to their detriment." The separate traders could portray themselves as the defenders of liberal trading activity and the African Company as a typically fraudulent corporation seeking government sponsorship to rob the independent trader, via speculative mania, of his hard-won trading gains.[37]

In March 1730, Parliament formally resolved—but again without a statute—that the British slave trade ought to remain unregulated and added, "The Trade and Navigation to *Africa* ought never to be charged with any Duty for the Maintenance of the *British Forts* and *Settlements* belonging to the Company." Such was the force of the public's countenance for deregulated slave trading by the mid-1730s that the African Company had to spell out each time it made an appeal to a public body that a free trade in slaves represented the best means to manage the slave trade. A plantation interest growing in importance by the 1730s and 1740s forced the African Company to tread very

---

37. R. A. Roberts, ed., *Manuscripts of the Earl of Egmont: Diary of Viscount Percival, afterwards First Earl of Egmont* ..., 3 vols. (London, 1920–1923), I, 51, 52. For the ridiculing of Richard Lockwood's candidacy for MP for City of London because of his directorships at the African Company and Royal Exchange Assurance Company, "by which many of your Brethren have been ruin'd," see *Daily Journal*, Apr. 3, 1722.

carefully in Parliament. As one African Company petitioner obsequiously announced, the African Company

> should be wanting in their Duty to their Country, If at the same time, that they beg leave to represent the difficulties and discouragements, which they have long labored under themselves They did not likewise express their Fears, that the laying any burthen on the said Trade in general would very much tend to discourage the Importation of such Supplyes of Negros from time to time into the Colonys and Plantations belonging to this Kingdom, as are necessarily required for their Support and Improvement.

Another pro-company pamphlet obediently described the deregulated slave trade as the *"Sense* of the *Nation."* The 1730s provided another opportunity for the separate traders to show that their efforts in the Africa trade debates of the 1690s and 1710s had persuaded public and political opinion that an unregulated slave trade equaled an "open" trade and that both were in the best interests of the nation. In sum, a free trade in enslaved humans supported the liberty of Englishmen. Parliament, however, agreed to offer public subsidies to the Royal African Company to support its forts. Throughout much of the 1730s and 1740s, the state maintained the company via annual payments of ten thousand pounds, which the company could spend on its forts. The separate traders had helped to garner public enthusiasm for the slave trade, and Parliament thus felt comfortable providing public funds to support it. It was certainly ironic that the separate traders' success at developing public support for the slave trade would lead to the state's providing substantial annual subsidies to their lobbying opponents to protect the national interest on the African coast.[38]

The African Company's reputation enjoyed another brief resurgence during the 1740s. French success in the Atlantic economy and the outbreak of the War of the Austrian Succession (1740–1748) endorsed the African Company's argument that a strong monopoly company could better confront French competition than a diffuse deregulated trade. The success of the French slave trade during these years (partly under the monopolistic management of the French Senegal Company in the 1740s) and the rapid development

---

38. The 1730 parliamentary resolution is quoted in [Malachy Postlethwayt], *The National and Private Advantages of the African Trade Considered: Being an Enquiry, How Far It Concerns the Trading Interest of Great Britain* . . . (London, 1746), 90–91. See also [AZ], *Letter to a Member of Parliament concerning the African Trade* (n.p., [1748]), 1. See also Minutes of the Court of Assistants, Apr. 10, 1729, T 70/93, 37 ("wanting in their Duty"); *The Case of the Royal African Company of England* [London, 1730], 19 (*"Sense* of the *Nation"*).

of Saint Domingue as the most efficient sugar-producing island precipitated the creation of a British interest group led by Julius Beckford, brother of William Beckford, the City of London grandee. The African Company deployed lobbyists with impressive Atlantic credentials such as Beckford and Jack Sharp, Jamaica's agent in Parliament, as the company's solicitors before the Board of Trade hearings in the mid-1740s. The company began to advocate once again for a monopoly to defend overseas trade from the encroachments of rival European nations with their own monopolies.[39]

It was Thomas Pelham-Holles, the duke of Newcastle and secretary of state for the Southern Department, who finally hammered the nails into the Royal African Company's coffin in a 1748 report to the Board of Trade. Newcastle explained that deregulation had hugely increased the scale of the trade and had secured an adequate supply of slaves for the mainland American colonies for the first time. He saw the 1712 expiration as the crucial turning point in the development of the slave trade: "From this time the Trade began to flourish and has gradually increas'd. In 1709 the Separate Traders had only 71 Ships; In 1727 they had 170 which carried 40,000 Negroes. The ships now employd from Great Brittain are 140, which Ships being larger than those formerly used carry upwards of 45,000 Negroes." He added that companies like the African Company were held in low esteem by the public because they were predisposed to commit fraud by manipulating their stock for insiders: "The Practice of all Companys shews that the first Adventurers do not fairly stand the Profit and Loss of their own Projects but by making fictitious Dividends out of their Principial tho they make no Profits, raise the nominal Value of their Stock and thereby draw unwary People into Ruin."[40]

Newcastle's influential verdict on the Royal African Company proved damning and helped silence the Beckford and Sharp axis. In 1750, Parliament finally created a regulated African trading company that enjoyed no real or pretended monopoly over the African trade and posed no threat to the interests of the independent slave traders. Two years later, the government wound up the Royal African Company. In April 1752, the African Company's "charter, . . . all books, papers, and writings" were stowed in two rented rooms at the Jerusalem Coffee House (the favored meeting place of East India Company merchants and officials) to await the historian.[41]

---

39. For the midcentury regulatory moment, see *The Importance of Effectually Supporting the Royal African Company of England Impartially Consider'd* . . . (London, 1744), 2, 7. For Julius Beckford's involvement, see Walter Edward Minchinton, ed., *Politics and the Port of Bristol in the Eighteenth Century: The Petitions of the Society of Merchant Adventurers, 1698-1803* (Bristol, 1963), 68.

40. Proceedings in Parliament, Add. MSS 33053, 293, British Library.

41. For the storage of the company's papers, see Minutes of the Bye Committee, Apr. 15, 1752,

THE MAINTENANCE OF the Royal African Company between 1712 and 1752 had sought mostly to generate income for the company's directors from stock market manipulation, and from the 1730s the source of these speculations was often public subsidy. Under the duke of Chandos's leadership from 1718 to 1723, however, the company made a viable attempt to manage Britain's trade with the unexplored African interior. The African Company, despite the quality of its personnel and the extent of its resources, failed in this endeavor because of the interference of the South Sea Company, the Portuguese, the betrayals of a group of wayward Cornish miners turned pirates, but mostly because local African power was too strong to allow a British organization to confiscate its natural resources. The British state's attempts to directly divert resources away from the separate traders' legislative vacuum and into statutory regulations like the South Sea Company proved, like the African Company's forays into gold mining in Africa, to be costly tropical burlesques.

The separate traders continued to use their political capital to protect their interests in the slave trade. They did not need to thwart the African Company's ambitions after 1712 because the company had largely conceded defeat in the competition to dominate the slave trade. The separate traders deregulated this trade and continued its growth under their guidance throughout the eighteenth century, as the duke of Newcastle attested. The separate traders' legislative vacuum reflected the breadth of public support for the slave trade. By the second quarter of the eighteenth century, the separate traders began to use their public support to achieve statutory means of protecting their slave-trading interests, including the Debt Recovery Act and the Molasses Act. The British state's determination to regulate the African trade was gathering pace. Because of the African Company's long period of commercial decline after 1712 and its continued political and corporate presence, the company's pro-regulation rationales would mutate into an argument that was to have anti-slavery connotations. Abolition would represent the ultimate form of statutory state regulation of the transatlantic trade in enslaved Africans. It is to that final feature of the politicization of the transatlantic slave trade that we now turn.

T 70/143, 135–136. For the legislation that wound up the African Company, see African Company Act (1750), 24 Geo. 2, c. 49.

SIX

The Legacies
Free to Enslave

The Royal African Company and the separate traders disagreed publicly about a lot of things. Their political disputes rose above one shared assumption, however: that the forced transportation of enslaved Africans to the British American colonies was legitimate, moral, and of national strategic importance. Both the African Company and the separate traders agreed that enslaved African labor was integral to the expansion of Britain's plantation economies. Broad participation in the Africa trade debates helped to portray African slaves as commodities indispensable for the successful development of the empire. Although they rarely mentioned it, both sides endorsed the views that Africans were culturally and ethnically different from Europeans and, for the most part, inferior as well. The politicization of the transatlantic slave trade that the Africa trade debates produced, however, allowed some of the long-established residual moral concern about slavery and slave trading to enter the mainstream political debate. This concern gravitated exclusively around and emanated largely from the Royal African Company and its vision of trade. Once the company had lost the central issue of the debate—who could conduct the slave trade in a way that satisfied the broadest public interest and uphold the natural right of Englishmen to trade—it began to leverage concern about the morality of slavery to buttress its political position. During the debates about the slave trade, the company's arguments in favor of monopoly closely resembled those isolated objections to the slave trade and slavery in the colonies that connected slavery to vice, avarice, and overconsumption. The survival of the African Company after the deregulation of the trade in 1712 ensured that this pro-monopoly argument would nurture the antislavery sentiments of others during the 1730s, 1740s, and 1750s.

The company would view its monopoly, not as a vessel for the coercive power of the state to prevent selfish merchants from dissolving the trade away, but as a regulatory mechanism that could curb the immoral activities of independent slave traders. Rather than intimidating Africans, the company would protect them. The commercial successes of the separate traders necessitated an argument for abolition that celebrated commerce. But, ambivalence toward the slave trade and slavery proposed that commerce had become disconnected from moral and humane imperatives and required reform. The African Company's traditional argument voicing suspicion of unregulated economic activity became, in the context of the company's continued interest in promoting Britain's trade with Africa, associated with a sentimentalized commerce. By the 1730s, this commerce connected its traditional pro-monopoly argument with the need to treat Africans with humanity, hospitality, and dignity, a dignity that remained attached to royalty and would be best upheld by the royally sponsored African Company. The Royal African Company's political disapproval of the separate traders' deregulated slave trade came, by the middle of the eighteenth century, to inform a desire to reform the trade's brutality via regulation, which, by the 1780s, had become a politicized argument for abolition.[1]

The following discussion assesses how the political disputes between the African Company and the separate traders helped produce from the 1680s to the 1760s the ideological and policy underpinnings for the antislavery movement that developed in the final third of the eighteenth century into full-blown abolitionism. The public, parliamentary setting for the debates between the separate traders and the African Company broadened the discussion beyond the narrow consideration of the management of the trade to the treatment of Africans. The dialogic impetus between company and traders also saw the refinement of their respective positions on regulation so that monopoly came to be seen as a potential means to rein in the slave trade's unique brutality. The company's long history in the eighteenth century and its corporate structure provided an institutional setting and a political issue that placed these antislavery views on the public, political agenda. In this way, the African Company's politicization of the transatlantic slave trade nurtured embryonic abolitionist language, ideas, and personnel. By the 1770s, antislavery campaigners began to associate the evils of slavery with an absence of regulation for the trade. To early proponents of abolitionism, independent slave traders had been given an excess of freedom to enslave.

IN 1690, an apologist for the Royal African Company argued that joint-stock organization of the slave trade provided the only means of regulating the behavior of the English slave traders on the African coast and of ensuring the humane treatment of the Africans: "It is only by means of an Incorpo-

---

1. Philip Gould, *Barbaric Traffic: Commerce and Antislavery in the Eighteenth-Century Atlantic World* (Cambridge, Mass., 2003), 34.

rated Company, that the *English* in their Dealing and Trafficking with the *Natives,* can be restrained to a due Observation of the Rules and Measures of Humanity, Truth, and Justice." What was meant by "Dealing and Trafficking" is unclear, but it is likely that the pamphlet refers to the growing concern about English involvement in the direct enslavement of Africans rather than about the purchase of the enslaved from African brokers, a practice known as "pilliarding." The "Gentleman in the City" who authored this pamphlet went on to allege that the independent slave traders' self-interest prevented the sort of impartial justice that could ensure the interests of humanity were upheld.

> For as Traders at random, do seldom propose any thing, besides and beyond their private ends, so it is easie to be imagined, on what Insolences, Frauds and Rapines, scattered and particular Men will venture, upon the hope and prospect of enriching themselves, when there is no Common and Established *Society* accountable for the miscarriage of every individual.

For the gentleman, the private interests of the independent traders would override the cause of humanity as a whole. Only a state-sponsored monopoly company could uphold "Humanity, Truth, and Justice."[2]

The African Company had not made such arguments before the start of the Africa trade debates in Parliament in 1690. This early African Company pamphlet shows to what extent the parliamentary audience wished to have all features of the trade examined. Public consideration of the slave trade allowed for discussions that interrogated every aspect of the trade. In this case, growing public concern about English participation in "man-stealing" bled into the public deliberations that had been initiated by the company's narrow interest in having its monopolistic charter endorsed. The need to satisfy a disinterested audience of Members of Parliament (MPs) who might consider the slave trade in any number of contexts, including the growing concern about the trade's immorality, could be appealed to with an equal number of considerations—in this case, the ways in which a monopolistic organization for the trade could better manage its brutality on the African coast. The gentleman also demonstrated that what would become the central disagreement in the debate—whether individual, self-interested merchants or a corporate society could better advance the national interest—could be recast in moral terms.[3]

---

2. *That the Trade to Affrica, Is Only Manageable by an Incorporated Company and a Joynt Stock, Demonstrated in a Letter to a Member of the Present House of Commons, by a Gentleman in the City* (London, 1690), 2.

3. [George Keith], *An Exhortation and Caution to Friends concerning Buying or Keeping of Negroes*

The gentleman supporter of the African Company understood the political benefits of styling the company as the upholder of a humanitarian approach to slave trading that other writers had wished for in the 1680s. Influential and articulate exponents of concern about the morality of slavery in the colonies deployed arguments that expressed suspicion of the centrality of commerce and interest to late-seventeenth-century society. These writers focused on the immorality of slavery in the American plantations rather than slave trading on the African coast. Their criticisms reflected similar values to those endorsed by the African Company, however. In 1680, the firebrand Anglican vicar, Morgan Godwyn, railed against the greed and false Christianity of the English, describing "INTEREST" as the English God. Godwyn's depiction of the English plantations evoked earlier English portrayals of the gold lust, godlessness, and cruelty of the Spanish in America. He suggested that English zeal had been, like the conquistadores, corrupted by the love of money:

> 'Tis true, their *Zeal* is said of late to be much abated. But this, as 'tis the Crime of some few, whose great *Wisdom* consisteth only in *getting of Money (the grand Antichrist of our English Nation,* which, in the very letter of the Text, they exalt, . . . above God and Religion:) So I doubt not but their *Impiety* will in time be better lookt into, and a stop be put to its further growth, at least there: And those *Mammonists* be obliged to a more Christian deportment and compliance with the universal practice of all Believers, especially of our *English Nation,* till now."[4]

In 1684, in *Friendly Advice, to the Gentlemen-Planters of the East and West Indies,* Thomas Tryon sought to expose the hypocrisy of the planters' claim to act in a Christian manner toward their slaves. But Tryon also predicted the African Company's criticism of the independent traders by depicting the plantation owners as humans whose innate virtues had been corrupted by interest, greed, and vice: "A false conceit of *Interest* has blinded their [the planters] Eyes and stopt their Ears, and rendred their Hearts harder than *Rocks of Adament.*" Tryon ventriloquized via a fictional slave to expose the planters' hypocrisy as Christians and blamed their failure to curb their excessive brutality on their in-

---

([New York], 1693), 7. For more on man-stealing, see Lawrence W. Towner, "The Sewall-Saffin Dialogue on Slavery," *William and Mary Quarterly,* 3d Ser., XXI (1964), 40–52.

4. Morgan Godwyn, *The Negro's and Indians Advocate, Suing for Their Admission to the Church; or, A Persuasive to the Instructing and Baptizing of the Negro's and Indians in Our Plantations, Shewing That as the Compliance Therewith Can Prejudice No Mans Just Interest; So the Wilful Neglecting and Opposing of It, Is No Less Than a Manifest Apostacy from the Christian Faith; to Which Is Added, a Brief Account of Religion in Virginia* (London, 1680), 83, 161.

ability to regulate their passions, despite their belief that their interests would help them achieve this regulation:

> How well you regulate your *Passions* (which is another thing you say Christian Doctrine teaches you) all the World sees, and we often *feel;* ... your Lusts duel one another, Covetousness fights with Luxury, Wantonness jostles Ambition, and Revenge is opposed by Cowardize; *Sence* gets above *Reason,* the *Man* is ridden by the *Beast.*

Just as to the African Company the separate traders would have their "Swill of Liberty" in deregulating the trade, for Tryon unregulated slavery had initiated the corrupting excesses of American avarice, often expressed in the intemperance of meat eaters and alcoholics. Slaveowning, however, was the ultimate form of overconsumption:

> They wantonly consume the Encrease and Product of our heavy Pains in Riot and Volumptuousness, in Superfluity, and all kinds of extravagant Vitiousness; their chief *Study* and *Philosophy* being to gratifie their liquorish Palates, and insatiate Paunches, and to enslave us with many intollerable Burthens; so that their Lamps are ready to be extinguished by their Superfluity and Excess of Oyl, whilst they make frequent and solemn *Feasts,* (that is, offer Sacrifices, and celebrate Festivals to their Idol *Belly-God-Paunch,* the Divinity which they chiefly adore).

African Company writers described the separate traders in a similar light: contorted by greed and interest and distracted from the true end of overseas trade, to uphold the public good.[5]

The African Company's vision for the slave trade also reflected Aphra Behn's criticism of plantation life. Behn's 1688 novel *Oroonoko* altered Tryon's depiction of the plantations as dens of corrupt consumption, to arenas for the jettisoning of the social distinctions that ought to be the lifeblood of a stable, civilized society. She contrasted the subordination of enslaved Africans with the heroic nobility of the novel's royal protagonist. A truth-telling infi-

---

5. [Thomas Tryon], *Friendly Advice, to the Gentlemen-Planters of the East and West Indies* ([London], 1684), 77, 123–124, 177; Robert Bleau, *A Letter from One of the Royal African Company's Chief Agents on the African Coasts* (n.p., [1714?]), [1] ("Swill of Liberty"). On Tryon, see also Philippe Rosenberg, "Thomas Tryon and the Seventeenth-Century Dimensions of Antislavery," *WMQ,* 3d Ser., LXI (2004), 609–642. Rosenberg perhaps underplays the ways in which Tryon's antislavery views derive from his critique of the excesses of unregulated trade. See also Kim F. Hall, "'Extravagant Viciousness': Slavery and Gluttony in the Works of Thomas Tryon," in Philip D. Beidler and Gary Taylor, eds., *Writing Race across the Atlantic World: Medieval to Modern* (New York, 2005), 93–111.

del—much like Tryon's slave spokesman—Oroonoko celebrated the dignity of monarchy more than the inherent dignity of mankind. For Behn, as for the African Company's pamphleteers, royalty was the protector of decency, humanity, virtue, and a well-ordered society.[6]

By the time of the parliamentary debates about the slave trade in the 1690s, the story of Oroonoko had found a larger audience thanks to Thomas Southerne's play of the same name, first performed in 1695. It modified features of Behn's novel in ways that reflect the content of the Africa trade debates. The slave trader, Captain Driver, procures Oroonoko in Angola, a region the separate traders had begun to trade with in the 1690s, rather than closer to the African Company's forts at Kormantine. Southerne also introduces a subplot about a pair of women seeking advantageous marriages in the colonies to further dramatize an important theme that African Company pamphleteers had alluded to: the inhumanity of unregulated market transactions. Like the African Company's publicists, Southerne criticized the financial revolution of the 1690s as favoring utility over enlightenment. Southerne, like Behn, watched with distaste as the quest for material gain subordinated notions of nobility and separated political economy from its social and moral foundations. Echoing the African Company's refrain about the separate traders as callous social climbers, Southerne depicts Captain Driver, who buys and sells Oroonoko, as low born, money obsessed, and shallow. As in company portrayals of independent slave traders, Captain Driver's ruthless pursuit of gain saw him lure Oroonoko into captivity under false pretenses, shunning conventions of hospitality and friendship. The implication that an unregulated market threatened royalty in ways that encouraged slave trading is evident throughout the play.

The connections Godwyn, Tryon, Behn, and Southerne drew between self-interested commerce, luxury, "extravagant Vitiousness," an absence of respect for social order, and American slavery recalled many of the Royal African Company's depictions of the independent slave trade. Tryon lobbied in the 1680s for reform of the American slave plantations. The company lobbied in 1690 for a trade that could support the interests of humanity on the African coast. Neither Tryon nor the company's gentlemanly supporter advocated for the end of slavery. They both sought to manage its excesses and believed that management would be good for the trade as a whole.

In the opening stages of the Africa trade debates and in a rather isolated

---

6. Aphra Behn, *Oroonoko; or, The Royal Slave* (1688) (Boston, 2000); Thomas Southerne, *Oroonoko*, ed. Maximillian E. Novak and David Stuart Rodes (Lincoln, Nebr., 1976). See also William Letwin, *The Origins of Scientific Economics: English Economic Thought, 1660-1776* (London, 1963), 147.

fashion, the political discussions of the future of the slave trade provided an outlet for the growing criticism of plantation slavery and unregulated slave trading that was, for all of these writers, the result of a society polluted by greed and selfishness. The openness of parliamentary debates in the 1690s helped to connect pamphlet concern about slavery with the formal, public consideration of the slave trade that the Africa trade debates involved. Moral concern with slavery also supplied another argument that company supporters could use to develop political support. The politics of the Africa trade debates would continue to provide a public outlet for calls for stronger state management of slavery. The African Company itself provided a corporate setting for these shared ideas that helped to detach them from particular individuals like Tryon and to transfer them into the middle of the eighteenth century. For, as a company supporter would later argue, only a fixed society could allow for the maintenance and transferal of such ideas, ideas ". . . which can never be maintain'd with Individuals or single Persons, who being Transient and Mortal."[7]

SEPARATE-TRADER pamphleteers did not express any concern about the morality of the slave trade during the parliamentary debates. Very few felt the need to justify the enslavement of Africans at all. In 1708, a London pamphleteer praised enslavement on philanthropic grounds:

> I cannot but think it a charitable and commendable, as well as a lawful Undertaking, to buy a Slave in *Guinea*, where the Severity of the Government has subjected him to a Discipline, that Flesh and Blood can scarce go thro; and to transport him to one of our Plantations, where he retains the Name of a Slave, but performs only the Work and Business of a Servant.

It was typical of the separate traders to use an argument in favor of American slavery that celebrated liberal government. They cited the barbarity of African society to justify the slave trade and praised English government and politics while doing so. This barbarity did not necessitate a monopoly company because a deregulated trade would help to extend the commendable charity of slave trading by transporting more slaves to the plantations and therefore converting more to the relative comforts of servitude. The same pamphleteering slave trader measured the barbarity of African society accord-

---

7. On a fixed society, see [Charles Davenant], *Several Reasons Proving, That Our Trade to Africa, Cannot Be Preserved and Carried on Effectually by Any Other Method, Than That of a Considerable Joint-Stock, with Exclusive Privileges* ([London, 1712?]), 2.

ing to Africans' inability to understand "Thoughts of Liberty, which few of them can attain to, and not many of them aspire after." This constitutional and ethnic deficiency made them ripe for and deserving of enslavement. According to this perverse formulation, it would be wrong for the separate traders to embrace deliberative government as the best means of advancing their own interests without extending the blessings of that government to the Africans by encouraging their enslavement and then transporting them.[8]

The African Company did not initially deny the separate traders' assertion that Africa was a barbarous place. Sir Dalby Thomas, the African Company's chief agent at Cape Coast Castle, also argued that Africans were unable to conceive of liberty or the benefits of English civilization after 1688. When reporting back to his London superiors, Thomas offered an assessment of the African peoples he had encountered: "[They have no] knowledge of liberty and property, nothing being more common than the strongest to dispose of and inslave the weakest, might is their right." According to Thomas's logic, an understanding and appreciation of liberty should prevent the desire to enslave. But he did not ruminate on the implications of his logic. Instead, the Africans' barbarity, or their inability to conceive of freedom, formed part of the African Company's justification for monopoly, because such barbarity required the intercession, via monopoly, of the coercive power of the state. Another pamphleteer echoed Thomas: "As the [African] Settlements are numerous, and under divers Petty Kings, they are seldom free from Differences amongst one or more of their Neighbours, ... Also they are illiterate People, and have not (or are they govern'd by) and Religion, Laws or Courts of Justice, or any civiliz'd Rules of Discipline."[9]

For the separate traders, the perceived despotic barbarity of African government justified their transportation to the plantations where a more benign government would improve their situation. For the African Company's supporters, the barbarity of African government existed in its fractured, unsettled quality (much like the separate traders) and in the unpredictable use of force. The company proposed that such an environment necessitated the unitary power that a joint-stock company could provide.[10]

Toward the end of the Africa trade debates, however, the political exchanges between the separate traders and the African Company led the latter

---

8. *Considerations upon the Trade to Guinea* (London, 1708), 27–30.

9. Sir Dalby Thomas to the Royal African Company, Nov. 26, 1709, Treasury (T) 70/175, 202. See also *The Falsities of the Private Traders to Africa Discover'd, and the Mischiefs They Occasion Demonstrated* . . . ([London, 1708]), 1; and [Davenant], *Several Reasons Proving*, 4.

10. See Anthony J. Barker, *The African Link: British Attitudes to the Negro in the Era of the Atlantic Slave Trade, 1550–1807* (London, 1978), 151.

to reconceptualize African barbarity. Instead of viewing Africans as barbarous despots, the company began to associate Africans with the barbaric commerce of the separate traders. Because the price of slaves increased after the deregulation of the trade, African vendors were seen as the principal beneficiaries of the trade, at least in England. In a 1707 letter to the company's Leadenhall Street Directorate, an African Company official at Cape Coast Castle, John Chaigneau, described the deregulation as favoring the Africans and depicted them in ways that the company had often portrayed the separate traders: "No people in the world (I believe) understand their interest better than the Blacks of the Gold-Coast." Another added, "They are Selfish and Perfidious to the last degree; and having no sence of Honour, or Religion to controle them, No contracts or promises on their Parts will Bind them." The company began to attribute the commercial success of the separate traders to their willingness to encourage the "truckling" of African vendors. One African Company official compared the separate traders' commercial attributes to a latent but vicious tropical disease that would remain dormant until activated by the germ of unregulated human trafficking: "The *Fantyns* are taught to trade [by the separate traders], and by Experience are Expert Merchants, if such a Term may be given to Cunning Tricking Villains, who now give the Law to their instructors, and make them meanly and basely truckle to them for every Thing." For the African Company, the absence of its joint-stock monopoly power had allowed the free pursuit of self-interest. The separate traders were the authors of an African barbarity expressed as self-interest rather than despotism. The African Company's argument about the importance of the coercive power of its monopoly on the West African coast would, by 1714, be used to protect and then civilize the Africans, not by transporting them to America as slaves (as the separate traders proposed), but by developing commercial contacts with the African interior.[11]

The African Company identified the separate traders' immoral participation in enslavement, or the kidnapping of Africans, as one of the principal obstacles to the development of civilized commerce with the African interior. Charles Davenant repeatedly provided examples of separate traders' forcibly

---

11. John Chaigneau to the Royal African Company, Apr. 2, 1707, quoted in Charles Davenant, *Reflections upon the Constitution and Management of the African Trade, etc.*, in Charles Whitworth, ed., *The Political and Commericial Works of That Celebrated Writer Charles D'avenant, L.L. D.* . . . , V (London, 1771), 195 (hereafter cited as Davenant, *Reflections*). For Davenant's belief that Africans enslaved British traders by price fixing, see 334. For the separate traders' spreading the disease of self-interest, see Bleau, *Letter*, [2]; and *Mr. Phipps's Speech to a Committee of the Honourable House of Commons, concerning the African Trade, March the 27th, 1712* (London, 1712), 4. For more on disease as an analogue to trade, see Gould, *Barbaric Traffic*, 152.

seizing African slaves rather than purchasing them. In his *Reflections upon the Constitution and Management of the African Trade*, Davenant quoted from a letter from Captain Bernard Ladman at Commenda: "As for trade, I have met with very little, the Blacks being afraid to come aboard English ships, they having been tricked by several [separate traders], . . . who, . . . did surprize and carry away with them 24 Negroes." Davenant also recorded the names of a group of separate traders who had been "with very gross and barbarous acts of inhumanity, seizing and taking away with them all the Negroes whom they could surprize along the coast, robbing canoes on the water, forcing women, boys and girls along with them from the shore, shooting at boats, and killing such Negroes as refused to answer their call." He used these accounts to equate the separate traders' free trade in slaves with "plundering, stealing, and sometimes killing."[12]

The African Company's depiction of the barbarous cruelty and immorality of the separate traders on the African coast was matched by testimony from the plantations that combined pro-company arguments with concern about the morality of the slave trade. For some pro-company writers, the African Company's monopoly could civilize slavery on the plantations as well as the slave trade on the African coast. In 1709, one pamphleteer fused Tryon's portrayal of a Caribbean society poisoned by luxury and Davenant's repeated accusation that the separate traders had barbarized the African coast with an argument in favor of the amelioration of slavery that derived from natural law. *A Letter from a Merchant at Jamaica* offered to show more of the "Iniquity of that [slave] Trade . . . than either the Planters or Merchants, the Company or Traders, will think it their Business to shew." The Jamaican merchant explained the brutalities of the plantations in civic humanist terms. "The Desire of possessing" and "Avarice and Luxury" led to slavery and its evil consequences. The *Letter* reserved special opprobrium for those slave traders who bypassed the African vendors to kidnap free Africans, declaring one to be an "odious Man-stealer." Unlike separate-trader pamphleteers in the dispute who invoked the natural right to trade in slaves, the merchant emphasized that slave purchases contravened natural law, the slaves' "plain and natural Right to Life and Liberty."[13]

The Jamaican merchant resented the colonies' lack of sound, disinterested

---

12. Davenant, *Reflections*, 185–186, 236, 237.

13. *A Letter from a Merchant of Jamaica to a Member of Parliament in London, Touching the African Trade* . . . (London, 1709) is introduced and reproduced in full in Jack P. Greene, "'A Plain and Natural Right to Life and Liberty': An Early Natural Rights Attack on the Excesses of the Slave System in Colonial British America," *WMQ*, 3d Ser., LVII (2000), 793–808 (quotations on 794, 799, 804, 806, 808).

government, which allowed for "what the *Caprice* and *Cruelty* of Men, *bounded by no* Fences of *human Law,* can invent and execute." Without sufficient control of the trade, attention could not be focused on the living and working conditions of slaves. The merchant's mention of the danger of having "so many Buyers" referred to the deregulated trade, and he emphasized the need for a shift to wise, state-sponsored government of the trade. The merchant appealed, via his correspondent, who he alleged had a "God-like Mind," to so "August an Assembly" as Parliament to provide assurances that "There is a God who governs the Earth, and restrains the Pride and Cruelty of wicked Men." But, in the end, the merchant advocated increasing the scale of the trade, not restricting its capacity. He suggested that reducing slavery's brutality with improved management might make economic sense: "Let them [Company and Separate Traders] study Ways and Means to preserve and increase it. It has never yet throve, nor do I believe ever will, till 'tis manag'd with more Justice and Humanity."[14]

The importance the author of the *Letter* placed on converting the slaves to Christianity offered a means of exchanging guilt about the trade for a civilizing mission that complemented the African Company's formal imperialist agenda. Other writers agreed. The intensification of political deliberations about the company from 1710 had allowed for the public to again insert moral compunction about the slave trade into the public debate. The Jamaica merchant, whoever he was, achieved some press coverage in early 1710. The Whig newspaper the *Observator* published "A Letter from a Gentleman relating to the African-Trade," which endorsed many of the merchant's concerns about the state of the slave plantations and the mistreatment of enslaved Africans there and highlighted the importance of slave baptism. The *Observator* promoted the baptism of slaves on the grounds that "tho' we have them in our own Power, and Opportunity to instruct them in our Faith, we designedly leave them in Ignorance, which is a plain Proof, that for the Labour of their Bodies, we suffer them to damn their Souls." The baptism of enslaved Africans proved especially appealing to Parliament, which, on two occasions, inserted a clause about it into proposed legislation with reassurances that bap-

---

14. Ibid., 799, 802, 803, 806, 808. Scholars tend to associate the *Letter*'s progressive tone with the Whigs and, therefore, the separate traders. Closer readings of the literature of the debate and the *Letter* suggest, however, that its author sympathized with the African Company because joint-stock organization offered a better means of policing and limiting the brutalities of the trade, as the company had advised at various points during the Africa trade dispute. Historians have failed to fully place the *Letter* within the context of the African trade debates. See ibid., 793–798; and Tim Keirn, "Monopoly, Economic Thought, and the Royal African Company," in John Brewer and Susan Staves, eds., *Early Modern Conceptions of Property* (London, 1995), 443.

tism would not threaten planters' human property. The *Observator* associated this desire to convert African slaves to Christianity with Anglican missionary societies like the Society for the Propagation of Christian Knowledge that had links with the African Company. Morgan Godwyn (as the *Observator* mentioned) had made calls for slave baptism from the 1680s, but widespread conversion of slaves did not begin in earnest until the eighteenth century. The newspaper connected its enthusiasm for slave baptism to the need for greater regulation and, by implication, the company: "That therefore there seems as much or more need to regulate this Matter, than to interpose between the contending Trader." By the early decades of the eighteenth century, writers sympathetic to the African Company could claim its monopoly came to provide a patriarchal structure to look after the spiritual needs of its human cargoes as much as it had been designed to protect the spiritual conditions of its employees. Again, the Africa trade debates helped to alter the interpretation of African barbarism: from a justification for monopoly that was coeval with the justification for enslavement to a justification for monopoly that helped in the civilization of Africans through baptism. The Christianizing of slaves, however, would aid the cause of slavery, rather than aid in its abolition. Parliamentary consideration in the eighteenth century might have helped to disabuse planters and merchants of the seventeenth-century maxim that baptism meant manumission.[15]

The Society for the Propagation of the Gospel in Foreign Parts had been strongly associated with the Society for the Reformation of Manners, which

---

15. *Letter from a Merchant of Jamaica*, in Greene, "'A Plain and Natural Right,'" *WMQ*, 3d Ser., LVII (2000), 807; "Letter from a Gentleman relating to the African-Trade," *Observator*, Jan. 28–Feb. 1, 1710. Parliament inserted clauses about slave baptism into proposed legislation in March 1710 and May 1712. The government made suggestions to encourage the conversion of slaves as early as 1701, but planters were recalcitrant because they believed Christianity to be inconsistent with enslavement (see "Council of Trade and Plantations to the Lords Justices," July 16, 1701, in W. Noel Sainsbury et al., eds., *Calendar of State Papers, Colonial Series, America and West Indies* . . . , 44 vols. [London, 1860–1969], XIX, no. 647, 354–361). See *Journals of the House of Commons*, I–LI (London, 1803), XVI, 372 (hereafter cited as *Commons Journals*); and "A Draught of a Bill for Converting the Negros in Plantations," MS 941, 72, Lambeth Palace Library, London. For the company's connections with the Society for the Propagation of Christian Knowledge, see Royal African Company to John Chamberlaine, Dec. 3, 1713, T 70/45, n.p. Rowland Tryon and William Tryon, who were the treasurers for the Society's Barbados plantations, were also African Company directors in 1713, 1714, 1715, 1717 (Rowland) and in 1720–1725 (William). Apologists for monopoly used the same rationale to support the East India Company in court; see *East India Company v. Sandys*, in "Pleadings and Judgments in the Case of the East India Company v. Thomas Sandys for Trading to the East Indies without License from the Company," Rawlinson Manuscripts, class C, no. 130, 34–35, Bodleian Library, Oxford. See also Travis Glasson, *Mastering Christianity: Missionary Anglicanism and Slavery in the Atlantic World* (Oxford, 2012), 47–50.

had worried since the 1690s about the morally enervating effect of unbridled commerce on society. The *Observator* therefore echoed the now familiar notion that unregulated trade had corrupted and dehumanized the Africans: "By the Temptation of a Market, the Negroes are induc'd to betray, steal, and make War upon one another." But, as with the Jamaica merchant, the *Observator* also advanced strident, Whiggish calls for the slave trade to come into line with national pride in British liberty and respect for the natural rights of mankind:

> Tis strange that we should be so partial as to think the Liberties of others is to be sacrific'd for us. We talk of national Sins: I could wish we had nothing of this to answer for. But really I do not see how we can in Justice expect either Peace or Safety, whilst we sport away others Lives, or treat Men like Dogs. . . .
> The African-Trade in Slaves, as manag'd, is an Invasion upon the Rights and Liberties of Mankind.[16]

In March 1711, as the Africa trade debates continued in Parliament, this Whiggish distaste for the commercial excesses of slavery and slave trading appeared in the *Spectator*. Richard Steele retold the story of Yarico, a high-born native American, and Thomas Inkle, a hard-headed London merchant, whose father "had taken particular Care to instill into his Mind an early Love of Gain, by making him a perfect Master of Numbers, and consequently giving him a quick View of Loss and Advantage, and preventing the natural Impulses of his Passions, by Prepossession towards his Interests." Inkle and Yarico had fallen in love and had eloped into some remote part of Barbados. Love had suppressed Inkle's interest until the two lovers strayed back "into English Territories, [when Inkle] began seriously to reflect upon his loss of Time, and to weigh with himself how many Days Interest of his Mony he had lost during his Stay with *Yarico*." "This Thought made the Young Man very pensive, and careful what Account he should be able to give his Friends of his Voyage." Inkle's solution is to turn himself into a separate trader: "Upon which Considerations, the prudent and frugal young Man sold *Yarico* to a *Barbadian Merchant*; notwithstanding that the poor Girl, in incline him to commiserate her Condition, told him that she was with Child by him: But he only made use of that Information, to rise in his Demands upon the Purchaser." Steele drew upon the traditions of Aphra Behn, Thomas Southerne, Charles Davenant, and the Jamaica merchant in dramatizing the inhumanity of slavery by

---

16. "Letter from a Gentleman relating to the African-Trade," *Observator*, Jan. 28–Feb. 1, 1710. Under John Tutchin, this newspaper had clear Whig leanings, but, after his death, it is likely Daniel Defoe and his hybrid party views came to influence the paper's tone.

noting that it intruded on privacy and supplanted romantic love with mercenary calculation. But Steele's vision of Thomas Inkle is also the African Company's vision of the archetypal separate trader: urban, interested, calculating, and callous. Here was a Whig, sentimental outburst against the slave trade that demonized the independent slave trader as the enemy of humanity and closely resembled Southerne's high Tory interpretation of *Oroonoko*.[17]

The African Company's increasing tendency to justify its monopoly to protect rather than overawe the Africans helped to humanize the Africans as much as it helped to demonize the deregulated trading model of the separate traders. For Charles Davenant and many other African apologists, the principal argument for monopoly had been to protect British interests from the savage natives. Losing the Africa trade debate led the company to resort to the opposite position, that the monopoly could help save some of the innocent, noble natives from the barbarous independent slave traders. For interlopers like William Wilkinson, the company's monopoly allowed it to treat patriotic English merchants worse than Turks. For company propagandists like Charles Davenant, the deregulation of the trade allowed separate traders to treat Africans inhumanely. The separate traders, wrote Davenant, "committed very gross abuses, inconsistent with the common rules of humanity, both with relation to the company and the natives on the coast of Africa." For African Company apologists, therefore, monopolistic regulation advanced the good of humanity.[18]

THE RESOLUTION OF the Africa trade debates in 1712 left the separate traders supreme in the slave trade. The Royal African Company endured and so did its pro-regulation argument for amelioration of the slave trade. Each new chapter in the company's history brought renewed political deliberations about its public role. From the 1730s, these political discussions enabled opponents of the slave trade, and the African Company itself, to nurture antislavery sentiment. The ambition of James Brydges, duke of Chandos, to develop the company's commercial ties with the African interior helped bridge the company's long-held desire to trade in nonhuman cargoes with the mid-eighteenth-century argument that the slave trade prevented Britain from realizing the enormous commercial potential of civilized trade with the African continent. This ambition led African Company officials, including Chandos, to

17. *Spectator*, no. 11 (Mar. 11, 1711), [2].
18. Davenant, *Reflections*, 237, 284. For the African Company's rationale of trying to save Britons from the barbarous natives, see, in particular, *Some Further Objections Humbly Offer'd to the Consideration of the Legislature, against the Bill, for Establishing the Trade to Africa, in a Regulated Company* (n.p., [1712?]), 1.

reject the company's earlier assumption of African savagery and to begin to consort with Africans as fellow human beings. Chandos's consultation in 1721 with two African princes about the African interior over dinner at his stately home, mentioned previously, provides an early example. Hospitality to and friendship with African royalty would become a trademark protoabolitionist gesture for the remainder of the eighteenth century.[19]

In the 1730s, as the African Company became the recipient of government subsidies, its promoters and officials advertised its role with reference to civilizing commerce and sentimental philanthropy. The company expressed the broader concern among many English people that Robert Walpole, the nation's prime minister, had inaugurated a political culture bereft of virtue and driven by special interests. The company attracted and developed individuals with views antagonistic to slavery. One of these, the founder of the Georgia colony, James Oglethorpe, became an African Company director and then, in 1732, subgovernor at the same time he steered his Georgia colony project through Parliament. Oglethorpe's plan for the Georgia colony shared many of the same values the African Company had developed since the 1690s: it worried about the social consequences of commercial society; it blamed the unregulated pursuit of self-interest for the corruption of society (the colony's motto was *Non sibi, sed aliis [Not for themselves, but for others]*); and it mistrusted the ability of legislative institutions to arbitrate between commercial interests. In the Georgia colony, industry was to operate virtuously, just as trade under the control of the Royal African Company was to put public interest before private interest. Oglethorpe also disapproved of slave trading and of slavery, a position the African Company had, by the 1730s, been forced into because of the commercial dominance of the separate traders. For Oglethorpe, though, it was the presence of slaves rather than the presence of independent slave traders that would precipitate the dissolution of a virtuous society. The Georgia project, like the African Company, preached the advantages to humanity of social control. Africa was a place of free people for whom transportation to the American colonies would "occasion the misery of thousands in Africa."[20]

19. "An Account of Strangers Dining at Cannons," Sept. 24, 1721, Stowe Manuscripts 59, n.p., Huntington Library, San Marino, Calif.

20. See Milton L. Ready, "Philanthropy and the Origins of Georgia," in Harvey H. Jackson and Phinizy Spalding, eds., *Forty Years of Diversity: Essays on Colonial Georgia* (Athens, Ga., 1984), 52. On the Georgia colony's dual charitable and commercial agendas, see Betty Wood, *Slavery in Colonial Georgia, 1730-1775* (Athens, Ga., 1984), 2; Geraldine Meroney, "The London Entrepôt Merchants and the Georgia Colony," *WMQ*, 3d Ser., XXV (1968), 231; and James Van Horn Melton, "From Alpine Miner to Low-Country Yeoman: The Transatlantic Worlds of a Georgia Salzburger, 1693-1761," *Past and Present*, no. 201 (November 2008), 110. See also Mark Stewart, "What Nature Suffers to

As the African Company's trading focus shifted to the African interior and to Africans as commercial contacts rather than barbarous heathens, Oglethorpe's connection with the company brought him together with Africans whose stories would, like Oroonoko's, come to play a critical part in developing public interest and sympathy for Africans. One of these Africans, a Gambian called Job Ben Solomon, attracted widespread comment. Despite his high social standing and education, Job had been captured by rival Africans and transported to Maryland by a separate trader, Captain Pyke. Job's education became apparent to his owners, and it then attracted the attention of Oglethorpe in London. The African Company interceded to allow Oglethorpe to purchase Job's freedom because "the said Negroe understands and writes Arabick and maybe of Service to the Company on giving him his Freedom and sending him to Gambia." The company then paid for his passage to London and accommodated him at Africa House on Leadenhall Street before financing his passage back to Africa, where he "landed at *James*-Fort . . . having been recommended in a particular Manner by the Company to their Governor and Factors in this Country, who were desired to use him with the greatest Civility and Respect." Job, as with the African princes who dined with Chandos, could be useful to the African Company's ambition to develop profitable commercial relationships with the African interior. But the writer of Job's memoirs, Thomas Bluett, hoped to elevate the hospitality shown to Job to a higher plane of morality and sentimental virtue.

> In many Instances of private Friendship, we are apt to be guided by our own private Interest; and very often the Exchange of good Offices among Friends, is little better than mere Barter, where an Equivalent is expected on both Sides. In most Acts of Charity and Compassion too, we may be, and very often are wrought upon by the undue Influence of some selfish View, and thereby we destroy in good measure the Merit of them: But in shewing Pity to Strangers, as such, and kindly relieving them in their Distress, there is not such Danger of being influenced by private Regards; nor is it likely that we are so. Here we act for God's sake, and for the sake of human Nature; and we seem to have no Inducement superior to the Will of Heaven, and the Pleasure that results from the Consciousness of a generous Respect for our common Humanity.[21]

Grow": *Life, Labor, and Landscape on the Georgia Coast, 1680–1920* (Athens, Ga., 1996), 33. For "misery of thousands," see Oglethorpe to the Trustees, Jan. 17, 1739, Egmont (Sir John Percival) Papers, 14203, part 2, 187, University of Georgia, Athens.

21. Minutes of the Court of Assistants, May 3, 1733, T 70/93, 243 ("sending him to Gambia");

For Bluett, the African Company's hospitality to Job was redolent of an inherently English instinct for charity to strangers and helped to promote the company's position and its association with sentimental hospitality that could offer commercial advantages but whose rationale derived, in spirit, from a rejection of morality that was in any sense transactional. The African Company's monopolistic charter had been founded in the 1670s on the assumption of amity with foreigners. By the 1730s, the need for public, political posturing saw the company begin to rebrand itself as a vessel for humane hospitality for Africans in Africa and in London.[22]

Oglethorpe's involvement with the African Company encouraged another author to combine an attempt to educate the public about the African coast with a celebration of the company's trading values of humanity and hospitality. Francis Moore, whom Oglethorpe appears to have brought into employment at the company, mentioned that Oglethorpe's management of the company in 1732 had aimed to avoid slave trading and to increase the honesty of its servants in Africa. The company dispatched Moore to "the *Gambra*" to pursue a voyage into the inlands parts of Africa. He laid great stress on the company's instruction to "make them a suitable Return, by his Fidelity in his Transactions for them, as well as *affable Behaviour to the Natives and Traders,* agreeable to his solemn Engagements." Not only did Moore emphasize *"affable Behaviour to the Natives and Traders,"* he also added a footnote: "A very necessary and important Direction, but too often disregarded by Men who have no Notion of Humanity or Justice." Moore hoped to advance the company's interest as well as its reputation as a vehicle for diplomacy, affability, and diplomacy on the African coast to contrast with the separate traders who, according to Moore, understood little about "Humanity or Justice."[23]

In response to the African Company's growing body of pamphlets and personnel that questioned the humanity, morality, and commercial sense of the slave trade, a captain for one of the leading separate traders, William Snelgrave, entered the debate in 1734. Snelgrave was Humphrey Morice's favored captain for his many slave-trading voyages. Snelgrave turned the sentimental company criticism of slave trading on its head by depicting scenes of African

---

Thomas Bluett, *Some Memoirs of the Life of Job, the Son of Solomon the High Priest of Boonda in Africa* . . . (London, 1734), 59–61, 63. See also *The Remarkable Captivity and Deliverance of Job Ben Solomon, a Mohammedan Priest of Bûnda, Near the Gambra, in the Year 1732,* in *A New General Collection of Voyages and Travels* . . . , 4 vols. (London, 1745–1747), II, 237.

22. For the company's traditional assumption of amity with foreigners, see the legal opinion of its charter by Thomas Corbett [December? 1677], in Calendar of State Papers, Domestic Series (SP), 29/398, 118, National Archives, Kew.

23. Francis Moore, *Travels into the Inland Parts of Africa* . . . (London 1738), in *Voyages and Travels,* II, 223.

barbarity to endorse the old pro-slavery argument that transportation improved the lives of enslaved Africans. He devoted much time to descriptions of human sacrifice, cannibalism, and brutal, pagan religious practices to develop his case. In the opening sections of his book, Snelgrave described the beginnings of a ritual sacrifice of an African child by a local, despotic ruler: the child was "tied by the Leg to a Stake driven in the Ground, the flies and other vermin crawling on him, and two Priests standing by." Snelgrave responded to the scene by quoting the abolitionist mantra of the golden rule, "Do to others as we desir'd to be done unto." Snelgrave used the market to manumit the boy as well as his mother in an act replete with humanitarian and sentimental significance. The purchaser of the slave, a Mr. Studely, was then able to preserve the family unit and, wrote Snelgrave, would be a "kind Master to them."[24]

Snelgrave's account prompted another former African Company employee, John Atkins, to write the first promotional account of the African Company's activity in Africa that included an unequivocal desire to have the trade in enslaved Africans ended. Published in 1735, Atkins's account was the first to depict the west coast of Africa under deregulated trade as Tryon had portrayed the plantations—a place of violence, disharmony, gluttony, and alcoholism. Gone were the portrayals—like those of Southerne, Defoe, and Steele—of the separate traders as the quintessence of economic rationality. For Atkins, the independent slave traders were

> loose privateering Blades, that if they cannot trade fairly with the Natives, will rob; but then don't do it so much in pursuance of that trading Advice, *(Amass Riches, my Son)* as to put themselves in a Capacity of living well, and treating their Friends, being always well pleased if they can keep their Stock *at Par,* and with their Profits purchase from time to time, Strong-beer, Wine, Cyder, and such Necessaries, of *Bristol* Ships, that more frequently than others put in there.

As with company descriptions of the double-dealing and dissembling techniques of the deregulated slave trade (and with Defoe's account of the separate traders' lobbying methods), Atkins portrayed the separate traders as thriving on falsehood and duplicity: "Your Reputation is secured by the diffidence of your Report, and you must resolve with him now upon a Price in your Slaves, not to outbid one another; but at the same time make as strong a Resolution not to observe it." In Atkins's account, as Philip Gould has shown, the separate

---

24. William Snelgrave, *A New Account of Some Parts of Guinea, and the Slave-Trade* . . . (London, 1734), x, xi.

trader (or, for Gould, just the slave trader) became the "rake" whose "arts" disrupt the civilized, social functions of commerce. Deregulated trade for Atkins as for Davenant promoted an atomized, private trade that eroded the nobler features of commercial activity.[25]

Atkins contrasted the luxuriant cruelty of the independent slave traders with the noble defiance and dignity of an African captive. He became one of the first commentators on the African coast to reference the Oroonoko type in his eyewitness account. He described one of the separate traders' slaves:

> I could not help taking notice of one Fellow among the rest, of a tall, strong Make, and bold, stern aspect. As he imagined we were viewing them with a design to buy, he seemed to disdain his Fellow-Slaves for their Readiness to be examined, and as it were scorned looking at us, refusing to rise or stretch out his Limbs, as the Master commanded; which got him an unmerciful Whipping from *Cracker's* own Hand [the separate trader], and had certainly killed him but for the loss he himself must sustain by it; all which the Negro bore with Magnanimity, shrinking very little, and shedding a Tear or two, which he endeavoured to hide as tho' ashamed of. All the Company grew curious at his Courage, and wanted to know of Cracker, how he came by him; who told us, that this same Fellow, called Captain *Tomba,* was a Leader of some Country Villages that opposed them, and their Trade, at the River *Nunes*.

Atkins's depiction of Captain Tomba allowed him to contrast the callous, mercenary brutality of the separate traders with the natural dignity and strength of the African victims of the slave trade. These distinctions were also at work in his narrative of the conquest of Ouidah, a large center for unregulated slave trading, by the king of Dahomey. The king's invasion had been revenge for the king of Ouidah's encouragement of pilliarding. The new king, as Atkins viewed it, had deployed a coercive but virtuous royal power to overcome the immoral self-interest of individual traders: "The King's Actions carry great Reputation, for by the destruction of this Trade, he relinquished his own private Interests for the sake of publick Justice and Humanity." Atkins then described that this king sought to contract with the Royal African Company for a profitable commerce in the interior that would involve the enslavement

---

25. John Atkins, *A Voyage to Guinea, Brasil, and the West-Indies* . . . (London, 1735), 40, 168–169; Gould, *Barbaric Traffic,* 28. For John Atkins's prior employment with the African Company, see Robin Law, "Dahomey and the Slave Trade: Reflections on the Historiography of the Rise of Dahomey," *Journal of African History,* XXVII (1986), 244.

of Africans, but not their transportation. Another African Company employee, Bulfinch Lambe, had attempted to publicly market this plan in 1731. For Atkins and Lambe, the African Company understood that its best interests existed in its willingness to promote friendly relations with African leaders and to shun human trafficking for commerce in African flora and minerals.[26]

Atkins's portrayal of the African coast helped him to work up to an early statement of abolition. His use of Oroonoko, his concern about the calculated self-interest and duplicity of the independent traders, and his enthusiasm for the company prefaced a clear desire to end the slave trade. Atkins declared of the deregulated trade:

> An extensive [slave] Trade, in a moral Sense, is an extensive Evil, obvious to those who can see how Fraud, Thieving, and Executions have kept pace with it. The great Excess in Branches feeding Pride and Luxury, are an Oppression on the Publick; and the Peculiarity of it in this, and the Settlement of Colonies are Infringements on the Peace and Happiness of Mankind.

Atkins challenged the pro-slavery argument that transportation benefited Africans by moving them from a barbaric, "poor" Africa and by preserving "them from Sacrifice and Cannibals, to convey them to a Land flowing with more Milk and Honey, to a better Living, better Manners, Virtue, and Religion." In the same way as the African Company dismissed the separate traders as selfish and greedy, Atkins noted that the pro-slavery position reflected an interpretation of a society that was obsessed with money. It was only possible to see the Africans as "poor" if you viewed everything in society through the lens of money, as people in "trading Republicks" did. Such a perspective was un-British; in Britain, people could detach society from wealth because they appreciated that poverty communicated virtue. As a result, "it is a barbarous Corruption to stile such [Africans as] poor." The deregulated trade had, for Atkins, barbarized the instinctive ability of Britons to view trade beyond exclusively economic ends.[27]

BY THE 1740S, the Royal African Company began to propose to use its charter for charitable purposes in Britain to reflect the humanitarian attitudes it

---

26. Atkins, *Voyage to Guinea*, 41–42, 121; Bulfinch Lambe, *Capt. Bulfinch Lambe's Scheme for Trade with the Emperor of Paupau* ([London, 1731]). The separate trader whom Atkins singled out as meting out cruel treatment to the noble slave was John Leadstone. Leadstone had complained of the company's barbaric treatment toward him in 1713. See *The Case of John Leadstone, a Private Trader Residing in Africa* (n.p., [1713]), 1.

27. Atkins, *Voyage to Guinea*, 149–150, 176, 178.

had begun to direct at Africans in Africa and on the American plantations. Again, this strategy formed part of the company's continued attempts to court political favor. It was part of a broader project at this time to unlock the virtuous potential of a trade to Africa and to respond to the desire for national regeneration based on charitable acts. In 1740, Mercator Honestus targeted the separate traders' argument that African barbarity justified the slave trade: "I don't doubt the Blacks are more civilized than they are generally represented, and it is very certain, that with some Pains they might become much more so." The author went on to suggest that the virtue and "pure Religion" of African societies could inspire Britain to revisit its own morality. With its joint-stock structure and its experience of African trade, the Royal African Company proposed to contribute to such a national, moral regeneration.[28]

The African Company was not the only corporation to attempt to promote its stock with disinterested, charitable acts. From the early years of the eighteenth century, promoters of charitable schemes had articulated the commercial benefits of philanthropy. These promoters used the corporation, which had traditionally expressed more than just economic motivations, to develop their schemes. Since the 1690s, philanthropists who had been inspired by the Society for the Reformation of Manners had believed the parish administration of charity via trusts, individual bequests, and almsgiving was inadequate and began, in the early eighteenth century, to advance the joint-stock corporation as a suitable vehicle for philanthropy. The corporation provided a charter that could assist longevity and investment for the project. It also brought philanthropy in line with business practice as charity came more and more to be seen as a way to satisfy commercial as well as philanthropic goals. An offshoot of the Society for the Propagation of the Gospel in Foreign Parts, the Society for the Promotion of Christian Knowledge began in the 1710s to develop Charity Schools for poor children, which used the joint-stock format. Similar organizations had been set up to manage the workhouses of early Georgian England. These organizations showed that the directors of chartered corporations fused the ideas of social sympathy and a well-ordered society with the traditional rationale for joint-stock investment.[29]

As the functions of joint-stock corporations multiplied in the early years of the eighteenth century, they began to serve explicitly social and cultural purposes, such as the 1719 Royal Academy of Music and the Company of Mine

---

28. Mercator Honestus, "A Letter to the Gentlemen Merchants in the Guinea Trade, Particularly Addressed to the Merchants in Bristol and Liverpool," *Gentleman's Magazine*, X (July 1740), 341.

29. Geoffrey Clark, *Betting on Lives: The Culture of Life Insurance in England, 1695-1775* (Manchester, 1999), 83.

Adventurers of England. Humphrey Mackworth, the leader of the Company of Mine Adventurers, articulated the public and charitable aims of his corporation, even detailing the amount of money the profits from the scheme would allow him to donate to the service of the poor. After the bursting of the South Sea Bubble in 1720–1721, the public worried about joint-stock companies' often dubious value in overseas trade and in domestic industry. Directors of joint-stock companies sought to reinvent the corporation as a suitable vehicle for an older tradition that noted the virtuous, often charitable, and sometimes pious aims of corporate activity. Socially sympathetic business, so the developers of these adventures argued, was good business.[30]

In the 1740s, these charitable movements again changed tack, shifting their priorities from the education and employment of the poor to schemes that would increase the nation's population and improve its morals. No philanthropic enterprise did more to embody this movement than Thomas Coram's Foundling Hospital, founded as a corporation in 1740 to nurture abandoned children. Coram's project combined Christian benevolence with mercantile zeal. It made its case as a corporation with reference to the imperative to regenerate the nation's morals, population, and commerce.[31]

During this time, the African Company proposed to contribute to this movement by resurrecting a project one of its directors, Sir Robert Sutton (who was also a subgovernor in the 1730s), had been involved with since 1725. Sutton had served with the Committee of Management of the Charitable Corporation for the Relief of the Industrious Poor (founded by charter in 1707). This corporation lent small sums to the laboring poor on pledges at legal, regulated rates of interest to prevent these unfortunates from falling into the hands of pawnbrokers, the unregulated bankers who provided cash in exchange for goods. The corporation ended in disgrace in 1732 once its intentions had been exposed as fraudulent in Parliament.[32]

Concern with the laboring poor and the size of the British population came, as it had done in the 1660s and 1680s, to offer the African Company an argument for its monopoly. With the Charitable Corporation in mind, the company sought statutory support for its charter in March 1748 with ref-

30. For the Royal Academy of Music, see Judith Milhous and Robert D. Hume, "New Light on Handel and the Royal Academy of Music in 1720," *Theatre Journal*, XXXV (1983), 149–167. For Mackworth, see Koji Yamamoto, "Piety, Profit, and Public Service in the Early Financial Revolution," *English Historical Review*, CXXVI (2011), 818.

31. This summary of the history of charitable institutions in the period relies on Donna T. Andrew, *Philanthropy and Police: London Charity in the Eighteenth Century* (Princeton, N.J., 1989), 8, 49, 54, 58.

32. For the history of the Charitable Corporation, see A. Mcf. Davis, "The Charitable Company of London," Massachusetts Historical Society, *Proceedings*, 3d Ser., XVIV (1910–1911), 646–656.

erence to a plan to regulate the pawnbroking sector. The promoters of the scheme argued that it would help "prevent the sale and disposal of stolen Goods and to ease and relieve the Necessities of many Thousands of poor and industrious People." The company proposed to reduce the pawnbrokers' rate of interest from "50, 40, and 30 *per Cent*" to 20 percent and to levy a 5 percent tax on a fully regulated pawnbroking industry that the company could use for its benefit for thirty-two years, primarily to remove the burden of supporting its West African forts from the taxpayers and place it onto the perennially unpopular pawnbroker. The plan would also help to support the population of laboring poor, who it was hoped by Oglethorpe and other African Company sympathizers could substitute for enslaved African labor in the American colonies.[33]

The Royal African Company had acquired a reputation as a financial manipulator, especially under the management of Sir Bibye Lake in the late 1720s and 1730s. Its scheme to regulate the panwbroking business aimed to deflect that charge with its focus on the activities of an unpopular financial institution. It also sought to combine concern about the poor, the welfare of the mass of the population, and crime with a reestablishment of its joint-stock capital. The proposal, however, was declared "wholly *unconstitutional*" by "*two great Men* in *Power*" (one of whom was very likely the duke of Newcastle, Thomas Pelham-Holles). Lampooning comments by "The Fool" in the *London Gazetteer* concluded that the scheme demonstrated only an "outside Shew of Public Spirit." Nonetheless, the company's attempts to improve their share price by appealing to public sympathy for disadvantaged groups confirms the growing prominence of a consciously benign commerce that could generate wealth, virtue, and labor simultaneously. This vision of commerce came to be central to the early antislavery mantra.[34]

As the Africa trade debates drew to a close in Parliament in 1750, one final pamphlet appeared that would combine all aspects of the company's plat-

---

33. For the company's pawnbroking scheme, see *Answers to the Objections against the Proposals of the Royal African Company for Settling the Trade to Africa in a Second Letter to a Member of Parliament* ([London], 1748), 4. On the levy, see *The Case of the Royal African Company of England and Their Creditors* (London, 1748), 12; *A Detection of the Proceedings and Practices of the Directors of the Royal African Company of England* . . . (London, 1749), 25.

34. Mr. O'Connor, *Considerations on the Trade to Africa, Together with a Proposal for securing the Benefits Thereof to This Nation* . . . (London, 1749), 52. For Sir Bibye Lake's use of East India Company bonds to prop up the Hudson's Bay Company in this period, see Michael Wagner, "Companies, Commerce, and Politics: The Hudson's Bay, Levant, and Russia Companies, 1714–1763" (D.Phil. thesis, Oxford University, 2012), 179–118. Another African Company director of long service, Solomon Ashley, was caught up in a fraud scandal concerning the York Buildings Company in 1735; see *London Gazetteer,* Jan. 27, 1749.

PLATE 4. *William Ansah Sessarakoo* [the Royal African]. By John Faber, Jr.
© National Portrait Gallery, London

form for antislavery opinion: celebrations of social hierarchy, monarchy, and the commercial benefits of kindness to strangers; suspicion of unregulated commerce and interested behavior; and the promotion of the corporation as a force for disinterested good and humanity. *The Royal African; or, Memoir of the Young Prince of Annamaboe* claimed to be a biography of the African prince William Ansah Sessarakoo, and it invoked the literary traditions of Oroonoko and the narratives of Job Ben Solomon. *The Royal African* also intervened to promote the Royal African Company during its final deliberations in Parliament. It made a pitch for the corporate management of civilized commerce with the African interior by placing the biography of the prince of Annamaboe in the context of the broader history of the African trade. The author blamed the enslavement of the prince on the separate traders, who, like Captain Driver, had no respect for social rank. He depicted the pro- and anti-slave-trade arguments, as the Africa trade debates had done, in constitutional terms. The author associated the Africans' monarchical government with freedom and prosperity. This benign monarchy was the source of sentimental, familiar warmth in African society: "No People in the World, generally speaking, express greater Kindness for their Offspring than they do." The separate-trader (and Dutch) attachment to liberal, deliberative government was conducive to the escalation of enslavement. Like Atkins, the author noted that Europeans too often chose to misconstrue African commercial acumen and the constitutional freedoms provided by African government as barbarism to justify the trade in human beings.[35]

The author alleged, as company officials had done earlier in the century, that deregulated trade with Africa had elevated interest above humanity and justice and corrupted and dissolved bonds of friendship between all parties in the slave trade, "for Interest is a universal Deity, the *Fettish,* as these People call it, of the Negroes, as much as of the *Europeans;* and notwithstanding any Ties of Friendship and old Acquaintance with the *African* Company's Servants." The separate traders' interest had become, by 1750, the essence of disloyalty, which fueled the immorality of the slave trade. As with Bluett and Atkins, the author of *The Royal African* proposed that sentimental hospitality (as promoted by the African Company) could produce commercial gains. Kindness and respect would serve mercantilist agendas, helping Britain improve its commercial position at the expense of its European rivals. The author used the example of the French African trade to promote joint stock, in this case as a better means to encourage respect for the Africans through commer-

---

35. *The Royal African; or, Memoirs of the Young Prince of Annamaboe . . .* (London, [1749]), iv, vii, viii, 18, 22, 27, 28–29, 35, 40, 45.

cially minded hospitality. As part of this example, he recounted the story of an African king who was hosted in France to receive an education and then returned to Africa to cement the bonds of friendship between his people and the French. The author compares the French example of hospitality of Africans to the English attempt with Prince William Ansah Sessarakoo. African Company officials had sought to provide passage for the prince to England for his education. But an unscrupulous separate trader, who had "the Reputation of being among the Number of the most clear-sighted and adroit Traders that ever visited the Coast of *Guinea*," kidnapped the prince and sold him into slavery in Barbados. The Royal African Company, depicted by the author as heroic, came to the rescue and interceded to obtain preferential trading terms from the ruler at Annamaboe at the expense of their French rivals.[36]

The essence of this heroism, so the author proclaimed, was the corporate format of the Royal African Company because it provided a structure that offered legal recourse to those in Africa and in Britain. The African Company's corporate structure ensured that the evil practices of the separate traders could be reined in.

> Thus this Affair terminated much to the Advantage of the Company, but so that they were obliged to take upon them the satisfaction of an Injury in which they had not the least Concern; and to this the Company will always be liable, because in *Africa,* as well as in *England,* they are considered as a corporate Body, to which Application may be always made, and who are at all Times answerable to the several *Negroe* Governments upon the Coast for the Conduct and Behaviour of the *British* Nation, which is a Point highly deserving Notice.

The episode also offered further evidence "of the important Consequences that attend a judicious and humane Behaviour towards distant and barbarous Nations." The author argued that such behavior was, as a matter of course, most easily promoted by corporations like the Royal African Company and cited the great seventeenth-century advocate of corporations, Sir Josiah Child. Child's justification for corporate monopolies, like the African Company's in the seventeenth century, was founded upon a belief in the barbarity of heathen traders. The position of the author of *The Royal African* that corporations could better offer respect and kindness to barbarian Africans would, it is fair to say, have surprised Child. The author's final comment also sits uneasily with the African Company's older portrayal of itself as a martial force, best suited to intimidate and awe barbaric Africans: "Our Humanity and Jus-

36. *The Royal African*, 31, 38.

tice should be as extensive, as either the Terror of our Navies, or the Attention we have to Trade. It is of as great Consequence to be esteemed, and to be loved, as to be dreaded or revered." By the mid-eighteenth century, however, promoters of the Royal African Company, like the author of *The Royal African*, viewed the deregulated trade as an opportunity to re-regulate because corporate management of the trade would allow the British, not the Africans, to overcome their barbarity—a barbarity that was (as it was for Davenant) the product of deregulation and the work of the separate traders. The statute that would dissolve the Royal African Company in 1750 designated for the first time that the practice of pilliarding Africans was to be a capital crime. But the new regulated African Company that was formed by the 1750 statute, the Company of Merchants Trading to Africa, would become an important pro-slavery lobbyist.[37]

AFTER THE ROYAL AFRICAN COMPANY'S dissolution in 1752, the former director of the company, Malachy Postlethwayt, proved to be the most important poster boy for the company's ambivalence toward the slave trade. An influential political economist, Postlethwayt had served as a director of the Royal African Company throughout 1744 and 1745 and was an assiduous participant at the meetings of the Court of Assistants. Postlethwayt also authored two influential pamphlets in favor of the company for which he was paid. In these, he promoted the joint-stock format in traditional terms as the surest means to finance forts and to uphold the interests of national commerce against the highly effective French trade in enslaved Africans at midcentury. Like his predecessor apologist for the African Company, Charles Davenant, Postlethwayt believed passionately in suppressing personal interest to develop the greatness of the nation. In these pamphlets, Postlethwayt also continued to articulate the African Company as the proper venue for advancing a British trade with the inland parts of Africa, as Davenant, Chandos, and Oglethorpe had done before him.[38]

In 1759, Postlethwayt, like the author of *The Royal African*, praised the royal prerogative as the best means to manage the African trade and cited the suc-

37. Ibid., 46, 48, 51–52. For the Company of Merchants Trading to Africa's pro-slavery position, see Glasson, *Mastering Christianity*, 185.

38. For the similarities between Davenant's and Postlethwayt's conceptions of the threats to national liberty posed by private interests, see Peter N. Miller, *Defining the Common Good: Empire, Religion, and Philosophy in Eighteenth-Century Britain* (Cambridge, 1994), 159, 165. For population, see [Malachy Postlethwayt], *The National and Private Advantages of the African Trade Considered: Being an Enquiry, How Far It Concerns the Trading Interest of Great Britain* . . . (London, 1746), 3. For anti-French and pro-inland trade, see [Postlethwayt], *The African Trade, the Great Pillar and Support of the British Plantation Trade in America* . . . (London, 1745), 10, 35.

cess the French had since the 1720s in using their monarchy to subsidize and manage the trade, rather than leave it to the caprice of individual merchants, as the English had done. He argued that the French African Company accounted for the resurgence in French trade in the middle of the eighteenth century: "WE have seen that France has upheld her African commerce by the weight and influence of an opulent company, a perpetuated company, supported and upheld by the crown of France by mighty privileges and immunities; by a company endowed with extensive privileges for ever." Postlethwayt repeated his earlier argument that a corporate management of the African trade provided the best means to develop commercial relations with the inland "bowels" of Africa. In the context of Postlethwayt's excitement about the commercial benefits of African trade, he nailed his colors to the mast as a fully fledged advocate of antislavery. "For my own part," he admitted, "I cannot help expressing my dislike to the slave-trade, and wish an end could be put to it." Anticipating a wave of protest linked to the question of who but African slaves would staff the plantations, Postlethwayt proposed the "numberless poor" of Europe. He later connected his plan to substitute white labor for enslaved African labor with the charitable projects that promoted population growth in Britain, such as Coram's Foundling Hospital, with which the African Company had sought to associate in the 1740s.

> Whether the territories of those European nations that are interested in the colonies and plantations in America, are not populous enough, or may not be rendered so, by proper encouragement given to intermarriages amongst them, and to the breed of foundling infants, to supply their respective colonies with labourers, in the place of negro slaves?[39]

The deregulated slave trade was thus a barrier to the realization of Postlethwayt's vision of a lucrative, humane commerce with the interior of Africa: "It will ever spirit up wars and hostilities among the negro-princes and chiefs, for the sake of making captives of each other for sale. This, therefore, will ever obstruct the civilizing of these people, and extending of the trade into the bowels of Africa, which, by the contrary means, might be easily practicable." The advantages of a vibrant commerce with Africa could only be realized with the help of "a great and powerful company, with exclusive privileges

---

39. Malachy Postlethwayt, *Great-Britain's Commercial Interest Explained and Improved; in a Series of Dissertations on the Most Important Branches of Her Trade and Landed Interest* . . . , 2d ed. (London, 1759), 203, 217, 268; Postlethwayt, *The Universal Dictionary of Trade and Commerce* . . . , 3d ed. (London, 1766), s.v. "English African Company."

and immunities." As a former director of the Royal African Company, Postlethwayt understood the challenges such a company would face, but his determination to promote one as a vehicle for his antislavery agenda, even after the dissolution of the African Company, confirms the extent to which, by the late 1750s, the mission of the company (and its royally sponsored monopolistic predecessors) had come full circle in almost a century, from one designed to promote human trafficking from Africa to one chartered to substitute for it. For Postlethwayt and the African Company, then, joint-stock monopolies provided the best means of advancing the mid-eighteenth-century Enlightenment project of a civilizing, improving form of commerce.[40]

Postlethwayt's reasons for the suitability of the corporate format were clear. The separate traders' freedom crusade had brought anarchy to the trade, and this anarchy had upset the African commerce: "But as our fondness for the words liberty and freedom sometimes lead to licentiousness, and even anarchy in government; so may not a too great eagerness for an universal freedom and liberty of trade carry us such lengths, that we may, at length lose all the trade we have?" It is revealing evidence of the power of the African Company's ideology, as developed since its foundation through political deliberations, that Postlethwayt could associate the company's suspicion of the separate trader's attachment to liberty more directly with an argument for the company than he could with an argument for the abolition of the slave trade, which he, by 1759, also favored. It also confirms, as Christopher Brown has noted, that Malachy Postlethwayt promoted regulation of the African trade as much to enlarge the British Empire as he did to revolutionize attitudes toward slavery.[41]

THE ROYAL AFRICAN COMPANY's politicization of the trade in enslaved Africans provided the context, the ideas, and the policies for the early political disputes about whether the trade ought to be ended. Celebrations of strong state intervention in the trade, of benign commerce with the interior of Africa, and of the sentimental benefits of regulated commerce all became important motifs for the early political secular incarnations of antislavery campaigning. The continual need to formulate a political argument to sustain its public appeal induced the African Company to associate its pro-regulation argument with early moral discomfort with the slave trade. By the 1730s, this political association tapped into and helped develop sentimental portrayals of alternative trading scenarios with Africa, without human trafficking and

---

40. Postlethwayt, *Great Britain's Commercial Interest*, 222, 268.

41. Ibid., 200, 210, 214, 218, 222, 235, 269; Christopher Leslie Brown, *Moral Capital: Foundations of British Abolitionism* (Chapel Hill, N.C., 2006), 274.

guided by humanity, hospitality, royalty, and the coercive force of state regulation bent on protecting the Africans from the evils of the separate traders. The company also sought to develop political and investment capital by involving itself in charitable projects to nurture the laboring poor and support their population. A vogue for civic-minded corporations and projects sustained the African Company despite its trading inanity and helped the company to consider charitable and moral corporate ventures. James Oglethorpe's consistent association of corporate means with moral aims and the association of both those means and aims with an ambivalent attitude toward African slavery suggest that the early proto-abolitionist platform owed some debt of inspiration to the Royal African Company.[42]

How might we place these ideas in the context of the broader history of abolitionism in the British Atlantic world? They do not change the importance of those pillars of the abolitionist cause: the development of an ethic of benevolence and the broader appreciation of the positive image of the African. The African Company was one of many institutions that celebrated this ethic and reconceptualized the public image of the African, building on Oroonoko to note the commercial benefits of hospitality to Africans in Britain and overseas. The abolitionist ideas nurtured by the Africa trade dispute directly informed the language of parliamentary intervention in the slave trade.

Slavery's exposure to the legislative process during the Africa trade debates from 1690 to 1713 broadened the terms of debate, which led to calls for slave baptism and sowed the seeds that blossomed half a century later as the abolitionist movement. Defeated in the slave trade, the African Company justified its existence with reference to its physical presence in Africa and the possibilities of gold mining and inland trade there. Here, again, the African Company provided some precedent for arguments by early antislavery advocates that a new postslavery trading commerce with Africa could help restore British economic fortunes once the American colonies had detached themselves from the British state. The company began to associate itself with campaigns such as the reform of the pawnbroking system and became the stable for some early, lukewarm critics of slavery such as James Oglethorpe and Malachy Postlethwayt. These debates placed the theme of government regulation of commerce at the center of the slavery issue. As a result, abolition, when it came,

---

42. Nicholas Hudson has also noted the force of some of these ideas often associated with conservative politics and their traction with early antislavery campaigns and thought. See Hudson, "'Britons Never Will Be Slaves': National Myth, Conservatism, and the Beginnings of British Antislavery," *Eighteenth-Century Studies*, XXXIV (2001), 559–576.

was unequivocally an act of regulation, not deregulation. This was the principal abolitionist legacy of the Royal African Company's portrayal of itself and its African trade.[43]

The separate traders' deregulated version of the slave trade became, after decades of petitioning and pamphleteering, the explanation for the evils of the trade. They had established their freedom to trade in enslaved humans and legitimated that right in popular, representative politics based on principles of liberty and individual rights of property. But, for the African Company, the separate traders came to be the public villains of the African trade, leaving it to the inherently callous, brutal, inhuman workings of the market. They, not the Africans, had barbarized the trade. Abolitionists focused on the provincial beneficiaries of the deregulated slave trade, writing letters to the merchants of Liverpool and Bristol. Absenteeism came under fire as a cause of the brutalities of the slave system. The deterritorialized Atlantic that had offered the separate traders a network of supporters came to be vilified for separating ownership from management and moral responsibility. The decentralized polity that had so assisted the separate traders thus came to be blamed for the evils of slavery.[44]

---

43. For the tradition that abolition formed part of a movement to deregulate various aspects of the British economy, see E. P. Thompson, *The Making of the English Working Class* (New York, 1964), 529. As Philip Gould noted, Thomas Jefferson proposed regulatory means to end slavery in the Declaration of Independence in 1776; see *Barbaric Traffic*, 13.

44. For the periodical that targeted the slave traders of Liverpool and Bristol, see *London Magazine; and Monthly Chronologer*, IX (1740), 493–494.

EPILOGUE

Confused Commemorations

Like the Royal African Company, the separate traders also established a legacy that influenced the movement to abolish the slave trade. Two features of the independent slave traders' political campaign from the 1690s would be central to the abolitionists' political campaign from the 1780s: their natural rights argument and their ideological commitment to communicating the breadth of popular support for their campaign. Abolitionists hewed the right to oppose slavery from the same natural rights rock as the separate traders had hewed the right to resist monopoly. As early as July 1740, the *Gentleman's Magazine* published a letter aimed at the slave traders of Bristol and Liverpool asserting that all men were born with the natural right to liberty. In 1755, Francis Hutcheson cited "liberty and property" as the two most important freedoms denied the enslaved. These were the ideals the separate traders had celebrated to develop the slave trade. But, by the 1780s, the abolitionists infused their argument about natural rights with the African Company's growing sentimental attachment to humanity. In doing so, the abolitionists' campaign would develop its central argument: the natural rights of Englishmen should be universalized and extended to enslaved Africans as human rights.[1]

The clashing ends of these natural rights arguments reflects the political structure for slave trading that the separate traders had engineered and the abolitionists would have to confront. This elusive, deregulated structure would prove difficult to dismantle. If there had been a statute to escalate the slave trade, abolition simply would have been a matter of repeal. As it was, the political campaign to deregulate the slave trade worked to persuade public opinion of the need for escalation without creating a statute to support it. Abolitionists would also have to overcome the pervasive acceptance of slavery among Britons without the means to focus on a discrete legislative expression of that acceptance. But, because of the separate traders' parliamentary triumph, the abolitionists understood that their cause would have to achieve vic-

---

1. Mercator Honestus, "A Letter to the Gentlemen Merchants in the Guinea Trade, Particularly Addressed to the Merchants in Bristol and Liverpool," *Gentleman's Magazine*, X (July 1740), 341; Francis Hutcheson, *A System of Moral Philosophy, in Three Books* (Glasgow, 1755), I, 300.

tory in Parliament and, because of the mid-eighteenth-century celebration of the humane imperatives of regulation, this parliamentary victory would have to be statutory.

To defeat and dismantle pro-escalation public opinion, the abolitionists would have to adopt the lobbying methods of the separate traders. The famous upswell of disinterested public opinion in favor of abolition had as its most notable and pertinent precedent the separate traders' effective cultivation of large-scale interested public opinion in support of the escalation of the slave trade. The abolitionists' promotion of its lobby's broad base of support, especially in petitioning, also reflects the separate traders' style of politics. The later phases of antislavery campaigning saw the movement embrace the separate traders' language of reform and their ideological and strategic commitment to popular mobilization in service of their cause. The abolitionists began to employ the separate traders' political means to achieve some of the ends that had been nurtured by the African Company. They espoused a broad-based mandate, reveled in the scale of their petitioning campaign, and promoted the effects their national endorsement would have on the moral sense of the nation. From the 1760s and 1770s, without the same American support in Parliament for the slave trade that had buttressed the separate traders' case, British public opinion could be rallied against the trade to celebrate the nation's inherent discomfort with enslavement and human trafficking.[2]

The political ideas and the strategies of the separate traders and the debt both owed to the constitutional changes of 1688–1689 meant that the Glorious Revolution provided a conflicted legacy for abolition. In 1788, Peter Peckard, the vice-chancellor of the University of Cambridge, proposed that Britain celebrate the centenary of the Glorious Revolution by abolishing its transatlantic slave trade. Peckard praised the revolution for producing "the inestimable blessings of Liberty Civil and Religious" in Britain and argued that the revolution had started a manumitting journey whose next destination should be the American plantations. Peckard therefore proposed that 1788 should "be a Jubilee of Commemoration . . . by extending the blessings we enjoy to those who are deprived of them; by breaking every yoke, and setting the poor Captive free." Peckard did not apprehend, however, that the "inestimable blessings of Liberty" the revolution had protected had been instrumental in accelerating England's involvement in the transatlantic slave trade.[3]

---

2. For the importance abolitionists attached to the wishes of the people, see Thomas Clarkson, *The History of the Rise, Progress, and Accomplishment of the Abolition of the African Slave Trade by the British Parliament*, 2 vols. (London, 1808), I, 470.

3. P[eter] Peckard, *Justice and Mercy Recommended, Particularly with Reference to the Slave Trade* (Cambridge, 1788), ix–x.

For the pro-slavery lobbyist and the scion of a prominent Liverpudlian separate-trading dynasty, Robert Norris, the connections between the liberties protected by the Glorious Revolution and that revolution's role in supporting slave-trade escalation provided further proof that slavery was a civilizing institution. Writing in 1789, Norris argued that the natural laws that supported the slave trade and slavery were just as valid as those the abolitionists believed undermined slavery. The 1698 act that had greatly enlarged the scale of England's slave trade was the product "of a parliament that had vindicated the natural rights of mankind" and reflected the involvement of a "king, who was the patron of liberty." Norris went on, in the style of a separate trader, to extol the part played by British business acumen and ingenuity:

> The principle which has raised the commerce and navigation of this country, and with them the landed interest and revenues of the kingdom, from inconsiderable beginnings to their present greatness, is the *right* which every man in it possesses, to carry on his own business, in the way most advantageous to himself and the society, without any sudden interruption in the pursuit of it; and the *consciousness* which he has, of the steady protection of the laws, in the prosecution of what has been shewn to be legal.

Countless pro-slavery petitions also attributed Britain's commercial success to the slave trade, as those of their separate-trader predecessors had done, and, in particular, to the "enterprising Spirit of the People"—a phrase that exemplifies the tone of the separate traders.[4]

Robert Norris's account of the slave-trading legacy of the Glorious Revolution is surely more insightful than Peter Peckard's. The revolution established the political conditions, lauded the political ideas, and allowed lobbyists to pioneer the political strategies that led to Europe's supreme, unregulated contribution to the largest forced intercontinental migration in human history. Its most cherished, popularly countenanced, and elastic notion, freedom, came to offer the justification for the design of this forced migration of enslaved African women, men, and children. But, because of the Royal African

---

4. Robert Norris, *A Short Account of the African Slave-Trade* (London, 1789), 22. For "enterprising Spirit of the People," see "A Petition of the Mayor, Aldermen, Bailiffs, and Common Council of the Town of Liverpool," May 20, 1789, in *Journals of the House of Commons*, I–LI (London, 1803), XLIV, 383. The separate traders' notion of economic self-interest as an encouragement to efficiency was, however, memorably deployed by Adam Smith in service of the abolitionist position: "The work done by freemen comes cheaper in the end than that performed by slaves," owing to the insufficient incentives provided for slaves. See Adam Smith, *An Inquiry into the Nature and Causes of the Wealth of Nations* (New York, 1994), 415.

Company's rearguard political campaign against the separate traders throughout the first half of the eighteenth century, their pro-regulation, humane, disinterested rhetoric provided much of the inspiration for the political will and some of the political rhetoric of the antislavery cause. Some of the sources for antislavery thought can therefore be found in the seventeenth-century justifications for monopolistic regulation of trade.

The Glorious Revolution allowed an unregulated transatlantic trade in enslaved Africans. Without that revolution, the African Company's monopoly would likely have endured. James II would have applied the power of an absolutist monarchy, including the Royal Navy, to support the company's monopoly. If the threat of seizure did not continue to dissuade prospective independent slave traders from assembling cargoes bound for Africa, the experience of seizure and a show trial before a vice-admiralty court would have convinced them never to attempt it again. The company could have maintained its impressive though restricted contribution to the transatlantic slave trade. Without the colonies' charters and assemblies, and a Parliament and Board of Trade receptive to their interests, the colonists' desire to improve their supply of African slaves by deregulating the African trade would have gone unheeded. The African Company could have sustained its creditor status to dominate its debtors in the Caribbean and to augment the power of James's Dominion of New England. The colonies, with a less abundant supply of African slaves, might have developed more slowly, and other, rival European powers could have improved their presence on the African coast and in the Caribbean and on the North and South American mainlands. This was the potential outcome that the Glorious Revolution and the separate traders to Africa succeeded in averting.

The Glorious Revolution deprived the African Company of the political support for its operations and effected administrative, political, cultural, and ideological changes that provided a platform for the assertion of grievances and an arena in which to sustain those assertions. A Parliament rendered sovereign within the English constitution after the Glorious Revolution encouraged provincial and colonial interests to assert themselves at the expense of bastions of metropolitan privilege like the Royal African Company. Britain's commercial society became more receptive to private economic activity and celebrated its inherent benefits to national well-being. Its interest group, the separate traders to Africa, proved themselves better able to align their economic agenda with the institutional landscape left by the Glorious Revolution and better able to master the procedural possibilities that revolution had allowed.

The victory of the separate traders was part of a changing balance of power in the British Atlantic that reflected the domestic implications of the Glorious Revolution. This change saw imperial initiative devolved to colonists who, by the end of the seventeenth century, began to develop the means to assert themselves politically within the metropolis. A new style of mediation emerged in the British Atlantic to match the new political culture of the mother country. The metropolis sought information from the colonies to inform imperial policy, which empowered colonial interests that had opposed the Royal African Company from its inception. Like the economics of slave trading itself, the politics of company opposition proceeded transatlantically. Although the separate traders prioritized certain trades at particular times, they represented a genuinely Atlantic grouping with deterritorialized interests. A parliamentary campaign guaranteed Britain's slave trading supremacy for the rest of the eighteenth century and helped to ensure that African slaves would be the mainland American colonies' chosen solution to their labor-supply problem.

Political ideas, institutions, and a changed political context provided the means for slave-trade escalation. The highly politicized and institutionally pluralist world of the post-1688 constitutional settlement allowed the English public to brand the company as a deplorable relic of a bygone age, whereas the separate traders became emblematic of every British citizen's right to trade. Common law encroachment on the royal prerogative and the Admiralty's traditional control over overseas territories allowed the separate traders to ground their campaign to expand slavery on the constitutional basis of the liberty of the subject. The company's demise appeared like the death throes of the Stuart monarchy. The additional million and a half (or so) enslaved Africans transported across the Atlantic after the demise of the Royal African Company sailed on the same Protestant wind as William of Orange. Their forced migration was the direct result of the institutional defenders of British liberty.

The Royal African Company's attempts to maintain its monopoly exposed the trade to constitutional disputes. These came to inform the polarized (at times partisan) ideas that the Africa trade debates in Parliament set into dialogue with one another. On one side, the African Company advanced that its monopoly was the best means to uphold a national interest vested in the state. This state could defeat European rivals, resist the barbarity of African vendors, and prevent the national interest from being subsumed by the corrupting influence of greed, avarice, and selfish passions. On the other side, the independent slave traders argued that their deregulated trade was the surest route to trade expansion, noted the part played by that expansive trade in protecting English national liberty, and viewed the national interest in terms of the extent of public participation in trade and in the parliamentary management of state economic regulation. The separate traders used Parliament and the common law to develop access to private, independent slave trading as a natural, English birthright. The economic results of their deregulation were no less contingent on political factors than the African Company's monopoly. Slave-trade expansion, like the slave-trade monopoly, was politically constituted.

These conflicting political ideologies came to be reflected in the political strategies of both disputants. The African Company, despite its entrenched political capital in the City of London and the lobbying advantages of its joint-stock structure, failed to adapt its political tactics to a new constitutional regulatory environment. Using their breadth of support throughout Britain and the colonies to block the company's regulatory statutes, the separate traders proved to be brilliant lobbyists, cultivating the Board of Trade and the pamphlet-reading public to legitimize their deregulated trade. They understood the new political context, developed ideas with broad appeal, and translated that broad appeal into a successful regulatory outcome. The introduction of politics into the slave trade gave the edge to the group more adept at promoting its interests as representative of British subjects as a whole. As a consequence, the Royal African Company's economic interests suffered along with its political defeat.

Politics broadened the focus of debate from the narrow interests of the African Company and the separate traders to discussions of national interest, constitutional rights, and the importance of broad involvement in state decision making about national economic regulation. Once the African Company lost the political battle to manage the slave trade in the early eighteenth century, it used political means to improve its public profile. This first involved attempts to help provide financial support for a state that had been deprived of slave-trading revenue by the separate traders' legislative vacuum by satisfying a contract with the highly politicized South Sea Company and then by proposing a new means of extracting nonhuman resources from the African continent during the financial mania of the South Sea Bubble. The company then shifted its political strategy by voicing some of the traditional arguments opposing the transatlantic slave trade in moral terms. Throughout the 1730s, 1740s, and 1750s, the company's political lobby absorbed contemporary enthusiasm for the sentimental depiction of Africans and of trade with the African interior to describe the company as a vessel for sentimental hospitality and as a force for managing the slave trade with more humanity. These arguments would underpin former African Company directors' later calls for political consideration of the possibility of ending the transatlantic slave trade. The full-scale British slave trade therefore began as well as ended with a flood of pamphlets and an army of lobbyists. The politicization of the transatlantic slave trade between 1660 and 1752 connects these two bookends in the story of the trade.

IN A MUCH-ANTICIPATED speech to the House of Commons that was designed to set the tone for Britain's bicentennial of the abolition statute in 2007, Prime Minister Tony Blair expressed "deep sorrow" about British involvement in the transatlantic slave trade on behalf of the British government. Blair stopped short of a full apology to avoid accepting official responsibility. He deployed a modicum of reflection to begin the long process of atonement. He wondered why it was that the slave trade emerged at a time when "the capitals of Europe and America championed the enlightenment of man." Rather than confront this well-posed conundrum head on, however, Blair was quick to retreat into a familiar truism and rush to the defense of modernity: "Racism, not the rights of man, drove the horrors of the triangular trade." But modernity and the liberal political institutions and ideologies that define it belie this defense. The "rights of man," or their more elastic substitute "freedom," contributed much to the escalation of the slave trade.[5]

This contribution is visible in institutional and ideological features of the political debates about the slave trade from the late seventeenth to the mid-eighteenth century. The emergence of unregulated slave trading in Britain illustrates the connection between an accelerating slave trade and the rise of more inclusive institutions after 1688 as well as the mindset of the individuals who conceived those institutions. Eighteenth-century Britons believed that the Glorious Revolution would protect their liberties. This belief became a missionary creed as Britain's control extended over territories outside the mother country. The king's prerogative and its jurisdiction over conquered American territories might have provided the legal space for colonial governments to legislate slavery in America, but the common law provided an essential contribution to the entrenchment of American slavery—it protected the right of all English subjects to trade in the enslaved. The rhetoric of liberty therefore represented more than a figleaf to obscure the darker side of empire. The assertion of individual freedoms gave rise to a politics of interest that equated the pursuit of self-advancement with the economic development of the nation. An unregulated, expanded slave trade was one important result of this new politics. Liberal institutions and ideas proved instrumental in escalating the worst injustices of British imperialism. The separate traders'

---

5. Hansard H.C. (House of Commons), Ministerial Statements, Nov. 28, 2006, vol. 453, pt. 8, col. 103WS.

victory in the Africa trade debates demonstrates that institutional and ideological changes explicitly connected to freedom *caused,* rather than merely assisted, the deregulation of the British slave trade.[6]

The separate traders escalated and expanded the British slave trade in the name of British liberty. With each new year of the political campaign to expand the slave trade, Anglo-Saxon people, ideals, institutions, and identity became more and more inseparable from the desire to celebrate the trafficking of enslaved Africans. This selective application of liberty to slave traders, but not, until the late eighteenth century, to enslaved Africans, confirms the prevalence of what we would call racial thinking. It also offers a new means of connecting the intention to develop the slave trade and slavery to the precise workings of politics in this period. The campaign's length, the number of people involved, the scale of petitioning, the number of pamphlets, justifications, arguments, and counterarguments that derived from the politicization of the slave trade provide enough information to show that British American society, values, and venerated political institutions promoted slavery long before the abolitionists began to criticize it. The campaign's rich detail reveals the social interest committed to developing the slave trade. The slave trade and slavery emanated from public policy that was mulled over by thousands of people for more than twenty-five years. An analysis of this public policy demonstrates that enslaved labor became embedded in the very fabric of democratic freedom and economic liberalism.

As much as Prime Minister Blair would have wished to deny it in 2007, the development of the slave trade and the establishment of American slavery cannot be separated from the development of modern society, its creeds and its institutions. The hallmarks of modern society—representative democracy, civil society, and individual interests—all bear the responsibility for slavery. In helping to expand slavery, freedom has incurred a debt. Freedom's role in helping to end the slave trade and slavery partially satisfies that debt. Placing freedom's debt into the story of the emergence of modern liberal society represents another part of the continuing reconciliation and reckoning.

---

6. Exposing the connection between Britain and the United States's attachment to freedom and their dependence on slavery has long been a concern of historians. David Eltis noted how broadly conceived values, social structures, and cultural topoi that were collapsed into a definition of liberty *assisted* the development of slavery. See David Eltis, *The Rise of African Slavery in the Americas* (New York, 2000), 2.

Appendix 1
Data Supplements for Annual Slave-Trading Voyages, 1672–1752

A. TOTAL SLAVE-TRADING VOYAGES, ROYAL AFRICAN COMPANY (RAC),
INDEPENDENT TRADERS (IT), AND SOUTH SEA COMPANY (SSC), 1673–1752

Year	RAC	IT	SSC	Total	RAC and SSC Market Share (%)
1673	1	0	0	1	100
1674	11	1	0	12	92
1675	15	3	0	18	83
1676	16	2	0	18	89
1677	10	7	0	17	59
1678	19	1	0	20	95
1679	20	3	0	23	87
1680	19	2	0	21	90
1681	27	5	0	32	84
1682	25	2	0	27	93
1683	26	13	0	39	67
1684	26	2	0	28	93
1685	22	2	0	24	92
1686	39	0	0	39	100
1687	35	1	0	36	97
1688	17	2	0	19	89
1689	21	0	0	21	100
1690	7	1	0	8	88
1691	9	6	0	15	60
1692	5	4	0	9	56
1693	7	3	0	10	70
1694	9	0	0	9	100
1695	10	5	0	15	67
1696	8	13	0	21	38
1697	8	19	0	27	30
1698	7	24	0	31	23
1699	6	45	0	51	12
1700	14	82	0	96	15
1701	10	118	0	128	8
1702	14	84	0	98	14
1703	12	32	0	44	27
1704	18	42	0	60	30
1705	18	36	0	54	33
1706	16	33	0	49	33

Year	RAC	IT	SSC	Total	RAC and SSC Market Share (%)
1707	8	31	0	39	21
1708	15	44	0	59	25
1709	12	27	0	39	31
1710	5	51	0	56	9
1711	2	45	0	47	4
1712	3	33	0	36	8
1713	5	37	0	42	12
1714	9	40	5	54	26
1715	3	54	5	62	13
1716	1	51	6	58	12
1717	0	70	9	79	11
1718	0	88	14	102	14
1719	2	90	9	101	11
1720	3	68	0	71	4
1721	10	45	1	56	20
1722	12	43	4	59	27
1723	15	33	6	54	39
1724	9	68	7	84	19
1725	2	74	15	91	19
1726	1	81	14	96	16
1727	1	68	4	73	7
1728	0	79	1	80	1
1729	2	108	1	111	3
1730	0	94	4	98	4
1731	1	104	5	110	5
1732	0	109	1	110	1
1733	0	83	0	83	0
1734	0	84	1	85	1
1735	0	63	0	63	0
1736	0	84	1	85	1
1737	0	131	1	132	1
1738	0	78	0	78	0
1739	0	109	0	109	0
1740	0	97	0	97	0
1741	0	76	0	76	0
1742	0	61	0	61	0
1743	0	60	0	60	0
1744	0	84	0	84	0
1745	0	34	0	34	0
1746	0	24	0	24	0
1747	0	59	0	59	0
1748	0	72	0	72	0
1749	0	88	0	88	0
1750	0	92	0	92	0
1751	0	96	0	96	0
1752	0	112	0	112	0

Annual Slave-Trading Voyages · 221

B. DESTINATIONS OF SLAVE-TRADING VOYAGES, 1672–1752

Year	Leeward Islands		Barbados		Jamaica		Mainland	
	N	%	N	%	N	%	N	%
1672	0	0	3	75	0	0	1	25
1673	0	0	1	100	0	0	0	0
1674	3	18	9	53	4	24	1	6
1675	3	17	11	61	4	22	0	0
1676	4	22	8	44	6	33	0	0
1677	3	18	8	47	5	29	1	6
1678	5	19	13	48	6	22	3	11
1679	10	29	12	35	8	24	4	12
1680	6	20	15	50	8	27	1	3
1681	14	29	23	48	11	23	0	0
1682	16	39	18	44	7	17	0	0
1683	5	9	33	60	16	29	12	2
1684	1	3	18	56	12	38	1	3
1685	4	12	14	41	16	47	0	0
1686	7	17	14	33	16	38	5	12
1687	5	13	17	44	13	33	4	10
1688	9	43	6	29	4	19	2	10
1689	7	33	6	29	7	33	1	5
1690	1	20	2	40	2	40	0	0
1691	0	0	7	41	10	59	0	0
1692	0	0	5	36	8	57	1	7
1693	1	9	3	27	6	55	1	9
1694	1	7	5	33	7	47	2	13
1695	3	21	7	50	2	14	2	14
1696	3	14	11	52	5	24	2	10
1697	1	4	21	88	0	0	2	8
1698	4	11	18	50	5	14	9	25
1699	3	7	14	33	21	49	5	12
1700	12	17	20	29	35	50	3	4
1701	20	18	40	36	44	40	7	6
1702	18	23	36	46	20	25	5	6
1703	6	19	11	34	13	41	2	6
1704	6	13	14	31	18	40	7	16
1705	6	12	12	24	18	37	13	27
1706	5	12	12	29	16	39	8	20
1707	3	9	5	15	17	52	8	24
1708	9	16	7	13	29	53	10	18
1709	5	21	5	21	12	50	2	8
1710	5	13	6	15	22	56	6	15
1711	5	12	8	20	25	61	3	7
1712	3	9	12	34	19	54	1	3
1713	13	25	16	31	20	38	3	6
1714	8	12	34	52	21	32	2	3
1715	10	18	37	66	5	9	4	7

Year	Leeward Islands N	%	Barbados N	%	Jamaica N	%	Mainland N	%
1716	9	19	26	55	9	19	3	6
1717	9	13	37	52	14	20	11	15
1718	2	2	41	45	26	29	22	24
1719	8	10	24	30	31	39	17	21
1720	1	2	14	26	26	49	12	23
1721	5	14	5	14	10	28	16	44
1722	8	17	9	19	28	58	3	6
1723	9	19	15	32	19	40	4	9
1724	17	24	18	25	28	39	9	13
1725	20	25	19	23	26	32	16	20
1726	22	24	17	18	32	35	21	23
1727	17	24	13	19	14	20	26	37
1728	11	16	18	26	27	40	12	18
1729	20	20	21	21	49	50	8	8
1730	22	24	15	16	45	49	10	11
1731	14	15	24	25	40	42	18	19
1732	5	5	15	16	55	59	18	19
1733	7	10	9	13	26	38	27	39
1734	8	11	14	20	26	37	22	31
1735	9	18	6	12	12	24	23	46
1736	18	26	9	13	11	16	30	44
1737	31	31	8	8	41	41	20	20
1738	18	29	5	8	19	31	20	32
1739	28	28	22	22	26	26	23	23
1740	17	21	13	16	31	39	19	24
1741	13	21	25	40	18	29	6	10
1742	7	14	11	22	20	41	11	22
1743	4	8	4	8	33	62	12	23
1744	14	21	8	12	35	51	11	16
1745	2	8	1	4	18	72	4	16
1746	0	0	4	13	18	60	8	27
1747	13	23	8	14	34	61	1	2
1748	21	32	4	6	39	59	2	3
1749	27	35	16	21	23	29	12	15
1750	23	27	33	39	13	15	15	18
1751	22	25	25	28	25	28	17	19
1752	6	6	29	29	30	30	36	36

C. ORIGINS OF SLAVE-TRADING VOYAGES, 1672–1752

Year	London N	London %	Liverpool N	Liverpool %	Bristol N	Bristol %	Colonies N	Colonies %
1672	1	50	0	0	0	0	1	50
1673	1	100	0	0	0	0	0	0
1674	11	92	0	0	0	0	1	8
1675	16	89	0	0	0	0	2	11
1676	18	100	0	0	0	0	0	0
1677	13	76	0	0	0	0	4	24
1678	19	95	0	0	0	0	1	5
1679	17	74	0	0	0	0	6	26
1680	18	86	0	0	0	0	3	14
1681	31	97	0	0	0	0	1	3
1682	25	93	0	0	0	0	2	7
1683	29	74	0	0	0	0	8	21
1684	26	93	0	0	0	0	2	7
1685	20	83	0	0	0	0	4	17
1686	35	90	0	0	1	3	2	5
1687	27	84	0	0	1	3	8	22
1688	16	84	0	0	0	0	3	16
1689	21	91	0	0	0	0	1	4
1690	8	100	0	0	0	0	0	0
1691	10	67	0	0	0	0	5	33
1692	8	89	0	0	0	0	1	11
1693	9	90	0	0	0	0	1	10
1694	7	64	0	0	0	0	3	27
1695	11	73	0	0	0	0	4	27
1696	10	48	2	10	0	0	9	43
1697	12	44	0	0	0	0	15	56
1698	19	61	0	0	1	3	10	32
1699	34	67	1	2	1	2	14	27
1700	65	68	3	3	3	3	24	25
1701	87	68	3	2	3	2	34	27
1702	65	66	1	1	2	2	30	31
1703	31	70	0	0	3	7	10	23
1704	41	68	0	0	2	3	15	25
1705	41	76	0	0	3	6	10	19
1706	28	57	0	0	6	12	14	29
1707	24	62	0	0	7	18	8	21
1708	35	59	0	0	10	17	14	24
1709	24	62	0	0	5	13	9	23
1710	24	43	2	4	20	36	9	16
1711	23	49	3	6	13	28	6	13
1712	23	64	0	0	9	25	4	11
1713	14	33	1	2	18	43	8	19
1714	18	33	4	7	19	35	11	20
1715	17	27	11	18	17	27	16	26
1716	22	38	7	12	16	28	9	16

224 · APPENDIX 1

Year	London		Liverpool		Bristol		Colonies	
	N	%	N	%	N	%	N	%
1717	38	48	9	11	19	24	11	14
1718	50	49	11	11	26	25	14	14
1719	49	49	10	10	28	28	11	11
1720	29	41	5	7	26	37	10	14
1721	24	43	0	0	29	52	3	5
1722	35	59	6	10	15	25	2	3
1723	28	52	2	4	19	35	5	9
1724	38	45	3	4	39	46	4	5
1725	43	47	4	34	7	41	7	8
1726	46	48	5	5	38	40	6	6
1727	30	41	7	10	29	40	6	8
1728	32	40	4	5	39	49	5	6
1729	36	32	12	11	48	43	14	13
1730	35	36	7	7	47	48	9	9
1731	41	37	15	14	49	45	4	4
1732	31	28	19	17	52	46	9	8
1733	24	29	10	12	34	41	15	18
1734	24	28	22	26	33	39	5	6
1735	14	22	13	21	28	44	6	10
1736	21	24	19	22	29	33	17	20
1737	31	23	33	25	53	40	15	11
1738	20	26	17	22	31	40	10	13
1739	18	17	36	33	40	37	14	13
1740	13	13	33	34	36	37	15	15
1741	7	9	25	33	35	46	9	12
1742	8	13	24	39	23	38	6	10
1743	4	7	21	35	24	40	11	18
1744	8	10	37	44	29	35	10	12
1745	4	12	20	59	6	18	3	9
1746	1	4	8	33	13	54	2	8
1747	4	7	24	41	24	41	4	7
1748	4	6	36	50	27	38	5	7
1749	3	3	39	44	33	38	12	14
1750	10	11	42	46	26	28	11	12
1751	5	5	42	44	21	22	24	25
1752	12	11	50	45	24	21	18	16

D. AFRICAN EMBARKATION POINTS FOR ENSLAVED
AFRICANS ON BRITISH SLAVE-TRADING VOYAGES, 1672–1752

Year	Senegambia and offshore Atlantic		Sierra Leone		Windward Coast		Gold Coast		Bight of Benin		Bight of Biafra and Gulf of Guinea Islands		West Central Africa and Saint Helena		Southeast Africa and Indian Ocean	
	N	%	N	%	N	%	N	%	N	%	N	%	N	%	N	%
72	0	0	0	0	0	0	0	0	0	0	1	100	0	0	0	0
73	0	0	0	0	0	0	0	0	0	0	0	0	0	0	0	0
74	1	11	0	0	0	0	4	44	0	0	4	44	0	0	0	0
75	0	0	0	0	0	0	5	38	2	15	6	46	0	0	0	0
76	0	0	0	0	0	0	5	25	1	5	10	50	2	10	2	10
77	0	0	0	0	0	0	7	54	0	0	5	38	1	8	0	0
78	1	6	0	0	0	0	5	28	5	28	4	22	2	11	1	6
79	2	7	0	0	0	0	4	15	5	19	10	37	1	4	5	19
80	2	9	0	0	0	0	4	17	5	22	9	39	3	13	0	0
81	4	11	1	3	0	0	4	11	5	14	11	31	5	14	5	14
82	4	14	0	0	0	0	3	11	10	36	8	29	3	11	0	0
83	5	12	2	5	0	0	4	10	12	29	6	15	5	12	7	17
84	5	16	1	3	0	0	2	6	10	32	4	13	6	19	3	10
85	3	12	0	0	0	0	3	12	8	32	5	20	3	12	3	12
86	7	18	1	3	0	0	2	5	15	38	6	15	7	18	2	8
87	5	13	1	3	0	0	3	8	13	33	7	18	7	18	3	8
88	3	18	2	12	0	0	2	12	5	29	3	18	1	6	1	6
89	2	10	1	5	0	0	1	5	8	38	4	19	5	24	0	0
90	0	0	0	0	0	0	0	0	3	33	3	33	2	22	1	11
91	6	46	0	0	0	0	0	0	4	31	1	8	2	15	0	0
92	2	17	0	0	0	0	3	25	3	25	1	8	3	25	0	0
93	1	8	2	15	0	0	2	15	3	23	3	23	1	8	1	8
94	1	9	0	0	0	0	2	18	3	27	1	9	3	27	1	9
95	3	19	1	6	0	0	5	31	3	19	3	19	0	0	1	6
96	1	9	2	18	0	0	2	18	2	18	1	9	3	27	0	0
97	2	13	0	0	0	0	7	44	2	13	3	19	0	0	2	13
98	1	5	2	9	0	0	4	18	5	23	4	18	1	5	5	23
99	4	27	1	7	0	0	2	13	3	20	3	20	1	7	1	7
00	4	13	0	0	0	0	10	33	5	17	7	23	3	10	1	3
01	2	11	1	5	1	5	1	5	4	21	3	16	7	37	0	0
02	2	7	0	0	1	3	8	28	3	10	9	31	6	21	0	0
03	2	7	1	4	0	0	15	56	4	15	1	4	4	15	0	0
04	2	5	0	0	0	0	18	49	12	32	5	14	0	0	0	0
05	2	9	0	0	0	0	14	64	4	18	2	9	0	0	0	0
06	2	6	0	0	0	0	19	59	8	25	2	6	1	3	0	0
07	3	14	2	9	0	0	11	50	2	9	3	14	1	5	0	0
08	3	9	1	3	0	0	23	70	5	15	0	0	1	3	0	0
09	4	24	0	0	0	0	8	47	1	6	1	6	3	18	0	0
10	0	0	0	0	2	7	17	59	5	17	5	17	0	0	0	0
11	2	9	0	0	0	0	16	70	1	4	2	9	2	9	0	0
12	0	0	0	0	0	0	6	75	2	25	0	0	0	0	0	0

APPENDIX 1

Year	Senegambia and offshore Atlantic		Sierra Leone		Windward Coast		Gold Coast		Bight of Benin		Bight of Biafra and Gulf of Guinea Islands		West Central Africa and Saint Helena		Southeast Africa and Indian Ocean	
	N	%	N	%	N	%	N	%	N	%	N	%	N	%	N	%
1713	5	16	0	0	0	0	16	52	8	26	2	6	0	0	0	0
1714	6	17	2	6	0	0	15	42	10	28	1	3	2	6	0	0
1715	8	22	0	0	0	0	17	46	6	16	3	8	3	8	0	0
1716	6	22	0	0	0	0	15	56	4	15	0	0	2	7	0	0
1717	4	13	0	0	0	0	18	56	3	9	3	9	2	6	2	6
1718	6	13	5	11	0	0	16	34	9	19	7	15	2	4	2	4
1719	2	5	4	10	0	0	12	29	9	21	10	24	2	5	3	7
1720	1	2	0	0	0	0	30	70	2	5	8	19	1	2	1	2
1721	3	9	2	6	0	0	18	51	1	3	4	11	2	6	5	1
1722	4	13	1	3	0	0	15	50	7	23	2	7	1	3	0	0
1723	4	13	1	3	0	0	6	19	10	31	2	6	9	28	0	0
1724	6	17	0	0	2	6	8	23	9	26	2	6	8	23	0	0
1725	4	14	2	7	0	0	11	38	3	10	3	10	6	21	0	0
1726	8	19	2	5	2	5	9	21	5	12	11	26	5	12	0	0
1727	5	17	5	17	0	0	10	33	4	13	1	3	4	13	1	3
1728	8	27	4	13	3	10	9	30	2	7	3	10	0	0	1	3
1729	9	19	2	4	1	2	19	40	3	6	11	23	3	6	0	0
1730	4	5	2	3	0	0	25	34	9	12	16	22	16	22	2	3
1731	10	15	4	6	3	4	21	31	5	7	14	21	11	16	0	0
1732	11	22	0	0	1	2	13	25	3	6	16	31	7	14	0	0
1733	9	35	0	0	0	0	2	8	0	0	5	19	10	38	0	0
1734	10	33	0	0	0	0	4	13	3	10	3	10	10	33	0	0
1735	2	12	0	0	0	0	2	12	1	6	3	18	9	53	0	0
1736	6	17	0	0	1	3	8	22	1	3	6	17	14	39	0	0
1737	6	14	0	0	2	5	7	17	0	0	4	10	23	55	0	0
1738	4	17	0	0	0	0	8	35	1	4	1	4	9	39	0	0
1739	5	11	0	0	1	2	9	20	2	5	9	20	18	41	0	0
1740	3	7	1	2	4	10	6	15	1	2	18	44	8	20	0	0
1741	3	14	4	19	0	0	5	24	0	0	9	43	0	0	0	0
1742	1	4	2	7	3	11	5	18	0	0	13	46	4	14	0	0
1743	6	18	1	3	0	0	4	12	1	3	19	58	2	6	0	0
1744	8	13	1	2	1	2	12	20	4	7	27	44	8	13	0	0
1745	2	22	1	11	0	0	0	0	2	22	4	44	0	0	0	0
1746	1	8	1	8	0	0	2	15	0	0	9	69	0	0	0	0
1747	0	0	0	0	3	21	1	7	0	0	4	29	6	43	0	0
1748	0	0	0	0	1	2	16	35	3	7	14	30	12	26	0	0
1749	3	5	0	0	0	0	12	19	3	5	30	48	14	23	0	0
1750	4	7	2	3	3	5	12	20	3	5	32	52	5	8	0	0
1751	6	8	3	4	6	8	21	29	2	3	31	42	4	5	0	0
1752	13	13	5	5	10	10	27	27	1	1	38	38	9	9	0	0

Note: Leeward Islands includes Nevis, Antigua, and Montserrat.
Source: The Trans-Atlantic Slave Trade Database (Voyages Data Set), "Estimates" spreadsheet (2010), http://www.slavevoyages.org/tast/database/download.faces#extended. These calculations use the imputed data.

Appendix 2
A Directory of Independent Slave Traders, 1672–1712

Abenaker, Elias
Abney, Sir Thomas
Abott, Richard
Acton, Richard
Adams, William
Agnew, Hugh
Ainsworth, John
Alford, Daniel
Alford, Isaac
Alford, Joseph
Ambrose, William
Andrews, George
Andrews, Oliver
Angley, Samuel
Anthony, Jane
Archer, Edward
Arminger, William
Arnalling, William
Arnold, Thomas
Arnold, William
Arthur, Edward
Arthur, Henry
Ash, Ralph
Ashfield, Thomas
Astley, Charles
Astley, Christopher
Atkins, Richard
Atkins, Robert
Aylett, Charles
Ayleward, Daniel
Aynesworth, Joseph
Ayres, John
Ayshford, Anthony
Bachelor, John
Baggs, Joseph
Baily, John
Baker, James
Baker, John
Baker, Nicholas

Baker, Stephen
Ball, James
Ball, Samuel
Bamber, John
Barber, Isaac
Barbot, James
Barbot, John
Barlow, Samuel
Barnes, Charles
Barnes, Joseph
Barons, George
Barr, William
Barrow, Jacob
Barton, John
Barwick, Samuel
Batchellor, Nicholas
Bates, John
Batson, Richard
Battyn, William
Baty, John
Beades, Mungee
Beasley, Edward
Becher, John
Beckford, Peter
Beckford, Robert
Beckles, Thomas
Bedwell, Maurice
Bendall, Captain Hopefor
Benson, Edward
Benson, Robert, Lord Bingley
Benson, Sir William
Berdoe, James
Berdoe, John
Berdoe, Samuel
Berkeley, Robert
Bernard, John
Bertles, John
Besonth, James
Bignall, James

Bill, Benjamin
Bingham, Joseph
Birkin, Abraham
Blair, John
Blinkerne, William
Bloome, Robert
Blumley, Richard
Bodwell, Maurice
Bolton, Samuel
Bond, Abell
Bond, Richard
Bond, Thomas
Bond, William
Bonham, Samuel
Bookey, John
Bortes, John
Bosely, Richard
Bosworth, Richard
Boughton, Stephen
Bourne, Patrick
Bowden, William
Boyre, Thomas
Brace, John
Bradshaw, Henry
Bray, Jonathan
Brent, John
Brerewood, Thomas
Brethaver, John
Brewster, Edward
Brewster, James
Brewster, Thomas
Briggs, Major
Bright, John
Bristow, Robert
Broad, William
Brock, Joseph
Bromley, Richard
Brook, John
Brook, Robert

Brooke, Joseph
Broome, John
Brough, Gervase
Brown, John
Brown, Peregrine
Brown, Philip
Brownbill, Thomas
Browne, William
Bruce, Michael
Bruro, Mish
Brusser, James
Bryant, John
Buckle, Daniel
Buckley, John
Bucknall, Reginald
Bullard, Benjamin
Bulling, Robert
Burle, Guy
Burridge, John
Burridge, John, Jr.
Burridge, Robert
Burridge, Walter
Burrow, John
Buttery, Charles
Buxton, John
Byam, Edward
Byne, John
Byrd, William, I
Cabibell, Peter
Cabibell, Stephen
Caine, Joseph
Canning, Nathaniel
Carey, John
Carle, John
Carlelosse, Robert
Carmitchell, Peter
Carne, Joseph
Carpenter, Gregory
Carpenter, Henry
Carpenter, Joseph
Carpenter, Thomas
Carr, Robert
Carrill, Robert
Carrington, Paul
Carter, Edwin
Carter, Robert
Carter, Thomas
Carter, Zebulon
Cary, Joshua

Cary, Richard
Cary, Thomas
Casamajor, Lewis
Caske, Thomas
Chantley, Edward
Chase, William
Chauncey, Charles
Chauncey, Richard
Chauncey, William
Chauwell, James
Cheeke, John
Cherry, William
Cheshire, John
Chester, Robert
Chew, Samuel
Cheyney (Ching), John
Churchey, Do
Clarke, Edward
Clarke, Thomas
Clarke, William
Clarkson, John
Clarkwood, Samuel
Clarmore, Jonathan
Clarson, John
Clayton, Richard
Clayton, William
Cleavly, Edward
Cleeve, Alexander
Cleeveland, John
Cleland, John
Clemenoe, John
Cliff, Henry
Coalthurst, Thomas
Coaster, Thomas
Cockett, Thomas
Cocks, Charles
Cocks, Robert
Coddrington, William
Cole, Elizabeth
Cole, John
Cole, Michael
Cole, Thomas
Cole, William
Coleman, Henry
Coleman, William
Coles, Thomas
Colleton, James
Collett, Joseph
Collingwood, John

Collins, John
Collins, Robert
Colston, Francis
Combs, Charles
Cooley, William
Cooper, William
Corbett, Francis
Corbin, Francis
Cordwent, Edward
Corker, Robert
Corker, Thomas
Corkin, John
Corlett, Robert
Corr, Ebenezer
Corr, Oliver
Corsley, John
Corthine, Joseph
Cotes, Robert
Coulon, Mouse
Courtney, Stephen
Courts, Thomas
Covant, John
Cox, Thomas
Creagh, David
Creagh, Stephen
Crooke, James
Cross, John
Crosse, Richard
Crouch, John
Croucher, John
Crowther, John
Cruickshank, Robert
Crumpe, Isaac
Crumpe, Margaret
Cuddon, Francis
Cuddon, Sir Thomas
Cuddon, Warner
Curtis, Edward
Curtis, Robert
Da Costa, Isaac
Dakins, Isaac
Danby, John
Daniel, Josiah
Darrall, John
Davenant, Roland
David, John James
Davidson, Robert
Davis, Henry
Davis, John

Directory of Independent Slave Traders · 229

Davis, Jonathan
Davison, John
Dawkins, Isaac
Day, James
Day, John
Day, Peter
De Lencey, Stephen
De Medina, Moses
De Mina, Moses
Deacon, William
Deane, Cornelius
Deane, John
Dearsley, John
Denew, John
Denton, Richard
Desher, John
Devonshire, Christopher
Diamond, Richard
Diamond, Robert
Diaz, Isaac
Dickinson, Caleb
Dodd, Edward
Dolling, Richard
Donning, George
Donning, John
Dove, Charles
Downing, George
Drake, Thomas
Draper, Thomas
Dring, Samuel
Drinkwater, Anthony
Druce, William
Dudley, Thomas
Duffield, Peter
Dunckley, Sir Robert
Duport, Simon
During, Charles
During, Samuel
Dyer, Edward
Dyer, John
Earle, John
Earle, Joseph
Easy, John
Edwards, Isaac
Edwards, Robert
Edwards, Thomas
Edwards, William
Egerton, Charles
Egerton, Robert

Elkins, William
Ellard, Charles
Ellard, John
Ellet, Ellen
Ellis, John
Ellis, Thomas
Elton, Abraham, Jr.
Elton, Jacob
Elwick, John
Elwick, Samuel
Emberley, William
Evans, Silianus
Evans, Thomas
Ewer, Roger
Eyres, Samuel
Eyton, James
Eyton, Richard
Fairman, Robert
Farmer, John
Farr, John
Faulkner, David
Fearleson, Lawrence
Fell, John
Fenlason, William
Ferguson, John
Fisher, Joseph
Fisher, William
Flight, Joseph
Ford, Phillip
Forty, Anthony
Forty, Henry
Foster, John
Foster, Thomas
Fowle, Joseph
Fowler, Christopher
Foxley, Thomas
Foye, Edward
Frampton, Thomas
Francia, Moses
Francis, James
Franco, Abraham
Franklyn, William
French, William
Frisby, Peregrine
Frost, William
Fry, John
Fryer, Andrew
Fulcher, Thomas
Galbraith, William

Galdy, Lawrence
Galdy, Lewis
Gale, Luke
Gardiner, William
Garthwaite, Nathaniel
Garvey, John
Gascoyne, Benjamin
Gates, Thomas
Gatton, Ebeneezer
Gawthorn, Roger
Genew, John
Gething, William
Gibb, William
Gibbon, John
Gibbons, Christopher
Gibson, William
Giles, John
Girdwood, George
Gladman, Jonathan
Godin, Stephen
Godman, John
Godman, William
Godwin, John
Goffe, William
Goodwin, John
Goodwin, Nicholas
Gore, Gerrard
Gore, Sir William
Gosfright, Francis
Gotley, Joseph
Gotley, Richard
Gough, James
Gould, James
Gracedieu, Sir Bartholomew
Green, James
Green, Thomas
Greene, Joseph
Greg, Edward
Gregory, William
Griell, David
Gries, Edward
Griffin, George
Griffin, Richard
Grimes, Barnard
Grosvenor, Richard
Grosvenor, William
Grout, John
Grubar, Francis
Grubar, Thomas

Gubbs, John
Gwillain, Nathaniel
Hackett, Robert
Hainton, Richard
Hall, Ezekiel
Hall, John
Hall, Urban
Hallam, Richard
Hally, Francis
Hamlin, Robert
Hamond, George
Handcock, William
Hangar, John
Hannay, James
Harbin, John
Harbin, Joseph
Hardy, Priscilla
Harford, Charles, Jr.
Harle, Edward
Harris, John
Harris, Philip
Harris, Richard
Harris, Robert
Harris, William
Harvey, George
Harwood, John
Hatley, Benjamin
Hawkesmore, Peter
Hawkesworth, Walter
Hawkins, Sir John
Hayes, John
Hayne, Cornelius
Haynes, Thomas
Hays, David
Hayward, Hugh
Hayward, Joseph
Heathcote, Sir Gilbert
Heathcote, John
Hedges, Joseph
Henriques, Joseph
Henvill, Richard
Herring, Benjamin
Heysham, Giles
Heysham, Robert
Heysham, William
Higgs, Caster
Hill, John
Hill, Thomas
Hillhouse, James

Hilliard, Richard
Hills, Thomas
Hillyard, John
Hilton, John
Hilton, Thomas
Hinton, Richard
Hoar, John
Hodges, Joseph
Hodges, Thomas
Hodgkin, Thomas
Holden, Joseph
Holder, Melisha
Holder, Richard
Holder, William
Holland, Richard
Hollander, Peter
Hollister, John
Hollister, Laurence
Holloway, John
Holmes, Richard
Hook, Abraham
Hopes, John
Hopewell, John
Hopkins, David
Hornby, Charles
Hotchkin, Thomas
Houghton, Francis
Houghton, George
Houghton, Richard
Houlditch, Abraham
Howard, Robert
Howell, Ben
Howes, George
Hubbard, John
Hudson, Kendall
Hudson, Thomas
Hunsden, John
Hunton, Isaac
Hurst, William
Hyde, Thomas
Imping, Philip
Ingleton, William
Ivy, David
Jackson, Francis
Jackson, Joseph
Jacobson, Henry
Jacobson, Theodore
James, Edward
James, John

James, Rice
James, Walter
James, William
Jamineau, Daniel
Jarrold, Edward
Jarrold, Robert
Jayne, John
Jefferies, Sir Jeffrey
Jeffry, Arthur
Jenkins, John
Johnson, John
Johnson, Lewis
Johnson, Nathaniel
Johnson, Sir Thomas
Johnson, William
Jones, Edward
Jones, John
Jones, Peregrine
Jones, Richard
Jones, Thomas
Jones, William
Jordan, Henry
Joy, Peter
Keckerboat, Ernestus
Kempthorne, Samuel
Kenagh, William
Kent, Baily
Kent, Charles
Kent, Walter
Kent, William
Keyser, Timothy
Kidgell, Nicholas
Kile, Nathaniel
King, William
Kingston, Kirkham
Kirkham, William
Knight, Richard
Lambert, John
Langdon, William
Lapthorne, Elizabeth
Lascelles, Edward
Lascelles, George
Lascelles, Robert
Law, Tarleton
Lea, John
Leaver, William
Ledford, John
Lee, Joshua
Lee, Richard

Lee, Thomas
Lett, Thomas
Letter, John
Levett, Sir Richard
Lewen, Marten
Lewin, Morde
Lewis, Daniel
Lewis, John
Lewis, William
Lidstone, Francis
Lillington, George
Litten, John
Living, Mordecai
Lloyd, Thomas
Lodge, Abraham
Loe, Charles
London, William
Lone, Giles
Lone, Samuel
Lone, William
Lopez, Andrew
Lopez, Jacob
Lott, Nicholas
Lovell, Bowyer
Loyd, John
Ludlam, Francis
Luke, John
Luny, John
Lutton, John
Lutwidge, Thomas
Lyell, Henry
Lyell, Robert
Lynch, Simon
Mackerell, John
Madan, Martyn
Maggot, William
Mahune, James
Maine, Strode
Major, Anthony
Mallinson (Milleson), John
Malthus, William
Mane, Elizabeth
Mann, Daniel
Mann, David
Marker, John
Markinsley, John
Marqnot, Peter
Marquett, Peter
Marshall, Joseph

Martin, Edward
Martin, Francis
Martin, George
Martin, Samuel
Martyn, Edward
Martyn, Joseph
Mason, George
Mason, Simon
Matthews, Jonathan
Matthews, Robert
Matthews, Roger
Matthews, Thomas
Matthews, William
Maxey, Benjamin
Maxwell, John
Mayhew, John
Mayle, Thomas
Mead, Thomas
Mears, Jacob
Mendez, Abraham
Mendez, Isaac
Mendez, Jacob
Mendez, Joseph
Mendez, Moses
Merrett, Solomon
Merring, John
Merritt, Thomas
Merryweather, Marlboro
Merryweather, Richard
Metcalfe, Peregrine
Mickelthwaite, Nathaniel
Miller, David
Miller, John
Millington, Francis
Mills, John
Milne, David
Milner, David
Milner, Isaac
Milner, James
Minson, Richard
Mitchell, Francis
Mitford, Cuthbert
Mitford, James
Mitford, John
Mockmedley, John
Moncriffe, Arthur
Montero, Anthony
Moore, Joseph
Moore, Thomas

Moore, William
Morgan, Francis
Morgan, Roger
Morice, Humphrey
Morice, Richard
Morton, John
Mosely, Charles
Mosely, Maurice
Mosely, William
Mott, John
Moulins, Robert
Muisken, Gerard
Munday, John
Murray, John
Musgrave, George
Nash, Guillaim
Nash, James
Neford, Joseph
Nelson, Thomas
Nelthorpe, George
Nerhulst, John
Newell, Ralph
Newman, Thomas
Newton, Thomas
Nicholls, Charles
Nicholls, Thomas
Nicholls, William
Nicholson, Edward
Nodin, Charles
Nolsbrough, Samuel
Normanton, John
Norris, Richard
Norton, John
Norwood, Benjamin
Nowell, Ralph
Nunez, David
Nurse, Henry
Nurse, Robert
Nutt, John
Nutt, William
Ogden, Thomas
Ongley, Sir Samuel
Orchard, Charles
Owen, John
Owen, William
Owley, Daniel
Oxley, Robert
Pack, Jonathan
Packer, Samuel

Pafford, William
Paggen, Paul
Paggen, Peter
Painfelt, James
Palmer, Anthony
Park, John
Parker, Edward
Parkin, John
Parkin, Joseph
Parkin, Thomas
Parmenter, John
Parrott, William
Pary, Richard
Paul, John
Peacock, John
Pearce, Edward
Pearson, Alex
Peck, George
Peck, Thomas
Peecke, John
Peers, George
Peloquin, Stephen
Penneck, William
Penny, Roger
Pentyre, Philip
Perrin, Thomas
Perry, Micajah
Pettitt, John
Pheasant, John
Philipse, Frederick
Phillips, Adolphus
Phillips, Francis
Phillips, Robert
Pickering, Charles
Pierce, Robert
Pindar, Paul
Pinkney, Thomas
Pitcarne, John
Pitts, Thomas
Plowman, Daniel
Plumb, Abraham
Plumley, John
Plumstead, Robert
Poole, Henry
Poole, Richard
Poole, Robert
Pope, Robert
Porter, James
Powis, Joseph

Pratt, John
Pratter, Edward
Prestons, John
Prideaux, Nicholas
Primate, Humphrey
Prince, John
Prince, Lawrence
Prissick, Charles
Prissick, Christopher
Proctor, Samuel
Prowde, John
Prowse, Roger
Pym, John
Quelch, Benjamin
Radley, Lintho
Ranson, Robert
Raper, Henry
Raymond, William
Read, James
Read, William
Reilly, Charles
Renardson, Charles
Renew, Peter
Reyly, William
Reynardson, Charles
Reynolds, Robert
Rhett, William
Rice, James
Richards, Sam
Richardson, Thomas
Richardson, William
Richmond, Silvester
Ridgell, Nicholas
Rigby, Thomas
Roach, John
Roberts, Edward
Roberts, Isaac
Roberts, William
Robinson, Samuel
Rock, John
Rock, Joseph
Rogers, Francis
Rogers, Thomas
Rogers, Woodes
Ronow, Peter
Rookes, John
Roope, Anthony
Rossignuolo, Domenio
Rous, Nathaniel

Rous, Nicholas
Rowley, John
Ruddock, Noblet
Russell, Edward
Russell, Henry
Russell, John
Rust, Walter
Ryan, Walter
Sadler, John
Sadler, Ralph
Sadler, Thomas
Sadlere, Charles
Saffard, William
Salter, John
Salter, Thomas
Salter, William
Sasquereau, Lewis
Saunders, Edmund
Saunders, William
Savage, Charles
Schuller, Roger
Scott, Benjamin
Scott, John
Scott, Thomas
Scott, William
Sealy, Robert
Searle, Edward
Searle, John
Searle, Jonathan
Searle, Owen
Selfe, John
Sellet, John
Shackle, Thomas
Shaw, Samuel
Shelswell, Thomas
Shephard, Thomas
Shepherd, Joshua
Shepherd, William
Shepney, William
Sherley, William
Sherwin, Henry
Short, John
Shubrick, Richard
Shute, Christopher
Shute, Giles
Silcarne, John
Silke, John
Simmonds, Thomas
Simpson, George

Directory of Independent Slave Traders · 233

Simpson, John
Simpson, Thomas
Sitwell, Francis
Skoopy, William
Slablin, Matthew
Sled, William
Slinsbey, Henry
Smaller, Samuel
Smallwood, John
Smally, Samuel
Smith, Daniel
Smith, George
Smith, Henry
Smith, James
Smith, John
Smith, Joseph
Smith, Joshua
Smith, Richard
Smith, Robert
Smith, Samuel
Smith, Thomas
Smith, William
Snablin, Matthew
Soames, Joseph
Soane, Samuel
Sorrel, John
Sorrel, Paul
South, Humphrey
South, John
South, Robert
South, Thomas
Southall, Robert
Southern, John
Spencer, Mary
Spooner, Mary
Spooner, Thomas
Stafford, John
Stafford, Joseph
Stanborough, Richard
Stanhope, Phillip
Stanley, Stephen
Starke, John
Starke, Thomas
Stevens, Edward
Stevenson, Alexander
Stevenson, Christopher
Stevenson, John
Stevenson, Thomas
Stone, Samuel

Storey, Samuel
Storey, William
Strange, David
Stratford, Joseph
Stringer, Robert
Stringer, Thomas
Strong, Benjamin
Stuckley, Silvester
Studdier, Robert
Styles, Thomas
Suttell, William
Sutton, John
Swettman, James
Tairmen, Robert
Tanner, John
Tayler, John
Taylor, Robert
Taylor, Thomas
Tenlason, Willam
Tennant, Henry
Terry, Benjamin
Theunemans, Simon
Thomas, Charles
Thomas, Daniel
Thomas, George
Thomas, John
Thomas, William
Thompson, John
Thompson, Richard
Thompson, Stephen
Thompson, Thomas
Thorn, Edward
Thornbury, Ben
Thornton, Richard
Throgmorton, James
Tindall, Owen
Tod, John
Torres, Jacob Lopes
Torriano, Nathaniel
Torriano, Ruoro
Tourney, Anthony
Towne, Richard
Townsend, Kingston
Travers, John
Travers, Samuel
Traworthy, James
Tray, Samuel
Treble, Joseph
Tryon, Rowland

Tryon, William
Tudor, Sarah
Tudway, Elizabeth
Tudway, Richard
Tunbridge, Robert
Turner, John
Turpin, Michael
Turville, John
Upton, John
Upton, Thomas
Valorisin, Manwell
Vanbrugh, Carleton
Verhulst, John
Wadding, Peter
Wade, Ford
Wags, Benjamin
Wagstaff, James
Walker, James
Walker, John
Walker, Thomas
Wallinger, Anthony
Walter, John
Walter, Richard
Walthall, Hanbury
Walthall, Simon
Walton, William
Ward, Thomas
Warkman, John
Warman, John
Warner, William
Warren, John
Warren, William
Wartham, Martie
Warwick, William
Waterhouse, David
Watkinson, Edward
Watson, Jonathan
Watson, Robert
Watts, Bridges
Watts, Richard
Watts, William
Way, Benjamin
Way, Joseph
Wayte, James
Wayte, Samuel
Weaver, William
Webley, John
Webster, Godfrey
Webster, William

Weldale, John
Wellon, William
Wenham, Thomas
West, Edward
Westerne, Maximilian
Wharton, Thomas
Whateley, Solomon
Whenham, Thomas
White, Ignatius
White, Michael
White, Robert
Wiggett, William
Wilde, Abraham

Wilde, Henry
Wilford, Thomas
Wilkinson, Margaret
Williams, Aaron
Williams, Edward
Williams, John
Williams, Thomas
Williamson, John
Willis, Francis
Willis, Richard
Wilson, Bigloy
Wilson, Robert
Winchcome, Thomas

Winder, Thomas
Winsor, Thomas
Wirkham, Nathaniel
Wise, Robert
Wittson, Thomas
Wood, Sampson
Wood, William
Woodcock, Hugh
Woodley, Joseph
Woolcock, Nicholas
Wright, Broughton
Young, William

Sources: Treasury (T) 70/1198–1199 and T 70/349–356; The *Trans-Atlantic Slave Trade Database (Voyages Data Set),* http://www.slavevoyages.org; Nigel Tattersfield, *The Forgotten Trade: Compromising the Log of the Daniel and Henry of 1700 and Accounts of the Slave Trade from the Minor Parts of England, 1698-1725* (London, 1998); and David Richardson, *Bristol, Africa, and the Eighteenth-Century Slave Trade to America,* I, *The Years of Expansion, 1698-1729,* Bristol Record Society, *Publications,* XXXVIII (Bristol, 1986).

Appendix 3
A Directory of Lobbying Independent Traders, 1678–1713

Archer, Edward
Arnold, William
Atkins, Robert
Baker, John
Ball, Guy
Barker, Jedediah
Barwick, Samuel
Bayley, Richard
Beckford, Peter
Beel, Jacob
Blackwell, John
Bound, Robert
Bradley, Benjamin
Brain, Benjamin
Brockman, William
Bromley, John, II
Brook, Robert
Brown, John
Brown, Peregrine
Bubb, John
Burges, Thomas
Burridge, John, Jr.
Burridge, John, Sr.
Campbell, Sir James
Cane, Richard
Carleton, Arden
Carleton, Edward
Carter, Edwin
Cary, John
Cary, Thomas
Chilton, Edward
Clark, Thomas
Clark, William
Clayton, William
Clutterbuck, William
Coleman, William
Colt, John Dutton
Corbin, John
Corbin, Thomas

Corrs, Godfrey
Corsley, John
Cotton, Sir Robert
Cruickshank, Robert
Crumpe, Richard
Cumming, Sir Alexander
Davers, Sir Robert
Davies, Isaac
Dawkins, John
Day, John
Day, Nathaniel
Day, Peter
Deane, Cornelius
Dockwra, William
Dodd, Edward
Earle, Joseph
Farr, John
Farrer, William
Field, James
Forty, Antony
Foster, Thomas
Freke, Philip
Galdy, Lawrence
Gardner, John
Gibbes, Henry
Godin, Stephen
Godman, John
Godman, William
Goodwin, John
Goodwin, Nicholas
Gracedieu, Sir Bartholomew
Groswold, Henry
Haltey, George
Hannay, James
Harris, Richard
Harris, William
Harrison, Benjamin, Jr.
Hartwell, Henry
Hatley, Benjamin

Hawkins, John
Hayne, Cornelius
Heath, William
Heathcote, Sir Gilbert
Henshaw, Benjamin
Heysham, Robert
Heysham, William
Hickes, John
Hill, John
Holder, Melisha
Holder, Richard
Hollander, Peter
Hollidge, James
Holmes, Richard
Hook, Abraham
Hooke, Francis
Houlditch, Abraham
Howard, Robert
Hutchinson, Charles
Ingleton, William
Jackson, Stephen
Jackson, William
James, Edward
Jeffreys, Edward
Johnson, William
Jones, Fred
Jones, Thomas
Kent, Charles
Lane, Robert
Lascall, Henry
Lascelles, Edward
Lawson, Gilfrid
Lee, Thomas
Levett, Sir Richard
Lillington, George
Littleton, Edward
Lloyd, Richard
Lloyd, Thomas
Loddington, John

Lomp, Hasemann
Lone, William
Long, James
Lowther, James
Lutwidge, Thomas
Major, Anthony
Martyn, George
Martyn, Joseph
Mascall, Timothy
Merritt, Thomas
Micklethwaite, Nathaniel
Mills, John
Milner, Isaac
Mitchell, Thomas
Molmoth, Francis
Montagu, George
Moore, Robert
Morgan, Christopher
Morice, Humphrey
Morice, John
Munday, John
Nelthorpe, George
Newman, Thomas
Nightingale, Jeffrey
Onslow, Thomas
Paggen, Peter
Palmer, Henry
Parrot, William

Pearse, Elias
Perry, Micajah
Portin, Richard
Pulteney, John
Radbourne, John
Ratbourne, Humphrey
Ridgley, Charles
Roberts, William
Rogers, Francis
Rooks, John
Rous, Nathaniel
Sail, John
Saunders, Peter
Saunders, William
Searle, Edward
Shepheard, Samuel, II
Sherrin, Samuel
Sherwin, Henry
Sitwell, Francis
Smallwood, John
Smith, John
Smith, Samuel
Smith, Thomas
South, Humphrey
Stevenson, Christopher
Suggitt, Thomas
Sutton, John
Swann, William

Swymmer, Anthony
Swymmer, John
Swymmer, William
Taylor, John
Taylor, Thomas
Thomas, John
Thomas, Tudor
Thomas, William
Thompson, Richard
Turner, John
Tyler, John
Vere, William
Vose, William
Walker, Robert
Walker, Thomas
Wallis, Samuel
Warren, Willam
Waterhouse, David
Way, Benjamin
Wayte, James
Webster, Godfrey
Whitchurch, Francis
Wilkinson, William
Wither, Thomas
Wood, William
Woodfine, Thomas
Yate, Robert
Yeomans, John Junior

Sources: *Journal of the Commissioners for Trade and Plantations* . . . , 14 vols. (London, 1920–1938), I–III; *Journals of the House of Commons,* I–LI (London, 1803), XI–XVI; *Journals of the House of Lords* (London, 1767–1830), XVI; T 70/175.

Appendix 4
A Directory of Royal African Company Directors, 1672–1750

Achesley, Roger
Acton, Francis
Acton, Robert
Affleck, Gilbert
Aleyn, Thomas
Andrewes, Sir Jonathan
Ashby, John
Ashley, John
Ashley, Solomon
Atkyns, Robert, Jr.
Baily, Arthur
Balle, Charles
Banks, Sir John
Barker, Edward
Barlow, George
Barton, George
Bathurst, Sir Benjamin
Beckford, Thomas
Bedford, Robert
Belasyse, Thomas, Viscount Fauconberg
Bellamy, John
Bence, John
Bendall, Captain Hopefor
Bennett, John
Benson, Robert, Lord Bingley
Benson, Samuel
Berkeley, Henry
Berkeley, Lord George
Betts, William
Beuzelin, Francis
Bird, Robert
Bladen, Martin
Blake, James
Bludworth, Sir Thomas
Blunt, Sir John
Bodicote, John
Bodicote, Thomas
Bohun, George

Bonnell, John
Boteler, Francis
Bouverie, William
Bradshaw, Thomas
Bradyll, Roger
Bridgen, Edward
Bristow, Robert
Brocas, Richard
Brown, John
Brydges, James, duke of Chandos
Buckworth, Sir John
Bull, James
Bull, John
Bulstrode, Edward
Burrell, Peter
Burroughs, William
Burton, John
Campbell, John
Carr, John
Cartwright, Jarvis
Cass, Sir John
Castleton, Nathaniel
Cater, John
Chappell, Roger
Child, Sir Josiah
Clarges, Sir Thomas
Clayton, Sir Robert
Cleeve, Alexander
Coalthurst, Thomas
Cole, Christian
Collet, Jonathan
Colleton, Sir Peter
Collett, Thomas
Collyer, Daniel
Colston, Edward
Comport, Robert
Cooke, John
Cooke, Nicholas

Cooke, Sir Thomas
Cooper, Anthony Ashley, earl of Shaftesbury
Corbet, William
Craddock, Richard
Cramond, Robert
Craven, William, earl of Craven
Crispe, Thomas
Crosby, George
Cruickshank, Robert
Cutting, John
Dandbridge, Francis
Danvers, Joseph
Dargeant, James
Darnall, Sir John
Dashwood, Francis
Dashwood, Sir Francis
Dashwood, Sir Samuel
Dashwood, Thomas
Davenant, Roland
Dawes, Sir Jonathan
Deane, James
Decker, Sir Matthew
Dekenver, John
Delme, Sir Peter
Des Bowerie, William
Deutry, Dennis
Dobyns, William
Done, Thomas
Drummond, John
Du Bois, John
Duncombe, John
Du Puy, Lawrence
Durley, Henry
Eckersall, James
Edmundson, James
Edwards, Francis
Edwards, Sir James

Edwards, Thomas
Elliott, William
Essington, John
Evance, Sir Stephen
Evans, John
Evans, Richard
Farrington, Thomas
Faure, Henry
Fawkener, William
Fazakerley, Sir William
Fellow, John
Finch, Daniel
Finch, William
Fleete, Sir John
Floyer, John
Foley, Edward
Ford, Sir Richard
Fotherby, Robert
Foxall, Zachariah
Gardiner, John
Gascoyne, Joseph
George II
Germain, Sir John
Goddard, James
Godolphin, Charles
Gohier, James
Gore, Sir William
Gorges, Ferdinando
Gouge, Edward
Graham, Colonel William
Gray, Sir James
Grey, Ralph, baron Grey of Werke
Grey, Thomas
Grosvenor, Seth
Hall, Thomas
Hall, Urban
Hallett, James
Hamilton, John
Hamond, Sir William
Hanbury, John
Hangar, John
Hardy, Charles
Harris, Thomas
Harrison, Edward
Hatsell, Lawrence
Hawles, Thomas
Hayes, Charles
Hayes, Daniel

Hayes, Francis
Hayne, Thompson
Heatley, Thomas
Herne, Frederick
Herne, Sir Nathaniel
Hickman, Nathaniel
Hill, Abraham
Hillersdon, Edward
Hodges, Sir William
Holland, Richard
Hopegood, Andrew
Hopegood, Andrew, Jr.
Hopegood, Sir Edward
Hopegood, Francis
Hopegood, Francis, Jr.
Hopkins, John
Horne, John
Houghton, Thomas
Houlditch, Abraham
Hughes, Edward
Hume, Benjamin
Humphreys, Orlando
Humphreys, Sir William
Hyde, Edward, earl of Clarendon
Ingram, Sir Arthur
Ivatt, William
James II
Jansen, Theodore
Jarret, William
Jasper, Edward
Jefferies, Sir Jeffrey
Jeffreys, Edward
Jeffreys, John
Jeffreys, Sir Robert
Jeffreys, Walter
Jermyn, Stephen
Johnson, James
Johnson, John
Johnson, Sir Henry
Johnson, William
Jolliffe, William
Jones, Samuel
Jorey, Joseph
Joy, Peter
Kennedy, Hugh
Kent, Griffith
King, Sir Andrew
Knight, John

Lade, John
Lake, Sir Atwill
Lake, Sir Bibye
Lake, Thomas
Lambert, John
Lancashire, Robert
Lancaster, William
Langhorne, Sir William
Lansdell, John
Laroche, John
Lawrence, Sir John
Lawton, John
Lee, Joseph
Lee, Ralph
Lee, William
Lethuillier, Sir John
Lloyd, Charles
Lockwood, Richard
Long, Charles
Lovibund, Edward
Lovibund, Henry
Lucie, Jacob
Manesty, Sprig
Mann, James
Marston, Thomas
Martin, Stephen
Martin, Joseph
Mason, William
Matthews, Sir John
Mead, John
Mead, Nicholas
Mead, Richard
Mead, Thomas
Mead, William
Meres, Sir John
Merle, John Anthony
Merry, John
Meyer, Sir Peter
Milner, Benjamin
Modyford, Charles
Monck, William
Moore, Arthur
Moore, Sir John
Morgan, Sir John
Morice, John
Mostyn, Richard
Mounteney, Nathaniel
Mounteney, Richard
Moyer, Samuel

Moyer, William
Murthwaite, Thomas
Naish, James
Neale, Henry
Negus, Francis
Newland, Sir Benjamin
Nicholls, Thomas
Nicholson, John
North, Captain John
North, Sir Dudley
Nurse, Henry
Oglethorpe, James
Ouchterlony, Alexander
Page, Sir Gregory
Panuwell, Thomas
Paramein, Sir Peter
Parsons, Henry
Paston, William, earl of Yarmouth
Pate, William
Peachey, Bolstrod
Pearse, Bert
Pearse, Thomas
Pendarves, Stephen
Periam, Benjamin
Perkins, Warner
Pery, John
Phillips, John
Pindar, Thomas
Pitts, Stephen
Polhill, Charles
Porten, James
Postlethwayte, Malacky
Powys, Richard
Priaulx, Paul
Price, William
Prichard, Sir William
Proby, Sir Peter
Radcliffe, Ralph
Raper, Henry
Revell, Thomas
Reynardson, Abraham
Reynardson, Joseph
Reynolds, Anthony
Richards, Henry
Roberts, Sir Gabriel
Roberts, William
Rudge, Edward
Rudge, John
Rustat, Tobias
Sambrooke, Sir Jeremy
Saunderson, Sir Thomas
Saunderson, Sir William
Savill, John
Searle, John
Sedgwick, Robert
Sedgwick, William
Shaw, Sir John
Shephard, Philip
Shepheard, Samuel
Sherard, Sir John
Short, John
Skinner, Israel
Skutt, Benjamin
Smith, Honorat
Smith, John
Smith, Sir James
Spackman, John
Speke, George
Spelman, John
Stamper, Robert
Stanier, Sir Samuel
Stevens, William
Stillingfleet, John
Storey, William
Sutton, Sir Robert
Tayler, John
Taylor, Joseph
Tench, Sir Fisher
Tench, Sir Nathaniel
Thomas, Sir Dalby
Thompson, Sir John
Thompson, [St.] Quentin
Tilson, John
Torriano, John
Townley, Francis
Traherne, Philip
Tryon, Rowland
Tryon, William
Tulse, Sir Henry
Tulson, Francis
Turner, Sir William
Tyson, Francis
Upton, John
Vanderesch, Thomas
Vansittart, Robert
Varnatty, Constantine
Vaughan, John
Vere, Charles
Verney, John, Viscount Fermanagh
Vernon, Thomas
Vyner, Sir Robert
Wachter, Jacob
Walcot, Humphrey
Waller, Edward
Ward, James
Warren, Nicholas
Warren, William
Watkins, Henry
Watts, Thomas
Westby, Wardell-George
Westerne, Robert
Whitcombe, Peter
Wilcock, Benjamin
Wilkinson, Philip
Williamson, Robert
Williamson, Sir Joseph
Wilshaw, Benoni
Wilshaw, Captain Francis
Windham, Wadham
Withers, Sir William
Wood, Robert
Woolfe, Joseph
Wren, Matthew
Wright, John
Young, Richard

Sources: K. G. Davies, *The Royal African Company* (London, 1957), index; Eveline Cruickshanks, Stuart Handley, and D. W. Hayton, eds., *The History of Parliament: The House of Commons, 1690-1715*, 5 vols. (Cambridge, 2002); Minutes of the Court of Assistants, T 70/76-99.

Appendix 5
Africa Trade Petitions to Parliament on the Royal African Company's Monopoly, 1690–1752

Date	Petitioner (to House of Commons, unless otherwise noted)	Position	Source
27.1.90	Royal African Company	Pro	*CJ*, X, 345
31.3.90	Royal African Company	Pro	*CJ*, X, 360
21.4.90	Clothiers of Suffolke and Essex	Anti	*CJ*, X, 382
21.4.90	Merchants of London, Merchants to the Coast of Barbary	Anti	*CJ*, X, 382
21.4.90	Planters and Merchants to Jamaica	Anti	*CJ*, X, 382
21.4.90	John Thrale, John Tutt, and Owners of the Ship *Delight*, of London	Anti	*CJ*, X, 382
22.4.90	Merchants and Planters Trading to and Interested in Barbadoes	Anti	*CJ*, X, 383
29.4.90	Thomas Byfield and Owners of the Ship *Henry and William*	Anti	*CJ*, X, 393
30.4.90	Benjamin Rawlins	Anti	*CJ*, X, 394
17.10.90	Royal African Company	Pro	*CJ*, X, 444
21.10.90	Merchants and Planters of Jamaica	Anti	*CJ*, X, 448
21.10.90	Clothiers of the Counties of Suffolke and Essex	Anti	*CJ*, X, 448
22.10.90	Mayor, Aldermen, and Common Council of Exeter	Anti	*CJ*, X, 449
30.10.90	Merchants and Planters of the Island of Barbadoes	Anti	*CJ*, X, 456
1.11.90	Company of Cutlers in Hallamshire, in the County of Yorke	Anti	*CJ*, X, 459
1.1.91	Royal African Company	Pro	*CJ*, X, 532
9.12.91	Mayor, Aldermen, and Common Councilmen of the City of Exeter	Anti	*CJ*, X, 579
24.1.94	Royal African Company	Pro	*CJ*, XI, 68
15.2.94	Mayor, Alderman, and Common Councilmen of Exeter	Anti	*CJ*, XI, ,96
19.2.94	Clothiers in and about Witney in the County of Oxon	Pro	*CJ*, XI, 100
30.11.94	Royal African Company	Pro	*CJ*, XI, 180
10.12.94	Planters and Merchants of Barbadoes	Anti	*CJ*, XI, 184
12.12.94	Merchants and Planters in Jamaica	Anti	*CJ*, XI, 186
20.12.94	Edmund Harrison, William Dockwra, John Thrale, Thomas Jones	Anti	*CJ*, XI, 190
25.3.95	Clothiers, Serge-Makers, Dyers, of Berkshire	Anti	*CJ*, XI, 281
25.3.95	Clothiers, Serge-Makers, Dyers, of Wiltshire	Anti	*CJ*, XI, 281
25.3.95	Clothiers, Serge-Makers, Dyers of Southwark	Anti	*CJ*, XI, 281
28.3.95	Makers of Stuffs, and Dyers of the City of Norwich	Anti	*CJ*, XI, 284

Date	Petitioner (to House of Commons, unless otherwise noted)	Position	Source
28.3.95	Clothiers, Dyers, of the County of York	Anti	CJ, XI, 284
30.3.95	Clothiers of Somerset	Anti	CJ, XI, 287
30.3.95	Clothiers of Gloucester	Anti	CJ, XI, 287
2.4.95	Clothiers of Devon	Anti	CJ, XI, 290
2.1.96	Royal African Company	Pro	CJ, XI, 375
28.2.96	Merchants and Planters of Virginia and Maryland	Anti	CJ, XI, 475
28.2.96	Merchants and Planters of Jamaica	Anti	CJ, XI, 475
3.3.96	Weavers and Dyers within the Borough of Kidderminster	Pro	CJ, XI, 486
17.3.96	Merchants of Plymouth Trading to Virginia and Maryland	Anti	CJ, XI, 518
26.3.96	Merchants and Other Traders of the Bristol	Anti	CJ, XI, 532
2.4.96	Sir Nicholas Crispe	Anti	CJ, XI, 542
24.11.96	Royal African Company	Pro	CJ, XI, 592
7.12.96	Merchants and Planters of Virginia and Maryland	Anti	CJ, XI, 616
7.12.96	Merchants and Planters in the Island of Jamaica	Anti	CJ, XI, 616
8.12.96	Merchants to South Barbary	Anti	CJ, XI, 617
8.12.96	Clothiers of the City of Bristol	Anti	CJ, XI, 618
11.12.96	Merchants of the City of London	Anti	CJ, XI, 622
29.12.96	Clothworkers of Shrewsbury	Pro	CJ, XI, 639
29.12.96	Weavers in and about Kidderminster	Pro	CJ, XI, 639
29.12.96	Mayor, Aldermen, and Common Council of Exeter	Anti	CJ, XI, 639
29.12.96	Merchants, and Other Traders of the City of Bristol	Anti	CJ, XI, 639
16.1.97	Royal African Company	Pro	CJ, XI, 663
8.2.97	Merchants and Planters of Barbadoes	Pro	CJ, XI, 696
11.3.97	Royal African Company	Pro	CJ, XI, 736
19.2.98	Merchants and Planters of Maryland in America	Anti	CJ, XII, 120
19.2.98	Merchants and Planters of Virginia and Maryland	Anti	CJ, XII, 120
21.2.98	Merchants and Planters of Jamaica	Anti	CJ, XII, 121
23.2.98	Mayor etc. and Merchant-Adventurers of Bristoll	Anti	CJ, XII, 125
28.2.98	Clothiers of Bristol	Anti	CJ, XII, 133
28.2.98	Planters and Merchants of Island of Barbadoes	Anti	CJ, XII, 133
28.2.98	Dyers of the City of London	Anti	CJ, XII, 133
19.3.98	Sir Nicholas Crisp, Baronet	Anti	CJ, XII, 166
19.3.98	Merchants in the Sugar-Plantations in America	Pro	CJ, XII, 166
19.3.98	Planters of His Majesty's Leeward Caribbee Islands	Pro	CJ, XII, 166
19.3.98	Inhabitants of Mountserrat	Pro	CJ, XII, 166
28.3.98	Sir Ralph Delavall	Neutral	CJ, XII, 181
31.3.98	Clothiers of Somersett	Neutral	CJ, XII, 185
31.3.98	Clothiers of Wiltshire	Neutral	CJ, XII, 185
2.4.98	Richard Dickinson	Neutral	CJ, XII, 190
25.5.98	Planters and Merchants of Virginia and Maryland to House of Lords	Anti	LJ, XVI, 297
26.5.98	Planters and Merchants of Jamaica to House of Lords	Anti	LJ, XVI, 299
27.5.98	Planters and Merchants of Cariby Islands in America to House of Lords	Pro	LJ, XVI, 300
28.5.98	Edward Carleton of London, Merchant to House of Lords	Neutral	LJ, XVI, 301

Date	Petitioner (to House of Commons, unless otherwise noted)	Position	Source
30.5.98	Planters in the Island of Barbados to House of Lords	Anti	LJ, XVI, 305
30.5.98	Planters Concerned in the Island of Barbados to House of Lords	Anti	LJ, XVI, 305
30.5.98	Mayor, etc. and Merchant Adventurers of Bristol to House of Lords	Anti	LJ, XVI, 305
8.2.07	Royal African Company	Pro	CJ, XV, 281
7.3.07	William Bishop	Neutral	CJ, XV, 328
10.3.08	Royal African Company	Pro	CJ, XV, 599
16.3.08	Separate Traders Trading to Barbadoes, and the Leeward Islands	Anti	CJ, XV, 612
23.3.08	Ship-wrights, etc. of London	Anti	CJ, XV, 625
23.3.08	Merchant-Adventurers of Bristol, Trading to Africa, the West Indies	Anti	CJ, XV, 625
23.3.08	Mayor, Aldermen, and Common Council of Exeter	Anti	CJ, XV, 625
25.3.08	Gun-Makers, etc. Metalworkers of Birmingham	Anti	CJ, XV, 631
20.1.09	Royal African Company	Pro	CJ, XVI, 64
20.1.09	Planters and Inhabitants of Barbados	Pro	CJ, XVI, 64
27.1.09	Separate Traders of London	Anti	CJ, XVI, 71
27.1.09	Mayor, Aldermen, Common Council of the City of Exeter	Anti	CJ, XVI, 71
28.1.09	Gun-Makers etc. of the City of London	Pro	CJ, XVI, 74
29.1.09	Separate Traders to Africa to Virginia and Maryland	Anti	CJ, XVI, 75
29.1.09	Shipwrights etc. of Wapping and Limehouse	Anti	CJ, XVI, 75
29.1.09	Merchants of the Montrosse	Anti	CJ, XVI, 75
1.2.09	Merchants of Edinburgh	Anti	CJ, XVI, 77
1.2.09	Separate Traders to Africa to Jamaica	Anti	CJ, XVI, 77
1.2.09	Planters of Nevis	Pro	CJ, XVI, 77
1.2.09	Dyers etc. of London	Pro	CJ, XVI, 77
2.2.09	Shipwrights etc. of London	Pro	CJ, XVI, 83
2.2.09	Society of Merchants-Adventurers of Bristol	Anti	CJ, XVI, 83
2.2.09	Weavers of Exeter	Pro	CJ, XVI, 83
2.2.09	Planters of Mountserrat	Pro	CJ, XVI, 83
2.2.09	Tradesmen and Ironworkers of Birmingham	Anti	CJ, XVI, 83
2.2.09	Merchants of the Burgh of Dundee	Anti	CJ, XVI, 83
3.2.09	Woollen Manufacturers of Kidderminster	Pro	CJ, XVI, 86
3.2.09	Tradesmen of London	Pro	CJ, XVI, 86
3.2.09	Mayor, Aldermen, and Common Council of the City of Bristol	Anti	CJ, XVI, 86
4.2.09	Dyers, Packers etc. of the City of London	Anti	CJ, XVI, 90
9.2.09	Merchants of Whitehaven	Anti	CJ, XVI, 98
9.2.09	Merchants of Inverness	Anti	CJ, XVI, 98
11.2.09	Merchants of Aberdeen	Anti	CJ, XVI, 102
11.2.09	Merchants of Lancaster	Anti	CJ, XVI, 102
18.2.09	Creditors of the Royal African Company	Pro	CJ, XVI, 112
19.2.09	Merchants of Chester	Anti	CJ, XVI, 114
25.2.09	Mayor, Aldermen, and Burgesses of the Corporation of Taunton	Anti	CJ, XVI, 124
4.3.09	Merchants of the City of Glasgow	Anti	CJ, XVI, 135

Date	Petitioner (to House of Commons, unless otherwise noted)	Position	Source
23.3.09	Royal African Company	Pro	*CJ*, XVI, 169
26.3.09	Creditors of the Royal African Company	Pro	*CJ*, XVI, 175
30.3.09	Creditors of the African Company	Pro	*CJ*, XVI, 179
31.3.09	Sir John Crisp, Baronet, and Charles Crisp, Esq.	Anti	*CJ*, XVI, 180
8.4.09	Creditors of the Royal African Company	Pro	*CJ*, XVI, 192
8.12.09	Merchants of London, Traders to Africa	Anti	*CJ*, XVI, 235
9.12.09	Planters of Barbadoes	Anti	*CJ*, XVI, 236
13.12.09	Mayor, Bailiffs, Burgesses and of Dartmouth	Anti	*CJ*, XVI, 240
15.12.09	Merchant-Adventurers of the City of Bristol	Anti	*CJ*, XVI, 242
15.12.09	Planters and Inhabitants of the Island of Barbadoes	Pro	*CJ*, XVI, 242
20.12.09	Mayor, Aldermen, Merchants, and Tradesmen of Liverpool	Anti	*CJ*, XVI, 246
10.1.10	Mayor, Aldermen, and Common Council of Exeter	Anti	*CJ*, XVI, 259
11.1.10	Planters of Nevis	Pro	*CJ*, XVI, 259
11.1.10	Tradesmen of Birmingham	Anti	*CJ*, XVI, 259
11.1.10	Shipwrights etc. of London	Anti	*CJ*, XVI, 260
11.1.10	Mayor, Magistrates, Common Council of Plymouth	Anti	*CJ*, XVI, 260
11.1.10	Royal African Company	Pro	*CJ*, XVI, 260
12.1.10	Merchants of Whitehaven	Anti	*CJ*, XVI, 261
12.1.10	Mayor, Aldermen, Burgesses of Bridgewater	Anti	*CJ*, XVI, 261
18.1.10	Shipwrights etc. of London	Pro	*CJ*, XVI, 267
19.1.10	Mayor, Aldermen of Bristol	Anti	*CJ*, XVI, 269
19.1.10	Packers, Dyers etc. of London	Anti	*CJ*, XVI, 269
24.1.10	Gun-Makers of London	Pro	*CJ*, XVI, 273
24.1.10	Dyers, Packers etc. of London	Pro	*CJ*, XVI, 273
11.2.10	Magistrates etc. Merchants of the City of Edinburgh	Anti	*CJ*, XVI, 308
11.2.10	Royal Boroughs of North Britain	Anti	*CJ*, XVI, 308
13.2.10	Creditors of the Royal African Company	Pro	*CJ*, XVI, 310
20.2.10	Creditors of the Royal African Company	Pro	*CJ*, XVI, 326
20.2.10	Creditors of the Royal African Company	Pro	*CJ*, XVI, 327
3.3.10	Royal African Company	Pro	*CJ*, XVI, 344
27.2.11	Adventurers and Creditors of the Royal African Company	Pro	*CJ*, XVI, 521
5.3.11	Merchants of London, Traders to Africa	Anti	*CJ*, XVI, 534
5.3.11	Planters and Merchants of Jamaica	Anti	*CJ*, XVI, 534
15.3.11	Inhabitants of the Town of Birmingham	Anti	*CJ*, XVI, 549
15.3.11	Shipwrights etc. of London	Anti	*CJ*, XVI, 549
15.3.11	Shipwrights etc. of Bristol	Anti	*CJ*, XVI, 550
15.3.11	Merchants and Liverpool	Anti	*CJ*, XVI, 550
15.3.11	Mayor, Aldermen, and Common Council, of Exeter	Anti	*CJ*, XVI, 550
15.3.11	Merchants of Lyme Regis	Anti	*CJ*, XVI, 550
15.3.11	Packers etc. of London	Anti	*CJ*, XVI, 550
15.3.11	Merchants and Planters of Carolina	Anti	*CJ*, XVI, 550
15.3.11	Mayor, Aldermen, and Common Council of the City of Bristol	Anti	*CJ*, XVI, 550
15.3.11	Merchants of Whitehaven	Anti	*CJ*, XVI, 551
15.3.11	Merchants, and Traders, of the City of Bristol, to Africa	Anti	*CJ*, XVI, 551

244 · APPENDIX 5

Date	Petitioner (to House of Commons, unless otherwise noted)	Position	Source
15.3.11	Shipwrights etc. of London	Pro	*CJ*, XVI, 551
15.3.11	Dyers etc. of London	Pro	*CJ*, XVI, 551
15.3.11	Woollen Manufactory in and about Kidderminster	Pro	*CJ*, XVI, 551
15.3.11	Gun-Makers of London	Pro	*CJ*, XVI, 551
19.3.11	Mayor, Bailiffs, Burgesses of Dartmouth	Anti	*CJ*, XVI, 561
2.4.11	Merchants of Edinburgh	Anti	*CJ*, XVI, 570
4.4.11	Mayor, Aldermen, and Burgesses of Taunton	Anti	*CJ*, XVI, 575
11.4.11	Royal African Company	Pro	*CJ*, XVI, 588
11.4.11	Wool Dealers in Totnes	Anti	*CJ*, XVI, 589
14.4.11	Wool Dealers in Ashburton	Anti	*CJ*, XVI, 595
17.4.11	Merchants of Minehead	Anti	*CJ*, XVI, 601
19.4.11	Merchants of Plymouth	Anti	*CJ*, XVI, 604
1.2.12	Merchants of London, Traders to Africa	Anti	*CJ*, XVII, 55
1.2.12	Planters, and Other Inhabitants of the Island of Barbadoes	Anti	*CJ*, XVII, 55
11.2.12	Merchants and Traders of the City of Bristol to Africa	Anti	*CJ*, XVII, 76
12.2.12	Royal African Company	Pro	*CJ*, XVII, 76
12.2.12	Town of Birmingham and Places Adjacent	Anti	*CJ*, XVII, 76
12.2.12	Merchants and Inhabitants of Liverpool	Anti	*CJ*, XVII, 76
12.2.12	Royal African Company and Creditors	Pro	*CJ*, XVII, 76
26.2.12	Mayor, Aldermen, and Common Council of Exeter	Anti	*CJ*, XVII, 112
26.2.12	Merchant Adventurers of Minehead	Anti	*CJ*, XVII, 113
11.3.12	Planters and Inhabitants of Nevis	Pro	*CJ*, XVII, 131
12.3.12	Mayor and Burgesses of Westbury in Wiltshire	Anti	*CJ*, XVII, 132
25.3.12	Inhabitants of Westbury	Pro	*CJ*, XVII, 153
27.3.12	Merchants and Planters of Carolina	Anti	*CJ*, XVII, 157
11.4.12	Royal African Company	Pro	*CJ*, XVII, 181
12.4.12	Creditors of the Royal African Company	Pro	*CJ*, XVII, 184
5.5.12	Creditors of the Royal African Company	Pro	*CJ*, XVII, 210
21.4.13	Merchants of London, Traders to Africa	Anti	*CJ*, XVII, 297
21.4.13	Merchants and Traders of the City of Bristol	Anti	*CJ*, XVII, 297
22.4.13	Merchants and Other Traders in the Town of Ashburton	Anti	*CJ*, XVII, 298
22.4.13	Mayor, Aldermen, and Common Council of Exeter	Anti	*CJ*, XVII, 298
23.4.13	Merchants of Kingsbridge	Anti	*CJ*, XVII, 299
23.4.13	Mayor, Aldermen, and Common Council of the City of Bristol	Anti	*CJ*, XVII, 299
23.4.13	Merchants, and Other Traders of Crediton	Anti	*CJ*, XVII, 299
23.4.13	Merchants, and Other Traders of Modbury	Anti	*CJ*, XVII, 299
23.4.13	Merchants and Inhabitants of Liverpool	Anti	*CJ*, XVII, 299
23.4.13	Mayor, Aldermen, and Inhabitants of Lancaster	Anti	*CJ*, XVII, 299
30.4.13	Inhabitants of Birmingham	Anti	*CJ*, XVII, 307
9.5.13	Royal African Company	Pro	*CJ*, XVII, 319
12.5.13	Woollen Manufacturers of Britain	Pro	*CJ*, XVII, 349
5.6.13	Planters of America	Pro	*CJ*, XVII, 403
5.6.13	Royal African Company	Pro	*CJ*, XVII, 403
17.6.13	Royal African Company and Creditors to House of Lords	Pro	*LJ*, XIX, 577

Date	Petitioner (to House of Commons, unless otherwise noted)	Position	Source
23.6.13	Royal African Company and Creditors to House of Lords	Pro	*LJ*, XIX, 583
21.5.14	Several Planters of the Sugar Colonies Now in Great Britain	Pro	*CJ*, XVII, 636
31.5.14	Merchants and Other Traders in Ashburton	Anti	*CJ*, XVII, 652
24.2.19	Creditors of Royal African Company	Pro	*CJ*, XIX, 280
18.2.30	Royal African Company	Pro	*CJ*, XXI, 447
15.2.31	Royal African Company	Pro	*CJ*, XXI, 625
31.1.44	Royal African Company	Pro	*CJ*, XXIV, 534
28.1.45	Royal African Company	Pro	*CJ*, XXIV, 724
31.1.46	Royal African Company	Pro	*CJ*, XXV, 48
13.2.47	Royal African Company	Pro	*CJ*, XXV, 286
16.2.48	Royal African Company	Pro	*CJ*, XXV, 526
14.3.48	Merchants of London	Anti	*CJ*, XXV, 565
24.3.48	Creditors of Royal African Company	Pro	*CJ*, XXV, 599
29.3.48	Mayor, Burgesses, Commonalty, of the City of Bristol	Anti	*CJ*, XXV, 604
29.3.48	Merchants-Adventurers of the City of Bristol	Anti	*CJ*, XXV, 604
22.12.48	Royal African Company	Pro	*CJ*, XXV, 676
19.1.49	Creditors of Royal African Company	Pro	*CJ*, XXV, 697
9.2.49	Several Merchants of London	Pro	*CJ*, XXV, 732–733
10.3.49	Merchants of Liverpool	Anti	*CJ*, XXV, 777
10.3.49	Merchant Venturers of Bristol	Anti	*CJ*, XXV, 777
9.5.49	Creditors of Royal African Company	Pro	*CJ*, XXV, 861
18.1.50	Royal African Company	Pro	*CJ*, XXV, 942
6.2.50	Merchants of London	Anti	*CJ*, XXV, 977
6.2.50	Mayor, Burgesses, Commonalty, of the City of Bristol	Anti	*CJ*, XXV, 977–978
6.2.50	Bristol Merchant Venturers	Anti	*CJ*, XXV, 978
6.2.50	Merchants of Liverpool	Anti	*CJ*, XXV, 978
9.2.50	Traders and Inhabitants of Manchester	Anti	*CJ*, XXV, 984
12.2.50	Borough of Wigan	Anti	*CJ*, XXV, 988
13.2.50	Tradesmen of Rippon	Anti	*CJ*, XXV, 993
13.2.50	Inhabitants of Preston	Anti	*CJ*, XXV, 993
15.2.50	Mayor, Aldermen, and Tradesmen of Coventry	Anti	*CJ*, XXV, 998
15.2.50	Mayor, Aldermen etc. of Appleby in Westmoreland	Anti	*CJ*, XXV, 998
15.2.50	Merchants of Plymouth	Anti	*CJ*, XXV, 998
19.2.50	Mayor, Aldermen etc. of Carlisle	Anti	*CJ*, XXV, 1003
19.2.50	Planters and Merchants of American Sugar Plantations	Anti	*CJ*, XXV, 1003–1004
20.2.50	Magistrates, Town Council, of Ayr in Scotland	Anti	*CJ*, XXV, 1005
20.2.50	Merchants and Traders of Chester	Anti	*CJ*, XXV, 1005
20.2.50	Principal Traders of the Borough of Newcastle under Lyme	Anti	*CJ*, XXV, 1005
20.2.50	Borough of Derby	Anti	*CJ*, XXV, 1005–1006
26.2.50	Kendall in Westmoreland	Anti	*CJ*, XXV, 1018
1.3.50	Inhabitants of Birmingham	Anti	*CJ*, XXV, 1023
13.3.50	Royal African Company	Pro	*CJ*, XXV, 1050

Date	Petitioner (to House of Commons, unless otherwise noted)	Position	Source
13.3.1750	Creditors of Royal African Company	Pro	*CJ*, XXV, 1050
5.3.51	Royal African Company	Pro	*CJ*, XXVI, 90
6.3.51	Creditors of Royal African Company	Pro	*CJ*, XXVI, 96
6.3.51	Company of Merchants Trading to Africa	Pro	*CJ*, XXVI, 96
25.3.51	Company of Merchants Trading to Africa	Pro	*CJ*, XXVI, 146
16.4.51	Creditors of Royal African Company	Pro	*CJ*, XXVI, 170
22.4.51	Creditor of Royal African Company	Pro	*CJ*, XXVI, 188
24.4.51	Alexander Grant and Richard Oswald of London	Anti	*CJ*, XXVI, 193–194
15.1.52	Company of Merchants Trading to Africa	Pro	*CJ*, XXVI, 366
17.1.52	Royal African Company	Pro	*CJ*, XXVI, 382
17.1.52	Creditor of the Royal African Company	Pro	*CJ*, XXVI, 383

Sources: *Journals of the House of Commons,* I–LI (London, 1803), X, XI, XII, XV, XVI, XVII, XXI, XIV, XXV, XXVI; *Journals of the House of Lords* (London, 1767–1830), XVI, XIX.

Acknowledgments

Many people helped me complete this book. I am obliged to the staff at the following libraries: the Huntington Library in San Marino, California, especially Mary Robertson; the Upper Reading Room and Duke Humphreys Library at the Bodleian Library in Oxford; the Vere Harmsworth Library and Rothermere American Institute in Oxford; Lincoln's Inn Library, the National Archives at Kew; the British Library at Saint Pancras; and, especially, the John D. Rockefeller, Jr. Library of Colonial Williamsburg, who provided a wonderful working environment in which I drafted the first version of this study.

I am indebted to all those who have supported me financially and logistically over the past decade. The Arts and Humanities Research Council, the rector, fellows, and staff of Lincoln College, Oxford (especially Peter McCullough, Juliet Montgomery, and Carmella Elan-Gaston), the Huntington and Rockefeller Libraries, and a benefaction from John Griffin all contributed to the completion of the doctoral research from which this monograph has developed. Subsequently, I benefited greatly from the munificence of a Junior Research Fellowship at Corpus Christi College, Oxford, and am extremely grateful to Colin Holmes, the late Ben Ruck Keene, and Sir Tim Lankester for providing a magnificent place to work and think. The School of History at the University of Kent has provided employment as a teacher of history and very generous allowances of time and money to conduct additional research. I thank Kenneth Fincham and Karl Leydecker for this opportunity and their patience in waiting for this book. I warmly record my gratitude here to the undergraduate students at Kent who participated in my special subject course, "Rise and Fall of Slavery in the Atlantic World," and who helped to shape my thinking in exciting weekly discussions, especially Paul Holder and Haig Smith. My own doctoral students, Oliver Ayers, Johan Garcia Zaldua, and David Veevers, have each offered me renewal as they grapple with their own research projects. Paul Donohoe and Michaela Alfred-Kamara of Antislavery International and Peter Twist and Christina Baxter of the City of London Guide Lecturers Association have all helped me to expand my audience as a historian.

The content and argument of this book have been nourished by the new perspectives and mental space provided by international travel. I am grateful to Doug Bradburn and John Coombs for hosting me at their 2007 symposium on Early Modern Virginia at Monticello, Virginia, and to friends and colleagues in Bamberg, especially Christa Jansohn and Stefan Eick. Repeated extended stays in Seoul at the Institute for the Study of History at Korea University allowed me a comfortable and supportive environment to revise later drafts. I am indebted to Professor Min, Kyoung Hyoun and Kim, Seung Woo for that experience. I also thank Martti Koskenniemi for the superbly staged workshops at the University of Helsinki that have provided fertile intellectual ground for a number of my ideas.

The supervisors of the D.Phil. thesis that was the starting point for this book, Perry Gauci and Peter Thompson, were and remain perfect mentors and excellent friends. Clive Holmes and Julian Hoppit intervened politely but firmly as my D.Phil. examiners. Their intervention also opened up important discussions about legal history with Jeffrey Hackney and Simon Douglas that have proved critical to my thinking. Perry Gauci's "Regulating the British Economy" workshops allowed me to test some of my ideas before an unrivaled team of scholars, including Bob Harris, Jane Humphries, Joanna Innes, Mark Knights, Philippe Minard, Steven Pincus, and James Vaughn, all of whom were charitable in their attention. My historian colleagues at Corpus Christi College, Oxford, James Howard-Johnston, Neil McLynn, Jay Sexton, and John Watts, all contributed to the intellectual backdrop against which this book's central thesis emerged. Colleagues, friends, and teachers who have encouraged, helped, and inspired include Ralph Austen, Toby Barnard, Andrew Beaumont, Richard Carwardine, Richard Drayton, Sir John Elliott, David Eltis, Paul Halliday, Jim Horn, Richard Huzzey, Mark Knights, Paul Langford, Ben Marsh, Joe Miller, Phil Morgan, Lindsay O'Neill, Peter Onuf, Guy Perry, Jim Robinson, Phil Stern, Abby Swingen, Alun Vaughan, Mike Wagner, Carl Wennerlind, Koji Yamamoto, and Nuala Zahedieh. I am grateful to all of them. I must reserve special thanks, however, for George Van Cleve, who from our first meeting almost ten years ago to the present day has offered his compelling energy, unrivaled clarity, exacting questions and standards, and invaluable insights, pointers, encouragement, and friendship. It was his reading of an early draft of this study that propelled it into this completed form.

I am extremely fortunate to have worked with the staff of the Omohundro Institute of Early American History and Culture throughout the conception and writing of this book—from the first academic conference paper I gave in Norwich in 2004, to my first academic article, to the citation checking, chart drawing, argument sharpening, and scheduling. The Institute has provided the setting, the intellectual compass points, the feedback, and the professionalism, especially Chris Grasso, Ron Hoffman, and Ginny Montijo Chew, that have given this project every possibility as a published work. Lastly, Fredrika Teute provided invaluable editorial guidance about the meaning and tone of academic writing.

I thank my family for remaining positive about this project's fruition, and my father, Andrew Pettigrew, for sharing his passion for ideas with me. My daughter, Marianne, also loves books, though she currently prefers eating them to reading. I hope this book (and what it represents) will provide food for thought for her as she grows older. I dedicate this book with much love to my wife, Gemma Shore, for liberating me throughout its creation by being resolutely and blissfully uninterested in every page.

Index

Abenaker, Elias, 74, 227

Aberdeen, 120, 121n, 242

Abolitionism: and Whig history, 3; and British national pride, 3; and politics, 3; and intention, 7; and Royal African Company, 7, 208–209; as an act of regulation, 177; and slave baptism, 190; and hospitality, 193; and the golden rule, 196; and John Atkins, 198; and Malachy Postlethwayt, 207; and the separate traders, 211–212; bicentennial of, 217; and British American values, 218. *See also* Antislavery; Pro-slavery arguments

Act for Making Effectual Such Agreement as Shall Be Made between the Royal African Company of England and Their Creditors (Creditors' Act), 153

Act of Union (with Scotland), 100, 101n, 116, 119

Act to Settle the Trade to Africa (1698 act), 13; expiration of, 17n, 44, 139, 140n, 148, 153, 155–156, 164, 176; as a Royal African Company victory, 37; terms of, 37; duties imposed by, 37; interlopers' contribution to, 38; as cause for craze in slave trading, 38; and Royal African Company's market share of the slave trade, 38; and prices of slaves, 38; and the separate traders, 118; and prohibition on office holding in the colonies, 128–129, 134. *See also* Deregulation of the slave trade

Admiralty, 2, 91, 215; and the seizure of interlopers in the slave trade, 1–2; and the Atlantic economy, 24; and Royal African Company, 26; statutory underpinnings of, 31. *See also* Civil law; Common law; Vice-admiralty courts

Africa House, 46, 67, 123, 137, 194

African interior: and trade, 154, 163–166, 171, 177, 187, 192–194, 197, 203, 206–207, 216. *See also* Antislavery; Chandos, James Brydges, duke of; Hospitality; Postlethwayt, Malachy

African plantations, 22, 134, 162–163, 166

Africans: culture and values of, 85, 111, 179, 186–187, 191, 198, 203, 205. *See also* Barbarity

Africa trade: defined, 8n

Africa trade debates, 6, 7, 36, 46, 49, 84, 108; and British imperial policy, 7–8; effects of, on slave trade, 11–16, 192; and American slavery, 14–15, 37, 179; beginning of, 33; and petitions, 33; and signatories on petitions, 33; and pamphlets, 33, 43; locations involved in, 33, 119; second stage of, 39; and Glorious Revolution, 89; and consent for the slave trade, 90, 132, 141, 175; and Daniel Defoe, 115; and colonial input, 133; and antislavery, 185, 203, 208; and the reconceptualization of African barbarity, 186–187, 190. *See also* Board of Trade; Deregulation of the slave trade; House of Commons; House of Lords; Lobbies; Politics; Slaves

Andrews, Sir John, 76

Andros, Sir Edmund, 25, 56

Anglican Church, 31, 138, 182, 190. *See also* Christianity

Anglo-Dutch War, second, 23

Angola, 169, 184, 171

Anne (queen of England), 39, 76, 138, 141, 144, 159, 162

Antigua, 68, 133n, 135, 137

Antislavery, 3–4; and Royal African Company, 150, 179–180, 192, 201, 203, 207–208, 214; and vice, 179, 182; and overconsumption, 183; and luxury, 183–184, 188; and liberty, 191, 211–212; and the separate traders, 212. *See also* Abolitionism; Pro-slavery arguments

Ashley, Solomon, 201n, 237
Asiento, 154, 160, 161
Atkins, John, 17–18, 18n, 171n; and depiction of the separate traders, 196; and Royal African Company, 196; and deregulation, 197; and pro-slavery, 198, 203; and trade with Africa, 203
Atkins, Sir Jonathan, 26, 88n
Atkins, Robert, 67, 73n, 233
Atlantic economy, 5–6, 24–25, 34, 40, 58, 60, 71, 82, 98, 175; integration of, by the separate traders, 59–60, 61n, 64, 71

Baker, John, 55n, 78, 227, 235
Bank of England, 79, 138–139, 158–159
Baptism: of slaves, 189–190, 208
Barbados, 25–26, 30, 36, 41, 50–53, 55, 55n, 68, 68n, 69, 72, 74n, 78, 120–121, 121n, 125–127, 129, 130, 133n, 134, 136, 137, 190n, 191, 204, 242
Barbarity: of Royal African Company, 1; of the Africans, 85, 97, 113, 140, 185–186, 196, 203–204, 215; of the separate traders, 187–188, 192, 205, 209; of pro-slavery arguments, 198–199. *See also* Atkins, John; Self-interest
Barnardiston, Sir Samuel, 53n
Barons, George, 65, 227
Barwick, Samuel, 55n, 227, 235
Bate, Raynes, 18n, 125, 129, 134, 136n, 154n
Bateman, Sir James, 76
Bathurst, Sir Benjamin, 45, 237
Bawden, John, 34, 50–51, 67
Beake v. Tyrell, 32n
Beckford, Julius, 176
Beckford, Peter, 134, 135n, 227, 235
Beehive (analogy), 94, 104; and Richard Harris, 94–95
Beeston, William, 128–129
Behn, Aphra, 83, 183–184, 191
Bennet, Henry, earl of Arlington, 25
Benson, Sir William, 75, 227
Berdoe, James, 75, 227
Berkshire, 57, 121n, 240
Bethlehem Hospital, 167

Bight of Benin, 15
Bilateral trade to Africa, 74. *See also* Triangular trade
Birmingham, 74n, 120–121, 242–245
Black majorities: fears of, in colonies, 35–36, 53. *See also* Slaves
Bladen, Martin, 168, 237
Blair, James, 56–57
Blair, Tony, 217–218
Blakiston, Nathaniel, 55n
Bluett, Thomas, 194–195, 203
Board of Trade: foundation of, 40; and House of Commons, 40; and the second stage of the Africa trade debates, 40; and Royal African Company, 40, 42, 131, 135; and deregulation, 40, 119, 127, 130; as an information-gathering body, 40, 131; and the separate traders, 40–41, 56, 62, 71, 76, 78–79, 81, 119, 127, 130, 137, 158–159, 214, 216; reports of, on the African trade, 40–41, 137, 146–147, 176; inquiries of, into slave trade, 94, 132, 173; and Charles Davenant, 95, 96n. *See also* Lords of Trade and Plantations
Bohun, George, 45, 237
Bolingbroke, Henry St. John, first Viscount, 172
Booth, Sir William, 55
Boyle, Henry, earl of Carleton, 168
Bracton, 90
Bradley, Benjamin, 77, 235
Brain, Benjamin, 55, 235
Brandenburg, 99
Bribery, 15, 116
Bridewell, 167
Bristol, 12–14, 46, 55n, 57, 58n, 65, 66, 74n, 78, 102, 105, 120–122, 154, 159, 164, 173, 196, 209, 211, 241–245
Bristol Society of Merchant Venturers, 80, 122, 242–243, 245
Bristow, Robert, 130n, 227, 237
British identity: and abolitionism, 3; and slavery, 218
Bromley, John, 77
Bromley, John II, 74n, 235

Brook, Robert, 61n, 66n, 73n, 227, 235
Brooke, Thomas, 57n
Brown, Peregrine, 66n, 67, 75, 78, 228, 235
Brue, Andre, 38
Bubb, John, 55, 235
Burridge, John, Junior, 65, 73n, 75n, 78, 228, 235
Burridge, John, Senior, 74n
Byfield, Thomas, 2n, 51, 55, 240

Cabal: involvement of, in Royal African Company, 25
Calico, 170
Cambridge University, 212
Campbell, Sir James, 74n, 235
Cannons, 169
Cape Blancoe, 37
Cape Coast (Cape Corsoe), 17
Cape Coast Castle, 1, 172, 186, 187
Cape Mount, 37
Cape of Good Hope, 37
Captivity, 1–2, 84, 184, 197, 206, 212. *See also* Slaves
Cardinal's Cap Tavern, 51
Carleton, Edward, 55–56, 235, 241
Carlisle, 77, 245
Carolinas, 25, 52
Carter, Thomas, 75, 228, 235
Carteret, Sir George, 25
Cary, John, 55n, 56, 58, 64, 128n, 235
Cary, Thomas, 55, 228, 235
Casamajor, Lewis, 75n, 228
Castell, Captain John, 1–2
Chaigneau, John, 187
Chamberlain v. Harvey, 36
Chandos, James Brydges, duke of: and Royal African Company, 144n, 154, 165–172, 174, 177, 192–194, 205, 237. *See also* African interior; Engraftment; Gold: mining of
Charitable Corporation, 200
Charity: slave trading as, 185; to Africans, 194–195; and Royal African Company, 198–200; and population growth, 206, 208. *See also* Antislavery; Charity Schools; Coram, Thomas; Postlethwayt, Malachy

Charity Schools, 199
Charles II, 4, 55–67; and Dutch competition, 22–23; and the taxing of the Atlantic economy, 24, 51; and support for Royal African Company, 25; and the dissolving of Parliament, 28
Charter government, 24
Chesapeake, 14, 15n, 55, 57–58, 64–66, 68, 69, 74n, 78, 80, 120, 131n. *See also* Maryland; Virginia
Chester, 120, 121n, 123, 242, 245
Chester, Edward, 135, 137
Chetwynd's Insurance Company, 166
Child, Sir Josiah, 167, 204, 237
Child, Sir Richard, Viscount Castlemain, 167–168
Chilton, Edward, 55–58, 235
Christianity, 89, 182–183, 189–190, 199–200. *See also* Anglican Church; Baptism
Churchill, James, duke of Marlborough, 165
Civic humanism, 96, 99, 188
Civilization: of society, 183, 186–187, 197; of commerce, 187, 192, 194, 197, 203, 207; of slavery, 188; of Africa and Africans, 190, 199, 206. *See also* African interior; Barbarity
Civil law, 24, 31. *See also* Admiralty; Vice-admiralty courts
Civil liberty, 107, 212
Civil List, 165–166
Civil rights, 107. *See also* Constitutional rights; Natural rights
Civil society, 218
Clarkson, Thomas, 4n
Clayton, William, 65, 74n, 78, 123, 124, 125n, 228, 235
Clifford, Sir Thomas, 25
Coalthurst, Thomas, 75, 228, 237
Coke, Roger, 29, 38, 90
College of William and Mary, 56–57
Colleton, Sir Peter, 25, 45, 237
Colonial agencies, 34, 71, 81
Colonies. *See* Barbados; Jamaica; Leeward Islands; Maryland; North American colonies; Virginia
Colston, Edward, 45, 237

Commerce, 91, 93, 109, 153, 163, 205, 213; and society, 106, 182, 184, 191, 197, 200, 203; and antislavery, 150, 180, 187, 201. *See also* African interior; Barbarity; Civilization; National interest; Self-interest; Society; State interest

Common law: in the empire, 26–27; and prerogative-sponsored monopolies, 30, 89, 142, 215; and review of Admiralty cases, 31, 215; and the slave trade, 31–33, 90, 215; and slavery, 37, 217. *See also* Admiralty; *East India Company v. Sandys*; *Nightingale v. Bridges*; Vice-admiralty courts

Company of Merchants Trading to Africa, 205

Company of Royal Adventurers (1663), 23

Company of Royal Adventurers Trading to Africa (1660), 22–23, 87

Competition: with the French, 7, 37, 175; imperfect, 19; with the Dutch, 22, 85; international, 23, 28, 96–97; within the English slave trade, 94, 109, 110, 142, 177

Consent: for slave trade deregulation, 22, 34, 48, 86, 90, 91, 140, 141, 173. *See also* Public, the

Consignment trade: defined, 34; and shift from direct trade, 34, 71–72, 137. *See also* Direct trade

Constitution, English: and the Africa trade debates, 4–7, 86; and monopolies, 23; and Royal African Company, 28, 87–88, 107, 140; and the separate traders, 34, 42, 44, 88–94, 99, 104–105, 117–119, 141–142, 149, 173, 212, 214–216; and Board of Trade, 40, 132, 135. *See also* Politics

Constitutional rights (political rights), 26, 86, 88, 90–92, 104, 106, 111, 119, 211, 216. *See also* Civil rights; Natural rights

Convention Parliament, 33

Cooke, Sir Thomas, 45, 46, 237

Coram, Thomas, 200, 206

Corbett, Thomas, 27

Corbin, Gawin, 57n, 133n, 136

Corbin, John, 55, 235

Corbin, Thomas, 55, 235

Cornhill, 67, 81

Corporation of London (City of London), 31, 45; the separate traders and, 45–46, 49, 64, 158–159; Royal African Company directors and, 45–46, 102, 216. *See also* London

Corporations, 107–108, 124, 165–166, 174; and philanthropy, 199–200, 203–204, 208. *See also* Corporation of London; East India Company; Monopolies; Royal African Company

Corseley, John, 55n

Cotton, 134, 170, 163

Country ideology, 95

Court, John, 57n

Court of Assistants (Royal African Company), 46–47, 205

Court of King's Bench, 30, 31, 89, 91. *See also* Common law

Court of Requests, 115

Courts of equity, 127

Coventry, Sir William, 25

Cowes, 66n

Craven, William, earl of Craven, 25, 237

Credit: extension of, by Royal African Company to colonists, 69–70, 96–97; of the nation, 139, 158, 160

Creditor power: of Royal African Company, 118, 128–129, 134–135, 214; of the separate traders, 135–136, 138

Creditors: of Royal African Company, 5, 39, 47, 79, 82, 103, 139, 153, 168, 242–246, 157. *See also* Act for Making Effectual Such Agreement as Shall Be Made between the Royal African Company of England and Their Creditors

Crispe, Elizabeth, 66

Crispe, Sir Nicholas, 66, 241

Crispe family, 23

Cross, John, 65, 228

Crowe, Mitford, 136–137

Cruickshank, Robert, 67, 78, 228, 235, 237

Cumberland, 77

Cumming, Sir Alexander, 74n, 235

Customs, 16, 28, 31, 52, 131n

Cutlers, 57, 240

Dahomey, 197
Dartmouth, 66n, 120–121, 243–244
Dashees, 15
Dashwood, Sir Francis, 46n, 237
Dashwood, Sir Samuel, 46n, 237
Davenant, Charles, 68; and the Africa trade debates, 40; and the separate traders, 49–50, 61, 67; and depiction of Royal African Company, 70; and the state interest, 94–99, 101, 134; and deregulated trade, 105, 197; and nonstatutory parliamentary resolutions, 146, 162; and the African interior, 162–163, 187, 188; and the moral imperatives of regulation, 187–188, 192, 197, 205. *See also* Civic humanism; National interest; State interest
Davers, Sir Robert, 74n, 76, 77n, 79, 130, 235
Dawkins, John, 53n, 235
Day, John, 78, 229, 235
Deane, Cornelius, 73n, 229, 235
Debt: of freedom, 8, 218; of colonies to Royal African Company, 15–16, 19, 25, 70, 87, 97, 127, 128, 214; of colonies to the separate traders, 129, 138, 156, 157; of government, 154, 158–159, 169; of Civil List, 165; of Royal African Company, 167. *See also* Credit; Creditor power; Creditors; Debt Recovery Act
Debt Recovery Act, 157, 177
Decentralization: of regulatory initiative, 65; of politics, 127, 209; of imperial initiative, 157. *See also* Empire, English / British; Politics; Regulation
Defoe, Daniel: and the Africa trade debates, 40, 50n, 70, 108, 115; and the separate traders, 83, 196; and Africa trade, 85, 110, 162, 163; and the Glorious Revolution, 116, 139; and political strategy, 117, 124–125, 145; and Robert Harley, 153–154, 160, 161n
Deregulation of the slave trade: and capacity, 11, 77; and geography, 12, 14; and the ethnic mixture of slave cargoes, 15; and expansion of sugar and tobacco industries, 16; and tax revenue for British state, 16; view of, by historians, 16–18, 21; causes of, 16–22; and the French, 20–21; and the Dutch, 21; and legislative inertia, 42–44; and public opinion, 43; as natural setting for the economy, 43, 105, 112; importance of 1712 expiration to, 44; broad public support for, 48–49, 57, 117–119, 142, 150, 174–175, 216; beneficiaries of, 59–60, 65, 108, 126, 143, 214; constitutional argument for, 91, 111; neo-Roman argument for, 99, 215; and the national interest, 101; and freedom, 104, 106; and society, 108; and competition, 109; and blame for the evils of slavery, 183, 192, 196–198, 203, 205, 206, 209; and abolition, 211. *See also* Act to Settle the Trade to Africa; Africa trade debates; Antislavery; Barbarity
Devon, 57, 121n, 241
Diamond, Robert, 75n, 229
Dickenson, Richard, 31–31, 36, 91, 241
Directors. *See* Royal African Company
Direct trade: defined, 34; and shift to consignment model, 34. *See also* Consignment trade
Dissenters, 51, 65, 138
Dockwra, William, 2n, 28, 31, 32, 34, 36, 51, 89, 91, 235, 240
Dockwra v. Dickenson, 31–32, 36, 91
Dodd, Edward, 73n, 78, 229, 235
Dominion of New England, 25, 214
Dorset, 50, 65
Driver, Captain (character, *Oroonoko*), 83, 184, 203
Drummond, John, 168n, 237
Du Puy, Lawrence, 25, 237
Dutch, 11, 21–23, 28, 30, 82, 85, 94, 99, 133, 134, 203
Dutch West India Company, 21
Duties: on slave imports, 15; on slave trade (10 percent duty), 37–39, 49, 54, 56, 59, 74, 118, 136, 139, 145, 153, 156, 174. *See also* Act to Settle the Trade to Africa; Taxation

Earle, Joseph, 65, 74n, 122, 229, 235
East India Company, 20, 25, 30–31, 32n, 42, 45, 51, 53n, 60, 62n, 64, 67, 73, 76, 89, 96n, 103, 112–113, 138, 144n, 160, 167, 176, 190n, 201n

East India Company v. Sandys, 30–31, 89, 190n
Economic growth: and deregulated trade, 85–86, 101; and security of property, 110. *See also* Deregulation of the slave trade
Edgware, 169
Elizabeth I, 22
Elton, Abraham, Junior, 65, 229
Empire, English / British: and abolition, 3, 7, 207; and political parties, 6; and freedom, 6, 217; and the Restoration, 24; and labor, 29; and the royal prerogative, 52, 88; and slave trading, 155–157, 179
Engraftment: of Royal African Company stock, 167–169
Enlightenment, 184, 217
Enslavement, 8; and antislavery, 181, 185–187, 190, 197, 203, 212
Essex, 52, 57, 121n, 143n, 145n, 158, 240
Exclusion Crisis, 28
Exeter, 46, 52, 57, 58n, 66n, 74n, 120, 121, 138n, 148, 240–244
Eyres, Samuel, 65, 229

Falmouth, 65, 66n
Farrer, William, 74, 235
Filibustering, 43, 117, 144. *See also* Legislative vacuum; Nonstatutory parliamentary rulings
Firearms, 62, 64n, 171
Fleet, Sir John, 46, 76, 238
Forts: of Royal African Company, 16–17, 37, 39, 49, 66, 79, 87, 97, 99, 116–117, 131–133, 143, 146–148, 155–156, 162, 169, 174–175, 184, 201, 205
France, 7, 11–13, 20–21, 30, 35, 37, 38, 45, 62n, 85, 99, 102, 157, 158, 166, 175, 203–206
Freedom: and slave-trade escalation, 2, 6–8, 37; and the Africa trade debates, 84, 104; as the enjoyment of property, 84, 211; as right to economic opportunity, 86, 105; as expressed constitutionally, 90; of the state, 95; to defend economic opportunity, 111–112, 217; of the press, 142; as explanation for brutalities of slavery, 180, 207, 209; and Africans' inability to comprehend, 186. *See also* Consent; Free trade; Liberty; Natural rights; Neo-Roman theory of free states
Freemen, 88, 90, 213n
Free trade, 6, 11, 15, 19, 27, 42, 57, 65, 73, 76–77, 82, 86–89, 91, 103, 106, 108, 111, 119, 123–124, 143–146, 148–149, 155–156, 159, 164, 174–175, 188, 209; defined, 35. *See also* Deregulation of the slave trade
French Guinea Company, 21
French Senegal Company, 21
Frigates, 1–2, 99

Galdy, Lawrence, 55n, 147n, 229, 235
Gambia, 1, 15, 23, 37, 194
Gambia River, 1
Gardner, John, 32n, 34, 50, 51, 53, 57, 58, 128n, 235
Gemmingen, Baroness, 168
General Court (Royal African Company), 30, 47, 165
Gentlemen Planters of Barbados, 51
George I, 164–165
George II, 238
Georgia, 193
Glasgow, 120, 121, 242
Glorious Revolution: and the separate traders, 5–6, 11, 31, 33, 48, 86, 89, 90, 127, 141, 213–215, 217; and Defoe, 115; and abolition, 212–214. *See also* Constitution, English; Politics
Gloucester, 57, 121, 241
Godin, Stephen, 68, 73n, 77, 78, 157, 229, 235
Godolphin, Charles, 46n, 238
Godwyn, Morgan, 182, 184, 190
Gohier, James, 130n, 238
Gold: English trade in, 8n, 22, 30, 37, 59n, 85, 109, 112, 164, 182; mining of, 160, 163, 166, 169–172, 177, 208; English lust for, 182
Gold Coast, 21, 37, 159, 187
Goodwin, John, 75, 78, 235, 239
Gore, Gerard, 162n
Gore, Sir William, 46, 229, 238
Gorges, Ferdinando, 25, 87n, 238
Gould, Nathaniel, 46n
Governor and Company of Adventurers of

London Trading to Gynney and Bynney, 23
Gracedieu, Sir Bartholomew, 55, 73–74, 229, 235
Grenville, John, earl of Bath, 23n
Grotius, Hugo, 87
Guy, Richard, 55n

Habeas corpus, 90
Hall, Urban, 76, 230, 238
Hallamshire, 57, 121, 240
Hallet, Colonel John, 50
Hampden case, 90
Handasyd, Thomas, 137
Hanoverian dynasty, 164
Harley, Robert, 52–53, 79, 115n, 127, 139, 150, 154, 159–161, 167
Harris, Richard, 66, 68, 76, 78–80, 94–95, 99, 137, 156–159, 169, 230, 235
Harrison, Benjamin, 55–56, 58
Harrison, Benjamin, Junior, 55n, 57–58, 235
Harrison, Edmund, 240
Hartwell, Henry, 55–58, 235
Hawkins, Sir John (Augustan), 55n, 230, 235
Hawkins, John (Elizabethan), 22
Hawley, Lord Francis, 25
Hayes, Daniel, 168n, 238
Heathcote, Sir Gilbert, 42–43, 53–55, 58, 60n, 63n, 64, 66, 72–73, 74n, 78, 127–128, 139, 144, 158–159, 160n, 230, 235
Herne, Frederick, 46n, 238
Herne, Sir Nathaniel, 46n, 238
Heysham, Robert, 61–62, 66n, 68, 72, 74n, 75n, 78–80, 103, 123–124, 136, 158–159, 230, 235
Heysham, William, 61, 63n, 72, 74n, 123, 125, 136, 230, 235
Hobbes, Thomas, 108
Hodges, Sir William, 45, 238
Holder, Melisha, 53, 55, 57–58, 230, 235
Hollander, Peter, 73n, 230, 235
Hollister, Laurence, 75n
Holt, Sir John, 31–32, 36–37, 66, 143–144. See also *Nightingale v. Bridges*
Honestus, Mercator, 199, 212

Hook, Abraham, 55n, 230, 235
Hooke, Robert, 170
Hospitality, 180, 184, 193–195, 203–204, 208, 216. *See also* Royalty
Houghton, John, 30
Houlditch, Abraham, 61n, 66n, 73n, 78, 230, 235, 238
House of Commons: and the Africa trade debates, 28, 40, 42, 52, 69, 80–81, 115, 128, 147, 217
House of Lords: and the Africa trade debates, 53, 70, 80, 161
Houstoun, James, 169, 171
Hudson's Bay Company, 20, 45, 201n
Huguenots, 64
Hutcheson, Francis, 211

Ideology. *See* Political ideology
Indentured servitude, 8n, 14, 35–36, 64n, 85
Indigo, 134, 163, 170
Inkle, Thomas (character, *Spectator*), 191–192
Interest groups. *See* Lobbies
Interlopers in the African trade: seizure of, 1–2, 16, 17n, 19, 20n, 25; in the courts, 26, 30–32, 49; in the colonies, 26–27; identification of, 51, 61, 64, 88–89, 92, 97, 113, 155, 161, 164. *See also* Separate traders to Africa
Inverness, 120–121, 242
Ivory (elephants' teeth), 8n, 57, 59n, 109, 112

Jackson, Joseph, 75n, 230
Jamaica, 14, 26–27, 35, 41, 52–53, 55, 57–58, 61n, 62, 65–66, 68, 69n, 72, 73n, 74n, 77–80, 120–121, 128, 133–134, 137, 145n, 156, 172, 176, 188–189, 191, 240–243
James II, 17, 21, 23–25, 28–31, 50, 52–53, 67, 87, 165, 214
Jamineau, Daniel, 66n, 74n, 75, 230
Jefferies, Sir Jeffrey, 46n, 75, 130n, 230, 238
Jeffreys, Edward, 46n, 235, 238
Jeffreys, George, 30, 89
Jeffreys, John, 46n, 75, 230, 238
Jerusalem Coffee House, 176
Johnson, William, 46n, 230, 235, 238
Joint-stock companies, 20, 28, 30, 32n, 62, 79,

116, 125, 132, 203, 205; and lobbying, 47, 216; and the royal prerogative, 87; as deliberative and associational, 93; and the national interest, 96, 112, 134; and civil liberty, 107; and social stability, 108; and gold mining, 163; and prevention of brutality in trade, 180, 186, 187; and moral regeneration, 199–201, 207. *See also* Corporations; East India Company; Hudson's Bay Company; Monopolies; National interest; Royal African Company
Jones, Fred, 55, 235
Jones, Thomas, 2n, 230, 240
Jorye, Joseph, 76
Jury, 2, 28, 87, 111

Kew Palace, 66
Kidderminster, 13, 57, 120–121, 241–242, 244
Kormantine, 23, 184

Labor: political arithmetic of, 29. *See also* Slave labor
Laboring poor, 200–201, 208
Lackitt, Widow (character, *Oroonoko*), 83
Ladman, Bernard, 188
Lake, Sir Bibye, 165, 201, 238
Lake, Mary, 165
Lake, Sir Thomas, 165, 238
Lambe, Bulfinch, 198
Lascelles, Edward, 68n, 73, 75n, 78, 230, 235
Law, John, 166
Lawson, Gilfrid, 74n, 77, 79, 235
Leadenhall Street, 46, 67, 187, 194
Leadstone, John, 154n, 198n
Leather: trade in, 119n
Leeward Islands, 41n, 52, 58, 68n, 69, 70n, 72, 77, 78, 80, 133n, 135, 137, 241, 242
Legislation, 3, 42, 86, 89, 118–119, 145, 147, 149, 154, 193, 208, 211. *See also* Regulation; Statutes
Legislative vacuum: for the slave trade, 6, 42–43, 111, 117–119, 142–145, 150, 154–155, 160, 177, 216. *See also* Deregulation of the slave trade; Freedom; Natural rights; Statutes

Leighton, Elias, 87–88
Levant Company, 45
Levett, Sir Richard, 66, 78, 231, 235
Liberalism: and slavery, 3, 8, 118, 174, 185, 203, 217–218. *See also* Freedom; Liberty
Liberty: to trade in slaves, 2, 8, 28, 82, 84–86, 91, 98, 104, 107, 111, 143, 145, 150, 175, 209, 215, 218; national, 85, 99, 102, 104, 111, 215, 218; to petition, 92; and monopolies, 105; as sanctity of property, 106, 107, 111; as intoxication, 106, 183; and statute, 142; and Africans, 186; and antislavery, 188, 191, 207, 211; and the Glorious Revolution, 212; and pro-slavery arguments, 213. *See also* Civil liberty; Freedom; Free trade
Licensing of the Press Act: expiration of, 43
Litigation: about the slave trade, 34, 50, 55. *See also* Admiralty; Common law
Littleton, Edward, 28–29, 36, 53, 56, 58, 73, 235
Liverpool, 12, 14, 65, 66, 74n, 77, 78, 120–121, 123, 124, 154, 159, 164, 173, 209, 211, 243–245
Lloyd, Richard, 74n, 235
Lloyd, Thomas, 73n, 231, 235
Lobbies: and the separate traders, 2, 5–6, 14–15, 22, 31, 34, 36, 39, 42–44, 47–53, 55, 58, 60–62, 64–65, 68, 71–77, 81–82, 110, 117–119, 122–124, 132, 138, 142–143, 145–146, 149, 155, 156, 158–159, 172–173, 196, 213, 216–217, 235–236; and Royal African Company, 8, 45–47, 126, 130, 138, 141, 146, 159–161, 175–176, 216; and constitutional rights, 109–111; and pro-slavery interests, 205, 213; and abolitionists, 212, 216. *See also* Deregulation of the slave trade; Royal African Company; Separate traders to Africa
Locke, John, 25
Lockwood, Richard, 46n, 168, 169, 174, 238
Lodge, Abraham, 75, 231
London, 12–13, 19, 23–24, 26, 28, 31, 34, 43, 45–46, 49, 50, 52, 54–58, 60–61, 64–68, 71–72, 77–78, 81, 94, 98, 101–102, 120–121, 123–124, 130, 132, 137, 158–159, 166–167, 169–170, 176, 185–186, 191, 194–195, 216, 240–246. *See also* Corporation of London
London Foundling Hospital, 200, 206

Long, Charles, 130n, 238
Lords of Trade and Plantations, 24, 26, 40. *See also* Board of Trade
Louis XIV, 86
Lowther, James, 74n, 77, 79, 236
Lutwidge, Thomas, 65, 231, 236
Luxury: in the Africa trade debates, 106, 183–184, 188. *See also* Antislavery; Vice
Lynn, Francis, 173

Machiavelli, Niccolo, 85, 93
Madeira, 68n, 75
Manchester, 170, 245
Mandeville, Bernard, 94–95
Man stealing, 181. *See also* Pilliarding
Manufacturing: interests of, 69, 100, 170
Martyn, John, 66n, 68, 72, 75n, 78–80, 231, 236
Mary II, 2
Maryland, 15, 55, 57n, 62, 64, 68n, 69n, 72, 73n, 121n, 131, 194, 241–242
Mascall, Timothy, 53n, 236
Mauditt, Jasper, 123, 125n
Maynard, Sir John: legal opinion of, 27
Members of Parliament, 40, 115, 181; and Royal African Company, 46; and the separate traders, 77
Merchants: opposition of, to Royal African Company, 2, 5, 11, 14, 28, 34–36, 38, 42, 48–53, 55, 57–60, 62, 64–72, 76–77, 80–81, 83, 86, 87, 92, 98, 100, 102, 132, 139, 156; political power of, 21, 34, 44, 104, 127, 130–131, 136, 157; support of, for Royal African Company, 46–47, 60, 96, 130, 132; as selfish, 179, 181, 206. *See also* Lobbies
Merrett, Thomas, 66n
Methuen, Peter, 168
Micklethwaite, Nathaniel, 55n, 236
Milner, Isaac, 55, 56, 62, 64, 66n, 71, 72, 75, 78–80, 131, 136, 231, 236
Miners: Cornish, 170–171, 177
Ministry (England / United Kingdom), 79, 119, 138–139, 141–142, 154, 159–162, 164–165, 168
Mississippi Scheme, 166
Mitchell, Francis, 77, 231

Modernity: and slavery, 3, 8, 217–218; and Royal African Company, 40; and the separate traders, 94, 158, 173; and freedom, 104. *See also* Liberalism
Molasses Act, 157, 177
Monarchy: and Royal African Company, 22–24, 47, 138–139, 141, 165–166, 214–215; and trade regulation, 42, 90, 141; dignity of, 184, 203; French, 206. *See also* Admiralty; Civil law; Royal prerogative; Vice-admiralty courts
Monck, George, duke of Albermarle, 23n
Monopolies: and Royal African Company, 2, 4–7, 11; as prone to inefficiency, 16–17; as politically constituted, 16–25, 27–36, 38–40, 42, 44–45, 47–48, 50, 53, 61, 65–66, 69, 76, 81–82, 150, 214–216; and an ordered society, 84, 108; ideological opposition to, 86–89, 91, 119, 123–124, 128, 137, 141, 145; as socially inclusive, 92–93; and the state interest, 95–98, 112, 116, 175–176; and trading opportunity, 100–105, 109; and civil liberty, 107; as property, 111, 114, 153, 155, 162; and antislavery, 179, 180–181, 185–190, 192, 200. *See also* Joint-stock companies; Regulation
Montagu, Charles, earl of Halifax, 161
Montagu, Edward, earl of Sandwich, 23n
Montagu, George, 74n
Montross, 121n, 242
Montserrat, 68n, 69, 120, 121n, 126, 133
Moore, Arthur, 46n, 164n, 238
Moore, Francis, 195
Morgan, Christopher, 55, 236
Morice, Humphrey, 16, 62, 63, 72–73, 74n, 75n, 78–80, 156–159, 169, 173, 195, 231, 236
Morice, John, 45, 236, 238
Morice, Nicholas, 16, 18
Mortality rates: of enslaved Africans, 17, 18n
Munday, John, 55–56, 231, 236
Muslin, 170

Nantes, 20
National interest, 67, 85, 87–88, 95–96, 98–102, 104–105, 111, 119–120, 123–124, 141, 175, 181, 215, 216. *See also* State interest

Natural law: and slave-trade escalation, 107, 213; and legislative vacuum, 142; and the amelioration of slavery, 188
Natural rights (of Englishmen), 7, 22, 90, 91, 143, 173, 191, 211, 213. *See also* Constitutional rights; Legislative vacuum; Property rights
Navigation Acts, 4n, 24, 85, 87. *See also* Regulation
Neo-Roman theory of free states, 99, 104. *See also* Freedom; Liberty
Nevis, 68–69, 70, 120–121, 133, 135, 137, 242–244
New England, 25, 68, 69n, 214
Newland, Sir Benjamin, 46n, 239
New York, 25, 41n, 68, 131n
Nicholson, Francis, 57n
Nicholson, John, 46, 239
Nightingale, Jeffrey, 28, 31–34, 50, 66, 89, 91, 142, 143, 236
Nightingale v. Bridges, 31–33, 66, 89, 91, 141n, 142–143. *See also* Common law; Holt, Sir John; Shower, Sir Bartholomew
Nine Years' War (King William's War, War of the Grand Alliance), 59, 62, 64, 102
Nonstatutory parliamentary rulings, 43, 145–149. *See also* Filibustering; Legislative vacuum
Norris, Richard, 77, 231
Norris, Robert, 213
North American colonies: as principal beneficiaries of deregulation, 4, 7n, 14, 35, 41, 46, 53, 55, 68, 69n, 74n, 77, 79, 122, 137, 176, 214–215; and the slave trade, 14–15. *See also* Chesapeake; Maryland; Virginia
Norwich, 57, 121n, 240
Nurse, Henry, 1, 231, 239

Observator, 189–191
Oglethorpe, James, 193–195, 201, 205, 208, 239
Oldmixon, John, 51
Onslow, Thomas, 74n, 77, 79, 236
Onslow's Insurance Company, 166
Orange Tree (ship), 1–2
Oroonoko (Behn), 183–184, 194, 197–198, 203, 208; dramatization of, by Thomas Southerne, 83, 184, 192
Ouidah, 197
Outports, 12, 61n, 65–66, 81, 101, 102, 164. *See also* Bristol; Dartmouth; Liverpool; Plymouth; Portsmouth; Whitehaven
Overconsumption, 183. *See also* Antislavery; Deregulation of the slave trade; Luxury; Vice
Owley, Daniel, 68, 231

Paggen, Katherine, 73
Paggen, Peter, 57, 62, 64, 71–73, 75n, 76, 78–80, 158, 159, 232, 236
Pamphlets: in the Africa trade debates, 15, 19, 29, 33, 36, 38, 43, 44, 47–49, 56, 58, 61, 66–67, 73, 80–81, 83–84, 88, 92–93, 96, 98–99, 100–106, 108–110, 118, 123, 125, 132, 133, 142–144, 146–149, 155, 156, 163, 172, 175, 181, 184–186, 188, 195, 201, 205, 209, 216–218. *See also* Africa trade debates
Parke, Daniel, 135
Parliament. *See* Africa trade debates; House of Commons; House of Lords; Lobbies; Members of Parliament; Petitions
Parties. *See* Political parties; Tory party; Whig party
Paston, William, earl of Yarmouth, 164, 239
Paterson, William, 161n
Pawnbroking, 200–201, 208
Peckard, Rev. Peter, 212–213
Pelham-Holles, Thomas, duke of Newcastle, 176–177, 201
Penn, William, 161n
Penneck, William, 65, 232
People, the, 86, 90–91, 96, 99, 104, 110, 116, 118, 124–125, 213, 218. *See also* National interest; Public, the
Perceval, John, earl of Egmont, 174
Perry, Micajah, 55–56, 75, 78, 103, 131, 136, 137, 232, 236
Petitions, 2, 7, 19, 22, 28–29, 31, 33–34, 42–44, 47–56, 58, 65, 69, 73, 75–77, 80–81, 83, 87, 91–92, 98–99, 101, 103–104, 115, 118–126, 128, 135–136, 141–145, 148, 162–163, 173–175,

209, 212–213, 218, 240–246; signatories on, 33, 48, 55, 76–77, 103, 123–125; cultivated, 50, 52, 58, 69, 80, 119, 121n, 124, 126, 145; spontaneous, 52, 125; neutral, 126, 241–242
Petyt, William, 29
Phelps, Thomas, 84
Philipse, Frederick, 68, 232
Phipps, James, 162n
Phipps, Thomas, 110
Pilliarding, 181, 197, 205. *See also* Man stealing
Pindar, Thomas, 130, 132–134, 139, 239
Pirates, 45, 50, 51, 171, 172, 177
Plague, 29
Plantation interest, 51, 76, 81, 130, 174. *See also* Lobbies
Plantations, 4, 7, 11, 22–23, 29, 41–42, 45, 53, 58, 79, 97, 100, 107, 112, 127, 129–130, 133–134, 162–163, 166, 182–186, 188–189, 196, 199, 206, 212. *See also* African plantations
Planters, 15, 16, 34, 35, 51–55, 57–58, 64, 69–71, 79–80, 87, 92–93, 109, 112, 125, 127, 129, 133, 136–137, 182, 188, 190
Plumstead, Robert, 68, 232
Plymouth, 65–66, 74, 120–121, 241, 243–245
Political ideology, 6, 34, 44, 50, 85, 91, 95, 102, 104–105, 111, 113, 119, 142, 143. *See also* Africa trade debates
Political parties: and the Africa trade debates, 5–6, 75, 83–85, 94, 115, 145, 148, 169, 203, 215
Political rights. *See* Constitutional rights
Political strategies: of the abolitionists, 3; of Royal African Company, 5, 47, 58, 102, 120, 124–125, 130, 134, 138–139, 141, 159, 161, 199, 216; of the separate traders, 6–7, 15, 19, 34, 48, 91, 99, 111, 117–119, 124, 127, 129, 142–146, 149
Politics: of the slave trade, 2–8, 13, 16, 20–22, 36, 44, 72, 82, 85–86, 105, 111, 115–116, 118, 120, 122, 124, 127, 158, 177, 179, 180, 185, 207, 209, 212, 215–218; transatlantic, 44, 71–72, 81–82, 86, 118, 127, 130–132, 137, 215
Population: of slaves in America, 11, 15, 35–37, 44, 154; of England, 29, 200–201, 208. *See also* Laboring poor; Slaves
Portsmouth, 65, 66n

Postlethwayt, Malachy, 205–207, 239; and antislavery, 206–207
Povey, Thomas, 25
Pratt, John, 68, 74, 232
Prichard, Sir William, 46n, 239
Primate, Humphrey, 68, 232
Prime minister, 169, 173, 193, 217–218
Privacy, 192
Privy Council, 24, 29, 40, 42, 43, 51, 87
Property, 2, 28, 31–32, 53, 84, 86, 89–90, 106, 110–111, 140, 143, 157, 186, 190, 209, 211. *See also* Monopolies; Slaves
Property rights, 32, 33, 37, 209. *See also* Natural rights
Proprietary government, 24, 161n
Pro-slavery arguments, 196, 198, 205, 213. *See also* Abolitionism; Antislavery
Provinces, 33, 46, 52, 65, 71, 119, 123, 125, 132
Public, the (the public good, the public interest), 22, 34, 46, 50, 70, 83–84, 86, 92, 96–97, 105–106, 109–111, 118–119, 122, 134, 143, 149, 150, 154, 157, 162, 173–175, 177, 183, 193–194, 198, 215–216. *See also* Consent
Public opinion, 43, 117, 124, 138, 139, 142, 145–146, 155–156, 175, 212
Public sphere, 43
Pulteney, John, 74n, 236
Pyke, Captain, 194
Pym, John, 68, 232

Race, 3, 7n, 35, 218
Redwood, 8n, 37, 59n
Regulated company, 35, 93, 116, 145, 147, 148
Regulation, 5–7, 21, 24, 34, 42, 57, 79, 86, 111, 118, 141, 145–146, 150, 160, 177, 180, 190, 192, 207–209, 212, 214, 216. *See also* Act to Settle the Trade to Africa; Dashees; Deregulation of the slave trade; Monopolies; Taxation
Restoration of the monarchy, 22, 24. *See also* Monarchy
Retailers: separate traders as, 49, 67, 98
Reynell, Carew, 29, 88
Ridgley, Charles, 55, 236
Roberts, Gabriel, 46n, 239
Robinson Crusoe (Defoe), 83

Rock, John, 68, 232
Roe, Richard, 28
Rogers, Francis, 55n, 77n, 78, 232, 236
Rous, Nathaniel, 55n, 56, 72, 73n, 75, 78, 232, 236
Royal African Company: charter of, 4–5, 18–20, 24–26, 28, 30–33, 37, 45, 49, 89, 91, 106, 110, 112, 117, 121, 128, 140, 141, 143, 148, 153–155, 166, 181, 195; shareholders (stockholders) of, 5, 17, 19, 25, 39, 46–47, 49, 51, 56, 82, 96, 103, 139, 162, 168; foundation of, 11, 17, 23, 30; and share of the slave trade, 11, 26, 30, 38, 135, 162; directors of, 17, 45–49, 60–62, 64, 67, 75–76, 95, 124, 130–132, 153, 161–162, 164, 165, 168, 174, 177, 187, 193, 199, 200, 205, 207, 216, 237–239; dishonest financial methods of, 17–19, 39; share (stock) price of, 19, 30, 47, 102, 156, 169, 172, 201; and minting of coins, 30; dividends of, 30, 39, 167, 176; and licenses to trade, 32, 33n; shares (stock) of, 35, 39, 45, 47–48, 75, 138, 162, 166–168, 172, 174, 176–177, 199; bonds of, 39, 153; corporate structure of, 46–47; and the army, 67; motto of, 88. *See also* African interior; Africa trade debates; Antislavery; Lobbies; Merchants; Political strategies; Royal prerogative; South Sea Company; State interest
Royal Exchange Assurance, 166, 174n
Royal Navy, 2, 30, 35, 214
Royal prerogative, 4, 5, 22–27, 31, 37, 44, 52, 65, 87–91, 100, 138–140, 142, 148, 205, 215, 217. *See also* Monarchy
Royalty, 180, 184, 193, 208
Rudge, Edward, 46n, 239
Rupert, Prince (Count Palatine of Rhine and duke of Bavaria), 23, 25
Russell, Francis, 127
Russia, 52, 53, 75
Russia Company, 20, 77

Sacheverell, Henry, 138–139
Sail, John, 55, 236
Saint Christopher (Saint Kitts), 68, 133n
Saint Domingue, 176

Saint George (ship), 26
Sandys, Thomas, 30–31, 89, 190n. *See also East India Company v. Sandys*
Scottish Darien Company, 37
Searle, Edward, 32n, 66n, 232, 236
Selden, John, 27
Self-interest, 5, 44, 59n, 85, 87, 91, 95–97, 99, 104–105, 111, 125, 126, 181, 184, 187, 193, 197–198, 213n. *See also* Commerce; Society
Senegal, 23
Senegal Adventurers, 23
Senegambia, 15
Separate traders to Africa: efficiency of, 17, 20, 71, 108, 111; as litigants, 34, 50, 55; identification of, 49–50, 52, 59, 60, 77, 82, 117; defined, 59n; leadership of, 60, 77–78, 80, 103; stereotypes of, 83, 184, 192, 196–198. *See also* Africa trade debates; Board of Trade; Interlopers in the African trade; Lobbies; Merchants; Political strategies
Sessarakoo, William Ansah, 202–204
Seymour, Sir Edward, 58n
Shaftesbury, Anthony Ashley Cooper, first earl of, 28, 237
Shareholders. *See* Royal African Company
Sharp, Jack, 176
Shepheard, Samuel, 46n, 74n, 76, 236, 239
Sheriff, 27, 46, 74
Sherrin, Samuel, 53n, 236
Sherwin, Henry, 55n, 232, 236
Ship captains: separate traders as, 18n, 58–59, 67, 91, 149
Shower, Sir Bartholomew, 89–90
Shrewsbury, 133n, 241
Sierra Leone, 170
Sitwell, Francis, 75n, 78, 233, 236
Slave labor, 14, 29, 68, 72, 82, 179, 201, 206, 218; price elasticity of, 39
Slave laws (colonial): and slave punishment, 35, 38; comparison of, with English slave law, 36; comparison of, with law of deregulation, 37. *See also* Slaves
Slave laws (English): comparison of, with colonial laws, 36–37. *See also* Common law; Slaves

Slavery, 3–4, 6–8, 15, 36–37, 84–85, 90, 104, 105, 177, 179–180, 182–185, 188–191, 193, 204, 207–209, 211, 213, 215, 217–218
Slaves (enslaved Africans), 3, 6, 7n, 11, 13, 15, 22, 26, 29, 36–37, 39, 44, 57, 59n, 61, 63–64, 91, 135, 142, 146, 150, 154, 158–159, 175, 177, 179, 183, 189, 196, 201, 205–207, 209, 211, 215, 217–218; demand for, 7, 8n, 11, 38–39, 58, 61, 64n, 68, 72, 96; prices of, 7n, 16, 18, 38, 39, 41, 47, 53, 79, 98, 126, 130, 133, 187, 196
Slave trade. *See* Deregulation of the slave trade; Royal African Company; Separate traders to Africa
Sloane, Hans, 169n, 170
Smith, Adam, 213n
Smith v. Brown and Cooper, 36
Snelgrave, William, 195–196
Social mobility: and independent slave trading, 60
Society, 8, 40, 48, 57, 76, 82–83, 89, 92–98, 102–104, 107–108, 173, 181–185, 188, 191, 193, 198, 203, 213, 214, 218. *See also* Commerce
Society for the Propagation of Christian Knowledge, 190
Society for the Propagation of the Gospel in Foreign Parts, 190, 199
Society for the Reformation of Manners, 106, 190, 199
Solomon, Job Ben, 194, 203
Somers, Sir John, 91, 92n
Somerset, 57, 121, 241
South Carolina, 68. *See also* Carolinas
Southerne, Thomas, 83, 184, 191–192, 196
South Sea Bubble, 169, 170, 172, 174, 200, 216
South Sea Company, 154, 156, 158, 160–162, 164, 166, 171, 172, 177, 216
Southwark, 121, 240
Spanish America, 22, 154, 160, 161, 182
Spectator (Addison and Steele), 191
Spencer, Charles, earl of Sunderland, 168
State: English / British, 4, 6–7, 15–16, 18, 24, 32–34, 40, 43, 46, 52, 67, 84–86, 88, 94–101, 104, 108, 110–113, 117–120, 127, 131–132, 134–135, 138–139, 150, 154–155, 157, 160, 162–163, 165–166, 172, 175, 177, 179, 181, 185–186, 207–208, 215–216; French, 21; African, 172. *See also* Regulation; State interest; Statutes
State interest, 37, 82, 87, 99, 163, 215. *See also* National interest
State of nature, 111
State subsidies: for Royal African Company, 155, 175, 193
Statute of Monopolies, 27
Statutes, 31, 33, 37, 38, 42–45, 48–49, 58, 59, 66, 71, 79–80, 86, 104, 105, 117–119, 123, 128, 133, 139, 141–143, 146, 148–149, 153, 156–157, 162, 174, 205, 211, 216–217. *See also* Regulation
Stede, Edwyn, 30, 127
Stewart, Thomas, 125, 155
Stock-jobbing politics, 102
Strategies. *See* Political strategies
Subject (of the crown), 4, 24, 27, 29, 32, 43, 86, 88, 90–92, 100, 102, 105–107, 130, 140, 144–145, 148, 156, 173, 216, 217; liberty of, 105, 107, 215. *See also* Constitutional rights; Monarchy
Suffolk, 29, 52, 53n, 57, 121n, 143n, 145n, 240
Sugar: trade in, 2, 12n, 16, 34, 51, 53, 55, 58–59, 61, 62, 65, 68, 75n, 77, 134, 176, 241, 245
Suicide, 1–2, 159
Sutton, Sir Robert, 200, 239
Swift, Jonathan, 172
Swinlowe, John, 28

Taxation, 15, 16, 21, 24, 51, 53, 90, 100, 102, 140, 142, 156, 157, 201. *See also* Duties; Regulation
Taylor, Joseph, 167, 168, 239
Taylor, Thomas, 55, 233, 236
Tench, Fisher, 46n, 76, 239
Tench, Thomas, 57n
Thomas, Sir Dalby, 51, 60, 130, 186, 239
Thomas, Tudor, 53n, 236
Thrale, John, 2n, 51–52, 240
Tobacco, 12n, 14, 16, 51, 55–59, 64–66, 75, 77, 81, 131, 136
Tobacco Adventure to Russia, 52, 75
Tomba, Captain, 197. *See also Oroonoko*
Tory party, 5, 123, 139, 158, 160, 161n, 192. *See also* Political parties

Tourney, Anthony, 66n, 74–75, 233
Tower Hamlets Ward, 76
Townshend, Charles, Viscount Townshend, 168
Travers, John, 75n, 233
Treasury, 24
Triangular trade, 74, 81. *See also* Bilateral trade to Africa
Tryon, Rowland, 190n, 233, 239
Tryon, Thomas, 182–185, 188, 196
Tryon, William, 190n, 233, 239
Turner, Sir William, 46n, 239
Turnor, Thomas, 27
Tutchin, John, 191n
Tutt, John, 2n, 240

Utrecht, Treaty of, 160

Vaughan, Lord John, 26
Vernon, Sir Thomas, 46n, 239
Vertical integration, 71. *See also* Atlantic economy
Vice, 106, 179, 182
Vice-admiralty courts, 24–25, 27–28, 31–32, 142, 214. *See also* Admiralty; Common law
Villiers, George, Lord Buckingham, 23n, 25
Virginia, 16, 18n, 30n, 37, 41n, 53, 55–58, 64, 68n, 69n, 73n, 101n, 121n, 131, 133, 136, 157n, 241, 242
Virginia Company, 30n, 112n

Walcot, Humphrey, 46n, 167, 239
Waller, Edward, 168, 239
Walpole, Robert, 164n, 165, 169, 173, 193
Wapping, 67n, 121n, 242
Warfare. *See* Nine Years' War; War of the Austrian Succession; War of the Spanish Succession

Warman, John, 55n, 233
War of the Austrian Succession, 175
War of the Spanish Succession (Queen Anne's War), 62, 102, 160, 165
Way, Benjamin, 55n, 65, 78, 137, 233, 236
Way, Joseph, 65, 75n, 233
Wayte, James, 53n, 66n, 75n, 78–80, 233, 236
Wealth, national, 5, 29, 34, 42, 82, 86–87, 89, 93–94, 98–99, 101–102, 104–105, 109–110, 118, 163, 205, 214
Webster, Godfrey, 77, 233, 236
West Country, 13, 65, 122
Westminster, 43, 115, 122, 127, 129
Whig history, 3, 4n
Whig party, 5, 22, 50, 51, 53n, 138–139, 189, 191–192. *See also* Political parties
Whitehaven, 64, 66n, 74n, 77, 120–121, 242–243
Wilkinson, Henry, 1, 2
Wilkinson, William, 1, 2, 84, 192, 236
William III, 2, 45, 86, 91, 138, 215
Williamsburg, Va., 16
Williamson, Sir Joseph, 25, 239
Wiltshire, 57, 121n, 240, 244
Withers, Sir William, 46, 76, 239
Witney, 57, 121n, 240
Wood, Thomas, 72
Wood, William, 73, 78, 234, 236
Wool, 28, 29, 42, 100, 109, 112, 121n, 148n, 242, 244
Wren, Matthew, 25, 239
Writ, 27

Yarico (character, *Spectator*), 191
Yate, Robert, 74n, 236
Yorke, Philip, 171n, 190n
Yorkshire, 57, 240, 241

www.ingramcontent.com/pod-product-compliance
Lightning Source LLC
Chambersburg PA
CBHW020644230426

43665CB00008B/304